WHO SANG WHAT
IN
ROCK'N'ROLL

500 REVERED, REVIVED
AND MUCH RECORDED
SONGS FROM THE
ROCK ERA

WHO SANG WHAT IN ROCK'N'ROLL

Alan Warner

BLANDFORD

First published in the UK in 1990 by Blandford,
an imprint of Cassell, Villiers House,
41/47 Strand,
London WC2N 5JE

Distributed in Australia by
Capricorn Link (Australia) Pty Ltd,
PO Box 665, Lane Cove, NSW 2066

British Library Cataloguing in Publication Data
Warner, Alan, 1943-
   Who sang what in rock 'n' roll.
   1. Rock music - Discographies
   I. Title
   016.78149166

            ISBN 0-7137-2082-4   Hardback
                 0-7137-2089-1   Paperback

Typeset in Rockwell by Creative Text and Communitype Ltd.
Printed in Great Britain by Bath Press, Avon.

Contents

Dedicated
to Dave Bartholomew and Hank Ballard
two legends of rhythm and blues who have left their indelible
marks on the history of rock 'n' roll

I count myself lucky that I have come to know both Dave and Hank
and deeply appreciate their friendship.

Also by Alan Warner
Celluloid Rock (with Philip Jenkinson) 1974
Who Sang What On The Screen 1984

Acknowledgements

This book would not have been possible without the unfailing support and enthusiasm from my wife and partner, Pat. She has always been my most valuable critic and her guidance through this book's various concepts and formats retained my sanity and sense of humour. Her organization of the book was invaluable.

Thanks go particularly to my agent, Jane Judd, who believed in me and found the right home for this book, and to Stuart Booth, our editor at Blandford, who shares my love of the music and its resulting trivia.

Thanks to the following:

Brady Benton (of BMI), Rick Coleman, Stuart Colman, Theresa MacNeil, Max Oates, Chris Peake, Billy Vera and Larry Zwisohn.

Photo Credits

Many of the illustrations in this book are original publicity photographs from the author's collection. Every effort has been made to credit their source; we apologise to anyone who has not been duly acknowledged.

Acuff-Rose Music 272; **Arista Records** 61; **Avco Records** 280; **CBS Special Products** 196, 285; **CBS Television** 193; **Charly Records** 42, 90 (Jerry Lee Lewis), 145, 158; **Columbia Pictures** 263; **Columbia Records** 116, 250 (Bob Dylan); **Constellation Records** 73; **Demon records** 29, 54 (Julie London), 253, 266; **DooTone Records** 74 (The Penguins); **EMI Music Publishing** 25, 43, 48, 57, 100, 149, 237, 271; **EMI Records** 16, 17, 34, 37, 52, 53, 72, 79, 83, 84, 99, 113, 114, 129, 130, 133, 141 (Lori Lieberman), 142, 148, 160, 162, 181, 185, 215, 219, 235, 241, 242, 244, 248, 250 (Irma Thomas), 255, 279, 283, 296, 300; **Epic Records** 92; **Grand National Films** 108; **Gusto Records** 60, 85; **Hudson Bay Music** 243; **Immediate Records** 184; **Irving Music** 87; **Janus Records** 91; **Jobete Music** 27, 59, 63, 69, 107, 275; **Laurie Records** 97; **London Records** 167; **MCA Records** 15, 39, 161, 164, 281; **Metro-Goldwyn-Mayer** 135, 147; **Mother Bertha Music** 251; **Motown Records** 67, 174, 189; **MPL Communications** 287; **Juggy Murray** 166; **Myers Music/Capano Music** 201; **Ode Records** 270; **Paramount Pictures** 141 (Roberta Flack); **Philles Records** 31; **PolyGram/Polydor/Phonogram Records** 28, 93, 131, 157, 190, 236, 254 (Billy Fury), 269, 301; **Regent Music** 220; **Del Shannon** 74 (Del & Johnny Tillotson), 205; **Specialty Records** 65, 144; **Trio & Alley Music** 66, 217, 233, 268; **20th Century Fox** 223; **United Artists Pictures** 204; **Warner-Chappell Music/Six Continents** 57 (WHY DO LOVERS); **WEA Records** 54 (Solomon Burke), 169, 229, 231, 260.

Lyric extracts by courtesy of the following copyright owners:

ABRAHAM MARTIN AND JOHN: Blue Ribbon Music; **BOOK OF LOVE:** EMI Music; **C'MON EVERYBODY:** Burlington Music; **GOOD ROCKIN' TONIGHT:** Lark Music; **LEADER OF THE PACK:** EMI Music; **MEMPHIS:** Jewel Music; **MY GENERATION:** Fabulous Music; **PIECE OF MY HEART:** Planetary-Nom Music; **SHAKE RATTLE AND ROLL:** Carlin Music/Campbell Connelly; **TRIBUTE TO BUDDY HOLLY:** Southern Music; **TUTTI FRUTTI:** ATV Music.

Introduction

I've always been obsessed by music and the more I discover, the deeper my passion for it grows. The trouble was, when I was growing up in Britain in the 1950s, the history of popular music was insufficiently documented. Pop music was often either MOR ballads and novelty songs straight out of the music-hall and an adjunct to the fast-fading dance band era, or what little rock 'n' roll we could get on the radio was mostly watered down for white, mass-market ears or discreetly chosen by those lords of censorship, the radio programme planners! OK, so I'm being unfair and probably I am unduly prejudiced; but the record industry had blinkers on when the dazzling bright lights of originality were breaking through the cracks. I was at EMI in London in the early 1960s and, before The Beatles and their contemporaries started ramming home the importance of roots music from across the Atlantic, availability of rhythm and blues classics was severely limited.

While I was at school, one of my favourite songs was JUST WALKING IN THE RAIN; Johnnie Ray's Columbia recording on British Philips was a Number One single in late 1956 and it was a firm favourite in my collection of 78s! Yet in those days, there was almost no way of knowing that this wasn't the original version of the song. Years later, I was to discover that it was first recorded in 1953 for Sun Records by a group of inmates of the Tennessee State Penitentiary, aptly named The Prisonaires. The impact of this latter-day discovery illustrates the reason that I instinctively track down the origins of songs: and my current work in the music-publishing field has only enhanced my respect for the writers and the original interpreters.

What led me to this book was that many rock 'n' roll reference books are laid out so that the reader can have easier access to the performers and the genres than to the actual songs. So it seemed time to begin to turn the spotlight on the real heart and soul of each record we buy.

Today, pop music is evolving and cross-pollinating more than ever. British group Simply Red recently unearthed not only the Gamble and Huff soul classic, IF YOU DON'T KNOW ME BY NOW (originally by Harold Melvin and The Blue Notes), but also IT'S ONLY LOVE, written by soul brother-and-sister act Jimmie and Vella Cameron who themselves once cut a glorious version of the Moody Blues' NIGHTS IN WHITE SATIN! Similarly, Billy Idol reintroduced TO BE A LOVER on his *Vital Idol* album; written by William Bell and Boooker T. Jones, TO BE A LOVER had been an R&B charter for Gene Chandler a full two decades earlier!

The same resurgence is happening in the movies; once, it seemed that Hollywood was only prepared to license proven hits as source music, but now the field has opened up dramatically. Former GoGo Belinda Carlisle reshaped The Cream's glorious testament, I FEEL FREE, on the soundtrack of "Licensed To Drive"; and that was Debbie Harry breathing new life into The Castaways' garage band classic, LIAR, LIAR, underneath the action in "Married To The Mob".

This book attempts to set the record straight on some memorable songs from rock 'n' roll's past, with particular emphasis on compositions from the 1950s and 1960s. There are a few points I would like to stress up front... firstly, this is *not* a chart book; there are some fine ongoing books which superbly track the course of hit records (they're listed in my bibliography section) and you'll find that when I show 'UK' or 'US Hits', only what are considered to be significant hit versions are indicated.

Secondly, this book can only be selective, both in terms of which songs are singled out and as far as how many 'other recordings' are listed. The songs chosen are among the best of the rock era but have in no way been judged as the absolute finest of their genre. Some such works to which I refer have been covered more extensively than we can begin to accommodate here and it should be noted that it was our intention to provide a mere brief indication of the range of performers who have interpreted the individual compositions chosen. Similarly, the motion pictures indicated are, by design, a random sampling of those which have featured relevant songs in on-screen performances or soundtrack uses.

In the majority of cases, record labels which are indicated in parenthesis following performers' names are the original companies from their country of origin. Therefore, a Brenda Lee record may be listed as being on 'Decca' rather than on 'Brunswick' because she is an American artist and US Decca was the originating label of the recording; however, if we are indicating the actual 'hit' performance of a Brenda Lee single in the UK, then it would show: UK Hit: Brenda Lee (Brunswick).

After each listing of US hit records, we show one of three classifications of American charts; this indicates significant performance by the individual recording on the black, pop and/or country charts. To this end, 'black' refers to that which contemporary record charts categorize as black music and also the various names under which the corresponding music has been listed over the years, including race, rhythm and blues, as well as soul music. The main thrust of the discussion in this book is related to pop and black music performances, whereas country music versions are only sporadically listed.

Finally, I would add that throughout the book, titles marked thus** indicate that these particular songs have their own individual entries.

My plan is to update and hopefully expand this concept in the future, so I would appreciate your sending any relevant additions, corrections and suggestions to me c/o my publisher – and I will endeavour to reply to you.

Alan Warner, Hollywood

Category Songs

The key songs in this book are presented alphabetically. A number of related categories and themes have been developed and explored and they occur at different places throughout the text. Again, these are purely selective and are not in any way ultimate listings. A number of these segments are devoted to representative lists of hits by certain composers; however, in the case of song-writing teams, space allows us only to highlight the output of each specific collaboration. In other words, the Goffin and King entry does not detail other writers with whom Gerry Goffin wrote or other collaborators of Carole King's.

The following are the individual categories developed in the book along with the song titles in whose entries they can be located:

Annie and Henry songs
  under WORK WITH ME ANNIE

Answer records
  under MY BOYFRIEND'S BACK

Bacharach and David songs
  under MAKE IT EASY ON YOURSELF

Hank Ballard songs
  under THE TWIST

Barry and Greenwich songs
  under RIVER DEEP, MOUNTAIN HIGH

Dave Bartholomew songs
  under I HEAR YOU KNOCKING

Based on the classics
  under IT'S NOW OR NEVER

Beach Boys' hits, covers of
  under GOOD VIBRATIONS

Beatles' remakes
  under DIZZY MISS LIZZY

Bee Gees' songs
  under TO LOVE SOMEBODY

Bert Berns songs
  under TWIST AND SHOUT

Chuck Berry songs
  under MEMPHIS

Otis Blackwell songs
  under ALL SHOOK UP

Pat Boone covers
  under AIN'T THAT A SHAME

James Brown songs
  under PLEASE, PLEASE, PLEASE

Boudleaux and Felice Bryant songs
  under BYE BYE LOVE

Car songs
  under MAYBELLENE

Cher/Sonny and Cher records
  under ALL I REALLY WANT TO DO

Christmas songs
  under MERRY CHRISTMAS BABY

Sam Cooke songs
  under ONLY SIXTEEN

Creedence in the movies
  under PROUD MARY

Dance songs
under DO YOU WANT TO DANCE

Jackie DeShannon songs
under WHEN YOU WALK IN THE ROOM

DeShannon and Sheeley songs
under BREAK-A-WAY

Death songs
under TELL LAURA I LOVE HER

Neil Diamond songs
under I'M A BELIEVER

Bo Diddley songs
under BO DIDDLEY

Willie Dixon songs
under I'M YOUR HOOCHIE COOCHIE MAN

Fats Domino songs
under AIN'T THAT A SHAME

Bob Dylan songs
under BLOWIN' IN THE WIND

Gamble and Huff songs
under DON'T LEAVE ME THIS WAY

Girl group records
under BABY I LOVE YOU

Girls' names in titles
under LONG TALL SALLY

Goffin and King songs
under UP ON THE ROOF

Graham Gouldman songs
under HEART FULL OF SOUL

The hits that got away
under SEE YOU LATER ALLIGATOR

Holland, Dozier and Holland songs
under HOW SWEET IT IS (TO BE LOVED BY YOU)

Buddy Holly covers
under LOVE'S MADE A FOOL OF YOU

John Lee Hooker songs
under BOOM BOOM

Instrumental hits
under TEQUILA

Instrumentals... with lyrics
under YOU CAN'T SIT DOWN

Jagger and Richards songs
under PAINT IT BLACK

Leiber and Stoller songs
under JAILHOUSE ROCK

Lennon and McCartney songs
under WITH A LITTLE HELP FROM MY FRIENDS

Little Richard songs
under TUTTI FRUTTI

Mann and Weil songs
under YOU'VE LOST THAT LOVIN' FEELIN'

John Marascalco songs
under RIP IT UP

Curtis Mayfield songs
under PEOPLE GET READY

Joe Meek classics
under JOHNNY REMEMBER ME

Monster songs
under MONSTER MASH

Motown covers
under DEVIL WITH A BLUE DRESS ON

Name-dropping songs
under SWEET SOUL MUSIC

Novelty songs
under WITCH DOCTOR

Roy Orbison songs
under OH PRETTY WOMAN

Parody records
under BEAT IT

Pomus and Shuman songs
under A TEENAGER IN LOVE

Elvis Presley hits, covers of
under SUSPICIOUS MINDS

Elvis Presley remakes
under SUSPICIOUS MINDS

Jerry Ragovoy songs
under CRY BABY

Jimmy Reed songs
under BABY WHAT YOU WANT ME TO DO

Reggae songs
under I SHOT THE SHERIFF

Smokey Robinson songs
under SHOP AROUND

Rolling Stones' remakes
under YOU BETTER MOVE ON

Sedaka and Greenfield songs
under BREAKING UP IS HARD
TO DO

Sequel songs
under IT'S MY PARTY

Sound effects in rock 'n' roll
under SEA CRUISE

Phil Spector classics
under DA DOO RON RON

Dusty Springfield hits
under SON OF A PREACHER
MAN

Bruce Springsteen songs
under PINK CADILLAC

Telephone songs
under CHANTILLY LACE

Allen Toussaint songs
under MOTHER-IN-LAW

Tribute songs
under TRIBUTE TO BUDDY
HOLLY

Bobby Vee records
under TAKE GOOD CARE OF
MY BABY

Vietnam songs
under UNIVERSAL SOLDIER

Vintage popular standards
under TOMORROW NIGHT

Muddy Waters songs
under MANNISH BOY

Wedding and marriage songs
under CHAPEL OF LOVE

Stevie Wonder Songs
under YOU ARE THE SUNSHINE
OF MY LIFE

The Songs A–Z

ABRAHAM, MARTIN AND JOHN
(Dick Holler)
'Has anybody here seen my old friend Abraham....'
Evocative folk-rock anthem, written as a tribute to Abraham Lincoln, Martin Luther King and John Kennedy. It marked a comeback (and a return to his original record label) for Dion (Di Mucci), formerly of Dion and The Belmonts. The song, which was written by the same writer as the very different SNOOPY VS. THE RED BARRON hit (by The Royal Guardsmen on Laurie two years earlier), also charted for Smokey Robinson and The Miracles and by black comedienne Moms Mabley. Later revived in a Top 10 medley (with WHAT THE WORLD NEEDS NOW IS LOVE) by disc-jockey Tom Clay narrating between portions of the two songs sung by The Blackberries (namely Clydie King, Venetta Fields and Billie Barnum).

US HITS: Dion (Laurie: 1968) Pop
           Smokey Robinson and
             The Miracles (Tamla:
             1969) Black & Pop
           Moms Mabley (Mercury:
             1969) Black & Pop
           Tom Clay: Medley with
             WHAT THE WORLD
             NEEDS NOW IS LOVE
             (Bacharach/David)
             (Mowest: 1971)
             Black & Pop

UK HIT: Marvin Gaye (Tamla
             Motown: 1970)

Other recordings: Harry Belafonte (RCA); Kenny Rogers (Liberty); Ray Charles (ABC).

AFTER MIDNIGHT
(J. J. Cale)
Originally recorded by J. J. Cale on a Liberty single in 1967, it has become adopted as one of Eric Clapton's most requested songs; Clapton himself re-recorded AFTER MIDNIGHT in 1988 for an American TV beer commercial.

US HITS: Eric Clapton (Atco: 1970)
             Pop
           J. J. Cale (Shelter: 1972
             Re-recording) Pop

Other recordings: Chet Atkins (RCA); Maggie Bell (Atlantic).

AIN'T GOT NO HOME
(Clarence Henry)
R&B novelty song written and recorded by New Orleans artist Clarence Henry; this was the first occasion on which he injected his croaking 'frog' voice, hence his

AIN'T GOT NO HOME
Clarence 'Frogman' Henry (with his ever-present mascot) whose other major hits included BUT I DO** (see separate entry) and YOU ALWAYS HURT THE ONE YOU LOVE (Roberts/Fisher), a 1940s ballad which Connie Francis revived in 1958, followed by Clarence Henry's Top 20 version three years later.

nickname. Song later revived by The Band on their *Moondog Matinee* album (Capitol: 1973), from which the single briefly charted. Performed in recent concerts by Billy Vera and The Beaters and also Joe Ely.

US HITS:　Clarence 'Frogman'
　　　　　Henry (Argo: 1956)
　　　　　Pop & Black
　　　　　The Band (Capitol: 1973)
　　　　　Pop

Other recordings: Buddy Holly (Coral); Sleepy LaBeef (Rounder); Bruce Channel (Smash); Carl Mann (Sun).

Sequel record: I FOUND A HOME by Clarence 'Frogman' Henry (Argo: 1957).

AIN'T NO MOUNTAIN HIGH ENOUGH

(Nickolas Ashford/Valerie Simpson) Joyously romantic R&B song written by singer–songwriters Ashford and Simpson. Originally planned as a solo for Tammi Terrell, it became the first of a series of successful duet sides teaming her with Marvin Gaye. Revived three years later by Diana Ross, it became her first Number One away from The Supremes.

Former Motown staff writers, Nickolas Ashford and Valerie Simpson's other hit songs include LET'S GO GET STONED by Ray

Charles (ABC: 1966), REACH OUT AND TOUCH (SOMEBODY'S HAND) by Diana Ross (Motown: 1970), YOU'RE ALL I NEED TO GET BY originally by Marvin Gaye and Tammi Terrell (Tamla: 1968) and later by Aretha Franklin (Atlantic: 1971), AIN'T NOTHING LIKE THE REAL THING** and their own smash SOLID (Capitol: 1984).

US HITS:　Marvin Gaye and Tammi
　　　　　Terrell (Tamla: 1967)
　　　　　Black & Pop
　　　　　Diana Ross (Motown:
　　　　　1970) Black & Pop
UK HITS:　Diana Ross (Tamla
　　　　　Motown: 1970)
　　　　　Boystown Gang
　　　　　(WEA: 1981)

Other recordings: Ashford and Simpson (Warner Bros); Marvin Gaye (Tamla); Odell Brown and The Organ-izers (Cadet); Stacy Lattisaw and Howard Hewett (Motown).

See: DEVIL WITH A BLUE DRESS ON for other Motown hits.

AIN'T NOTHING LIKE THE REAL THING

(Nickolas Ashford/Valerie Simpson) More Ashford and Simpson magic that worked wonders (after AIN'T NO MOUNTAIN HIGH ENOUGH) for Marvin and Tammi. Later it was a Top 50 charter for Aretha Franklin, and a moderate-sized hit for Donny and Marie Osmond.

US HITS:　Marvin Gaye and Tammi
　　　　　Terrell (Tamla: 1968)
　　　　　Black & Pop
　　　　　Aretha Franklin (Atlantic:
　　　　　1974) Black & Pop
　　　　　Donny and Marie
　　　　　Osmond (Polydor:
　　　　　1977) Pop

ASHFORD & SIMPSON

OLID

AIN'T NO MOUNTAIN HIGH ENOUGH
Ashford and Simpson who began as a Motown staff song-writing team and graduated into performing artists in their own right!

UK HIT: Marvin Gaye and Tammi
            Terrell (Tamla Motown:
            1968)

Other recordings: Ashford and Simpson
(Warner Bros); The Jackson 5
(Motown); Chris Christian and Amy
Holland (Boardwalk); Diana Ross and
Marvin Gaye (Motown); Barry
Manilow (RCA); Angela Bofill
(Arista); Marv Johnson and Carolyn
Gill (Nightmare).

See: AIN'T NO MOUNTAIN HIGH
ENOUGH for other Nickolas Ashford
and Valerie Simpson songs.

See: DEVIL WITH A BLUE DRESS
ON for other Motown hits.

AIN'T THAT A SHAME
(Antoine Domino/Dave
Bartholomew)
Fats Domino's giant breakthrough
song – up until then, his initial twelve
hits had been R&B charters which
didn't crossover to the pop listings.
Covered by Pat Boone who reached
Number One on the hit parade (as
the pop chart was known in those
days!) with his jerky, pubescent
version which clearly lacked the
appetizingly rhythmic roll of Fats'
original, that was initially titled AIN'T
IT A SHAME.
    The Domino sound sparked a trail
of 22 million-sellers, led off by 1949's
THE FAT MAN (Domino/
Bartholomew) and continuing
through to the early 1960s.
    Fats performed AIN'T THAT A
SHAME himself in the movie "Shake,
Rattle and Rock!" (AIP: 1956) and his
1955 record was heard on the
soundtrack of "American Graffiti"
(Universal: 1973); however, MCA's
Graffiti soundtrack album contains a
bastardized version of the original
master with a chanting girl chorus
which had been added on in later
years!
    Among the most recent covers is
a version by Paul McCartney on his
EMI album specifically recorded for

AIN'T THAT A SHAME!
Well should he smile! Fats Domino cut hit after hit
after hit in the 1950s and early 1960s. His songs
were either originals which he usually wrote with
Dave Bartholomew, or choice oldies like
BLUEBERRY HILL (Lewis/Stock/Rose) (Imperial:
1956).

release in Russia.

US HITS: Fats Domino (Imperial:
            1955) Black & Pop
            Pat Boone (Dot: 1955) Pop
            The Four Seasons
            (Vee-Jay: 1963) Pop
            Hank Williams, Jr (MGM:
            1971) Country
            Cheap Trick (Epic: 1979)
            Pop
UK HITS: Pat Boone (London: 1955)
            Fats Domino (London:
            1957)
            The Four Seasons
            (Stateside: 1963)

Other recordings: Dave
Bartholomew (Imperial); John
Lennon (Capitol); Bill Medley
(Liberty); Brownsville Station
(Private Stock); Bobby Rydell

(Cameo); Bill Black's Combo (Hi); Tanya Tucker (MCA); Roy Clark (Churchill); Frances Faye (Imperial).

Pat Boone Covers
Pat Boone's white versions of black songs also included AT MY FRONT DOOR (CRAZY LITTLE MAMA) (Moore/Abner Jr) originally by The El Dorados (Vee-Jay: 1955), I'LL BE HOME (Washington/Lewis) first by The Flamingos (Checker: 1956), Ivory Joe Hunter's own I ALMOST LOST MY MIND (MGM: 1950), TWO HEARTS (Williams/Stone) originally by The Charms (DeLuxe: 1955), plus the Little Richard classics, LONG TALL SALLY (Johnson/Blackwell/Penniman)** and TUTTI FRUTTI (Penniman/LaBostre/Lubin)**.

Fats Domino songs
Fats Domino left a lasting impression on many rock 'n' rollers from his contemporaries in the 1950s to The Beatles in later years, whose LADY MADONNA (Lennon/McCartney) single is one of their most affectionate tributes and which the Fat Man himself recorded for Reprise.
　　Among the cover versions of other Fats Domino songs:

ALL BY MYSELF by The Johnny Burnette Trio (Coral: 1956)
BLUE MONDAY** by Dave Edmunds (Regal Zonophone: 1971)
EVERY NIGHT ABOUT THIS TIME by Little Richard (Little Star: 1962)
THE FAT MAN by Robbie Robertson with Gary Busey and Dr John in the movie, "Carney" (Lorimar: 1980) and on the soundtrack album (Warner Bros)
GOIN' TO THE RIVER by Chuck Willis (Okeh: 1953)
I WANT YOU TO KNOW by The Everly Brothers (Warner Bros: 1960)
I'M GONNA BE A WHEEL SOMEDAY** by Los Lobos on the

soundtrack of "A Fine Mess" (Columbia: 1986) and on the soundtrack album (Motown)
LET THE FOUR WINDS BLOW** by Roy Brown (Imperial: 1957)
MY GIRL JOSEPHINE by Billy Vera (Midsong: 1976)
WALKING TO NEW ORLEANS by Brenda Lee (Decca: 1960)

Of the above songs, all are Antoine Domino/Dave Bartholomew compositions except EVERY NIGHT ABOUT THIS TIME (Domino), I'M GONNA BE A WHEEL SOMEDAY (Hayes/Domino/Bartholomew) and WALKING TO NEW ORLEANS (Domino/Bartholomew/Guidry).

See: I HEAR YOU KNOCKING for other Dave Bartholomew songs.

AIN'T TOO PROUD TO BEG
(Eddie Holland/Norman Whitfield)
Part of a four-song 'Apollo Medley' with GET READY (Robinson), MY GIRL (Robinson/White) and THE WAY YOU DO THE THINGS YOU DO (Robinson/Rogers) recorded by Daryl Hall and John Oates with David Ruffin and Eddie Kendrick on their Live At The Apollo album (RCA: 1985). Sung in another medley with PUT YOURSELF IN MY PLACE (Holland/Dozier/Holland) by Rick Astley (RCA).

US HITS:　The Temptations (Gordy: 1966) Black & Pop
　　　　　The Rolling Stones (Rolling Stones: 1974) Pop
UK HIT:　The Temptations (Tamla Motown: 1966)

Other recordings: Diana Ross and The Supremes and The Four Tops (Motown); Rick Astley (RCA); David Ruffin (Motown); Jimmy James and The Vagabonds (Pye).

See: DEVIL WITH A BLUE DRESS ON for other Motown hits.

ALL ALONG THE WATCHTOWER
(Bob Dylan)
Originally recorded by Bob Dylan
on his *John Wesley Harding* album
(Columbia: 1967), he also included it
in his *Live at Budokan* LP (Columbia:
1978). It became a major part of the
repertoire of Jimi Hendrix whose
studio version was heard on the
soundtrack of "Where The Buffalo
Roam" (Universal: 1980).

US HIT: The Jimi Hendrix
Experience
(Reprise: 1968) Pop
UK HIT: The Jimi Hendrix
Experience
(Track: 1968)

Other recordings: XTC (Geffen);
Dave Mason (Columbia); Alan Bown
(Music Factory); TSOL (Geffen);
Frank Marino and Mahogany Rush
(Columbia); Nashville Teens (UK
Decca); Barbara Keith.

See: BLOWIN' IN THE WIND for
other Bob Dylan songs.

ALL I HAVE TO DO IS DREAM
(Felice Bryant/Boudleaux Bryant)
Though they've each recorded
separately, and consciously didn't
work together for a number of years,
Don and Phil Everly were a hugely
successful duo, their close country-
based harmonies hugging the pop
charts around the world from the late
1950s to the mid-1960s.

Most of their early hits were
written by Felice Bryant and her
husband, Boudleaux, including this,
their second US Number One,
following WAKE UP LITTLE
SUZIE**.

US HITS: The Everly Brothers
(Cadence: 1958)
Pop & Country
Richard Chamberlain
(MGM: 1963) Pop
Glen Campbell and
Bobbie Gentry
(Capitol: 1970) Pop &

Country
Andy Gibb and Victoria
Principal (RSO: 1981)
Pop
UK HITS: The Everly Brothers
(London: 1958)
Glen Campbell and
Bobbie Gentry
(Capitol: 1969)

Other recordings: Roy Orbison
(Monument); Paul Anka (RCA); The
Nitty Gritty Dirt Band (UA); Gary
Lewis and The Playboys (Liberty);
R.E.M. Soundtrack (IRS); Juice
Newton (Capitol); Cliff Richard (UK
Columbia).

See: BYE BYE LOVE for other
Boudleaux and Felice Bryant songs.

ALL I REALLY WANT TO DO
(Bob Dylan)
From the composer's *Another Side
Of Bob Dylan* album (Columbia:
1964) came this song which was
hotly contested for chart stakes by
both Cher and The Byrds. Cher won
the Stateside battle, even though it
was her first-ever hit, while The
Byrds had come off a Number One
with Dylan's MR. TAMBOURINE
MAN**.

US HITS: Cher (Imperial: 1965) Pop
The Byrds (Columbia:
1965) Pop
UK HITS: Cher (Liberty: 1965)
The Byrds (CBS: 1965)

Other recordings: The Hollies
(Parlophone); The Four Seasons
(Philips); The Everly Brothers (RCA).

Cher/Sonny and Cher records
ALL I REALLY WANT TO DO was
the first record released under the
name 'Cher', but she had had two
previous solo singles, one called
RINGO, I LOVE YOU (Spector/
Poncia/Andreoli) produced by Phil
Spector (Annette: 1964) and DREAM
BABY, not the Roy Orbison song, but
a Sonny Bono composition and

production, released on Imperial in 1964 and credited to 'Cherilyn'. She and Sonny had also cut some sides as 'Caesar And Cleo', including THE LETTER (Harris/Terry Jr), on Vault in '63 and LOVE IS STRANGE (Baker/Smith/Robinson) for Reprise in '64, pre-dating their 'Sonny and Cher' singles which began with BABY DON'T GO (Bono) (Reprise: 1964) and I GOT YOU BABE (Bono) (Atco: 1965).

See: BLOWIN' IN THE WIND for other Bob Dylan songs.

ALL RIGHT NOW
(Paul Rodgers/Andy Fraser)
The finest hour of British rock band Free, originally part of their third album, *Fire and Water* (Island: 1970). Song has been revived several times; it charted briefly in the States for Rod Stewart and in the UK by Pepsi and Shirlie.

UK HITS:	Free (Island: 1970)
	Free (Island: 1973 Re-
	release)
	Pepsi and Shirlie
	(Polydor: 1987)
US HIT:	Free (A&M: 1970) Pop
	Rod Stewart (Warner
	Bros: 1985) Pop
	Lea Roberts (UA: 1975)
	Pop & Black

ALL SHOOK UP
(Otis Blackwell/Elvis Presley)
Elvis' first British Number One. Originally recorded by David Hill (Aladdin: 1956) on the same session as he cut another Otis Blackwell tune, MELODY FOR LOVERS. Revived by Suzi Quatro as a single on Bell in 1974 which appeared briefly on the back end of the US charts.
  Performed by Ry Cooder on the soundtrack of the Tom Cruise movie, "Cocktail" (Touchstone: 1988).

US HIT:	Elvis Presley (RCA:1957)
	Black & Pop
UK HIT:	Elvis Presley (HMV: 1957)

Other recordings: Jeff Beck Group (Epic); Suzi Quatro (Bell); Otis Blackwell (Inner City); Albert King (Stax); Pat Boone (Dot); Sandy Nelson (Imperial); Brian Hyland (ABC Paramount); Steve Marriott (Aura).

See: ROCK AROUND THE CLOCK for the SWING THE MOOD record.

Otis Blackwell songs
One of the breakthrough black composers of the 1950s, Otis was also a singer–pianist and made records of his own. Among the hit records of other Otis Blackwell songs are:

BREATHLESS by Jerry Lee Lewis (Sun: 1958)
DON'T BE CRUEL** (written with Elvis Presley) (see note below) by Elvis Presley (RCA: 1956)
FEVER** (with Eddie Cooley) by Little Willie John (King: 1956)
GREAT BALLS OF FIRE** (with Jack Hammer) by Jerry Lee Lewis (Sun: 1958)
HANDY MAN** (with Jimmy Jones) by Jimmy Jones (Cub: 1960)
HEY LITTLE GIRL (with Bobby Stevenson) by Dee Clark (Abner: 1959)
JUST KEEP IT UP by Dee Clark (Abner: 1959)
NINE TIMES OUT OF TEN (with Waldense Hall) by Cliff Richard (UK Columbia: 1960)
ONE BROKEN HEART FOR SALE (with Winfield Scott) by Elvis Presley (RCA: 1963)
PARALYZED by Elvis Presley (RCA: 1957)
RETURN TO SENDER (with Winfield Scott) by Elvis Presley (RCA: 1962)

NB: Co-writers of songs are shown throughout this book, but it does not always follow that the names indicated actually contributed to those copyrights. In the majority of cases where Elvis Presley's name appears as a writer, it is generally acknowledged that this was simply an agreed arrangement for him to be given credit without any actual involvement in the song's creation.

ALL YOU NEED IS LOVE

(John Lennon/Paul McCartney)
The Beatles' flower-children anthem, written for and basically recorded during a 'live' telecast from EMI's Abbey Road Studios in London on 25 June 1967. John sang the lead vocal and over-dubbed a new vocal track after the transmission.

The back-up musicians and singers on the session included such special guests as Mick Jagger, Keith Richards, Graham Nash, Keith Moon, Gary Leeds and Marianne Faithfull.

The resulting single was released in England on 7 July and it raced up to the Number One chart position as it also did in the States. George Martin's arrangement opens up with the initial strains of the French national anthem, a typical slice of Beatle humour.

Featured on the soundtrack of the Beatles' cartoon movie, "Yellow Submarine" (Apple: 1968) and by the cast in the musical, "Sgt. Pepper's Lonely Hearts Club Band" (Universal: 1978).

UK HIT: The Beatles (Parlophone: 1967)
US HIT: The Beatles (Capitol: 1967) Pop

An extract from the original Beatles master was included in THE BEATLES MOVIE MEDLEY, a specially edited single which made the charts on both sides of the Atlantic in 1982.

Other recordings: The 5th Dimension (Bell); The Osmond Brothers (Barnaby); Frannie Golde (Atlantic); Eddie Chacon (Columbia).

See: WITH A LITTLE HELP FROM MY FRIENDS for other Lennon and McCartney songs.

ALLEY OOP

(Dallas Frazier)
Crazy, nonsensical rock 'n' roll song written by country artist Dallas Frazier. Original version (which topped the charts) was by The Hollywood Argyles (their lead singer was Gary Paxton). There were two notable covers at that time, first by Dante and The Evergreens, who made the Top 20, also by The Dyna-Sores who barely scraped in the Top 75.

The Kingsmen's hit ANNIE FANNIE (Easton) (Wand: 1965) and SURFIN' SANTA (Denos/Paxton) by Lord Douglas Byron (Dot: 1954) both borrowed the tune to ALLEY OOP.

US HITS: The Hollywood Argyles (Lute: 1960) Pop
              Dante and the Evergreens (Madison: 1960) Pop
              The Dyna-Sores (Rendezvous: 1960) Pop
UK HIT: The Hollywood Argyles (London: 1960)

Other recordings: The Royal Guardsmen (Laurie); The Beach Boys (Capitol); George Thorogood and The Destroyers (EMI America); The Bonzo Dog Doo Dah Band (Parlophone); The Tams (MGM South); Brian Poole and The Tremeloes (UK Decca).

The ghost of ALLEY OOP stayed with Gary Paxton for quite some time; a single on the small Los Angeles Paxley label called YOU. BEEN TORTURING ME (Guilbeau/ Cotton/Williams/Moore) was credited to the Hollywood Argyles with Gary 'Alley-Oop' Paxton! In '62, he cut a song called ALLEY OOP WAS A TWO-DAB MAN (Macrae/ Paxton) for Liberty, who released his version of SPOOKY MOVIES (Stone) in 1963, just a few months after Bobby Pickett's legendary MONSTER MASH★★ had come out for the first time on Paxton's own label, Garpax!

The Hollywood Argyles' hit of ALLEY OOP was produced by Kim Fowley, who also produced the early '60s hits POPSICLE AND ICICLES by the Murmaids and NUT ROCKER by B. Bumble and The Stingers. The Dante and The Evergreens cover was an early Herb Alpert/Lou Adler production, prior to the formation of A&M Records.

Composer Dallas Frazier was also a country performer in his own right, recording the original version of his ELVIRA for Capitol in 1965, sixteen years before the Oak Ridge Boys' hit on MCA. Dallas also wrote THERE GOES MY EVERYTHING, recorded by both Engelbert Humperdinck (UK Decca: 1967) and Elvis Presley (RCA: 1971), as well as the country classic, SON OF HICKORY HOLLER'S TRAMP, which charted for O. C. Smith (Columbia: 1968).

ALWAYS ON MY MIND
(Wayne Carson Thompson/Mark James/Johnny Christopher)
Co-written by Wayne Carson Thompson who wrote THE LETTER for The Box Tops, ALWAYS ON MY MIND was originally released in the States as the flipside of Elvis Presley's hit SEPARATE WAYS (RCA: 1973). In England, ALWAYS was promoted as an A-side and made it into the Top 10.

US HITS: Willie Nelson (Columbia: 1982) Pop & Country
           The Pet Shop Boys (Manhattan: 1988) Pop
UK HITS: Elvis Presley (RCA: 1972)
           Willie Nelson (CBS: 1982)
           Elvis Presley (RCA: 1985 Re-release)
           The Pet Shop Boys (EMI: 1988)

Other recordings: Joe Simon (Compleat); Brenda Lee (Decca).

Composers of the above song include Mark James, who also wrote HOOKED ON A FEELING★★ and SUSPICIOUS MINDS★★ as well as THE EYES OF A NEW YORK WOMAN, a hit for B. J. Thomas (Scepter: 1968) and IT'S ONLY LOVE which charted for both B. J. Thomas (Scepter: 1969) and Elvis Presley (RCA: 1971). Wayne Carson Thompson also wrote THE LETTER★★ as well as The Box Tops' second hit, NEON RAINBOW (Mala: 1967).

ANGEL OF THE MORNING
(Chip Taylor)
Powerful ballad immortalized by petite Merrilee Rush, produced in Memphis by Chips Moman. Originally covered in Britain by former member of The Ikettes, P. P. Arnold. Revived successfully in the States by Juice Newton, providing her first solo hit since leaving Silver Spur. Song was also a mini country hit for Connie Eaton (Chart: 1970). The Merrilee Rush original was featured on the soundtrack of the 1977 movie, "Fingers".

Like another Chip Taylor hit, I CAN'T LET GO, the original version of ANGEL IN THE MORNING was recorded by Evie Sands (Cameo: 1967).

US HITS: Merrilee Rush and The Turnabouts (Bell: 1968) Pop
           Juice Newton (Capitol: 1981) Pop & Country
UK HITS: P. P. Arnold (Immediate: 1968)
           Mary Mason: Medley with another Chip Taylor song, ANY WAY THAT YOU WANT ME (Epic: 1977)

Other recordings: Nina Simone (RCA); Chip Taylor (Buddah); Bettye

Swan (Capitol); Olivia Newton-John (MCA); Skeeter Davis (RCA); Billie Davis (UK Decca).

See: WILD THING for other Chip Taylor songs.

ANY DAY NOW

(Burt Bacharach/Bob Hilliard)
Sub-titled MY WILD BEAUTIFUL BIRD. Ronnie Milsap's version was a Number One country record in 1982.

US HITS: Chuck Jackson (Wand: 1962) Black & Pop
Ronnie Milsap (RCA: 1982) Pop & Country

Other recordings: Elvis Presley (RCA); Percy Sledge (Atlantic); Burt Bacharach (A&M); Don Gibson (ABC).

See: MAKE IT EASY ON YOURSELF for songs written by Burt Bacharach with Hal David.

ARE YOU LONESOME TONIGHT

(Roy Turk/Lou Handman)
One of Elvis Presley's most romantic records was of this 1920s song which had been revived in 1959 by girl singer Jaye P. Morgan. Her MGM single was a moderate seller reaching just outside the American Top 50.

Elvis came out of the army and cut the song in April 1960. In the middle of the record, he spoke a few of the lines, heightening the song's sentimental quotient and most probably sending scores of his female fans into erotic frenzy!

US ROCK   Jaye P. Morgan (MGM:
ERA HITS: 1959) Pop
Elvis Presley (RCA: 1960) Black & Pop
Donny Osmond (MGM: 1973) Pop
UK ROCK   Elvis Presley (RCA: 1961)
ERA HITS: Elvis Presley (RCA: 1977 Re-release)

Elvis Presley (RCA: 1982 Re-release)

Other recordings: Don Gibson (MCA); Frank Sinatra (Reprise); Merle Haggard (MCA).

Answer records: OH HOW I MISS YOU TONIGHT by Jeanne Black (Capitol: 1960)
YES I'M LONESOME TONIGHT by Thelma Carpenter (Coral: 1960) by Dodie Stevens (Dot: 1960)

See: TOMORROW NIGHT for other Vintage popular standards.

AS TEARS GO BY

(Mick Jagger/Keith Richards/Andrew Oldham)
Marianne Faithfull was the dolly-bird girlfriend of Mick Jagger; their relationship continuously made headlines, particularly when she accompanied the Stones on overseas trips. In addition to making records, she acted; her most memorable appearance was in the movie "Girl On A Motorcycle" (1968), but gained recognition not for her dramatic role but rather for her costume on screen which was explained by the overseas release title: "Naked Under Leather".

Re-recorded by The Rolling Stones (actually Mick Jagger and Orchestra) as 'Con Le Mie Lacrime' for Italian Decca: 1966.

AS TEARS was Marianne's first hit song of which she sang an a cappella version in the Jean-Luc Godard film, "Made In The U.S.A." (Contemporary: 1966).

UK HIT: Marianne Faithfull: (UK Decca: 1964)
US HITS: Marianne Faithfull (London: 1964) Pop
The Rolling Stones (London: 1965) Pop

AT THE HOP
(Johnny Madara/Artie Singer/David White)

Teen dance song (originally written as DO THE BOP) which was the first US chart-topper of 1958 for Danny and The Juniors. They were a four-man white group from Philadelphia, and appeared reprising this, their biggest hit, in the movie "Let The Good Times Roll" (Columbia: 1973). Song was originally covered by Nick Boone, Pat's younger brother, alias Nick Todd. Featured by Flash Cadillac and The Continental Kids on the soundtrack of "American Graffiti" (Universal: 1973).

It was Sha Na Na's rousing performance of AT THE HOP on the soundtrack of the "Woodstock" movie (Warner Bros: 1970), which first brought them to national attention in the US. The group's saxophone player, Lenny Baker, had been a member of Danny and The Juniors' band.

US HITS: Danny and The Juniors (ABC/Paramount: 1958) Pop
Nick Todd (Dot: 1958) Pop
UK HITS: Danny and The Juniors (HMV: 1958)
Danny and The Juniors (ABC: 1976 Re-release)

Other recordings: Flash Cadillac and The Continental Kids (Epic); Chubby Checker (Parkway); Sha Na Na (Buddah).

Sequel records: AFTER THE HOP by Bill Pinkney (Sun: 1958)
BACK TO THE HOP by Danny and The Juniors (Swan: 1961)

See: ROCK AROUND THE CLOCK for the SWING THE MOOD record.

BABY I LOVE YOU
(Phil Spector/Jeff Barry/Ellie Greenwich)

A much-loved girl group anthem of the early sixties, BABY I LOVE YOU was first immortalized by The Ronettes, led by Ronnie Spector, then wife of the famed songwriter/producer. The song just had to return; and come back it did, firstly via a version by Welsh revivalist Dave Edmunds – it turned out to be his second hit after I HEAR YOU KNOCKING (Dave Bartholomew/Pearl King)** although they were over two years apart – which Edmunds himself produced; then, for their 1980 Phil Spector-produced *End Of The Century* album, New York's own Ramones brought it back to the charts one more triumphant time.

Featured in the Broadway musical of Ellie Greenwich songs, "Leader Of The Pack" (1985).

US HITS: The Ronettes (Philles: 1964) Black & Pop
Andy Kim (Steed: 1969) Pop
UK HITS: The Ronettes (London: 1964)
Dave Edmunds (Rockfield: 1973)
The Ramones (Sire: 1980)

Other recordings: Roberta Flack and Donny Hathaway (Atlantic), *Leader Of The Pack* cast album (Elektra).

See: RIVER DEEP, MOUNTAIN HIGH for other Jeff Barry and Ellie Greenwich songs.

Girl group records
A selection of other classic girl group songs*:

ABOUT MY BABY (I COULD WRITE A BOOK) (Stone) by The

S SURE THE BOY I LOVE

Words and Music by
BARRY MANN and CYNTHIA WEIL

Recorded by THE CRYSTALS

on PHILLES Records

ALDON MUSIC INC. • NEVINS-KIRSHNER ASSOCIATES, INC.

60¢

06120

Pandoras (Liberty: 1967)

BABY IT'S YOU (David/Bacharach/
Williams)** by The Shirelles
(Scepter: 1962)

BABY LOVE (Holland/Dozier/
Holland) by The Supremes
(Motown: 1964)

CHAINS (Goffin/King) ** by The
Cookies (Dimension: 1962)

CHAPEL OF LOVE** (Spector/
Barry/Greenwich) by The Dixie
Cups (Red Bird: 1964)

DA DOO RON RON (Spector/Barry/
Greenwich)** by The Crystals
(Philles: 1963)

DANCING IN THE STREET (Gaye/
Stevenson) ** by Martha and The
Vandellas (Gordy: 1964)

DON'T SAY NOTHING BAD ABOUT
MY BABY (Goffin/King) by The
Cookies (Dimension: 1963)

EASIER SAID THAN DONE (Linton/
Huff) by The Essex (Roulette:
1963)

GIRLS ARE OUT TO GET YOU
(Mayfield) by The Fascinations
(Mayfield: 1967)

GIVE HIM A GREAT BIG KISS
(Morton) by The Shangri-Las (Red
Bird: 1964)

HE'S A REBEL (Pitney) by The
Crystals (Philles: 1962)

HE'S SO FINE (Mack) by The
Chiffons (Laurie: 1963)

HE'S SURE THE BOY I LOVE (Mann/
Weil)** by The Crystals (Philles:
1962)

(LOVE IS LIKE A) HEAT WAVE
(Holland/Dozier/Holland)** by
Martha and The Vandellas
(Gordy: 1963)

I LOVE HOW YOU LOVE ME
(Mann/Kolber) by The Paris
Sisters (Gregmark: 1961)

I WANNA LOVE HIM SO BAD
(Barry/Greenwich) by The Jelly
Beans (Red Bird: 1964)

I'M INTO SOMETHING GOOD
(Goffin/King)** by Earl-Jean
(Colpix: 1964)

IT'S GONNA TAKE A MIRACLE
(Randazzo/Weinstein/Stallman)**
by The Royalettes (MGM: 1965)

IT'S MY PARTY (Weiner/Gluck Jr/
Gold)** by Lesley Gore
(Mercury: 1963)

LEADER OF THE PACK (Morton/
Barry/Greenwich)** by The
Shangri-Las (Red Bird: 1964)

THE LOCO-MOTION (Goffin/
King)** by Little Eva (Dimension:
1962)

LOOK IN MY EYES (Barrett) by The
Chantels (Carlton: 1961)

A LOVER'S CONCERTO (Linzer/
Randell) by The Toys (Dynovoice:
1965)

MASHED POTATO TIME (Dobbins/
Garrett/Holland/Bateman/Gorman/
Cohen) by Dee Dee Sharp
(Cameo: 1962)

MAYBE (Goldner) by The Chantels
(End: 1958)

MY BOYFRIEND'S BACK (Feldman/
Goldstein/Gottehrer)** by The
Angels (Smash: 1963)

MY GUY (Robinson)** by Mary
Wells (Motown: 1964)

NEEDLE IN A HAYSTACK
(Whitfield/Stevenson) by The
Velvelettes (V.I.P: 1964)

ONE FINE DAY (Goffin/King)** by
The Chiffons (Laurie: 1963)
PLEASE MR POSTMAN (Dobbins/
Garrett/Holland/Bateman/
Gorman)** by The Marvelettes
(Tamla: 1961)
POPSICLES AND ICICLES (Gates)
by The Murmaids
(Chattahoochee: 1963)
REMEMBER (WALKIN' IN THE
SAND) (Morton)** by The
Shangri-Las (Red Bird: 1964)
SALLY GO ROUND THE ROSES
(Sanders/Stevens) by The Jaynetts
(Tuff: 1963)
THE SHOOP SHOOP SONG (IT'S IN
HIS KISS) (Clark)** by Betty
Everett (Vee-Jay: 1964)
STAY AWHILE (Hawker/Raymonde)
by Dusty Springfield (Philips:
1964)
STOP! IN THE NAME OF LOVE
(Holland/Dozier/Holland) by The
Supremes (Motown: 1965)
TELL HIM (Russell)** by The
Exciters (UA: 1962)
THEN HE KISSED ME (Spector/
Barry/Greenwich)** by The
Crystals (Philles: 1963)
(TODAY I MET) THE BOY I'M
GONNA MARRY (Spector/
Greenwich/Powers) by Darlene
Love (Philles: 1963)
TONIGHT'S THE NIGHT (Dixon/
Owens) by The Shirelles (Scepter:
1960)
THE WAH-WATUSI (Mann/Appell)
by The Orlons (Cameo: 1962)
WHENEVER A TEENAGER CRIES
(Maresca) by Reparata and The
Delrons (World Artists: 1965)
WILL YOU LOVE ME TOMORROW
(Goffin/King)** by The Shirelles
(Scepter: 1961)
ZIP A DEE DO DAH (Gilbert/
Wrubel)** by Bob B. Soxx and
The Blue Jeans (Philles: 1963)

* The 'Girl Group Sound' of the late 1950s and
the 1960s is not limited to all-girl groups such as
The Supremes, The Crystals, etc. It can refer to
certain records by solo girls or even mixed-sex
groups such as The Exciters which comprised
three girls and one guy, or even The Essex
who were one girl and three guys. The 'sound'
is more important than the make-up.

BABY I LOVE YOUR WAY
(Peter Frampton)
British guitarist–singer Peter
Frampton's second single hit from
1976 which was featured on his
phenomenally successful double
album *Frampton Comes Alive!*
(A&M: 1976). Revived in 1988 by Will
To Power in a medley with Lynyrd
Skynyrd's FREE BIRD, the song
which had twice been a hit for the
Southern hard rock band, in 1974
and 1977, on MCA. Frampton's song
was also revived by the late Walter
Jackson on his producer Carl Davis'
Chi-Sound label, and was the lead-in
track on their *I Want To Come Back
As A Song* album (Chi-Sound: 1977).

UK HITS: Peter Frampton
(A&M: 1976)
Will To Power: Medley
with FREE BIRD
(Van Zandt/Collins)
(Epic: 1988)
US HITS: Peter Frampton
(A&M: 1976) Pop
Walter Jackson (Chi-
Sound: 1977) Black
Will To Power: Medley
with FREE BIRD
(Van Zandt/Collins)
(Epic: 1988) Pop

BABY I NEED YOUR LOVING
(Brian Holland/Lamont Dozier/Eddie
Holland)
Few artists have the luck to record
such a powerful song for their first
release, but this was indeed the Four
Tops' initial record on Motown. An
anthem that has understandably
stayed with them through their long
career, BABY I NEED YOUR
LOVING was actually an even
bigger chart success when it was
re-made by Johnny Rivers, who, with
his producer Lou Adler, released
two consecutive remakes of Motown
classics: BABY followed by THE

ded by THE FOUR TOPS on Motown Records

BY, I NEED YOUR LOVING

By EDDIE HOLLAND, LAMONT DOZIER and BRIAN HOLLAND

JOBETE

75¢

J-04236

BABY I NEED YOUR LOVING
The Four Tops, it seems, will go on forever, whether people remix and sample their golden hits or not! Led by the lead singer Levi Stubbs (*top left*), their early Motown hits were all original compositions, but they later turned in some fine cover versions of classic hits, such as WALK AWAY RENEE (Calilli/Lookofsky/Sansone), IF I WERE A CARPENTER (Hardin) and IT'S ALL IN THE GAME (Dawes/Sigman) (see also RIVER DEEP MOUNTAIN HIGH).

TRACKS OF MY TEARS. The original British cover of BABY I NEED YOUR LOVING was by Liverpool group The Fourmost, whose biggest claims to fame were hit records of the Lennon/McCartney song HELLO LITTLE GIRL and a non-Beatle tune called LITTLE LOVING (Alquist).

US HITS: The Four Tops (Motown: 1964) Black & Pop
            Johnny Rivers (Imperial: 1967) Pop
UK HIT: The Fourmost (Parlophone: 1964)

One of the later Shirelles singles, SHA LA LA (Taylor/Mosley) (Scepter: 1964), was a huge remake smash for Manfred Mann in both Britain (HMV: 1964) and the States (Ascot: 1965).

See: MAKE IT EASY ON YOURSELF for other songs written by Burt Bacharach with Hal David.

BABY LET'S PLAY HOUSE
(Arthur Gunter)
A rockabilly classic that went, not from blues to rock 'n' roll, but from country to blues to rock 'n' roll. The idea came from I WANT TO PLAY HOUSE WITH YOU (RCA), a Number One country hit in 1951. Bluesman Arthur Gunter wrote it in 1954 for a recording on Excello, which is the version Elvis Presley heard and subsequently covered the following year for Sun.

The song became Elvis' first national chart success, on the country hit parade in the summer of '55.

US HIT: Elvis Presley (Sun: 1955)
            Country

Song later recorded under the title I WANNA PLAY HOUSE WITH YOU by Buddy Holly (Coral: 1955). The Johnny Burnette Trio recorded essentially the same song as OH BABY BABE (Coral: 1956).

Other recordings: Rachel Sweet (Stiff); John Prine (Asylum); Sleepy Labeef (Sun).

John Lennon borrowed part of the BABY LET'S PLAY HOUSE lyric for RUN FOR YOUR LIFE (Lennon/ McCartney) on the Beatles' *Rubber Soul* album (Parlophone: 1965).

BABY PLEASE DON'T GO
(Joe Williams)
Classic blues song from the Mississippi Delta singer–songwriter, Big Joe Williams. Written in 1929, it has been recorded by many artists

HERE COMES THE NIGHT
Irish R&B band Them featuring Van Morrison broke into the UK Top 10 with BABY PLEASE DON'T GO (Williams), but HERE COMES THE NIGHT went even higher.

including Muddy Waters, who included it on his 'live' set on the Beserkley label. It was also one of the theme songs of the classic British rock 'n' roll TV show, "Ready, Steady, Go", the Rediffusion production which started the week-end for millions of viewers in the late 1960s.

The original single by Them was featured on the soundtrack of "Good Morning Vietnam" (Touchstone: 1987) and on the subsequent soundtrack album (A&M: 1988).

UK HIT: Them (UK Decca: 1965)

Other recordings: The Chambers Brothers (Fantasy); AC/DC (Atco) Ted Nugent (Epic); Tom Rush (Prestige); Dion (Columbia); Willie and The Poor Boys (Passport); The Amboy Dukes (Mainstream); Arlo Guthrie (Tomato); Eric Andersen (Vanguard); Georgie Fame and The Blue Flames (UK Columbia).

BABY WHAT YOU WANT ME TO DO
(Jimmy Reed)
Among bluesman Jimmy Reed's most recorded songs. Performed by Elvis Presley on his TV show, "Elvis", in 1968. Sung by The Righteous Brothers in the teen musical, "Beach Ball" (AIP: 1965).

US HIT: Jimmy Reed (Vee-Jay: 1960) Black & Pop

Other recordings: The Righteous Brothers (Philles); Them with Van Morrison (UK Decca); Erma Franklin (Solid Gold); Wishbone Ash (MCA); Elvis Presley (RCA); Hot Tuna (Grunt); Etta James (Argo); Peter and Gordon (Capitol); Little Richard (Modern); The Byrds (Columbia); The Everly Brothers (Warner Bros); Jerry Lee Lewis (Mercury); Freddy Fender; and many others.

Jimmy Reed songs
The Rolling Stones performed various Reed compositions in their early days and some of these performances (such as AIN'T THAT LOVING YOU BABY and BRIGHT LIGHTS, BIG CITY**) found their way onto bootlegs. On the other hand, HONEST I DO was legitimately released (UK Decca). No blues band repertoire was, or is, complete without a selection of Reed numbers.

Another Jimmy Reed classic which had some key cover versions is SHAME, SHAME, SHAME by the Merseybeats (Fontana: 1964), Bryan Ferry (Island: 1976) and by a contemporary of Reed's, Jimmy McCracklin (Art-Tone: 1962). Reed is also remembered for his 1961 R&B seller, BIG BOSS MAN (Smith/Dixon)**.

BAND OF GOLD
(Ronald Dunbar/Edith Wayne)
Motown's ace songwriting team of Holland, Dozier and Holland split from Berry Gordy's label around 1968 and eventually formed their own labels, Hot Wax and Invictus. One of their first hits was BAND OF GOLD, though it fell short of reaching the coveted Number One slot on the American charts – an honour afforded the following year's WANT-ADS (Johnson/Perkins/Perry) by The Honey Cone.

BAND OF GOLD
A former band singer who'd worked with Bob Crosby and Quincy Jones, luscious Freda Payne gave Invictus Records their first major hit.

BAND OF GOLD was also a major dance hit in the clubs and was performed by Modern Romance on the soundtrack of *Party Party* (A&M Sound Pictures: 1982).

US HIT: Freda Payne (Invictus: 1970) Black & Pop
UK HIT: Freda Payne (Invictus: 1970)

Other recordings: Belinda Carlisle (IRS); Sylvester (Megatone); Bonnie Tyler (Columbia).

In part of what has become a growing trend of original artists adding 'guest' vocals to contemporary remakes of their old hits, Freda Payne sang with Belinda Carlisle on her BAND OF GOLD revival (IRS: 1986). Similar appearances have been logged in by Gene Pitney with Mark Almond on SOMETHING'S GOTTEN HOLD OF MY HEART (Cook/Greenaway) and Cliff Richard with the cast of a TV show on "The Young Ones".

See: HOW SWEET IT IS for other Holland/Dozier/Holland songs.

BANG A GONG
See: GET IT ON

BARBARA ANN
(Fred Fassert)
'Baa-baa-baa, baa-baa-barann'
Nonsense singalong intro to this east coast doo-wop classic, originated by The Regents and then immortalized by Dean Torrance (of Jan and Dean) singing lead on the Beach Boys' version.

US HITS:	The Regents (Gee: 1961) Black & Pop
	The Beach Boys (Capitol: 1966) Pop
UK HIT:	The Beach Boys (Capitol: 1966)

Other recordings: Jan and Dean (Liberty); The Who (Track).

BAREFOOTIN'
(Robert Parker)
Written by New Orleans saxophonist Robert Parker after performing at a University of Alabama fraternity party in which everyone took off their shoes when they danced.
Performed in a 1987 Huey Lewis

and The News concert in Paris by Huey along with special guests, Bruce Springsteen and Bob Geldof.

| US HIT: | Robert Parker (Nola: 1966) Black & Pop |
| UK HIT: | Robert Parker (Island: 1966) |

Other recordings: Pete Townshend (Atco); Wilson Pickett (Atlantic); The Fantastic Johnny C (Phil L.A. of Soul); Zoot Money and His Big Roll Band (UK Columbia); Kate Taylor; The Alan Price Set (UK Decca); The Marvelettes (Tamla).

BE MY BABY
(Phil Spector/Ellie Greenwich/Jeff Barry)
The first and finest of all the Ronettes singles, and arguably the best-ever girl group anthem. Revived by certain artists including Jody Miller, who had a Top 20 country hit in 1972 on Epic; yet it's virtually impossible to overshadow the power of the original.
   In 1986, Ronnie Spector (original lead singer of The Ronettes) sang an extract from BE MY BABY; it was part of a hit single she made with Eddie Money of the song TAKE ME HOME TONIGHT (Vale/Leeson), on Columbia.
   The Ronettes' original version was heard on the soundtrack of The Who's "Quadrophenia" (Who Films: 1979), and in the Danish movie, "Twist And Shout" in 1986. Much earlier, The Ronettes themselves were seen performing the song in the concert movie, "The Big TNT Show" (American International: 1966).

US HITS:	The Ronettes (Philles: 1963) Black & Pop
	Andy Kim (Steed: 1970) Pop
UK HIT:	The Ronettes (London: 1963)

BE MY BABY
Who could resist such an invitation, particularly
when it came from the sexy Ronettes, led by
Ronnie Spector (*centre*), wife of producer whiz-kid
supreme Phil Spector.

Other recordings: Ellie Greenwich (Verve); The Bay City Rollers (Arista); John Lennon (Capitol); Carmen Appice (Pasha); Susie Allanson (Warner Bros); Cissy Houston (Janus); Shaun Cassidy (Warner Bros); The Searchers (Pye); The Shirelles (Scepter); Tommy Roe (ABC/Paramount); Ian Whitcomb and Bluesville (Tower); Rachel Sweet; The Honeys (Rhino); *Leader Of The Pack* Cast (Elektra).

See: RIVER DEEP, MOUNTAIN HIGH for other Jeff Barry and Ellie Greenwich songs.

BEAT IT
(Michael Jackson)
From Michael Jackson's ground-breaking, earth-shattering *Thriller* album (Epic: 1982), BEAT IT was the second of his three Number One singles of '83. With a guitar solo by Eddie Van Halen, BEAT IT literally beat all its competition!

US HIT: Michael Jackson (Epic: 1983) Black & Pop
UK HIT: Michael Jackson (Epic: 1983)

Parody record: EAT IT by Weird Al Yankovic (Rock 'n' Roll: 1984).

Parody records
Weird Al Yankovic had been around for a while, cutting one-off parodies such as MY BOLOGNA on Capitol in 1979, which lampooned MY SHARONA (Averre/Fieger), the brief shining light for The Knack that same year. Al's additional strength is that he successfully pantomimes the whole persona of many of the acts whose hits he parodies; in EAT IT, he adopts not only a military uniform reminiscent of Michael Jackson's, but he also brilliantly impersonates Jackson's dance steps and complete routine from the original "Beat It" video.

Yankovic's other contemporary song parodies include GIRLS JUST WANT TO HAVE LUNCH based on GIRLS JUST WANT TO HAVE FUN (Hazard) by Cyndi Lauper, LIKE A SURGEON based on Madonna's hit LIKE A VIRGIN (Steinberg/Kelly), RICKY which borrowed from Toni Basil's MICKEY (Chinn/Chapman), and WHOLE LOTTA LUNCH, derived from Led Zeppelin's WHOLE LOTTA LOVE (Bonham/Jones/ Page/Plant)**. 'Weird Al' did not invent song parodies, but he has created his own individual style of presentation whereby the video plays an integral role in the whole execution of his humour.

British group The Barron Knights used to construct medleys of topical parodies based on then-current pop songs; these continued into the 1980s, but it was their singles in the mid to late 60s which were understandably anticipated and remembered. CALL UP THE GROUPS (UK Columbia: 1964) about the pop groups being drafted into the service was their first and arguably their best effort.

On this, they adapted portions of NEEDLES AND PINS (Nitzsche/ Bono), YOU WERE MADE FOR ME (Murray), I WANNA BE YOUR MAN (Lennon/McCartney), DIANE (Pollack/Rapee), BITS AND PIECES (Clark/Smith) and TWIST AND SHOUT (Russell/Medley) to allow them to point fun at The Searchers, Freddie and The Dreamers, The Rolling Stones, The Bachelors, Dave Clark Five and, of course, The Beatles.

Though The Barron Knights developed their own style and were intrinsically British, CALL UP THE GROUPS was a gentle lift of a 1962 American parody chart single called THE BIG DRAFT by The Four Preps. Although the Knights played gigs just like any of the other pop groups of their day (and were, incidentally, on the bill of one of those famed Beatles' Christmas shows in London at the Astoria Theatre, Finsbury

Park), the bulk of their repertoire was parodies and speciality numbers. By contrast, the Preps had achieved a significant reputation for their own hits of comparatively straight pop singles; two of their records even went Top 10 in the States, namely 26 MILES (SANTA CATALINA) (Larson/Belland) (Capitol: 1958) and its successor, BIG MAN (Larson/Belland) later that same year, which had really put them on the map.

Their first and definitely their best send-up single was MORE MONEY FOR YOU AND ME, recorded 'live' for their *On Campus* album (Capitol: 1961). Group member Glen Larson, who went on to become a major creator–producer of networked TV drama series, explained that President Kennedy's Peace Corps could use the services of several outstanding vocal groups; that was the set-up and the Preps then wove together parodies of MR BLUE (Blackwell), ALLEY OOP (Frazier)**, SMOKE GETS IN YOUR EYES (Kern/Harbach), TOM DOOLEY (arr. Guard) and A TEENAGER IN LOVE (Pomus/Shuman)** and other songs to link together barbs aimed at The Fleetwoods, Hollywood Argyles, Platters, Kingston Trio and Dion and The Belmonts.

I also recall a British rock 'n' roll parody which pre-dated even The Barron Knights. Just prior to becoming a pop star with BE MY GIRL (Singer) (Parlophone: 1956), actor–TV host Jim Dale released a send-up of Lonnie Donegan's own skiffle smash, ROCK ISLAND LINE (UK Decca: 1956), which was called PICCADILLY LINE!

Country music had its own parody originators in Homer and Jethro who adapted many kinds of popular songs, particularly for their RCA record releases which included HOW MUCH IS THAT HOUND DOG IN THE WINDOW (1953) and a version of The Beatles' I WANT TO HOLD YOUR HAND in 1964.

Another more recent group of US mickey-takers (as they'd be called in England) are Big Daddy, an eight-man unit of doo-wop parodists who studiously displace classic rock 'n' roll songs into unrelated periods and styles; for instance, they took Michael Jackson's BILLIE JEAN and set it against a rockabilly backdrop à la Gene Vincent's BE-BOP-A-LULA; similarly, their UK hit, DANCING IN THE DARK (Making Waves: 1985), moulded the Bruce Springsteen song into the way that Pat Boone might perform it.

Finally, honourable mention must be made of Stan Freberg, whose radio shows and comedy albums were highlights of the late 1950s American entertainment scene. His GREEN CHRISTMAS (Capitol: 1958), lampooning the commercialization of the holiday season, is a classic, as are his explorations into the then emerging rock 'n roll scene: HEARTBREAK HOTEL coupled with ROCK ISLAND LINE (Capitol: 1956), SH-BOOM (Capitol: 1954), THE OLD PAYOLA ROLL BLUES (Capitol: 1960) and even his salute to the calypso craze, BANANA BOAT (DAY-O) (Capitol: 1957)...like, crazy man!

Where relevant, parody songs are listed throughout; for instance, LEADER OF THE LAUNDROMAT is shown under LEADER OF THE PACK.

BE-BOP-A-LULA
(Gene Vincent/Sheriff Tex Davis) Deejay 'Sheriff' Tex Davis co-wrote Gene 'The Screaming End' Vincent's breakthrough rocker. Performed by Gene and His Blue Caps in the rock movie, "The Girl Can't Help It" (20th Century Fox: 1956).

US HITS: Gene Vincent and His Blue Caps (Capitol: 1956) Black & Pop

BE-BOP-A-LULA

Classic shot of Gene Vincent and His Blue Caps performing BE-BOP-A-LULA in the all-star rock 'n' roll musical film, "The Girl Can't Help It" (20th Century Fox: 1956). With his rockabilly-based rhythms, Gene Vincent moaned and screamed his way through a series of great singles, but Capitol were never able to repeat the success.

| | The Everly Brothers (Cadence: 1960) Pop |
| UK HIT: | Gene Vincent and His Blue Caps (Capitol: 1956) |

Other recordings: Jerry Lee Lewis (Sun); John Lennon (Apple); The Five Cards Stud (Red Bird). Also included in The Beatles' live recordings made in Hamburg (AFE).

BIG BOSS MAN

(Al Smith/Luther Dixon)
Classic blues first recorded by Jimmy Reed. It formed the major part of a SOUL HOOTENANNY medley single by Gene Chandler (Constellation: 1964).

| US HITS: | Jimmy Reed (Vee-Jay: 1961) Black |
| | B. B. King (MCA: 1985) Black |

Other recordings: Jerry Lee Lewis (Mercury); Freddy Fender (ABC);

Elvis Presley (RCA); The Pretty Things (Fontana); Charlie Rich (Epic); The Grateful Dead (Warner Bros); The Astronauts (RCA); Erma Franklin (Bang); The Animals (UK Decca); The Standells (Vee-Jay); Sleepy Labeef (Sun); John Hammond (Vanguard); The Graham Bond Organization (Charly).

See: BABY WHAT YOU WANT ME TO DO for other Jimmy Reed songs.

THE BIG HURT
(Wayne Shanklin)
'Miss' Toni Fisher originally sang THE BIG HURT and her record is memorable because it was the first time that the track of a commercial record was electronically 'phased'. Song was successfully covered in Britain by Maureen Evans; she was one of the artists who also appeared on Embassy, the label whose budget 'cover' versions of all the current pop hits were sold in major UK branches of F. W. Woolworth, years before the chain began stocking regular full-price products.

US HIT: Miss Toni Fisher (Signet: 1959) Pop
UK HITS: Miss Toni Fisher (Top Rank: 1960)
Maureen Evans (Oriole: 1960)

Other recordings: Del Shannon (Liberty); Vikki Carr (Columbia).

BILLIE JEAN
(Michael Jackson)
The second single to be lifted from Michael Jackson's mega-hit album, *Thriller* (Epic: 1982), it made Number One on both sides of the Atlantic.

US HITS: Michael Jackson (Epic: 1983) Black & Pop
Club House: Medley with the Steely Dan song DO IT AGAIN (Atlantic: 1983) Pop

UK HIT: Michael Jackson (Epic: 1983)

Other recordings: Slingshot (Quality: 1983) whose version is also arranged in a medley with DO IT AGAIN (Becker/Fagen).

Answer record: SUPERSTAR by Lydia Murdock (Team).

In 1989, Stock, Aitken & Waterman produced a major UK hit revival of BLAME IT ON THE BOOGIE (Jackson/Jackson/Krohn) with local artists, Big Fun. The original US hit of the song was by The Jacksons on Epic in 1978.

BLOWIN' IN THE WIND
(Bob Dylan)
Archetypal Dylan protest song from his second album, *Freewheelin' Bob Dylan* (Columbia: 1963). Adopted by the civil rights movement, it remains one of his most recorded songs. A Top 3 single for Peter, Paul and Mary, it was another Top 10 hit when revived by Stevie Wonder.
Performed by Bob Dylan in the 1972 film, "Concert For Bangladesh" (20th Century Fox: 1972).

US HITS: Peter, Paul and Mary (Warner Bros: 1963) Pop
Stevie Wonder (Tamla: 1966) Black & Pop
UK HITS: Peter, Paul and Mary (Warner Bros: 1963)
Stevie Wonder (Tamla Motown: 1966)

Other recordings: Sam Cooke (RCA); The Hollies (EMI Parlophone); Bobby Darin (Capitol); The Staple Singers (Fantasy); Marlene Dietrich (Capitol); The Seekers (EMI); Jackie DeShannon (Imperial); Odetta (RCA); Nina and Frederik (UK Columbia); Cher (Imperial); The Edwin Hawkins Singers (Buddah); New Christy Minstrels (Columbia); Duke Ellington (Reprise); Lester Flatt and Earl

Scruggs (Columbia); Joan Baez
(A&M); The Kingston Trio (Capitol);
Lena Horne (20th Century); Glen
Campbell (Capitol); Walter Jackson
(Okeh).

Bob Dylan songs

Dylan's own self-written hit records
include: LIKE A ROLLING STONE
and POSITIVELY 4TH STREET
(1965), RAINY DAY WOMEN NOS.
12 AND 35 (1966), LAY LADY LAY
(1969) and KNOCKIN' ON
HEAVEN'S DOOR (1973). Among the
hit records of other Bob Dylan songs:

ALL ALONG THE WATCHTOWER**
by The Jimi Hendrix Experience
(Track: 1968)
ALL I REALLY WANT TO DO** by
Cher (Imperial: 1965)
by The Byrds (Columbia: 1965)
DON'T THINK TWICE, IT'S ALL
RIGHT by Peter, Paul and Mary
(Warner Bros: 1963)
by The Wonder Who (aka The
Four Seasons) (Philips: 1965)
A HARD RAIN'S GONNA FALL** by
Bryan Ferry (Island: 1973)
IF YOU GOTTA GO, GO NOW by
Manfred Mann (HMV: 1965)
IT AIN'T ME BABE** by Johnny
Cash (Columbia: 1964)
by The Turtles (White Whale:
1965)
JUST LIKE A WOMAN by Manfred
Mann (Fontana: 1966)
THE MIGHTY QUINN** by Manfred
Mann (Fontana: 1968)
MR TAMBOURINE MAN** by The
Byrds (Columbia: 1965)
MY BACK PAGES by The Byrds
(Columbia: 1967)
SHE BELONGS TO ME by Rick
Nelson (Decca: 1969)
THIS WHEEL'S ON FIRE** by Julie
Driscoll, Brian Auger and The
Trinity (Marmalade: 1968)
by Siouxsie and The Banshees
(Wonderland: 1987)
THE TIMES THEY ARE
A-CHANGIN'** by The Ian
Campbell Folk Group

(Transatlantic: 1965)
by Peter, Paul and Mary (Warner
Bros: 1964)

Among the most recent revivals of
Dylan compositions is a live version
by Guns N' Roses of KNOCKING ON
HEAVEN'S DOOR (Geffen: 1989).

BLUE MONDAY
(Antoine Domino/Dave
Bartholomew)
First recorded by Smiley Lewis for
Imperial in December 1953.
Subsequently cut by label-mate Fats
Domino who performed it in the
classic rock 'n' roll movie, "The Girl
Can't Help It" (20th Century Fox:
1956).

US HIT: Fats Domino (Imperial:
            1956) Black & Pop
UK HIT: Fats Domino (London:
            1957)

Other recordings: The Crickets
(Liberty); Buddy Holly (Coral);
Johnny Morisette (Sar); Frances Faye
(Imperial); Georgie Fame (UK
Columbia); Dave Edmunds (MAM);
Johnny Lee (Warner Bros); Bruce
Channel (Smash); Two Brothers
(Imperial); Delbert McClinton
(ABC).

See: I HEAR YOU KNOCKING for
other Dave Bartholomew songs.

BLUE MOON
(Richard Rodgers/Lorenz Hart)
Here's proof of the longevity of a
great song. Long before rock 'n' roll,
it was written under the title of THE
BAD IN EVERY MAN for Shirley
Ross to sing in a 1934 MGM drama
called "Manhattan Melodrama".
Re-written as BLUE MOON, it
became the theme tune of a radio
series called "Hollywood Hotel" and
was a best-seller for such artists as
Benny Goodman and singer Al
Bowlly with Ray Noble and His
Orchestra. In 1949, Mel Torme took

it back to the charts and sang it in the movie story of its composers, called "Words And Music". Over subsequent years it has been heard in various other movies, including Fellini's "8½", Martin Scorsese's "New York New York" in which it was sung by Robert DeNiro and Mary Kay Place, and in the 1978 screen version of "Grease" when it was sung by Sha Na Na. However, the latter interpretation was styled after the 1960 doo-wop version by The Marcels, immortalized by bass-singer Fred Johnson's 'dang-a-dang dang' introduction.

We got to see The Marcels performing BLUE MOON in one of those rush-out-a-movie-while-the-dance-craze-is-hot productions, "Twist Around The Clock" (Columbia: 1961) which also boasted Chubby Checker and Dion. It was The Marcels' record that jumped out of the soundtrack of Floyd Mutrux's 1971 documentary "Dusty And Sweets McGhee", but the tune's adaptability was finally etched in celluloid in 1980 when director John Landis used three different versions (by The Marcels, Bobby Vinton and Sam Cooke) on the soundtrack of "An American Werewolf In London" (Universal: 1981).

Probably the moodiest of all versions was Elvis Presley's, cut during his sessions for Sam Phillips' Sun label, in July 1954, with Elvis strumming his own acoustic guitar.

US ROCK ERA HITS:	Elvis Presley (RCA: 1956) Pop
	The Marcels (Colpix: 1961) Black & Pop
	Herb Lance and the Classics (Promo: 1961) Pop
	The Ventures (Dolton: 1961) Pop
UK ROCK ERA HITS:	Elvis Presley (HMV: 1956)
	The Marcels (Pye International: 1961)
	Showaddywaddy (Arista: 1980)

Other recordings: Jackie Wilson (Brunswick); Cliff Richard (UK Columbia); Bobby 'Blue' Bland (Duke); Ella Fitzgerald (Verve); Bob Dylan (Columbia); Conway Twitty (MGM); Dizzy Gillespie and Roy Eldridge (Verve); Ivory Joe Hunter (MGM); Frank Sinatra (Capitol); Billy Eckstine (MGM); Benny Goodman (Columbia).

See: TOMORROW NIGHT for other vintage popular standards.

BLUE SUEDE SHOES
(Carl Lee Perkins)
Elvis Presley's second UK hit was a cover of BLUE SUEDE SHOES issued simultaneously with Carl Perkins' own original version! A rockabilly mover, the song was a dance-hall

BLUE MOON
You have to love The Marcels; any record which begins with the doo-wop phrase 'Bomp ba-ba-bomp, ba-ba, ba-ba, bomp' and makes you want to come back for more, has to have its heart in the right place! This was the 1961 international hit revival of the old 1930s song. The Marcels have changed personnel over the years but one of the key ingredients is the resonant bass voice of Fred Johnson (*bottom right*). Incidentally, the group's follow-up singles were of other standard songs including SUMMERTIME (Gershwin/Heyward), HEARTACHES (Klenner/Hoffman) and MY MELANCHOLY BABY (Norton/Burnett).

favourite for years, and, released back-to-back with Elvis' version of Little Richard's TUTTI FRUTTI, it was certainly high on the King's list of priorities when picking tunes for his stage act in later years. Elvis also sang it on the soundtrack of "G.I. Blues" in 1960. The Carl Perkins original tune was featured on the soundtrack of "Porky's Revenge" (20th Century Fox: 1985) and Carl himself sang it in the concert movie, "Johnny Cash – The Man, His World, His Music" (Continental: 1969).

US HITS: Carl Perkins (Sun: 1956)
          Black, Pop & Country
          Elvis Presley (RCA:1956)
          Pop
          Boyd Bennett and His
          Rockets (King: 1956)
          Pop
          Johnny Rivers (UA: 1973)
          Pop
UK HITS: Carl Perkins (London:
          1956)
          Elvis Presley (RCA: 1966)

Other recordings: Eddie Cochran (Liberty); Willie Nelson (Plantation); Merle Haggard (MCA); Cliff Richard (Columbia); Jimi Hendrix (Polydor); Bill Haley and His Comets (Sonet); Billy 'Crash' Craddock (MCA); Jerry Lee Lewis (Mercury); Roy Hall (Decca); The Plastic Ono Band (Apple); Ry Cooder (Warner Bros); Albert King (Stax); Sam 'The Man' Taylor; Pee Wee King.

BLUEBERRY HILL

(Al Lewis/Larry Stock/Vincent Rose)
Fats Domino definitely found his thrill on BLUEBERRY HILL, a 1940 song once sung by cowboy Gene Autry in a movie and originally serenaded into the bestsellers of the day by big band leader Glenn Miller.

The Domino version was recorded in the summer of 1956 at a session in Los Angeles. Fats forgot the lyric in the middle of the song, so they

recorded the whole track in separate sections which were then edited together, a process not in regular use at that time. Producer Dave Bartholomew took the tape and put it on Imperial president Lew Chudd's desk, saying 'That's all we've got.' The label wanted to release something new on Fats Domino and so they released BLUEBERRY HILL which turned out to be one of his biggest-ever hits!

This wasn't the only vintage song which Fats issued as a single; over the years, he charted with several other ballads from the pre-rock era, including: MY BLUE HEAVEN (Whiting/Donaldson), WHEN MY DREAMBOAT COMES HOME (Friend/Franklin), WHAT'S THE REASON I'M NOT PLEASING YOU (Hatch/Tomlin/Poe/Grier), COQUETTE (Kahn/Lombardo/Green), MARGIE (Davis/Conrad/Robinson), and RED SAILS IN THE SUNSET (Kennedy/Williams).

Fats modelled his version after fellow New Orleans legend, Louis Armstrong's 1949 version which, in an odd turnabout, was re-released in competition with Fats' version on the charts.

US ROCK   Fats Domino (Imperial:
ERA HITS: 1956) Black & Pop
           Louis Armstrong (RCA:
           1956) Pop
UK ROCK   Fats Domino (London:
ERA HITS: 1956)
           John Barry Orchestra
           (UK Columbia: 1960)
           Fats Domino (UA: 1976
           Re-release)

Other recordings: The Beach Boys (Reprise); Charles Brown (Mainstream); Dave Clark Five (UK Columbia); Little Richard (Vee-Jay); Cliff Richard and The Shadows (UK Columbia); Mose Allison (Prestige); Elvis Presley (RCA); The Walker Brothers (Philips); Ray Charles (ABC/Paramount); Jerry Lee Lewis (Mercury); The Everly Brothers

(Warner Bros); The Soul Sisters
(Sue).

See: TOMORROW NIGHT for other
vintage popular standards.

BO DIDDLEY
(Ellas McDaniel)
Bo Diddley's self-penned R&B
classic which influenced many of the
British beat groups of the 60s.
Diddley performed it himself in the
1970 D. A. Pennebaker concert
movie, "Toronto Pop", an edited
version of which was released in
1972 as "Keep On Rockin". Song also
featured by Bo Diddley on the
soundtrack of "Fritz The Cat"
(Cinemation: 1972). Finally, another
rock movie performance was
Diddley singing it in "Let The Good
Times Roll" (Columbia: 1973).

Bo Diddley later updated the
song, re-cutting it for Chess as BO
DIDDLEY 1969.

US HIT: Bo Diddley (Checker:
            1955) Black
UK HIT: Buddy Holly (Coral: 1963)

Other recordings: Bob Seger
(Capitol); The Royal Guardsmen
(Laurie); Art Neville (Cinderella);
Chubby Checker (Parkway);
Bobby Vee (Liberty); Tim
Hardin (Columbia); New
York City Band (American
International); Little Richard
(Demand); Art Neville
(Sansu).

Bo Diddley songs
R&B guitarist–singer Bo Diddley was
the classical composer of the British
beat group repertoires of the
mid-1960s. Five of the first eleven
(unreleased) songs which The
Rolling Stones recorded were those
of the master. The Yardbirds, The
Pretty Things (who named
themselves after a Bo Diddley song)
and The Animals (who wrote the
tribute, STORY OF BO DIDDLEY)
were especially indebted to the
genius of the 'chunka-chunka' beat.
This is what Johnny Otis, who used
the same rhythm for WILLIE AND
THE HAND JIVE, called the 'Shave
and a haircut, six bits' sound.

Other versions of Bo Diddley
songs include:

BEFORE YOU ACCUSE ME by
    Creedence Clearwater Revival
    (Fantasy: 1971)
DIDDY WAH DIDDY (written with
    Willie Dixon): by Captain
    Beefheart (A&M: 1966)
    by The Remains (Epic: 1966)
HERE 'TIS by The Yardbirds (UK
    Columbia: 1965)
HEY BO DIDDLEY by The Animals
    (1963)

BO DIDDLEY
Hey, Bo Diddley! Many of us got
to know Bo and his rocking
rumba rhythms via his
appearances in London and on
British television during the
1960s R&B beat boom.

I CAN TELL by Johnny Kidd and
The Pirates (HMV: 1962)
by The Pirates (Warner Bros: 1977)
by Ray Anton and the Peppermint
Men (UK Columbia: 1963)
I'M A MAN** by The Who
(Brunswick: 1965)
by The Yardbirds (UK Columbia:
1965)
I'M ALRIGHT by The Rolling Stones
(UK Decca: 1965)
MAMA KEEP YOUR BIG MOUTH
SHUT by The Pretty Things
(Fontana: 1965)
MONA (I NEED YOU BABY) by
Quicksilver Messenger Service
(Capitol: 1969)
by The Rolling Stones (UK Decca:
1964)
by The Nashville Teens (UK
Decca: 1964)
OH YEAH by The Shadows Of
Knight (Dunwich: 1966)
PRETTY GIRL by The Yardbirds
(UK Columbia: 1964)
by The Pretty Things (Fontana:
1965)
ROAD RUNNER by The Gants
(Liberty: 1965)
by The Pretty Things (Fontana:
1965)
by The Animals (UK Columbia:
1965)
WHO DO YOU LOVE** by Juicy
Luicy (Vertigo: 1970)

For a taste of the real thing, check
out Bo Diddley's performance in
"The Big TNT Show" (AIP: 1966), in
which he performs his own BO
DIDDLEY and ROAD RUNNER.

BOOK OF LOVE
(Warren Davis/Charles Patrick/
George Malone)
'Oh I wun-der, wun-der, who?!' sang
The Monotones, asking perhaps the
ultimate rock 'n' roll question. The
song was inspired by a toothpaste
commercial.
    East-coast R&B song which was a

major 1958 success for one-hit wonder
group, The Monotones. Songwriters
Jeff Barry and Ellie Greenwich
revived the song under their alias,
The Raindrops, for Jubilee in 1964.

US HIT: The Monotones (Argo:
             1958) Black & Pop
UK HIT: The Mudlarks (UK
             Columbia: 1958)

A two-boy, one-girl British group,
The Mudlarks had previously made
the local charts with their cover of
LOLLIPOP (Ross/Dixon) which was
originally made popular in the States
by The Chordettes (Cadence: 1958).

BOOM BOOM
(John Lee Hooker)
After BOOGIE CHILLUN, this is
probably the most recognized of
bluesman John Lee Hooker's songs,
popularized during the 1960s beat
boom by Eric Burdon and The
Animals, whose early repertoire
included not only Hooker tunes but
also DON'T LET ME BE
MISUNDERSTOOD and HOUSE OF
THE RISING SUN, both blues
standards which are covered in their
own separate entries here. Hooker's
own Vee-Jay recording of BOOM
BOOM was a minor hit on the US
singles chart. Hooker's songs were
part of every British R&B group in
the 1960s; and BOOM BOOM stands
the test of time featuring in Bruce
Springsteen's live set in 1989.

US HITS: John Lee Hooker (Vee-
            Jay: 1962) Black & Pop
            The Animals (MGM: 1965)
            Pop

Other recordings: The Yardbirds
(Polygram).

John Lee Hooker songs
Versions of other John Lee Hooker
songs include:

BOOGIE CHILLUN by John Lee
Hooker (Sensation: 1950)

by John Lee Hooker and Canned
Heat (Liberty: 1970)
CRAWLIN' KING SNAKE BLUES by
The Doors (Elektra: 1971)
DIMPLES (written with James
Bracken) by The Allman Brothers
Band (Capricorn: 1974)
by The Spencer Davis Group
(Fontana: 1965)
GOIN' UPSTAIRS by Sam Samudio
(Atlantic: 1971)
I'M MAD by The Animals (UK
Columbia: 1964)
ONE BOURBON, ONE SCOTCH,
ONE BEER by George Thorogood
and The Destroyers (EMI
America: 1986)
SERVES YOU RIGHT TO SUFFER
by The J. Geils Band (Atlantic:
1971)

BORN IN THE USA
(Bruce Springsteen)
Opening song and title track from
Bruce Springsteen's seventh album
(Columbia: 1984). A version by The
Stanley Clarke Band was a mini US
Black hit in mid-1985 on Epic.

US HIT: Bruce Springsteen
            (Columbia: 1985) Pop
UK HIT: Bruce Springsteen (CBS:
            1985)

Parody record: BORN IN EAST L.A.
by Cheech and Chong, a Top 50
Chart Single on MCA in 1985.

See: PINK CADILLAC for other
Bruce Springsteen songs.

BORN TO BE WILD
(Mars Bonfire)
Pivotal song from the great rock
music soundtrack for the Peter
Fonda/Dennis Hopper motorcycle
movie, "Easy Rider" (Columbia:
1969). Song was covered by Wilson
Pickett who made the lower rungs of
the pop and black charts (Atlantic:
1969).

Performed by Blue Oyster Cult in
their concert movie with Black
Sabbath, "Black And Blue" (Daltyn:
1980).

US HIT: Steppenwolf (Dunhill:
            1968) Pop
UK HIT: Steppenwolf (Stateside:
            1969)

Other recordings: Blue Oyster Cult
(Columbia); Cult (Sire); Lizzy Borden
(Capitol); Zodiac Mindwarp and The
Love Reaction (Polydor); Riot
(Capitol); Eclipse (Casablanca);
Wilson Pickett (Atlantic).

BORN TO BE WILD was just one of a
group of songs revived by Wilson
Pickett; see also entries on HEY JOE,
HEY JUDE, LAND OF 1000 DANCES,
STAGGER LEE, SUGAR SUGAR and
YOU KEEP ME HANGIN' ON.
Another tune with a previous life was
MUSTANG SALLY (Rice) which had
originally charted for Sir Mack Rice
(Blue Rock: 1965) and was then
released by The Young Rascals on
the flipside of their GOOD LOVIN'**
seller (Atlantic: 1966) prior to
Wilson's crossover hit version of
MUSTANG that same year on the
same label!

THE BOY FROM NEW YORK CITY
(John Taylor)
'Ooh-wah, ooh-wah, cool, cool, Kitty'
sing the four male members of The
Ad Libs as they cajole lead singer
Mary Ann Thomas into telling them
about her uptown lover who looks so
cute 'in his mohair suit'! Adam White,
in his liner for *The Red Bird Story*
album (Charly: 1987), recounts Jerry
Wexler naming the group The Ad
Libs after a New York club, though
the record label wanted to call them
The Cheerios after a breakfast
cereal.

US HITS: The Ad Libs (Blue Cat:
            1965) Black & Pop
            Manhattan Transfer
            (Atlantic: 1981) Pop

UK HIT: Darts (Magnet: 1978)

Recorded as THE GIRL FROM NEW YORK CITY by Unit Four Plus Two (UK Decca).

THE BOY FROM NEW YORK CITY
Four boys (and one girl) from New York City, namely The Ad Libs.

BREAK-A-WAY
(Jackie DeShannon/Sharon Sheeley)
An uptempo turnaround for New Orleans singer Irma Thomas (Imperial: 1964). Complete with handclaps and backup chanting chorus, it had the feeling of the 1960s girl-group sound and was perfect for British actress–comedienne–singer Tracey Ullman's timely revival almost two decades later. Her single went Top 5 in England and made it into the lower rungs of the US Pop 100.

UK HIT: Tracey Ullman (Stiff: 1983)
US HIT: Tracey Ullman (MCA: 1984) Pop

Other recording: Beryl Marsden (UK Columbia).

DeShannon and Sheeley songs
Singer–songwriter Jackie DeShannon wrote many songs with Sharon (Shari) Sheeley who was Eddie Cochran's fiancée when the rocker died in 1960. Four of their compositions were successfully recorded by Brenda Lee: DUM DUM (Decca: 1961), HEART IN HAND (Decca: 1962), SO DEEP (Decca: 1962) and HE'S SO HEAVENLY (Decca: 1963).

Another winning DeShannon/Sheeley collaboration was (HE'S) THE GREAT IMPOSTOR, a US hit for The Fleetwoods (Dolton: 1961). Sharon Sheeley was probably the first female composer of the 1950s to achieve a Number One rock and pop record...it was POOR LITTLE FOOL by Ricky Nelson (Imperial: 1958).

See: WHEN YOU WALK IN THE ROOM for other Jackie DeShannon songs.

BREAKFAST IN BED
(Donnie Fritts/Eddie Hinton)
One of 1988's best reggae-based singles featured a song that has already had several lives.

Written by keyboard player Donnie Fritts and guitarist Eddie Hinton, the first released version was by British singer Dusty Springfield, from the same *Dusty In Memphis* album which had also produced her Top 10 single SON OF A PREACHER MAN (Hurley/Wilkins). American R&B singer Baby Washington followed with a version (Cotillion: 1969), but it was Dusty's version which eeked on to the back end of Billboard's Hot 100. Among the first-known reggae versions was one by Lorna Bennett (Island: 1973) which, though never making a dent on any pop charts, made an impression on many, including members of UB40. They had already joined forces with Chrissie Hynde for a successful re-working of I GOT YOU BABE (Bono)** in 1985 and, three years later, they teamed up with the lead singer of The Pretenders once more.

UK HIT: UB40 with Chrissie Hynde
           (Dep International:
           1988)
US HIT: UB40 with Chrissie Hynde
           (A&M: 1988) Pop

Other recordings: James Taylor (Apple); Angela Stewart (Brotherhood Music); Jack Wilson (Up Tempo); Peter Straker (Polydor); Floyd Cramer (RCA).

BREAKING UP IS HARD TO DO
(Neil Sedaka/Howard Greenfield)
One example of the great Neil Sedaka pop ballads and a first-class example of the rare occasions on which a Top 10 hit song is re-cut successfully by the same artist.

US HITS: Neil Sedaka (RCA: 1962)
           Black & Pop
           The Happenings (B. T.
           Puppy: 1968) Pop
           Lenny Welch
           (Commonwealth
           United: 1970) Black &
           Pop
           The Partridge Family
           (Bell: 1972) Pop
           Neil Sedaka (Rocket:
           1976) Pop
UK HITS: Neil Sedaka (RCA: 1962)
           The Partridge Family
           (Bell: 1972)

Other recordings: Jivin' Gene (Mercury); Johnny Preston (Mercury); Sha Na Na (Buddah); The Carpenters (A&M); Brian Poole and The Tremeloes (UK Decca); Shelley Fabares (Colpix); The Four Seasons (Philips).

Parody: In 1984, the American Bell Telephone system was broken up into separate companies. The American Comedy Network constructed a parody of BREAKING

UP IS HARD TO DO under the title BREAKING UP IS HARD ON YOU, aka DON'T TAKE MA BELL AWAY FROM ME. The single was released by Critique Records.

BREAKING UP IS HARD TO DO
STAIRWAY TO HEAVEN was another of Neil Sedaka's early single hits on RCA. With his writing partner Howard Greenfield, he also wrote some key hits for Connie Francis. Greenfield later teamed up with Carole King to compose CRYING IN THE RAIN for The Everly Brothers.

Sedaka and Greenfield songs
Among the hit records of other Neil Sedaka and Howard Greenfield songs:

ANOTHER SLEEPLESS NIGHT by
    Jimmy Clanton (Ace: 1960)
CALENDAR GIRL by Neil Sedaka
    (RCA: 1961)
THE DIARY by Neil Sedaka (RCA:
    1959)

FALLIN' by Connie Francis (MGM: 1958)
FRANKIE by Connie Francis (MGM: 1959)
HAPPY BIRTHDAY, SWEET SIXTEEN by Neil Sedaka (RCA: 1961)
I GO APE by Neil Sedaka (RCA: 1959)
LITTLE DEVIL by Neil Sedaka (RCA: 1961)
LOVE WILL KEEP US TOGETHER by The Captain and Tennille (A&M: 1975)
NEXT DOOR TO AN ANGEL by Neil Sedaka (RCA: 1962)
OH CAROL** by Neil Sedaka (RCA: 1959)
STAIRWAY TO HEAVEN by Neil Sedaka (RCA: 1960)
STUPID CUPID by Connie Francis (MGM: 1958)
WHERE THE BOYS ARE by Connie Francis (MGM: 1961)
YOU MEAN EVERYTHING TO ME by Neil Sedaka (RCA: 1960)

Known primarily as both a singer and a songwriter, Neil Sedaka played percussion on Bobby Darin's DREAM LOVER (Darin) (Atco:1959) and chimes on The Willows' original of CHURCH BELLS MAY RING (Craft/The Willows) (Melba: 1956).

BRIDGE OVER TROUBLED WATER
(Paul Simon)
Many regard BRIDGE OVER TROUBLED WATER as Simon and Garfunkel's best-ever recording. It was one of their three Number One singles between 1965 and 1970 and was the title track of a hugely successful album. The majestic sweep of its melody, usually ushered in by a piano intro, was transposed into many varying styles including both R&B and country as listed below.

US HITS: Simon and Garfunkel (Columbia: 1970) Pop
Aretha Franklin (Atlantic: 1971) Black & Pop
Buck Owens (Capitol: 1971) Country
Linda Clifford (RSO: 1979) Black & Pop
UK HITS: Simon and Garfunkel (CBS: 1970)
Linda Clifford (RSO: 1979)

Other recordings: Elvis Presley (RCA); Roberta Flack (Atlantic); Gladys Knight and The Pips (Soul); Chet Atkins and Jerry Reed (RCA); Quincy Jones (A&M); Boots Randolph (Monument); Stevie Wonder (Tamla); King Curtis (Atco); The Jackson 5 (Motown); Chairmen Of The Board (Invictus); Smokey Robinson and The Miracles (Tamla); Cilla Black (Parlophone); Jessi Colter and Waylon Jennings (RCA); The Supremes (Motown); The Five Blind Boys Of Alabama (Wand); Willie Nelson (Columbia).

Parody: Not so much of the song, but English folksinger-cum-comedian Trevor Crozier, anxious to identify the county town of his Somerset base, entitled his 1970s album *Trouble Over Bridgwater.*

BRIGHT LIGHTS, BIG CITY
(Jimmy Reed)
Bluesman Jimmy Reed's classic urban celebration which was performed by Donald Fagen on the soundtrack of "Bright Lights, Big City" (UA: 1988); the movie, which starred Michael J. Fox, was based on a book by Jay McInerney, not on the song.

US HITS: Jimmy Reed (Vee-Jay: 1961) Black & Pop
Sonny James (Capitol: 1971) Country

Other recordings: Them with Van Morrison (UK Decca); The Animals (UK Columbia); The Persuasions.

See: BABY WHAT YOU WANT ME TO DO for other Jimmy Reed songs.

BRING IT ON HOME TO ME
(Sam Cooke)
Piano-driven blues ballad which Sam Cooke sang, supported by fellow gospel-trained singer, Lou Rawls. Actually based on a churchy regional seller by Charles Brown together with Amos Milburn called I WANT TO GO HOME (Ace: 1959). Brown recalls: '(Sam Cooke) came to see me in Newport, Kentucky. I was doing "I Want To Go Home"...Amos and I had done that and it was a very popular thing in Ohio...Sam said, "Charles, we're gonna do that when you come out to California." When I did come out there, I didn't go to the session, I went to the races!'

US HITS: Sam Cooke (RCA: 1962)
           Black & Pop
           The Animals (MGM: 1965)
           Pop
           Eddie Floyd (Stax: 1968)
           Black & Pop
UK HITS: The Animals (UK
           Columbia: 1965)
           Rod Stewart
           (Mercury:1974)

Other recordings: Joe Simon (Vee-Jay); John Lennon (Capitol); Mickey Gilley (Playboy); Dave Clark Five (UK Columbia); Lou Rawls (Capitol); Bill Haley and His Comets (Sonet); Dave Mason (Columbia); Tony Orlando (Elektra); Van Morrison (Warner Bros); Sonny Terry and Brownie McGhee (A&M); Diana Ross and The Supremes (Motown); Aretha Franklin (Atlantic); Eddie Floyd (Stax); Little Richard (Modern); Sonny Boy Williamson (Chess); Millie (Fontana).

Answer record: I'LL BRING IT ON HOME TO YOU by Carla Thomas (Atlantic: 1962).

See: ONLY SIXTEEN for other Sam Cooke songs.

BROWN-EYED HANDSOME MAN
(Chuck Berry)
Chuck Berry recorded his own original version and the song was a Top 5 country hit thirteen years later by Waylon Jennings. It didn't become a hit in Britain until 1963, when a posthumous release of a previously unissued track by Buddy Holly took the song up to Number Three.

US HITS: Chuck Berry (Chess:
           1956) Black
           Waylon Jennings (RCA:
           1969) Country
UK HIT: Buddy Holly (Coral: 1963)

Other recordings: Elvis Presley (Sun); Wanda Jackson (Capitol); Tanya Tucker (MCA); Bobby Vee (Liberty); Jerry Lee Lewis (Smash); John Hammond (Atlantic); Taj Mahal; Mitch Ryder (Dynovoice); Johnny Rivers (Imperial).

See: MEMPHIS for other Chuck Berry songs.

BUT I DO
(Robert Guidry/Paul Gayten)
Clarence Henry's first record, AIN'T GOT NO HOME (Henry)** never happened in Britain, but his two big ballads which followed were big hits on Pye who had the Argo product for the UK. BUT I DO was co-written by Robert Guidry, a.k.a Bobby Charles, the guy who also gave us SEE YOU LATER ALLIGATOR**.

US HIT: Clarence 'Frogman'
           Henry (Argo: 1961)
           Black & Pop
UK HIT: Clarence 'Frogman'
           Henry (Pye
           International: 1961)

Other recordings: Bobby Charles (Rice 'N' Gravy); Tommy Roe (Monument); The Walker Brothers (Philips); Bobby Vinton (Epic); Frankie Avalon (Reprise).

Clarence Henry's follow-up hit on both sides of the Atlantic was YOU ALWAYS HURT THE ONE YOU LOVE (Roberts/Fisher), a 1940s song made popular originally by The Mills Brothers.

BYE BYE LOVE
(Boudleaux Bryant/Felice Bryant)
The song that started it all for The Everlys. Wesley Rose, head of the Acuff-Rose publishing house, had been told about Don and Phil by guitarist Chet Atkins; Rose became their manager and had two of his staff writers come up with a song for The Everly Brothers. Performed by Ben Vereen and Roy Scheider in Bob Fosse's semi-autobiographical movie, "All That Jazz" (20th Century Fox: 1979).

US HITS: The Everly Brothers
(Cadence: 1957) Black,
Country & Pop
Webb Pierce (Decca:
1957) Country
Philippe Wynne: Medley
with: WAIT 'TIL
TOMORROW (Fantasy:
1983) Black
UK HIT: The Everly Brothers
(London: 1957)

Other recordings: George Harrison (Capitol); Kenny Vance (Gold Castle); Rita Coolidge (A&M); Simon and Garfunkel (Columbia); Ray Charles (ABC/Paramount); Earl Scruggs (Columbia); Connie Francis and Hank Williams Jr (MGM); The Newbeats (Hickory); Dale and Grace (Montel); The Righteous Brothers (Moonglow); Barbara Fairchild and Billy Walker (Paid); Moe Bandy and Joe Stamply (Columbia).

Boudleaux and Felice Bryant
The Everlys cut the following other songs by The Bryants:

POOR JENNY (Cadence: 1959)
PROBLEMS (Cadence: 1958)
TAKE A MESSAGE TO MARY
(Cadence: 1959)
WAKE UP LITTLE SUSIE**
(Cadence: 1957)

They also recorded these titles, written by Boudleaux Bryant on his own:

ALL I HAVE TO DO IS DREAM**
(Cadence: 1958)
BIRD DOG (Cadence: 1958)
DEVOTED TO YOU (Cadence: 1958)
LIKE STRANGERS (Cadence: 1960)
LOVE HURTS** (Warner Bros: 1960)

C

C. C. RIDER
See: SEE SEE RIDER

CALIFORNIA DREAMIN'
(John Phillips/Michelle Phillips)
The song which prompted the Rolling Stones' then producer–manager Andrew Oldham to take out an ad in the "New Musical Express" (25 March 1966 edition) saying that it (CALIFORNIA DREAMIN') is 'more relative to today than the general election which can only bring more bigotry, unfulfilled promises and the ultimately big bringdown'. While also adding that he had nothing to do with the record...'I just like it', Oldham concluded: 'CALIFORNIA DREAMIN' won't put the country back on it's feet but it will give you a helluva lift for two minutes and thirty two seconds and sometimes that can be a long time'. Whether they heeded Oldham's words or not, the British record buyers put the single in the charts, though the Mamas and Papas found greater UK success with three later releases: MONDAY, MONDAY (Phillips) also in 1966 and DEDICATED TO THE ONE I LOVE (Pauling/Bass)** and CREEQUE ALLEY (Phillips/Gilliam), both from 1967.

US HITS: The Mamas and The Papas
(Dunhill: 1966) Pop

Bobby Womack (Minit:
1969) Black & Pop
America (American
International: 1979) Pop
The Beach Boys (Capitol:
1986) Pop
UK HITS: The Mamas and The
Papas (RCA: 1966)
Colorado (Pinnacle: 1978)

Other recordings: George Benson
(CTI); Melanie (Midsong); The
Seekers (UK Columbia); Jose
Feliciano (RCA); Bill Black's Combo
(Hi); Barry McGuire (Dunhill).

CALIFORNIA GIRLS
(Brian Wilson)
From the carefree period of the
Beach Boys' *Summer Days (And
Summer Nights!)* album (Capitol:
1965), from which HELP ME
RHONDA was also lifted,
CALIFORNIA GIRLS with its
memorable keyboard intro remains
one of the archetypal beach party
anthems. Adding more than a
passing dab of authenticity, Beach
Boy Carl Wilson contributed to the
backup vocals on David Lee Roth's
very successful remake of
CALIFORNIA GIRLS, two decades
after the original was first released.

US HITS: The Beach Boys (Capitol:
1965) Pop
David Lee Roth (Warner
Bros: 1985) Pop
UK HIT: The Beach Boys (Capitol:
1965)

Other recordings: Leif Garrett
(Atlantic); The Chipmunks (Liberty);
Jan and Dean (Rhino).

See: GOOD VIBRATIONS for other
Beach Boys hits.

CAN I GET A WITNESS
(Brian Holland/Lamont Dozier/Eddie
Holland)
Britain was so unprepared for the
Motown sound, but its disciples in
the form of local promotion man

Tony Hall and groups like The
Stones and The Beatles gradually
changed all that. Yet it didn't happen
overnight. Marvin Gaye's CAN I GET
A WITNESS, a joyous gospel
statement, driven by its underlying
12-bar blues rhythm, emerged
triumphantly on *The Rolling Stones*
(UK Decca: 1964), the group's debut
album. Other British artists were
performing the song, but Marvin
only got brief bites at the UK chart
with HOW SWEET IT IS (Holland/
Dozier/Holland)** in '68 and then
with the same writers' LITTLE
DARLING, I NEED YOU in '66 (a
song which would later be covered
by The Doobie Brothers); it wasn't
until I HEARD IT THROUGH THE
GRAPEVINE** soared to Number
One in 1969 that Marvin Gaye finally
became a household name in the UK.

US HITS: Marvin Gaye (Tamla:
1963) Black & Pop
Lee Michaels (A&M:
1971) Pop
UK HIT: Sam Brown (A&M: 1989)

Other recordings: The Rolling Stones
(UK Decca); Gloria Jones (Minit);
Lulu and The Luvvers (UK Decca);
Stevie Wonder (Tamla); Diana Ross
and The Supremes (Motown); Dusty
Springfield (Philips).

Answer record: NOW I'VE GOT A
WITNESS (Phelge) by The Rolling
Stones (UK Decca: 1964).

CAN'T HELP FALLING IN LOVE
(Hugo Peretti/Luigi Creatore/George
Weiss)
Performed by Elvis Presley in his
"Blue Hawaii" movie (Paramount:
1961). Actually based on PLAISIR
D'AMOUR* by French classical
composer Giovanni Martini.

US HITS: Elvis Presley (RCA: 1962)
Pop
Al Martino (Capitol: 1970)
Pop
Corey Hart (EMI
America: 1987) Pop

UK HITS: Elvis Presley (RCA: 1962)
Andy Williams (CBS: 1970)

Other recordings: We Five (A&M); Bob Dylan (Columbia); Shirley Bassey (UA); Engelbert Humperdinck (Epic).

* Recorded as PLAISIR D'AMOUR by Marianne Faithfull (UK Decca); PLAISIR D'AMOUR also crops up in the most unusual places; for example, actor James Woods sings a few lines in the movie, "Best Seller" (Orion: 1987).

CHAINS
(Gerry Goffin/Carole King)
'My baby's got me locked up in chains' chanted The Cookies, three New York girls, one of whom (Earl-Jean) would later go solo and cut the original of I'M INTO SOMETHING GOOD (Goffin/King)** which was successfully covered by Herman's Hermits. CHAINS was picked up by The Beatles who used it on their *Please Please Me* album on Parlophone in 1963.

US HIT: The Cookies (Dimension: 1962) Black & Pop

UK HIT: The Cookies (London: 1963)

Other recordings: Carole King (Capitol); Stanky Brown (Sire); The Orlons (Cameo).

See: UP ON THE ROOF for other Gerry Goffin and Carole King songs.

CHANTILLY LACE
(J. P. Richardson)
'Hello, Baby...this is the Big Bopper speaking...'
 J. P. Richardson's spoken introduction to his only Top 10 single, the song of which is also preceded by the Bopper's famous line 'Oh baby, you know what I like!'
 Only 28 when he died, Richardson was killed in the same 1959 plane crash that took the lives of Buddy Holly and Ritchie Valens; in fact, the single was still on the British hit parade when the tragedy occurred.
 Another of J.P.'s songs, RUNNING BEAR, was an international smash for Johnny Preston (Mercury: 1959) while his WHITE LIGHTNING charged for George Jones (Mercury: 1959) and was performed by Eddie Cochran and Gene Vincent on the British "Boy Meets Girls" TV show in 1960.

US HIT: The Big Bopper
(Mercury: 1958) Pop
Jerry Lee Lewis
(Mercury: Country)
UK HIT: The Big Bopper
(Mercury: 1958)

Other recordings: Bruce Channel (Smash); Shorty Long (Soul); Don Lang and His Twisters (UK Decca); Rene and Rene (ABC)

Answer record: BOPPER 48-6609 by Donna Dameron (Dart: 1959)

CHAINS
The Cookies sang on records with some of the Brill Building writers, including Carole King, and it was through her that they were the back-up voices on Little Eva's THE LOCOMOTION.

Telephone songs
Other R&B/R&R songs referring to
telephone calls and/or using the
telephone sound effect include:

BEECHWOOD 4-5789 (Stevenson/
Gordy/Gaye) by The Marvelettes
(Tamla: 1962)
CALL OPERATOR 210 (Dixon) by
Floyd Dixon (Aladdin: 1952)
DON'T HANG UP (Mann/Appell) by
The Orlons (Cameo: 1962)
DON'T LOSE MY NUMBER (Collins)
by Phil Collins (Atlantic: 1985)
867-5309/JENNY (Keller/Call) by
Tommy Tutone (Columbia: 1982)
HOT LINE (Perren/St Lewis) by The
Sylvers (Capitol: 1976)
I'M NOT IN LOVE (Gouldman/
Stewart) by 10CC (Mercury: 1975)
LILLIE MAE (Clayton) by Tony Allen
(Aladdin: 1957)
MEMPHIS** by Chuck Berry
(Chess: 1958)
MR TELEPHONE MAN (Parker Jr)
by New Edition (MCA: 1985)
NAME AND NUMBER
(Curiosity/Skinner) by Curiosity
(Mercury: 1989)
OPERATOR (Spivery) by Manhattan
Transfer (Atlantic: 1975)
OPERATOR (Watson/Calloway/
Calloway/Lipscomb) by Midnight
Star (Elektra: 1985)
RIKKI, DON'T LOSE THAT NUMBER
(Becker/Fagen) by Steely Dan
(ABC: 1974)
(619) 239-K.I.N.G. (Nixon) by Mojo
Nixon (Enigma: 1989)
634-5789 (SOULSVILLE, USA)
(Cropper/Floyd) by Wilson
Pickett (Atlantic: 1966)
TELEPHONE LINE (Lynne) by
Electric Light Orchestra (UA:
1977)
YELLOW KIMONO (TOKYO TIME)
(Lyle) Lyle-McGuinness Band
(Cool King: 1983)
plus the great country song HE'LL
HAVE TO GO (Allison/Allison),
recorded by Jim Reeves (RCA:
1960) along with its answer
version, HE'LL HAVE TO STAY
by Jeanne Black (Capitol: 1960).

CHAPEL OF LOVE
(Phil Spector/Jeff Barry/Ellie
Greenwich)
'Going to the chapel' is how the three
Dixie Cups began their
unaccompanied opening phrase to
this, another of the memorable girl-
group hits of the 1960s. Their original
single was heard on the soundtrack
of the Vietnam-war movie "Full Metal
Jacket" (Warner Bros: 1987) and the
song was performed by Bette Midler
in her movie, "Divine Madness"
(Warner Bros: 1980).

The Dixie Cups' original manager
was Joe Jones, remembered for his
own hit record of YOU TALK TOO
MUCH (Roulette: 1960); as such,
you'll see Joe's name listed on the
credits of another of the Dixie Cups'
hits, IKO IKO**.

US HIT: The Dixie Cups (Red
          Bird: 1964) Black & Pop
UK HIT: The Dixie Cups (Pye
          International: 1964)

Other recordings: The Crystals
(Philles); The Beach Boys (Brother);
Bette Midler (Atlantic); The Ronettes
(Philles); Penny Marshall and Cindy
Williams (Atlantic); Frankie Avalon
in a medley with I'M GONNA GET
MARRIED (Price/Logan) (De Lite);
Ellie Greenwich (Verve); *Leader of
the Pack* Cast (Elektra).

See: RIVER DEEP, MOUNTAIN
HIGH for other Jeff Barry and Ellie
Greenwich songs.

Wedding songs
Other memorable R&B/R&R
'wedding' and 'marriage' songs
include:

DOWN THE AISLE OF LOVE
(Haymon/Carr/Cristi/Holmes/
Sexton/Scott) by The Quin-Tones
(Hunt: 1958)
I WANT TO GET MARRIED
(Walton/Sanders) by The
Delicates (Challenge: 1964)
I WISH THAT WE WERE MARRIED

(Weiss/Lewis) by Ronnie and The
Hi-Lites (Joy: 1962)
I'M GONNA GET MARRIED (Price/
Logan) by Lloyd Price
(ABC/Paramount: 1959)
MATRIMONY (Madison/Williams) by
Tiny Tip and The Tip Tops
(Chess: 1962)
WEDDING BELL BLUES (Nyro) by
5th Dimension (Soul City: 1969)
WHEN WE GET MARRIED (Hogan)
by Larry Graham (Warner Bros:
1980)
by The Intruders (Gamble: 1970)
WHERE WERE YOU (ON OUR
WEDDING DAY?) (Price/Logan/
Patton) by Lloyd Price
(ABC/Paramount: 1959)

C'MON EVERYBODY
(Eddie Cochran/Jerry Capehart)
'When you hear the music you just
can't sit still, If your brother won't
rock, then your sister will.'

Eddie Cochran's classic rocker and
one of the finest youth anthems of the
1950s. Originally written and first
recorded under the title LET'S GET
TOGETHER. In 1988, it was adapted
for a 501 Jeans commercial, depicting
Eddie and his girlfriend/songwriter,
Sharon Sheeley. The popularity of
the TV ad propelled EMI's reissue of
the original mono single into Britain's
Top 20.

US HIT: Eddie Cochran (Liberty:
            1959) Pop
UK HITS: Eddie Cochran (London:
            1959)
            Eddie Cochran (EMI:
            1988 Re-release)

Other recordings: Humble Pie
(A&M); The Gants (Liberty); Ray
Allen and The Upbeats (Sinclair);
NRBQ (Columbia); The Sex Pistols
(Virgin).

See: ROCK AROUND THE CLOCK
for the SWING THE MOOD record.

COME GO WITH ME
(Clarence E. Quick)
All-time doo-wop classic. The Del-
Vikings, who were part white, part
black, performed COME GO WITH
ME in the rock musical, "The Big
Beat" (Universal: 1957).

US HITS: The Del-Vikings (Dot:
            1957) Black & Pop
            Dion (Laurie: 1963) Pop
            The Beach Boys (Caribou:
            1982) Pop

Other recordings: Sha Na Na
(Buddah); The Chants (Cameo).

COME ON, LET'S GO
(Ritchie Valens)
The first song to chart for the late
Ritchie Valens, though in America its
remake version by the Rick
Derringer-led McCoys fared better.
   Performed by The Paley Brothers
in "Rock 'n' Roll High School" (New
World: 1979). Performed by Los
Lobos for the Valens biopic, "La
Bamba" (Columbia: 1987).

US HITS: Ritchie Valens (Del-Fi:
            1958) Pop
            The McCoys (Bang: 1966)
            Pop
            Los Lobos (Slash: 1987)
            Pop
UK HITS: Tommy Steele (UK
            Decca: 1958)
            Los Lobos (Slash/London:
            1987)

Other recordings: Gary US Bonds;
Paley Brothers and The Ramones (Sire).

COME SOFTLY TO ME
(Gary Troxel/Gretchen Christopher/
Barbara Ellis)
One of two huge 1959 Number One
songs in America (the other was MR
BLUE) for the soft-spoken, almost
whispering, vocal trio known as The
Fleetwoods. They wrote this
themselves and their original scored

big in Britain where it outran big time opposition from Frankie Vaughan and The Kaye Sisters. The previous year had seen Vaughan successfully cover another west coast teen ballad, GONNA GET ALONG WITHOUT YOU NOW (Kellem) which had originally scored for Patience and Prudence (Liberty: 1956).

US HITS: The Fleetwoods (Dolton: 1959) Pop
            Ronnie Height (Dore: 1959) Pop
UK HITS: The Fleetwoods (London: 1959)
            Frankie Vaughan and The Kaye Sisters (Philips: 1959)
            The New Seekers (Polydor: 1972)

Other recordings: Percy Sledge (Atlantic), Brenton Wood (Cream); Sandy Posey (MGM); Paul and Paula (Philips); Jane Olivor (Columbia); Richard Barrett and The Chantels (Gone); Craig Douglas (Top Rank); Billy 'n' Sue (aka: Lesley Gore and Oliver) (Crewe).

COME TOGETHER
(John Lennon/Paul McCartney)
Classic Beatles' song which Tina Turner sang on the soundtrack of "All This And World War II" (20th Century Fox: 1976). Performed by Aerosmith in the movie adaptation of "Sgt Pepper's Lonely Hearts Club Band" (Universal: 1978) and by Michael Jackson in his full-length video, "Moonwalker" (CBS Music Video: 1988), released theatrically in certain countries.

US HITS: The Beatles (Apple: 1969) Pop
            Ike and Tina Turner (Minit: 1970) Black & Pop
            Aerosmith (Columbia: 1978) Pop
UK HIT: The Beatles (Apple: 1969)

Other recordings: George Benson (A&M); Diana Ross and The Supremes (Motown); Ben E. King (Atlantic); Sarah Vaughan (Atlantic); Mary Wells (Jay-Gee); George Duke (Pacific Jazz); Dionne Warwick (Scepter); Booker T. and The M.G.'s (Stax); The Brothers Johnson (A&M); Gladys Knight and The Pips (Soul); John Lennon (Capitol).

See: WITH A LITTLE HELP FROM MY FRIENDS for other John Lennon and Paul McCartney songs.

CORRINA, CORRINA
(J. M. Williams/Bo Chatman)
1920s blues song, also known as CORRINNE, CORRINNA.
    CORRINA, CORRINA gave blues legend Joe Turner his only Top 40 hit and the Ray Peterson version was one of Phil Spector's first productions.
    Big Joe Turner's version inspired Taj Mahal to write an adaptation of the same theme, calling it simply CORINNA and including it on his *Recycling The Blues* album (Columbia: 1972).

US HITS: Joe Turner (Atlantic: 1956) Black & Pop
            Ray Peterson (Dunes: 1960) Pop
UK HIT: Ray Peterson (London: 1961)

Other recordings: Bob Dylan (Columbia); Bill Haley and His Comets (Decca); Steppenwolf (Dunhill); Jesse Colin Young (Warner Bros); Merle Haggard and The Strangers (Capitol); Dean Martin (Reprise); Jimmy Witherspoon (Fantasy); Sleepy Labeef (Sun); Mississippi John Hurt (Vanguard); Lloyd Price (ABC); Merrill Moore (Capitol); Piano Red (Arhoolie); Siegall Schwall Band (Wooden Nickel); Bob Wills and His Texas Playboys (Columbia).

CRIMSON AND CLOVER
(Tommy James/Peter Lucia)
The biggest hit for Tommy James and The Shondells, co-written by the Shondells' drummer, Peter Lucia. Song was successfully revived by former member of the all-girl Runaways, Joan Jett; her record was co-produced by Ritchie Cordell who not only was Tommy James' former producer but also was the composer of I THINK WE'RE ALONE NOW, the Tommy James hit of 1967 which was a big hit again for Tiffany twenty years later!

US HITS: Tommy James and The Shondells (Roulette: 1969)
           Joan Jett and The Blackhearts (Boardwalk: 1982)
UK HIT: Joan Jett and The Blackhearts (Epic: 1982)

In Britain, the Joan Jett record made the Top 75, but failed to reach the Top 50; however, her previous single, I LOVE ROCK 'N' ROLL (Hooker/Merrill), was a Top 5 UK hit and demonstrates the unusual ways in which artists sometimes find the songs they record. On a visit to Britain, Joan Jett was listening to the radio and heard the original version of I LOVE ROCK 'N' ROLL; it was by the group The Arrows on the B-side of a single on Mickie Most's RAK label.
    In the States, Joan Jett's follow-up success to CRIMSON AND CLOVER was her cover of another British song, namely DO YOU WANNA TOUCH ME (OH YEAH) (Glitter/Leander), originally by Gary Glitter (Bell: 1973).

CRY BABY
(Bert Russell/Norman Meade)
Much-revered R&B producer Jerry Ragovoy (aka Norman Meade) joined forces with composer Bert

CRY BABY
Garnet Mimms (*seated*) and The Enchanters with their gospel-laden, wailing epic record of the Jerry Ragovoy/Bert Berns classic song. Dionne Warwick was one of the background singers on this milestone 1963 session.

Berns (aka Bert Russell) and together they created one of the finest soul records of the early 1960s. Garnet Mimms later went solo under Ragovoy's guidance, but on CRY BABY and three other hit singles, he fronted The Enchanters who, for this song, were augmented by some session singers including, Garnet recalls, Dionne Warwick. The revival by rock's Janis Joplin was from her classic *Pearl* album (Columbia: 1971) and the song was also heard in the rockumentary film, "Janis" (Universal: 1975).

US HITS: Garnet Mimms and The Enchanters (UA: 1963)
           Black & Pop

Janis Joplin (Columbia: 1971) Pop

Other recordings: Klique (MCA); The Mad Lads (Stax).

Jerry and Garnet collaborated on the song ANYTIME YOU WANT ME, recorded by The Who on the B-side of their first US single release (Decca: 1965).

Jerry Ragovoy songs

Among the hit records of other Jerry Ragovoy songs are:

BABY DON'T YOU WEEP by Garnet Mimms and The Enchanters (UA: 1963)

I'LL TAKE GOOD CARE OF YOU (written with Bert Berns) by Garnet Mimms (UA: 1966)

A LITTLE BIT NOW (A LITTLE BIT LATER)
The Majors first broke through with A WONDERFUL DREAM (Meade/Marshall), but it was their follow-up, A LITTLE BIT NOW which received more lasting attention when it was revived five years after their original version: this time by the British group The Dave Clark Five.

A LITTLE BIT NOW (A LITTLE BIT LATER) by The Dave Clark Five (Epic: 1967)
by The Majors (Imperial: 1962)

ONE GIRL (with Bert Berns) by Garnet Mimms (UA: 1967)

PATA PATA (with Miriam Makeba) by Miriam Makeba (Reprise: 1967)

PIECE OF MY HEART (with Bert Berns)** by Big Brother and The Holding Company with vocal by Janis Joplin (Columbia: 1968)
by Erma Franklin (Shout: 1967)

STAY WITH ME (with George Weiss)** by Lorraine Ellison (Warner Bros: 1966)

TIME IS ON MY SIDE (with James Norman)** by The Rolling Stones (London: 1964)

WHAT'S IT GONNA BE (with Mort Shuman) by Dusty Springfield (Philips: 1967)

A WONDERFUL DREAM by The Majors (Imperial: 1962)

(Some Jerry Ragovoy songs are credited to his pseudonyms, Norman Meade and Norman Margulies.)

See: TWIST AND SHOUT for other Bert Berns songs.

CRY ME A RIVER

(Arthur Hamilton)
Torch song with which actress–singer Julie London not only began her career, but also was virtually responsible for putting west-coast label, Liberty Records, on the map. In the rock musical, "The Girl Can't Help It" (20th Century Fox: 1956), Tom Ewell is obsessed by Julie London and, as he stumbles around his house in a daze, visions of Julie appear in a succession of sultry poses and stunning gowns, while she sings to her record of CRY ME A RIVER!

Joe Cocker performed the song in his legendary Fillmore East recording from the soundtrack of "Mad Dogs And Englishmen" movie

Julie London

julie is her name

CRY ME A RIVER

Julie London was the voice that put Liberty Records on the map in 1955. This was one of her eye-catching poses that accompanied her original sultry albums! Married to jazz pianist Bobby Troup, who wrote the GIRL CAN'T HELP IT title song which Little Richard sang on the movie soundtrack, actress–singer Julie is in semi-retirement since she and her husband finished work on the TV series "Emergency" (1972–1977), though she did sing MY FUNNY VALENTINE (Rodgers/Hart) on the soundtrack of the Burt Reynolds movie, "Sharkey's Machine" (Orion: 1981).

(MGM: 1971). First-class example of an easy listening ballad being tailored for a raw, soulful rock interpretation.

Years later, a British girl called Mari Wilson recreated the look of the 1960s (complete with a beehive hairstyle) and, apart from her JUST WHAT I ALWAYS WANTED Top 10 hit (Compact: 1982), her biggest selling record was her revival of CRY ME A RIVER.

US HITS: Julie London (Liberty: 1955) Pop
            Joe Cocker (A&M: 1970) Pop
UK HITS: Julie London (London: 1957)
            Mari Wilson (Compact: 1983)

Other recordings: Sam Cooke (RCA); Joan Baez (Portrait); Long John Baldry (UA); Sonny Stitt (Prestige); Crystal Gayle (UA); George Benson and Jack McDuff (Prestige); Barbra Streisand (Columbia).

CRY TO ME
(Bert Russell)
Heart-wrenching soul ballad produced and written by Bert Berns under his usual pseudonym, Bert Russell; it marked Solomon Burke's

CRY TO ME
Preacher-turned-singer Solomon Burke pioneered country soul even before Ray Charles with a song called JUST OUT OF REACH (OF MY TWO EMPTY ARMS) (Stewart) on Atlantic in 1961, which EMI covered with MOR singer, Donald Peers. Solomon's next release was CRY TO ME, Bert Berns' exceptional soul ballad into which Burke poured every ounce of his remarkable talent.

finest hour at Atlantic Records and years later, Solomon's original record was heard on the soundtrack of "Dirty Dancing" (Vestron: 1987). The Rolling Stones turned in another memorable version on their *Out Of Our Heads* album (UK Decca: 1965).

It was Solomon Burke for whom the phrase 'Country Soul' was virtually invented, particularly after his best-selling JUST OUT OF REACH (OF MY TWO EMPTY ARMS) (Stewart) which had been previously recorded by Eddy Arnold (RCA) and Patsy Cline (Decca).

US HITS: Solomon Burke (Atlantic: 1962) Black & Pop
Betty Harris (Jubilee: 1963) Black & Pop
Loleatta Holloway (Aware: 1975) Black
UK HIT: The Pretty Things (Fontana: 1965)

Other recordings: Professor Longhair (Atlantic); Freddie Scott (Shout); Garnet Mimms (UA).

See: TWIST AND SHOUT for other Bert Berns songs.

CRYING

(Roy Orbison/Joe Melson)
Among the most recorded of Roy Orbison's slow ballads. Re-cut by Roy, duetting with k. d. lang, on the soundtrack of the teen comedy movie, "Hiding Out" (De Laurentis: 1987).

US HITS: Roy Orbison (Monument: 1961) Pop
Jay and the Americans (United Artists: 1966) Pop
Don McLean (Millenium: 1981) Pop
UK HITS: Roy Orbison (London: 1961)
Don McLean (EMI: 1980)

Other recordings: Ronnie Milsap (Warner Bros); Del Shannon (Liberty); Stephanie Winslow

(Warner Bros); Waylon Jennings (Aura); Roy Orbison and k. d. lang.

Another Roy Orbison classic was recorded for a contemporary motion picture; IN DREAMS which he wrote and charted with in 1963 (Monument) was featured in David Lynch's movie, "Blue Velvet" (De Laurentis: 1986). In return, David Lynch directed the star-studded Orbison cable TV tribute, "Roy Orbison and Friends: A Black And White Night" (Cinemax: 1988). Roy performed both CRYING and IN DREAMS in this special which is currently available on home video.

CRYING IN THE CHAPEL

(Artie Glenn)
One of the great 'church' songs which can be sanctimonious and inappropriate in the wrong hands, but was perfect when handled by Sonny Til, lead tenor of The Orioles, and bettered only by Elvis Presley, whose majestic voice was tempered down to a sparse, gentle tone. The original version was by country artist Darrell Glenn and it was initially also covered by such as cowboy Rex Allen, Ella Fitzgerald plus a white singer on RCA, June Valli. In Britain, it was originally covered by singer Lee Lawrence. Elvis' version was one of the highlights of his best-selling inspirational album, *How Great Thou Art* (RCA: 1967).

US HITS: Darrell Glenn (Valley: 1953) Pop & Country
The Orioles (Jubilee: 1953) Black & Pop
Rex Allen (Decca: 1953) Country
Elvis Presley (RCA: 1965) Pop
UK HITS: Elvis Presley (RCA: 1965)
Elvis Presley (RCA: 1977 Re-release)

Other recordings: Johnny Burnette (Liberty); Don McLean (UA); The Persuasions (Flying Fish); Roy

Hamilton (MGM); Little Richard (Atlantic); Mahalia Jackson (Columbia); Al Martino (Capitol); Sonny Til (RCA); Adam Wade (Epic); The Penguins.

CUPID

(Sam Cooke)
One of Johnny Nash's very popular reggae singles was his revival of this Sam Cooke song. Besides the hits listed below, Johnny Rivers' 1965 version made it into the back end of the Top 100 in the States. Sam Cooke's original record was featured on the soundtrack of Joe Dante's fantasy adventure film, "Innerspace" (Warner Bros: 1987).

US HITS: Sam Cooke (RCA: 1961)
      Black & Pop
      Johnny Nash (JAD: 1970)
      Pop
      Dawn (Elektra: 1976) Pop
      The Spinners: Medley
      with I'VE LOVED YOU
      FOR A LONG TIME
      (Zager) (Atlantic: 1980)
      Black & Pop
UK HITS: Sam Cooke (RCA: 1961)
      Johnny Nash (Major
      Minor: 1969)
      The Detroit Spinners:
      Medley with I'VE
      LOVED YOU FOR A
      LONG TIME (Zager)
      (Atlantic: 1980)

Other recordings: Diana Ross and The Supremes (Motown); Frankie Avalon (Chancellor); Graham Parker (Demon).

NB: To avoid confusion with Liverpool folk group The Spinners, British releases of records by the American 'Spinners' altered their billing to 'The Detroit Spinners'.

See: ONLY SIXTEEN for other Sam Cooke songs.

D

DA DOO RON RON (WHEN HE WALKED ME HOME)

(Phil Spector/Jeff Barry/Ellie Greenwich)
One of the finest hours of the Phil Spector-produced girl group, The Crystals, featuring lead singer LaLa Brooks. Song performed by The Electricians (aka Brinsley Schwarz with Dave Edmunds) in the movie, "Stardust" (EMI: 1974). Also featured in the Broadway show, "Leader Of The Pack", which was built around the songs of Ellie Greenwich.

US HITS: The Crystals (Philles:
      1963) Pop
      Shaun Cassidy (Warners:
      1977) Pop
UK HITS: The Crystals (London:
      1963)
      The Crystals (Warner-
      Spector: 1974 Re-
      release)

Other recordings: Billy J.Kramer (Parlophone); The Ikettes (Modern) The Chiffons (Laurie); The Searchers (Pye); Ian Matthews (Vertigo); Brian Poole (UK Decca); Carpenters (A&M); Darlene Love (Rhino); Bette Midler (Atlantic); "Leader Of The Pack" Cast (Elektra); The Raindrops (Jubilee); The Four Pennies (Philips); Bo Donaldson and The Heywoods (Family); The Aztecs (World Artists).

See: RIVER DEEP, MOUNTAIN HIGH for other Jeff Barry and Ellie Greenwich songs.

Phil Spector classics

Phil Spector is one of rock's finest-ever producers, whose haunting 'wall of sound' recordings delivered spine-tingling, emotion-packed singles, many of which are top-dollar collectors' items in their original

West-coast trio, The Paris Sisters were originally produced by Phil Spector. They re-cut their most famous hit I LOVE HOW YOU LOVE ME in 1968 for Capitol (photo/courtesy of Michael Ochs).

form. He also master-minded a various-artist Christmas album which remains rock's finest seasonal concept.

The following is a brief selection of Phil Spector productions which have become rock classics:

BABY I LOVE YOU (Spector/ Greenwich/Barry)** by The Ronettes (Philles: 1964)

BE MY BABY (Spector/Greenwich/ Barry)** by The Ronettes (Philles: 1963)

(THE BEST PART OF) BREAKIN' UP (Spector/Poncia/Andreoli) by The Ronettes (Philles: 1964)

CHRISTMAS (BABY PLEASE COME HOME) (Spector/Barry/ Greenwich) by Darlene Love (Philles: 1963)

CORINNA, CORINNA (Williams/ Chapman)** by Ray Peterson (Dunes: 1960)

EVERY BREATH I TAKE (Goffin/ King) by Gene Pitney (Musicor: 1961)

HE'S A REBEL (Pitney) by The Crystals (Philles: 1962)

HE'S SURE THE BOY I LOVE (Mann/ Weil)** by The Crystals (Philles: 1962)

I LOVE HOW YOU LOVE ME (Mann/Kolber) by The Paris Sisters (Gregmark: 1961)

PRETTY LITTLE ANGEL EYES (Boyce/Lee)** by Curtis Lee (Dunes: 1961)

RIVER DEEP, MOUNTAIN HIGH (Spector/Greenwich/Barry)** by Ike and Tina Turner (Philles: 1966)

THEN HE KISSED ME (Spector/ Greenwich/Barry)** by The Crystals (Philles: 1963)

why do lovers break each others hearts?

by phil spector • ellie greenwich • tony powers

recorded by bob b. soxx and the blue jeans on philles records

january music corp.

A SCHROEDER MUSIC CORPORATION

CIMINO PUBLICATIONS INCORPORATED

.60

Another of Phil Spector's legendary groups was Bob B.Soxx and The Blue Jeans who were (*left to right*) Bobby Sheen, Darlene Love and Fanita James. Darlene's other Spector work is explained in the accompanying entry on this song. WHY DO LOVERS was originally covered in Britain by HMV's Beverly Jones and was a hit for Showaddywaddy years later (Arista: 1980).

TO KNOW HIM IS TO LOVE HIM
(Spector)** by The Teddy Bears
(Dore: 1958)
(TODAY I MET) THE BOY I'M
GONNA MARRY (Spector/
Greenwich/Powers) by Darlene
Love (Philles: 1963)
UNCHAINED MELODY (North/
Zaret) by The Righteous Brothers
(Philles: 1962)
UNDER THE MOON OF LOVE
(Boyce/Lee)** by Curtis Lee
(Dunes: 1961)
UPTOWN (Mann/Weil) by The
Crystals (Philles: 1962)
WAIT 'TIL MY BOBBY GETS HOME
(Spector/Greenwich/Barry) by
Darlene Love (Philles: 1963)
WALKIN' IN THE RAIN (Spector/
Mann/Weil)** by The Ronettes
(Philles: 1964)
WHY DO LOVERS BREAK EACH
OTHER'S HEARTS (Spector/
Greenwich/Powers) by Bob
B.Soxx and The Blue Jeans
(Philles: 1963)
YOU'VE LOST THAT LOVIN'
FEELIN' (Spector/Mann/Weil)**
by The Righteous Brothers
(Philles: 1964)
ZIP-A-DEE-DOO-DAH (Wrubel/
Gilbert)** by Bob B. Soxx and
The Blue Jeans (Philles:1963)

Spector also produced the original
version of BLACK PEARL
(Spector/Levine/Wine) by Sonny
Charles & The Checkmates Ltd.
(A&M: 1969); that same song was a
UK hit the following year for rock
steady performer Horace Faith
(Trojan: 1970).

DADDY'S HOME
(James Sheppard/William Miller)
Slow, melodic ballad that was
originally a doo-wop hit by its
composer James 'Shep' Sheppard.
DADDY'S HOME was actually an
answer song to A THOUSAND
MILES AWAY which Shep and
partner William Miller wrote for The

Heartbeats, a 1957 song that had
been revived on the charts in 1960.
None of the earlier versions were a
hit in England before Cliff Richard
took it to Number Two in the first
week of December, 1981.

US HITS: Shep and The Limelites
(Hull: 1961) Pop & Black
Chuck Jackson and
Maxine Brown (Wand:
1967) Pop & Black
Jermaine Jackson
(Motown: 1973) Pop &
Black
Cliff Richard (EMI
America: 1982) Pop
UK HIT: Cliff Richard (Columbia:
1981)

Other recordings: The Jackson 5
(Motown); Princess and The Doo
Rags (Columbia).

Answer record: DADDY'S HOME
BUT MOMMA'S GONE by The
Monotones (Hull: 1961).

DANCING IN THE STREET
(Marvin Gaye/William Stevenson/Ivy
Jo Hunter)
The second of two million-sellers
(the first was HEAT WAVE) by
Martha and the Vandellas,
DANCING IN THE STREET was
another milestone in the early days
of Berry Gordy's record empire.
Martha and The Vandellas' hit was
featured on the soundtrack of
"Heaven Help Us" (1985), and a new
recording by Animotion was heard
in "Girls Just Want To Have Fun –
The Movie" (New World: 1985) the
same year. Mick Jagger and David
Bowie teamed together for a revival
version, for which they shot a video
which was premiered on the historic
"Live Aid" worldwide telecast in
1985.

US HITS: Martha and The
Vandellas (Gordy:
1964) Black & Pop
Van Halen (Warner Bros:
1982) Pop

Recorded by MARTHA and THE VANDELLAS on Gordy Records

DANCING IN THE STREET

By WILLIAM STEVENSON and MARVIN GAYE

75¢

DANCING IN THE STREET
Martha (*top right*) and The Vandellas enjoyed the first hit on DANCING IN THE STREET; it was the group's fourth major single, following COME AND GET THESE MEMORIES, HEAT WAVE and QUICKSAND, all written by Holland/Dozier/Holland.

	Mick Jagger and David Bowie (EMI America: 1985) Pop
UK HITS:	Martha and The Vandellas (Stateside: 1964)
	Martha and The Vandellas (Tamla Motown: 1969 Re-release)

Other recordings: Neil Diamond (Columbia); Trax (Polydor); Laura Nyro and LaBelle (Columbia); The Kinks (Pye); Brenda Lee (Decca); The Everly Brothers (Warner Bros); The Dovells (Event); The Critters (Kapp); Irma Thomas (Rounder); Donald Byrd (Blue Note); Ramsey Lewis (Cadet); The Grateful Dead (Arista); Teri De Sario and K.C. (Casablanca); Little Richard (Reprise); Cilla Black (Parlophone); The Walker Brothers (Philips); Jackie Lee (Mirwood); The Mamas and The Papas (Dunhill); The Missing Links (MCA).

See: DEVIL WITH A BLUE DRESS ON for other Motown hits.

DARK END OF THE STREET
(Dan Penn/Chips Moman)
(AT THE) DARK END OF THE STREET became one of the 1960s' most influential soul songs, courtesy of James Carr's breathtaking performance on the Bell-distributed Goldwax label. Another of Dan Penn's songs that same year, 1967, was BROADWAY WALK which was among Bobby Womack's first recordings for Minit.

US HIT:	James Carr (Goldwax: 1967) Black & Pop

Other recordings: Aretha Franklin (Atlantic); Flying Burrito Bros (A&M); Linda Ronstadt (Capitol); Oscar Toney Jr (Bell); Clarence Carter (Atlantic); Percy Sledge (Atlantic); Ry Cooder (Reprise); Dorothy Moore (Malaco); Roy Hamilton; The Kendalls (Mercury); Moving Hearts (MCA).

Other Penn and Moman successes include DO RIGHT WOMAN – DO RIGHT MAN which charted for Aretha Franklin (Atlantic: 1967), and I'M YOUR PUPPET by James and Bobby Purify (Bell: 1966). With Spooner Oldham, Dan Penn wrote OUT OF LEFT FIELD (a 1967 charter for Percy Sledge on Atlantic), CRY LIKE A BABY which was The Box Tops' smash on Bell in 1968, plus the gospel song SWEET INSPIRATION, aptly recorded by The Sweet Inspirations, the female quartet which included Cissy Houston, on Atlantic in 1968.

DAY TRIPPER
(John Lennon/Paul McCartney)
One of the great Beatle classics,
released back-to-back with WE
CAN WORK IT OUT. The double-
sided single reached Number One
in England on 18 December 1965,
holding that spot four weeks.
   Performed by Julian Lennon in his
video: "Stand By Me: A Portrait Of
Julian Lennon" (MCA: 1985).

US HITS: The Beatles (Capitol:
               1966) Pop
             The Vontastics (Saint
               Lawrence: 1966) Black
             Anne Murray (Capitol:
               1975) Pop
UK HITS: The Beatles (Parlophone:
               1965)
             Otis Redding (Stax: 1967)

Other recordings: Jimi Hendrix and
Curtis Knight (51 West); Vanilla
Fudge (Atlantic); Mae West
(Capitol); Jose Feliciano (RCA);
Nancy Sinatra (Reprise); Herbie
Mann (Atlantic); Ramsey Lewis Trio
(Cadet); Cheap Trick (Epic); The
McCoys (Bang); Lulu (UK Columbia);
Dee Irwin and Mamie Galore
(Liberty); James Taylor (Columbia);
Joe Cocker (A&M); Whitesnake
(Geffen).

See: WITH A LITTLE HELP FROM
MY FRIENDS for other John Lennon
and Paul McCartney songs.

DEDICATED TO THE ONE I LOVE
The Five Royales, who recorded the very first
version and whose record The Shirelles heard
before they cut their cover, scored big with two
songs in 1953 on the R&B charts: BABY DON'T DO
IT and HELP ME SOMEBODY, both written by
group member Lowman Pauling.

DEDICATED TO THE ONE I LOVE
(Lowman Pauling/Ralph Bass)
Original version was by The Five
Royales, an R&B quintet out of North
Carolina, of which Lowman Pauling
was singer and lead guitarist. Girl
group The Shirelles heard The Five
Royales' record (King: 1957) and
re-arranged the song for their first
release on Scepter, the label owned
by their school friend's mother
Florence Greenberg. The Shirelles'
version was a minor success in '59
but a much bigger hit when it was
re-issued on the strength of WILL

YOU LOVE ME TOMORROW
(Goffin/King)**, their first US
Number One. King also re-released
The Five Royales' record in '61 and it
made the lower rungs of the
Stateside pop chart.
   Song is now a standard and is
often revived; actress–singer
Bernadette Peters charted briefly
with a stylish version from her *Now
Playing* (MCA: 1981) album on which
she also revived Little Anthony and
The Imperials' classic, TEARS ON
MY PILLOW (Lewis/ Bradford).

US HITS: The Shirelles (Scepter:
            1961 Re-release) Black
            & Pop
            The Mamas and The Papas
            (Dunhill: 1967) Pop
            The Temprees (We
            Produce: 1972) Black
UK HIT: The Mamas and The
            Papas (RCA: 1967)

Other recordings: Stacy Lattisaw
(Cotillion); The Nocturnes (UK
Columbia); Bernadette Peters
(MCA).

Another Lowman Pauling song
originally recorded by The Five
Royales (King: 1957) was the song
THINK which James Brown
successfully covered twice, in 1960
on Federal and in 1973 on Polydor. It
has recently been used as the theme
song over the opening credits of the
CBS Television series, "Almost Grown".

DEVIL WITH A BLUE DRESS ON
Mitch Ryder not only scored with a medley of
Shorty Long's DEVIL and Little Richard's GOOD
GOLLY MISS MOLLY, but he also took another
Richard Penniman classic back to the charts;
Ryder's producer Bob Crewe merged JENNY,
JENNY with the blues standard SEE SEE RIDER
and came up with JENNY TAKE A RIDE, a Mitch
Ryder hit on New Voice in 1966.

DEVIL WITH A BLUE DRESS ON
(William Stevenson/Frederick Long)
Originally co-written and recorded
by the late Shorty Long, who also
recorded FUNCTION AT THE
JUNCTION (Holland/Dozier/Long)
and HERE COMES THE JUDGE
(Long/Brown/DePasse). Long's
original version in 1964 was also the
very first release on the Motown-
owned Soul label.
    Song re-popularized by Bruce
Springsteen in live performances
and subsequently performed by him
in the concert film, "No Nukes"
(Warner Bros: 1980).

US HITS: Mitch Ryder and The
            Detroit Wheels:
            Medley with GOOD
            GOLLY MISS MOLLY
            (Blackwell/Marascalco)
            (New Voice: 1966) Pop
            Pratt and McClain
            (Reprise: 1976) Pop

Other recordings: Bruce Springsteen
(Columbia); The Soul Survivors
(Decca).

Motown covers
Songs which emanated originally
from the Motown stable seem to be
revived more often than from any
other source. Other key covers of
songs which were first recorded by
Motown acts include:

AIN'T NO MOUNTAIN HIGH
    ENOUGH (Ashford/Simpson)** by
    Diana Ross (Motown: 1970)
AIN'T TOO PROUD TO BEG
    (Holland/Whitfield)** by The
    Rolling Stones (Rolling Stones:
    1974)
BABY I NEED YOUR LOVING
    (Holland/Dozier/Holland)** by
    Johnny Rivers (Imperial: 1967)
CAN I GET A WITNESS (Holland/
    Dozier/Holland)** by Sam Brown
    (A&M: 1989)
COME SEE ABOUT ME (Holland/
    Dozier/Holland) by Nella Dodds
    (Wand: 1964)
    by Jr Walker and The All Stars
    (Soul: 1967)
originally by The Supremes
    (Motown: 1965)
DANCING IN THE STREET (Gaye/

Stevenson)** by Mick Jagger and
David Bowie (EMI America: 1985)
DO YOU LOVE ME (Gordy Jr)** by
The Dave Clark Five (UK
Columbia: 1963)
by Brian Poole and The
Tremeloes (UK Decca: 1963)
GOING TO A GO GO (Robinson/
Moore/Rogers/Tarplin) by The
Rolling Stones (Rolling Stones:
1982)
originally by The Miracles (Tamla:
1966)
HE WAS REALLY SAYIN'
SOMETHIN' (Whitfield/Stevenson/
Holland) by Bananarama (re-titled
REALLY SAYING SOMETHING)
(Deram: 1982)
originally by The Velvelettes (V.I.P:
1965)
HEAVEN MUST HAVE SENT YOU
(Holland/Dozier/Holland) by
Bonnie Pointer (Motown: 1979)
originally by The Elgins (V.I.P: 1966)
I CAN'T HELP MYSELF (Holland/
Dozier/Holland)** by Donnie
Elbert (Avco: 1972)
I HEARD IT THROUGH THE
GRAPEVINE (Whitfield/Strong)**
by Creedence Clearwater Revival
(Fantasy: 1976)
I SECOND THAT EMOTION
(Robinson/Cleveland)** by Japan
(Hansa: 1982)
by Alyson Williams (Def Jam:
1989)
I WISH IT WOULD RAIN
(Whitfield/Strong) by The Faces
(Warner Bros: 1973)
originally by the Temptations
(Gordy: 1968)
IT'S THE SAME OLD SONG
(Holland/Dozier/Holland) by K.C.
and The Sunshine Band (T.K.:
1978)
originally by The Four Tops
(Motown: 1965)
MORE LOVE (Robinson) by Kim
Carnes (EMI America: 1980)
originally by The Miracles (Tamla:
1967)
MY GIRL (Robinson/White)** by
Otis Redding (Atlantic: 1965)
OOH OOH BABY (Robinson/Moore)

by Linda Ronstadt (Asylum: 1978)
originally by The Miracles (Tamla:
1965)
PLEASE MR POSTMAN (Dobbins/
Garrett/Holland/Bateman/
Gorman)** by The Carpenters
(A&M: 1975)
REACH OUT I'LL BE THERE
(Holland/Dozier/Holland)** by
Gloria Gaynor (MGM: 1975)
SHOP AROUND (Gordy Jr/
Robinson)** by The Captain and
Tennille (A&M: 1976)
STANDING IN THE SHADOWS OF
LOVE (Holland/Dozier/Holland) by
Deborah Washington (Ariola:
1978)
originally by The Four Tops
(Motown: 1966)
TAKE ME IN YOUR ARMS (ROCK
ME A LITTLE WHILE) (Holland/
Dozier/Holland) by The Doobie
Brothers (Warner Bros: 1975)
by Johnny Rivers (UA: 1973)
originally by Kim Weston (Gordy:
1965)
TEARS OF A CLOWN (Cosby/
Robinson/Wonder) by The Beat (2
Tone: 1979)
originally by Smokey Robinson and
The Miracles (Tamla: 1970)
THIS OLD HEART OF MINE
(Holland/Dozier/Holland/Moy)**
by Rod Stewart (Riva: 1975)
TOO BUSY THINKING ABOUT MY
BABY (Whitfield/Strong/Bradford)
by Mardi Gras (Bell: 1972)
originally by Marvin Gaye (Tamla:
1969)
THE TRACKS OF MY TEARS
(Robinson/Moore/Tarplin)** by
Johnny Rivers (Imperial: 1967)
by Linda Ronstadt (Asylum: 1976)
by Colin Blunstone (PRT: 1982)
WHAT BECOMES OF THE
BROKENHEARTED (Riser/Dean/
Washington)** by Dave Stewart
with Colin Blunstone (Stiff: 1981)
WHAT DOES IT TAKE (TO WIN
YOUR LOVE)
(Bristol/Bullock/Fuqua) by Kenny
G. (Arista: 1988)
originally by Junior Walker and The
All Stars (Soul: 1969)

WHERE DID OUR LOVE GO
(Holland/Dozier/Holland) by
Donnie Elbert (London: 1972)
by Manhattan Transfer, in a
medley with JE VOULAIS TE
DIRE (Grosz/Jonasz) (Atlantic:
1978)
originally by The Supremes
(Motown: 1964)
WHEREVER I LAY MY HAT
(THAT'S MY HOME)
(Gaye/Strong/Whitfield) by Paul
Young (CBS: 1983)
originally by Marvin Gaye (Tamla:
1969)
YOU CAN'T HURRY LOVE (Holland/
Dozier/Holland)** by Phil Collins
(Atlantic: 1983)
YOU KEEP ME HANGIN' ON
(Holland/Dozier/Holland)** by
Vanilla Fudge (Atco: 1967)
by Kim Wilde (MCA: 1986)

YOU'RE ALL I NEED TO GET BY
(Ashford/Simpson)** by Aretha
Franklin (Atlantic: 1971)
YOU'VE MADE ME SO VERY
HAPPY (Gordy/Holloway/Wilson)
by Blood, Sweat and Tears
(Columbia: 1969)
originally by Brenda Holloway
(Tamla: 1967)
YOU'VE REALLY GOT A HOLD ON
ME (Robinson) by Eddie Money
(Columbia: 1978)
originally by The Miracles (Tamla:
1962)

NB: The above is only a partial list.
Also, original versions are indicated
alongside the songs which do not
have their own separate entry in this
book; for a listing of the original
recording of songs marked**, please
refer to the song title in our main
section.

By comparison, Van McCoy's WHEN
YOU'RE YOUNG AND IN LOVE is a
song that took a completely opposite
route in that it was a hit for a Motown
act after it had charted for a non-
Motown group. The first record on
WHEN YOU'RE YOUNG was by
Ruby and The Romantics (Kapp:
1964), but it was more successful by
The Marvelettes (Tamla: 1967). This
was, incidentally, not the only time
when Ruby and The Romantics lost a
hit song; when producer Allen
Stanton was mixing their version of
HURTING EACH OTHER (Geld/
Udell) at A&M, Richard Carpenter
heard the tune and asked if he and
his sister could record it if Ruby's
single didn't happen. The
Carpenters' version was
subsequently a huge hit (A&M:
1972).
Little Eva (Harris), whose 1962
smash single was Goffin/King song
THE LOCO-MOTION**, recorded a
medley of two Motown classics, GET
READY** and UPTIGHT
(EVERYTHING'S ALRIGHT)**. Little
Eva's medley was released on the
MGM-distributed Spring label in
1968.

Motown covers have not only been recorded as individual cover tracks and singles; some were part of entire album concepts, in and outside the Motown family. On Motown itself, Bonnie Pointer cut extended versions of five classics for a 1979 album simply called *Bonnie Pointer;* the tunes were: I CAN'T HELP MYSELF, JIMMY MACK,COME SEE ABOUT ME and NOWHERE TO RUN plus one of my favourite girl-group songs, WHEN THE LOVELIGHT STARTS SHINING THROUGH HIS EYES,an early Supremes hit (Motown: 1963).

Ruby Turner's British album, *The Motown Song Book* (Jive: 1988) was perhaps the most ambitious tribute yet. She remade ten songs and on four of them enlisted the aid of their original recording artists as in-studio guests; these very special combinations were BABY I NEED YOUR LOVIN' featuring The Four Tops, JUST MY IMAGINATION (RUNNING AWAY WITH ME) (Whitfield/Strong) featuring The Temptations, HOW SWEET IT IS (TO BE LOVED BY YOU) featuring Junior Walker, and WHAT BECOMES OF THE BROKENHEARTED with Jimmy Ruffin.

See: I'M GONNA MAKE YOU LOVE ME as an example of a non-Motown song being revived by a Motown artist.

DIDN'T I (BLOW YOUR MIND THIS TIME)

(Tom Bell/William Hart)
This slab of sultry soul was successfully revived by teen quintet New Kids On The Block, though the song was originally released on the B-side of their HANGIN' TOUGH (Starr) single. With their previous release, COVER GIRL (Starr), still in the charts in America, the group logged three single sides in the Top 40 in one week!

The song had already experienced one '80s revival by Millie Jackson.

US HITS: The Delfonics (Philly Groove: 1970) Black & Pop
Millie Jackson (Spring: 1980) Black
New Kids On The Block (Columbia: 1989) Pop
UK HIT: The Delfonics (Bell: 1971) Pop

Other recording: Aretha Franklin (Atlantic)

Thom Bell was a significant writer-producer of late 1960s and 1970s soul ballads, the trademarks of which were rich orchestrations and quivering vocals. His other hits for The Delfonics included LA-LA MEANS I LOVE YOU (1968), BREAK YOUR PROMISE (1968) and READY OR NOT HERE I COME (1969), all on Philly Groove and co-written with William Hart. Then for The Stylistics on Avco, he co-wrote a series of smashes including BETCHA BY GOLLY WOW (Bell/Creed) (1972), I'M STONE IN LOVE WITH YOU (Bell/Creed/Bell) (1972), BREAK UP TO MAKE UP (Bell/Creed/Gamble) (1973) and YOU MAKE ME FEEL BRAND NEW (Bell/Creed), released in 1974.

DIRTY WATER

(Ed Cobb)
The Standells zapped around various companies recording such as movie themes and dance songs; they were even in the teen flick, "Riot On Sunset Strip" (AIP: 1967). But their finest hour was the punkish DIRTY WATER on Capitol's subsidiary label, Tower.

Writer Ed Cobb was an original member of the 1950s vocal group, The Four Preps; his other songs include EVERY LITTLE BIT HURTS by Brenda Holloway (Tamla: 1964) and TAINTED LOVE**.

US HITS: The Standells (Tower: 1966) Pop
The Inmates (Polydor: 1980) Pop

DIZZY MISS LIZZY
(Larry Williams)
Larry Williams' third successive hit, completing his hat-trick of girl-inspired novelty rockers which he'd begun with SHORT FAT FANNIE and BONY MORONIE, both in 1957. Sung by John Lennon on the fourth Beatles album *Help* (Parlophone: 1965). Featured also by the Plastic Ono Band on their *Live Peace In Toronto 1969* album (Apple: 1969).

US HIT: Larry Williams (Specialty: 1958) Pop

Other recordings: Cliff Richard (UK Columbia); Kingsize Taylor and The Dominoes (UK Decca); The Escorts (Fontana)

DIZZY MISS LIZZY
Larry Williams was born in New Orleans but was a resident of Los Angeles until the day he took his own life in 1980. His best-known sides were recorded for Specialty, but he also cut a first-class duet with Johnny 'Guitar' Watson; it was a version of Cannonball Adderley's hit, MERCY, MERCY, MERCY (Zawinul/Levy/Levy) (Okeh: 1967).

Beatles' remakes
DIZZY MISS LIZZY was one of a stream of American songs covered by The Beatles on their early albums. Following is a list of some of the classics they recorded along with the original versions:

ACT NATURALLY (Russell/Morrison) by Buck Owens (Capitol: 1963). In 1988 Buck Owens and former Beatle Ringo Starr teamed up for a new version of ACT NATURALLY.
ANNA (GO TO HIM) (Alexander) by Arthur Alexander (Dot: 1962)
BABY IT'S YOU (Bacharach/David/Williams)** by The Shirelles (Scepter: 1962)
BAD BOY (Williams) by Larry Williams (Specialty: 1959)
BOYS (Dixon/Farrell) by The Shirelles (Scepter: 1960)
CHAINS (Goffin/King)** by The Cookies (Dimension: 1962)
DEVIL IN HIS HEART (Drapkin) by

The Donays (Brent: 1962)
EVERYBODY'S TRYING TO BE MY BABY (Perkins) by Carl Perkins (Sun: 1958)
HEY HEY HEY HEY (GOING BACK TO BIRMINGHAM) (Penniman) by Little Richard (Specialty: 1958)
HONEY DON'T (Perkins) by Carl Perkins (Sun: 1956)
KANSAS CITY (Leiber/Stoller),** originally: K. C. LOVIN' by Little Willie Littlefield (Federal: 1952)
LONG TALL SALLY (Johnson/Blackwell/Penniman)** by Little Richard (Specialty:1956)
MATCHBOX (Perkins) by Carl Perkins (Sun: 1957)
MR MOONLIGHT (Johnson) by Dr Feelgood and The Interns (Okeh: 1962)*

MONEY (THAT'S WHAT I WANT)
(Bradford/Gordy Jr)** by Barrett
Strong (Anna: 1959)
PLEASE MR POSTMAN (Dobbins/
Garrett/Holland/Bateman/
Gorman)** by The Marvelettes
(Tamla: 1961)
ROCK AND ROLL MUSIC (Berry)**
by Chuck Berry (Chess: 1957)
ROLL OVER BEETHOVEN (Berry)**
by Chuck Berry (Chess: 1956)
SLOW DOWN (Williams)** by Larry
Williams (Specialty: 1958)
TWIST AND SHOUT (Russell/
Medley)** by The Top Notes
(Atlantic: 1961)
WORDS OF LOVE (Holly)** by
Buddy Holly (Coral: 1957)
YOU REALLY GOT A HOLD ON ME
(Robinson)** by The Miracles
(Tamla: 1962)

* Dr Feelgood was the 1960s alias for Willie
Perryman. As 'Piano Red', he cut the original of
his RIGHT STRING BUT THE WRONG YO-YO
on RCA in 1951. As 'Dr Feelgood', he did it
once more for Okeh, along with DOCTOR
FEELGOOD (Smith), MISTER MOONLIGHT
and his own BALD-HEADED LENA, which The
Lovin' Spoonful included on their *Daydream*
album (Kama Sutra: 1966).

Price 60c

DO WAH DIDDY DIDDY
Manfred Mann, with lead singer Paul Jones
(*centre*), pose outside EMI House in Manchester
Square, London; they were HMV artists when they
covered DO WAH DIDDY DIDDY.

DO WAH DIDDY DIDDY

(Jeff Barry/Ellie Greenwich)
The perfect song to sing as you're
'Walking down the street'! It was
Manfred Mann's (with Paul Jones
singing) third British hit and the
group's only record to top the charts
on both sides of the Atlantic.
Manfred did other covers as well,
including SHA LA LA (Mosely/
Taylor) originally by The Shirelles
(Scepter: 1964), COME
TOMORROW (Elgin/Augustus/
Phillips) which Marie Knight first
recorded (Okeh: 1962), and OH NO
NOT MY BABY (Goffin/King), a song
first recorded by Maxine Brown
(Wand: 1964).
    The group then almost seemed to
go through a metamorphosis, no
longer covering girl singers, but
contemporary male-originated songs

such as Bob Dylan's THE MIGHTY
QUINN, though they also drew on
softer material such as Tommy Roe's
own SWEET PEA and some home-
grown songs like SEMI-DETACHED
SUBURBAN MR JAMES (Stevens/
Carter).
    The Exciters should not have been
surprised when DO WAH was
covered, because they were pipped
to the hit parade post in England in
1962/63, when their biggest success,
TELL HIM (Russell), was challenged
and finally outrun by a version from
local girl Billie Davis on UK Decca.
Down the line, when they had
switched labels to Bang, The

Exciters took revenge and covered someone else's song, A LITTLE BIT OF SOAP – originally by The Jarmels (Laurie: 1961) and covered in the UK the the Brooks Brothers – and, ironically, it was written by Bert Russell (aka Bert Berns), the composer of TELL HIM!

DO WAH DIDDY DIDDY was featured in the Broadway musical built around the songs of Ellie Greenwich titled "Leader Of The Pack" (1985).

US HITS: The Exciters (UA: 1964)
            Black & Pop
            Manfred Mann (Ascot:
            1964) Pop
UK HIT: Manfred Mann (HMV:
            1964)

Other recordings: Andrew Gold (Asylum); The Jelly Beans (Red Bird).

See: RIVER DEEP, MOUNTAIN HIGH for other Jeff Barry and Ellie Greenwich songs.

DO YOU BELIEVE IN MAGIC?
(John Sebastian)
One of the great rock 'n' roll anthems. John Sebastian and the other members were re-grouped to perform the song in his movie, "One-Trick Pony" (Warner Bros: 1980). They had originally sung MAGIC in the 1965 concert movie, "The Big TNT Show."

US HITS: The Lovin' Spoonful
            (Kama Sutra: 1965) Pop
            Shaun Cassidy (Warner
            Bros: 1978) Pop

Other recordings: The Pack (UK Columbia); Cher (Imperial); John Cougar Mellencamp; Barry McGuire (Dunhill).

DO YOU LOVE ME?
(Berry Gordy Jr)
Product from the Motown labels was first licensed in Britain to Oriole, a label that was eventually bought out by CBS. Try as they could, and Oroiole did try with DO YOU LOVE ME, they just couldn't break any of the early examples of the Detroit sound. DO YOU LOVE ME is a first-rate dance record and really came into its own via the soundtrack of a

DO YOU LOVE ME,
'Watch me now!' The original line-up of The Contours as they were when their dance classic was first released on Gordy in 1962.

movie made decades later! It had been heard in the gang movie, "The Wanderers" (Warner Bros: 1979), but it was the huge success of "Dirty Dancing" (Vestron: 1987) which brought new-found fame to The Contours; their classic original track was not just on the movie's soundbed and on the soundtrack album, but the single was successfully reissued and to top it all off, a 1980s line-up of The Contours toured with a stage version of "Dirty Dancing"! Strictly speaking, it wasn't a straight reissue, because Motown edited out the false ending from the original single.

US HITS: The Contours (Gordy: 1962) Black & Pop
           The Dave Clark Five (Epic: 1964) Pop
           The Contours (Motown: 1988 Re-release) Pop

UK HITS: The Dave Clark Five (UK Columbia: 1963)
           Brian Poole and The Tremeloes (UK Decca: 1963)
           Deep Feeling (Page One: 1970)

Other recordings: Smokey Robinson and The Miracles (Tamla); The Blues Brothers (Atlantic); The Hollies (Parlophone); Faron's Flamingos (Oriole); Diana Ross and The Supremes and The Temptations (Motown); Chubby Checker and Dee Dee Sharp (Cameo).

See: DEVIL WITH A BLUE DRESS ON for other Motown hits.

DO YOU WANT TO DANCE?

(Bobby Freeman)
Classic invitation from young R&B singer, Bobby Freeman, which is also known as DO YOU WANNA DANCE? Bobby's original record was featured on the soundtracks of "American Graffiti" (Universal: 1973), "Big Wednesday" (US TV Title: "Summer Of Innocence") (Warner Bros: 1978), and "Rock 'N' Roll High

School" (New World: 1979).

US HITS: Bobby Freeman (Josie: 1958) Black & Pop
           Del Shannon (Amy: 1964) Pop
           The Beach Boys (Capitol: 1965) Pop
           Bette Midler (Atlantic: 1973) Pop

UK HIT: Cliff Richard (UK Columbia: 1962)

Other recordings: The Ramones (Sire); Johnny Rivers (Imperial); The Mamas and The Papas (Dunhill); John Lennon (Capitol); Caesar and Cleo (aka Sonny and Cher) (Reprise); Jan and Dean (Rhino); Toni Basil (Chrysalis); Jack Reno (Target).

Bobby Freeman later cut some other dance records including C'MON AND SWIM (Stewart/Coman) (Autumn: 1964) and (I DO THE) SHIMMY SHIMMY (Shubert/Massey) (King: 1960).

Dance records

Other key R&B/R&R dance records include:

BAREFOOTIN' (Parker)** by Robert Parker Jr (Nola: 1966)
CISSY STRUT (Neville/Nocentelli/ Porter Jr/Modeliste Jr) by The Meters (Josie: 1969)
COME ON DO THE JERK (Whited/ Moore/Rogers/Robinson) by The Miracles (Tamla: 1964)
COOL JERK (Storball) by The Capitols (Karen: 1966)
THE DANCE ELECTRIC by Andre Cymone (Columbia: 1985)
DANCING IN THE STREET (Gaye/ Stevenson)** by Martha and The Vandellas (Gordy: 1964)
DISCO INFERNO (Green/Kersey) by The Trammps (Atlantic: 1977)
DO YOU LOVE ME (Gordy Jr)** by The Contours (Gordy: 1962)
MASHED POTATO TIME (Dobbins/Garrett/Holland/Bateman/ Gorman/Cohen)** by Dee Dee

recorded by THE MIRACLES on Tamla Records

OME ON, DO THE JERK

ONALD WHITED, WARREN MOORE, ROBERT ROGERS and WILLIAM ROBINSON

JOBETE MUSIC CO., INC.

75¢

The Miracles had recorded the great dance song,
MICKEY'S MONKEY (Holland/Dozier/Holland)
(Tamla: 1963) and, towards the end of 1964, came
out with COME ON, DO THE JERK.

Sharp (Cameo: 1962)
THE DUCK (Nelson/Sledge) by
Jackie Lee (Mirwood: 1966)
THE FLY (Madara/White) by
Chubby Checker (Parkway: 1961)
HI-HEEL SNEAKERS
(Higgenbotham)** by Tommy
Tucker (Checker: 1964)
HITCH HIKE (Gaye/Paul/Stevenson)
by Marvin Gaye (Tamla: 1963)
HUCKLEBUCK WITH JIMMY
(Pierce) by The Five Keys
(Aladdin: 1951)
THE HUSTLE (McCoy) by Van
McCoy (Avco: 1975)
THE JERK (Julian) by The Larks
(Money: 1964)
LET HER DANCE (Fuller) by The
Bobby Fuller Four (Liberty: 1965)
LET'S STOMP (Feldman/Goldstein/
Gottehrer) by Bobby Comstock

(Lawn: 1963)
LET'S TURKEY TROT (Goffin/Keller)
by Little Eva (Dimension: 1963)
LET'S TWIST AGAIN (Mann/Appell)
by Chubby Checker (Parkway:
1961)
NEUTRON DANCE (Willis/
Sembello) by The Pointer Sisters
(Planet: 1985)
NOBODY BUT ME (Isley/Isley/Isley)
by The Isley Brothers (Wand:
1962); by The Human Beinz
(Capitol: 1967)
PAPA-OOM-MOW-MOW (Frazier/
White/Wilson Jr/Harris)** by The
Rivingtons (Liberty: 1962)
THE PHILLY FREEZE (Hayes/Jones)
by Alvin Cash and The Registers
(Mar-V-Lus: 1966)
PONY TIME (Covay/Berry) by
Chubby Checker (Parkway: 1961)
STREET DANCE by Break Machine
(Sire: 1984)
THE STROLL (Lee/Otis) by The
Diamonds (Mercury: 1957)
TIGHTEN UP (Bell/Butler) by Archie
Bell and The Drells (Atlantic:
1968)
THE TWIST (Ballard)** by Chubby
Checker (Parkway: 1960)
WALKING THE DOG** (Thomas) by
Rufus Thomas (Stax: 1963)
THE WAH WATUSI (Mann/Appell)
by The Orlons (Cameo: 1962)
WALK THE DINOSAUR (Was/Was/
Jacobs) by Was (Not Was)
(Chrysalis: 1988)
THE WATUSI (Hall/Temple/Johnson)
by The Vibrations (Checker: 1961)
WILLIE AND THE HAND JIVE
(Otis)** by The Johnny Otis Show
(Capitol: 1958)

(See also under THE TWIST, where
we list a group of hit records born
out of the Twist craze itself.)

And, just in case you think that the
originator of The Twist didn't create
any other dance songs, check the
following Hank Ballard titles out:
THE COFFEE GRIND, THE
CONTINENTAL WALK, THE
FLOAT, THAT LOW DOWN MOVE,

THE SWITCH-A-ROO;
and the (truly) immortal HOOCHIE
COOCHIE COO – hear the
seemingly ageless Ballard still doing
this live at the Hammersmith Palais
London on the 1988 Charly album.

DOCTOR MY EYES
(Jackson Browne)
Ironically to date, the biggest UK hit
single by California-based singer–
songwriter Jackson Browne is
someone else's song, namely STAY
(Williams)**. But his songs have
been successful for other artists,
including DOCTOR MY EYES, which
had an unlikely cover version from
The Jackson 5.

US HIT:	Jackson Browne (Asylum: 1972) Pop
UK HIT:	The Jackson 5 (Tamla Motown: 1973)

DON'T BE CRUEL
(Otis Blackwell/Elvis Presley)
One of the breakthrough Elvis songs,
he sang it on a memorable TV
appearance on "The Ed Sullivan
Show" in January 1957. The record
marked the Jordanaires' first
appearance as Presley's backup
singers and was ushered by that
now-classic bass line, played by Bill
Black who went on to chart with his
own group's version. Though Elvis
did not sing DON'T BE CRUEL in
any of his own movies, it is featured
in the 1981 docudrama "This Is Elvis".
Song was originally offered to The
Four Lovers (with Frankie Valli).

US HITS:	Elvis Presley (RCA: 1956) Pop
	Bill Black's Combo (Hi: 1960) Pop
	The Judds (RCA: 1987) Country
	Cheap Trick (Epic: 1988) Pop
UK HITS:	Elvis Presley (HMV: 1956)

	Bill Black's Combo (London: 1960)
	Billy Swan (Monument: 1975)
	Elvis Presley (RCA: 1978) Re-release

Other recordings: Jerry Lee Lewis
(Sun); Albert King (Stax); Devo
(Enigma); Otis Blackwell (Inner
City); Barbara Lynn (Jamie); Mike
Berry (Polydor).

Parody record: DON'T BE MAD by
Simon Crum (aka country singer
Ferlin Husky) (Capitol: 1963)

DON'T LEAVE ME THIS WAY
(Kenny Gamble/Leon Huff/Cary
Gilbert)
First recorded by Harold Melvin and
The Blue Notes (Philadelphia
International: 1975), when their
featured vocalist was Teddy
Pendergrass.
  Song's initial US chart action didn't
come until Thelma Houston's version
was released at the end of 1976 and
the single went to Number One on
both the R&B and Pop charts.
Revived in the 1980s by British duo
The Communards, who later also
resurrected NEVER CAN SAY
GOODBYE**.

US HITS:	Thelma Houston (Tamla: 1977) Black & Pop
	The Communards (MCA: 1986) Pop
UK HITS:	Harold Melvin and The Blue Notes (Philadelphia International: 1977)
	Thelma Houston (Motown: 1977)
	The Communards (London: 1986)

Gamble and Huff songs
Composers–producers Kenny
Gamble and Leon Huff were the
most prolific creators of soul music in
the 1970s and the output on their
Philadelphia International label

underlined the Gamble and Huff trademark known as the Philly sound. Leon wrote BACK STABBERS with Gene McFadden and John Whitehead for The O'Jays (Philadelphia International:1972), while Kenny collaborated with Theresa Bell and Jerry Butler to write BRAND NEW ME with which Dusty Springfield charted (Atlantic: 1969) and he also co-wrote BREAK UP TO MAKE UP with Thom Bell and Linda Creed, resulting in a smash for The Stylistics (Avco: 1973); but together, Gamble and Huff wrote a slew of significant R&B hits including:

COWBOYS TO GIRLS by The
   Intruders (Gamble: 1968)
DROWNING IN THE SEA OF LOVE
   by Joe Simon (Spring: 1972)
EXPRESSWAY TO YOUR HEART by
   Soul Survivors (Crimson: 1967)
FOR THE LOVE OF MONEY by The
   O'Jays (Phil. Int'l: 1974)
   by Bulletboys (Warner Bros: 1989)
HEY, WESTERN UNION MAN by
   Jerry Butler (Mercury: 1968)
I CAN'T STOP DANCING by Archie
   Bell and The Drells (Atlantic:
   1968)
IF YOU DON'T KNOW ME BY NOW
   by Harold Melvin and The Blue
   Notes (Phil. Int'l: 1972)
   by Simply Red (Elektra: 1989)
LOVE TRAIN by The O'Jays (Phil.
   Int'l: 1973)
ME AND MRS. JONES by Billy Paul
   (Phil. Int'l: 1972)
PUT YOUR HANDS TOGETHER by
   The O'Jays (Phil. Int'l: 1974)
T.S.O.P.(THE SOUND OF
   PHILADELPHIA), by MFSB
   Featuring The Three Degrees
   (Phil. Int'l: 1974)
WHEN WILL I SEE YOU AGAIN by
   The Three Degrees (Phil. Int'l:
   1974)
YOU'LL NEVER FIND ANOTHER
   LOVE LIKE MINE by Lou Rawls
   (Phil. Int'l: 1976)

IF YOU DON'T KNOW ME BY NOW was not Simply Red's first cover;

their initial UK hit was a revival of MONEY'S TOO TIGHT (TO MENTION)(Valentine/Valentine/ Wiggins) (Elektra: 1985), originally by The Valentine Brothers (Bridge: 1982).

DON'T LET ME BE MISUNDERSTOOD
(Bennie Benjamin/Gloria Caldwell/ Sol Marcus)
Third biggest of the British hit singles by The Animals was this song, originally recorded by Nina Simone (Philips: 1964). Eric Burdon and the rest of the group were seen performing the song in the Associated British pop music extravaganza, "Pop Gear" (1965), which was released in the US as "Go Go Mania!"

UK HITS: The Animals (UK
               Columbia: 1965)
            Santa Esmerelda with
               Leroy Gomez (Philips:
               1977)
            Elvis Costello and The
               Attractions (F-Beat: 1986)
US HITS: The Animals (MGM: 1965)
               Pop
            Santa Esmerelda With
               Leroy Gomez
               (Casablanca: 1977) Pop

Other recordings: Brian Auger and Julie Tippetts (Warner Bros); Susan Carter (Verve).

NB: Disco group Santa Esmeralda followed their revival of DON'T LET ME BE MISUNDERSTOOD with another former Animals song, THE HOUSE OF THE RISING SUN**.

DON'T WORRY BABY
(Brian Wilson/Roger Christian)
A romanticized car song with Brian Wilson taking a breathtaking lead vocal. Most of the cover versions changed the car lyrics. Recorded in 1974 by California Music (Equinox)

which were Brian Wilson, Bruce Johnston and Terry Melcher.

US HITS: The Beach Boys (Capitol: 1964) Pop
B. J. Thomas (MCA: 1977) Pop

Other recordings: Bryan Ferry (Island); The Tokens (Buddah); Papa Doo Run Run (RCA); Keith Moon (Polydor); Good Vibrations (Millenium); The Ivy League (Pye).

DONNA
(Ritchie Valens)
Originally this was the ballad side of the late Ritchie Valens' most famous single (the rocking flip was LA BAMBA**). DONNA climbed way up to the Top 3 and remains one of that era's most plaintive love songs, covered then in England by Kim's father, Marty Wilde.

Performed by Los Lobos in the Ritchie Valens' biopic, "La Bamba" (Columbia: 1987).

US HIT: Ritchie Valens (Del-Fi: 1958) Pop
UK HITS: Ritchie Valens (London: 1959)
Marty Wilde (Philips: 1959)

Other recordings: Cliff Richard (UK Columbia); Gary Glitter; David Johansen (Blue Sky).

Answer record: A LETTER TO DONNA (Feldman/Goldstein/ Ottawa) by The Kittens (Unart: 1959)

DRINKIN' WINE SPO-DEE-O-DEE
(Granville McGhee/J. Mayo Williams)
An early Atlantic R&B success, co-written and originally sung by Stick McGhee and His Buddies. McGhee was the brother of blues singer Brownie McGhee.

US HITS: Stick McGhee (Atlantic: 1949) Black
Wynonie Harris (King:

DRINKIN' WINE SPO-DEE-O-DEE
The late R&B pianist-singer Amos Milburn didn't record DRINKIN' WINE SPO-DEE-O-DEE, but he did cut a string of other notable drinking songs including BAD BAD WHISKEY (Davis), THINKING AND DRINKING (Merritt), GOOD GOOD WHISKEY (Davis), LET ME GO HOME WHISKEY (Henri), VICIOUS VICIOUS VODKA (Smith) and ONE SCOTCH, ONE BOURBON, ONE BEER (Toombs), all for Aladdin Records between 1950 and 1954. Milburn recorded for Motown in 1963 and in his last years, re-cut several of his hits for producer Johnny Otis.

1949) Black
Lionel Hampton (Decca: 1949) Black
Jerry Lee Lewis (Mercury: 1973) Pop

Other recordings: Charlie Daniels (Epic); Johnny Otis (Alligator); Jerry Lee Lewis (Sun); Sid King (Rollin' Rock); The Pirates (Warner Bros); The Johnny Burnette Trio (Coral); Carl Perkins (Sun); Malcolm Yelvington (Sun).

DUKE OF EARL
(Eugene Dixon/Earl Edwards/ Bernice Williams)
Masterful doo-wop song, co-written by Eugene Dixon (aka Gene Chandler) who had been lead singer of Chicago group, The Dukays. Sadly, the original record never made it in Britain, but revival group

DUKE OF EARL

"Duke, duke, duke, duke of earl" sang Gene Chandler way back then, but here he is minus his top hat, white tie and monocle! He later cut several fine soul duets with Barbara Acklin and then with Jerry Butler.

Darts gave the song belated UK chart success seventeen years later.

US HIT: Gene Chandler (Vee-Jay: 1962) Black & Pop

UK HIT: Darts (Magnet: 1979)

Other recordings: Wayne Fontana and The Mindbenders (Fontana), New Edition (MCA).

Answer records: DUCHESS CONQUERS DUKE by The Conquerors (Lu Pine: 1962) DUCHESS OF EARL by The Pearlettes (Vee-Jay: 1962) by Bobbie Smith & The Dream Girls (Big Top: 1962) THE GIRL WHO STOPPED THE DUKE OF EARL by Dorothy Berry (Little Star: 1962) I STOPPED THE DUKE OF EARL by The Upfronts (Lummtone: 1962) WALK ON WITH THE DUKE (Carter/Finizo/Nahan/Pesta/Pirollo/

Spano) by The Duke Of Earl (aka Gene Chandler) (Vee-Jay: 1962)

Gene Chandler memorably performed DUKE OF EARL in the movie, "Don't Knock The Twist" (Columbia: 1962), resplendent in top hat, white tie and cape. He became a major R&B recording artist of the 1960s and 1970s, and among his many hits was a remake of one of his own discs, RAINBOW (Curtis Mayfield), with which he first charted on Vee-Jay in 1963, but then re-cut during a 'live' performance two years later; Constellation released the single which was billed as RAINBOW '65 (Part 1) and it was another major R&B seller, outcharting the first version. Incidentally, the remakes didn't stop there, because Gene Chandler gave it one final shot as RAINBOW '80 when he was on 20th Century. Not that he was alone in placing the year in the title of his own covers, for when Del Shannon travelled to London to record with producer Andrew Oldham over two decades ago, he re-cut his biggest hit as RUNAWAY '67 (Liberty).

EARLY IN THE MORNING

(Lonnie Simmons/Rudolph Taylor/ Charles Wilson)

US HITS: The Gap Band (Total Experience:1982) Black & Pop

             Robert Palmer (EMI: 1988) Pop

UK HIT: The Gap Band (Mercury: 1982)

Robert Palmer's other remakes have included TRICK BAG by New

Orleans' master guitarist, Earl King, and TAKE MY HEART (YOU CAN HAVE IT IF YOU WANT IT) (Smith/ Taylor/Brown/Deodato), one of the biggest sellers by Kool and The Gang (De-Lite: 1981). He also covered Moon Martin's BAD CASE OF LOVING YOU (DOCTOR, DOCTOR), a minor hit for him in 1979.

EARTH ANGEL
The Penguins, whose EARTH ANGEL remains one of America's all-time favourite oldies. A significant example of prime west coast doo-wop from Dootsie Williams' DooTone Records in 1954.

EARTH ANGEL
Johnny Tillotson (*left*) seen here on one of his UK visits in the 1960s with fellow stateside chartmaker, Del Shannon, revived not only EARTH ANGEL but Johnny Ace's PLEDGING MY LOVE (it was the flipside of EARTH ANGEL), along with the Hank Williams country classics, I'M SO LONESOME I COULD CRY and I CAN'T HELP IT (IF I'M STILL IN LOVE WITH YOU) (Courtesy: ABC Television).

EARTH ANGEL
(Jesse Belvin/Curtis Williams/Gaynel Hodge)
All-time favourite 1950s doo-wop ballad, memorably recorded by The Penguins for Dootsie Williams' west coast-based Dootone label. Song co-written by Jesse Belvin (see also under GOODNIGHT MY LOVE), Curtis Williams of The Penguins, and Gaynell Hodge, an R&B session singer in Los Angeles in the '50s.

Covered initially by The Crew-Cuts, a white Canadian group who also 'borrowed' KO KO MO**, Nappy Brown's 1955 Savoy hit DON'T BE ANGRY (Brown/Madison/ McCoy) and The Nutmegs' hit STORY UNTOLD (Griffin/Wilson) (Herald: 1955).

EARTH ANGEL charted for the following as well as by both Johnny Tillotson and The Vogues in 1960 and 1969 respectively, though neither version made it into the US Top 40. The most recent revival, by New Edition, was heard on the soundtrack of "The Karate Kid Part II" (Columbia: 1986).

US HITS: The Penguins (Dootone:
           1954) Black & Pop
           The Crew-Cuts (Mercury:
           1955) Pop
           Gloria Mann (Sound:
           1955) Pop
           The Vogues (Reprise:
           1969) Pop
           New Edition (MCA: 1986)
           Black & Pop

UK HIT: The Crew-Cuts (Mercury: 1955)

Other recordings: Johnny Tillotson (Cadence); Sha Na Na (Buddah); Bobby Vee (Liberty); Aaron Neville (Passport); The Four Seasons (Philips).

ENDLESS SLEEP
(Jody Reynolds/Dolores Nance)
Singer–guitarist Jody Reynolds came up with this, one of the great American 'death' songs. Jody's original record lost out first time round in Britain to Marty Wilde's cover, but a 1979 re-release on Lightning gave him a minor UK seller after all.

US HIT: Jody Reynolds (Demon: 1958) Pop
UK HIT: Marty Wilde (Philips: 1958)

Other recordings: Hank Williams Jr (MGM); Danny Kortchmar (Asylum); Leo Kottke (Chrysalis).

See: TELL LAURA I LOVE HER for other death songs.

EVE OF DESTRUCTION
(P. F. Sloan/Steve Barri)
Vividly descriptive lyric about the state of the world was written by Phil Sloan and Steve Barri, who wrote a slew of other hits including SECRET AGENT MAN (for Johnny Rivers) (Imperial: 1966), A MUST TO AVOID for Herman's Hermits (UK Columbia: 1965) and TAKE ME FOR WHAT I'M WORTH, a hit for The Searchers (Pye: 1965).

Sloan and Barri recorded under various names, most notably The Fantastic Baggys, a studio surf group (see also under our entry for the song SUMMER MEANS FUN). Barry McGuire came out of the The New Christy Minstrels, a folk group formed by Randy Sparks, whose early members also included Kenny Rogers and Kim Carnes; the Christys

scored an international hit with GREEN GREEN (McGuire/Sparks) (Columbia: 1963).

US HIT: Barry McGuire (Dunhill: 1965) Pop
UK HIT: Barry McGuire (RCA: 1965)

Other recordings: The Turtles (White Whale); The Dickies (A&M); The Pretty Things (Trax).

Answer record: DAWN OF CORRECTION (Madara/White/ Gilmore) by The Spokesmen (Decca: 1965)

EVERLASTING LOVE
(Buzz Cason/Mac Gayden)
Proving that not everything out of Tennessee is a country song, EVERLASTING LOVE was co-written by Buzz Cason who, as 'Garry Miles' had earlier covered a British song, namely LOOK FOR A STAR (Anthony).

Written for a British horror flick, LOOK FOR A STAR was sung on the original soundtrack by Garry Mills, a British singer who recorded for the Top Rank label.

EVERLASTING LOVE was originally covered in England by Love Affair who took it all the way to Number One. There have been two best-selling re-makes including a duet by Floridian actor Rex Smith and Ohio-born singer Rachel Sweet; Rachel was signed by Britains' Stiff label and cut a number of remakes on her own, including Del Shannon's I GO TO PIECES, the Carla Thomas soul classic B-A-B-Y (Hayes/Porter), plus one of Dusty Springfield's chestnuts, STAY AWHILE (Hawker/ Raymonde).

US HITS: Robert Knight (Rising Sons: 1967) Black & Pop
Carl Carlton (Back Beat: 1974) Black & Pop
Rex Smith and Rachel Sweet (Columbia: 1981) Pop

UK HITS: Robert Knight
                (Monument: 1968)
            Love Affair (CBS: 1968)
            Robert Knight
                (Monument: 1974 Re-
                release)
            Rex Smith and Rachel
                Sweet (CBS: 1981)
            Sandra (Siren: 1988)

Other recording's: Narvel Felts
(MCA); U2 (Island).

Robert Knight's only other UK hit
was by the same writers as
EVERLASTING LOVE; titled LOVE
ON A MOUNTAIN TOP
(Cason/Gayden), it reached the
British Top 10 (Monument: 1973) and
the song was revived in 1989 by
Sinitta as the follow-up to another
remake: her version on Fanfare of
Maxine Nightingale's RIGHT BACK
WHERE WE STARTED FROM
(Tubbs/Edwards). Maxine's original
was released on United Artists in
1975.

EVERYTHING I OWN
(David Gates)
Originally featured on the fourth
Bread album *Baby I'm-A Want You*
(Elektra: 1972), this ballad by the
group's founder David Gates has
proven to be Bread's most enduring
song, along with MAKE IT WITH
YOU (1970), BABY I'M-A WANT
YOU (1971) and that same year's IF;
the latter also made it to Number
One in the UK by TV actor Telly
Savalas (MCA: 1975). Ken Boothe's
reggae version of EVERYTHING I
OWN was also a British chart-topper.

US HIT: Bread (Elektra: 1972) Pop
UK HITS: Bread (Elektra: 1972)
            Ken Boothe (Trojan: 1974)
            Boy George (Virgin: 1987)

Other recordings: D. Moet and
X-Calibur (Big One).

FEEL SO GOOD
(Leonard Lee)
Also known as FEEL SO FINE.
Everybody's All-American Shirley
and Lee 'broke up' and 'reunited' on
a number of singles (see my story
explaining sequel songs under IT'S
MY PARTY) and this was among
their best 'getting together' lyrics.
    Their original record was featured
on the soundtrack of the Dennis
Quaid – Jessica Lange movie,
"Everybody's All-American" (Warner
Bros: 1988).

US HITS: Shirley and Lee (Aladdin:
                1955) Black
            Johnny Preston (Mercury:
                1960) Pop
            Bunny Sigler: Medley
                with LET THE GOOD
                TIMES ROLL (Lee/
                Goodman) (Parkway:
                1967) Pop
UK HIT: Johnny Preston (Mercury:
                1960)

Other recordings: Rick Nelson and
The Stone Country Band (Decca);
Slade (Polydor).

FEELIN' ALRIGHT
(Dave Mason)
A Traffic song by Dave Mason which
has been heavily re-recorded.
Originally featured on *Traffic*, their
second album (Island: 1968).
    The Joe Cocker version, which he
performed in *Mad Dogs And
Englishmen* (MGM: 1970), featured
Leon Russell on guitar with Merry
Clayton and Brenda Holloway
supplying backup vocals and, when
A&M first released it as a single in
1969, it made the lower regions of
the charts; the 1971 re-issue saw it
climb into the Top 40.

US HITS: Grand Funk Railroad
                 (Capitol: 1971) Pop
                 Joe Cocker (A&M: 1972
                 Re-release) Pop

Other recordings: Rare Earth (Rare
Earth); Maxine Weldon
(Mainstream); The Osmonds (MGM);
Dave Mason (Columbia).

FEVER
(Eddie Cooley/John Davenport)
The late R&B singer Little Willie
John (he died in 1958 at the age of
30) cut the original FEVER in 1956.
Two years later, Peggy Lee turned it
into a million-selling song, via an
arrangement by her husband–
conductor Dave Barbour. Another
bandleader, Louis Prima, and his
then-wife Keely Smith, featured
FEVER in their 1959 musical movie
"Hey Boy, Hey Girl", while The
McCoys (of HANG ON SLOOPY
fame) returned it to the best-seller
lists six years later. Little Willie
John's original was featured on the
soundtrack of the movie "Big Town"
(Columbia: 1987; Soundtrack:
Atlantic).

US HITS: Little Willie John (King:
                 1956) Black & Pop
                 Peggy Lee (Capitol:1958)
                 Black & Pop
                 The McCoys (Bang: 1965)
                 Pop
UK HITS: Peggy Lee (Capitol: 1958)
                 Helen Shapiro (Columbia:
                 1964)
                 The McCoys (Immediate:
                 1965)

Other recordings: Rita Coolidge
(A&M); Elvis Presley (RCA); The
Cramps (IRS); Buddy Guy
(Vanguard); Bobby Bland (MCA);
King Curtis (Prestige); The Hassles
(UA); Sylvester; Little Nell (A&M);
Isaac Hayes (Polydor); Boney M
(Atco); Ronnie Laws (Bluenote);
Madleen Kane (Warner Bros);
Esther Phillips (Kudu); Little Caesar
and The Romans (Del Fi); Joe
Cocker (Capitol).

THE FIRST CUT IS THE DEEPEST
(Cat Stevens)
One-time Ikette Pat Arnold had a
mini UK hit with FIRST CUT and Cat
Stevens' own version followed a few
months later on his second album,
New Masters (Island: 1968). Keith
Hampshire's version made a little
noise on the US charts in the spring
of '73, but Rod Stewart's record is the
one that really made the song
memorable on both sides of the
Atlantic.

UK HITS: P. P. Arnold (Immediate:
                 1967)
                 Rod Stewart (Riva: 1977)
US HIT: Rod Stewart (Riva: 1977)*
                 Pop

Other recording: The Koobas (UK
Columbia).

Understandably, the majority of
songs in this book are American
compositions, but the longevity of
British rock tunes cannot be
underestimated. Beyond the ongoing
presence of the Beatles' and Rolling
Stones' songs, a steady stream of
contemporary revivals is occurring.
Rod Stewarts' own first Number One
song from 1971, MAGGIE MAY
(Stewart/Quittenton), was recently
cut by Wet Wet Wet (Precious:
1989), and Mott The Hoople leader
Ian Hunter's solo hit from '75, ONCE
BITTEN TWICE SHY was turned into
a huge stateside hit by Great White
(Capitol: 1989), while ex-Kiss lead
guitarist Ace Frehley who had
earlier (1979) charted over there
with a cover or Russ Ballard's song,
NEW YORK GROOVE (which itself
had been a UK hit for Hello on Bell
in 1975), re-emerged in 1989 with a
new version of ELO's DO YA
(Lynne); the latter was a U.S. seller
for Electric Light Orchestra (UA:
1977), though the song itself started
life with Jeff Lynne and Roy Wood's
earlier band, The Move, when it was
released as the B-side of
CALIFORNIA MAN (Wood). Also,
offering further proof that Americans

are looking at earlier British hits, teen heart-throb Michael Damian (on Cypress) soared to the top of the US charts with an updated version of David Essex's own first hit of 1973, ROCK ON.

A FOOL IN LOVE
(Ike Turner)
The song that started it all. As legend would have it, Ike had set up the session and the singer who'd been booked for the date failed to show; Tina – Annie Mae Bullock – stepped in and a legend was born.

Listen to the original version and you'll see what I mean...her emotive, unaccompanied opening phrase 'Ooh, there's something on my mind...won't somebody please tell me what's wrong' sets the track alight, pulverizing the listener into almost total disbelief! Then in comes Ike's hand-picked Ikettes as the song takes off rhythmically and they chant backwards and forwards with Tina.

Often re-recorded (on both 'live' and subsequent studio albums) but never bettered, the original master must have sent shivers down Sue Records' president Juggy Murray's spine as he picked it up for national and international distribution.

US HIT: Ike and Tina Turner (Sue: 1960) Black & Pop

Recent events and Tina Turner's spectacular 1984 comeback have taken away somewhat from Ike's significant musical achievements; aside from discovering and nurturing the early careers of Howlin' Wolf and B. B. King, he put together a session which produced what is regarded by many as one of the first rock 'n' roll classics: the astounding ROCKET 88 (Chess: 1951), which gave artist and writer credit to Jackie Brenston, a tenor player with Ike's Kings Of Rhythm band. His time as 'scout' and fixer in the early days of Sun Records and for the Bihari

Brothers' Modern/Kent labels was truly a major contribution to R&B music.

In addition to A FOOL IN LOVE, Ike wrote all the other early Ike and Tina hits with the exception of IT'S GONNA WORK OUT FINE (McCoy/McKinney). Another of Ike's compositions, I'M BLUE (THE GONG-GONG SONG) was the biggest Ikettes single (Atco: 1962), the original version of which was used by John Waters on the soundtrack of his movie, "Hairspray" (New Line: 1988).

A FOOL SUCH AS I
(Bill Trader)
Also known as (NOW AND THEN THERE'S) A FOOL SUCH AS I. First recorded by country singer Hank Snow (RCA: 1952), it was covered successfully back then by Jo Stafford (Columbia: 1953).

US ROCK   Elvis Presley (RCA:
ERA HITS: 1959)Black & Pop
                 Bob Dylan (Columbia:
                 1974) Pop
UK ROCK   Elvis Presley (RCA:
ERA HIT: 1959)

Other recordings: Tommy Edwards (MGM); Jim Reeves (RCA); Tasty Licks (Rounder); The Robins (RCA); Bill Haley and His Comets (Decca).

FOR YOUR PRECIOUS LOVE
(Jerry Butler/Richard Brooks/Arthur Brooks)
Timeless R&B ballad, first recorded in 1958 by The Impressions whose line-up included lead singer Jerry Butler (who left the group shortly after), co-writers Richard and Arthur Brooks, and Curtis Mayfield who became the mainstay of The Impressions while they were on ABC/Paramount and later, on his own label, Curtom.

Curtis wrote most of their other big hits, including IT'S ALL RIGHT

A FOOL IN LOVE
Classic early 1960s shot of Ike and Tina Turner during the time they were recording for Sue and being managed by that label's president, Juggy Murray.

(1963), PEOPLE GET READY (1965) and WE'RE A WINNER (1967), as well as AMEN, the adaptation of an old folk tune on which he and Johnny Pate collaborated and which appeared in the Sidney Poitier movie, "Lillies Of The Field" (UA: 1963).

US HITS: Jerry Butler and The
          Impressions (Abner:
          1958) Black & Pop
          Garnet Mimms and The
          Enchanters (UA:1964)
          Black & Pop
          Jerry Butler (Vee-Jay:
          1966 Re-recording)
          Black

Oscar Toney Jr (Bell: 1967) Black & Pop

Other recordings: Jackie Wilson and Count Basie (Brunswick); Linda Jones (All Platinum); Roy Hamilton (MGM); Otis Redding (Atco); David Allan Coe (Columbia); Michael McDonald (Warner Bros).

FRIDAY ON MY MIND
(Harry Vanda/George Young) Harry and George were two members of The Easybeats, the British group which was extremely popular in Australia in the mid-to-late 1960s.

UK HITS:	The Easybeats (UA: 1966)
	Gary Moore (Ten: 1987)
US HIT:	The Easybeats (UA: 1967)
	Pop

Other recordings: David Bowie (RCA); Peter Frampton (A&M); The Shadows (UK Columbia); Peter Doyle (RCA); Curves (Allegiance); Straight Shooter (Sky).

    Another Vanda/Young song, GOOD TIMES, which The Easybeats cut on a 1967 session, was revived for the soundtrack of the comic-vampire movie, "The Lost Boys" (Warner Bros: 1987), by INXS and Jimmy Barnes; their single became a Top 50 hit in the States on Atlantic. Harry & George also wrote and recorded WAITING FOR A TRAIN, the disco smash released under Flash and The Pan, one of their varied post-Easybeats disguises, released in Britain appropriately on the Easybeat label in 1983.

FUNKYTOWN
(Steven Greenberg) One of the last disco-era hits, FUNKYTOWN was written, played and produced by Steven Greenberg and sung by former Minnesota beauty queen, Cynthia Johnson. Australian group Pseudo Echo injected a hard-rock feel to the song

for their Top 10 remake seven years later.

US HITS:	Lipps, Inc. (Casablanca: 1980) Pop & Black
	Pseudo Echo (RCA: 1987) Pop
UK HIT:	Lipps, Inc. (Casablanca: 1980)

G

GET A JOB
(Earl Beal/Raymond Edwards/ William Norton/Richard Lewis) Timeless doo-wop classic written and sung by a four-man group from Philadelphia. The song's memorable bass line 'Sha-na-na-na' is from where America's most popular 1950s revival group took their name, omitting just one of the syllables!

    The Silhouettes, who recently won a court battle to regain control of their song, were one of three perfect one-hit wonder acts on the US charts; along with The Hollywood Argyles (for ALLEY OOP**) and The Elegants, with LITTLE STAR (Venosa/Picone) (Apt: 1958) as well as IN THE YEAR 2525 (Evans) by Zager and Evans (RCA: 1969), they rose to the Number One slot, but never again entered the bestsellers with any follow-up or subsequent release.

    The Silhouettes could at least be proud that that they inspired a competing version of their song by the legendary black vocal group of the 1940s, The Mills Brothers! Their original record was heard on the soundtrack of "Stand By Me" (Columbia: 1986).

US HITS:	The Silhouettes (Ember: 1958) Black & Pop

The Mills Brothers (Dot:
1958) Pop

Other recordings: The Tams.

Answer record: GOT A JOB (Gordy/
Carlo/Robinson) by The Miracles
(Tamla: 1958).

GET IT ON
(Marc Bolan)
Also known as BANG A GONG, this
was one of the great T. Rex songs
written by that British group's
founder/leader, the late Marc Bolan.
The Power Station revival featured a
superstar line-up including members
of Duran Duran, and Robert Palmer
singing lead. T. Rex performed it in
their documentary film, "Born To
Boogie" (Apple: 1972).

US HITS: T. Rex (Reprise: 1972)
Pop
Witch Queen (Roadshow:
1979) Pop
Power Station (Capitol:
1985) Pop
UK HITS: T. Rex (Fly: 1971)
Power Station
(Parlophone: 1985)

Of the other T. Rex songs, the most
recently revived also included
CHILDREN OF THE REVOLUTION
(Bolan) by both Violent Femmes
(Slash) and Baby Ford (Rhythm
King).

GET READY
(William Robinson)
GET READY was the last of the
many hits Smokey Robinson wrote
and produced for The Temptations.
It was unusual in that it was an
upbeat number for Smokey, which
he wrote specifically for his sweet-
voiced protégé in the Temps, Eddie
Kendricks. Four years later the
rock/soul group, Rare Earth, took
advantage of the song's hard edge
and had a top US hit on the Motown
subsidiary named especially for

them. They followed it with another
Temptations song, (I KNOW) I'M
LOSING YOU.

US HITS: The Temptations (Gordy:
1966) Black & Pop
Rare Earth (Rare Earth:
1970) Black & Pop
King Curtis and The
Kingpins (Atco: 1970)
Black
Syl Johnson (Twinight:
1971) Black
UK HIT: The Temptations (Tamla
Motown: 1969)

Other recordings: Smokey Robinson
(Tamla); Tom Jones (UK Decca); The
Supremes (Motown); Wishbone Ash
(MCA); Angela Cole (Motown);
Daryl Hall and John Oates with
David Ruffin and Eddie Kendrick
(RCA).

See: DEVIL WITH A BLUE DRESS
ON for other Motown hits.

See: SHOP AROUND for other
Smokey Robinson songs.

GET TOGETHER
(Chester Powers)
A flower-power peace anthem that
didn't become a major hit until two
years after the so-called 'Summer Of
Love'. The Youngbloods version was
originally released in '67, when it
was a minor hit, but its reissue two
years later catapulted the record
into the Top 5.
  Crosby, Stills, Nash and Young
performed the song in the concert
movie, "Celebration At Big Sur" (20th
Century Fox: 1971), and Jesse Colin
Young sang it in the charity concert
movie, "No Nukes" (Warner Bros: 1980).

US HITS: We Five (A&M: 1965) Pop
The Youngbloods (RCA:
1969 Re-release) Pop

Other recordings: Jefferson Airplane
(RCA); John Denver (Mercury); The
Staple Singers; The Carpenters
(A&M); Anne Murray (Capitol); H. P.
Lovecraft (Philips).

GIMME SOME LOVIN'

(Steve Winwood/Muff Winwood/
Spencer Davis)
Second of the Spencer Davis Group
trio of huge single hits in the UK:
Jackie Edwards' song, KEEP ON
RUNNING was the first (Fontana:
1965) and rounding out the batch
was I'M A MAN (Fontana: 1967),
co-written by Stevie Winwood with
one of the Group's producers, Jimmy
Miller.

Song was revived (briefly on the
US charts) by Traffic, the band which
Stevie (then Steve) Winwood formed
after the break-up of the Spencer
Davis unit. The Blues Brothers
(actors Dan Aykroyd and John
Belushi) performed it in their "The
Blues Brothers" movie (Universal:
1980), and the Spencer Davis
original was heard on the soundtrack
of "Who'll Stop The Rain" (UK Title:
"The Dog Soldiers") (UA: 1978).

UK HIT: The Spencer Davis Group
            (Fontana: 1966)
US HITS: The Spencer Davis Group
            (UA: 1967) Pop
            Traffic (UA: 1971) Pop
            The Blues Brothers
            (Atlantic: 1980) Pop

Other recordings: The Alessi
Brothers (A&M); Kongas (Polydor);
Olivia Newton-John (MCA); The
Sunset Bombers (Ariola
America);Rubicon (20th Century);
Morningstar (Columbia).

THE GIRL CAN'T HELP IT

(Bobby Troup)
Not only was "The Girl Can't Help It"
the best of the early rock 'n' roll
movies, but this was the best of the
early rock 'n' roll movie-title songs!
Written by Bobby Troup, husband of
Julie London, it was sung over the
opening credits by Little Richard
backed by The Dave Bartholomew
Band. In 1988, it was a hit for
Dépèche Mode on Sire, who cut it as
part of a medley with BEHIND THE
WHEEL (Gore).

Before the film's opening titles,
Tom Ewell appears on the screen
standing next to a juke-box; as he is
introducing the picture, the box
suddenly blasts into life, booming out
the Little Richard version of the title
song.

US HIT: Little Richard (Specialty:
            1957) Black & Pop
UK HIT: Little Richard (London:
            1957)

Other recordings: Delaney and
Bonnie and Friends (Atco); Darts
(Magnet); Ray Anthony and His
Orchestra (Capitol); Alan Dale
(Coral); The Fourmost (Parlophone);
Flash Kahan (Capitol); Wayne
Fontana and The Mindbenders
(Fontana).

Recorded as THE BOY CAN'T HELP
IT by Bonnie Raitt (Warner Bros).

Bobby Troup's most famous
composition was (GET YOUR KICKS
ON) ROUTE 66, a major song for Nat
'King' Cole (Capitol: 1946); in the
rock era, it was recorded by The
Rolling Stones (UK Decca), Asleep
At The Wheel (Capitol), Them
featuring Van Morrison (UK Decca)
and Earth Quake (Beserkely).

GLORIA

(Van Morrison)
Van Morrison's first successful song,
recorded by his Irish R&B group
Them, was covered by the Chicago
punk band, Shadows Of Knight, who
had the significantly larger hit in the
US.

Patti Smith sang it in the film
"Blank Generation" (Poe Visions:
1976). Van Morrison performed it
himself in "Van Morrison In Ireland"
(Bill Graham Presents: 1980).

US HITS: Them (Parott: 1965) Pop
            The Shadows Of Knight
            (Dunwich: 1966) Pop
            The Doors (Elektra: 1983)
            Pop

Other recordings: Van Morrison

(Warner Bros); Santa Esmeralda
(Casablanca); Jimi Hendrix
(Reprise); Patti Smith Group (Arista).

GLORIA

(Leon Rene)
Romantic ballad which charted in
1948 for The Mills Brothers, but it is
primarily remembered as a rhythm-
and-blues classic. Johnny Moore's
Three Blazers, featuring Charles
Brown, cut the original version for
Exclusive in 1946 and, though it was
never a national hit, the song
inspired The Cadillacs to revive it on
Josie in 1954. It was this later version
which influenced a number of other
recordings and, after the group's
SPEEDOO hit, remains the most
popular of all The Cadillacs'
numbers. Incidentally, their original
label wrongly credited the writing of
GLORIA to Esther Navarro, the
composer of SPEEDOO, and that
name still surfaces on re-recordings
from time to time.

Other recordings: The Passions
(Audicon); Vito and The Salutations
(Rayna); The Manhattan Transfer
(Atlantic).

See: TOMORROW NIGHT for other
vintage popular standards.

Composer of GLORIA was Leon
Rene, head of one of the first key
black-owned record labels,
Exclusive. He and his brother Otis
co-wrote such standards as
SOMEONE'S ROCKING MY
DREAMBOAT and Louis Armstrong's
theme song, called WHEN IT'S
SLEEPY TIME DOWN SOUTH as
well as I SOLD MY HEART TO THE
JUNKMAN which got a new lease on
life in 1962 when The Blue-Belles
(led by Patti LaBelle) took their
version into the US Top 20
(Newtown)! On his own, Leon's songs
included Bobby Day's hit, ROCKIN'
ROBIN (Class: 1958), which was a
huge hit all over again in 1972 for
young Michael Jackson (Motown).

SPEEDOO actually pronounced 'Speedo', the song
was based on the nickname of The Cadillacs' lead
singer, Earl Carroll (*top left*). Like many groups of
that era who are still performing, personnel has
changed, but Earl is still with them today, singing
both SPEEDOO and Leon Rene's timeless ballad,
GLORIA.

GO NOW!

(Milton Bennett/Larry Banks)
An R&B song, rescued from
obscurity by British group, The
Moody Blues for their first hit single.
The original record on GO NOW!
was by Bessie Banks (Tiger: 1964).

US HIT: The Moody Blues
            (London: 1965) Pop
UK HIT: The Moody Blues (UK
            Decca: 1964)

Other recordings: Wings (Capitol);
Denny Laine (Takoma); Cher
(Imperial).

GOIN' OUT OF MY HEAD

(Teddy Randazzo/Bobby Weinstein)
Written by Teddy Randazzo for Little

Anthony, the artist he was producing for Don Costa's record label. Song was also a minor US chart hit for Frank Sinatra (Reprise: 1969) and in England, it was a brief Top Forty success for Dodie West (UK Decca: 1965).

US HITS: Little Anthony and The
               Imperials (DCP: 1965)
               Black & Pop
               The Lettermen (in a
               medley with
               CAN'T TAKE MY
               EYES OFF YOU
               (Crewe/Gaudio)
               (Capitol: 1968) Pop

Other recordings: Esther Phillips (Kudu); Ella Fitzgerald and Duke Ellington (Verve); Gloria Gaynor (Polydor); Vikki Carr (Liberty).

GOOD GOLLY MISS MOLLY

(Robert Blackwell/John Marascalco) Nobody could ever accuse Richard (Little Richard) Penniman of being slow in coming forward. Most of his hits were songs about girls (LONG TALL SALLY, JENNY JENNY, LUCILLE, etc.) and GOOD GOLLY was a typical rocker delivered with Richard's powerhouse delivery. His original hit version was heard on the soundtrack of "The Flamingo Kid" in 1984. Mitch Ryder featured the song in a 1966 medley with DEVIL WITH A BLUE DRESS ON**. Though the song was written for and first recorded by Little Richard, the first-released single of GOOD GOLLY MISS MOLLY was by The Valiants (Keen: 1957).

Little Richard used it also in one of his own medleys for a single recorded and released in Britain in 1977, along with another Blackwell–Marascalco composition, RIP IT UP.

US HITS: Little Richard
               (Specialty:1958) Black
               & Pop
               Swinging Blue Jeans
               (Imperial: 1964) Pop

GOIN' OUT OF MY HEAD
Little Anthony and The Imperials' R&B magic began with such late 1950s hits as TEARS ON MY PILLOW (Lewis/Bradford) - revived by Kylie Minogue on a Number One single in early 1990 - and SHIMMY SHIMMY KO-KO BOP (Smith). Their second 'wave' began in 1964 with I'M ON THE OUTSIDE (LOOKING IN) (Randazzo/Weinstein), and their classic ballad.

               Mitch Ryder and The
               Detroit Wheels (New
               Voice: 1966) Pop
UK HITS: Little Richard (London:
               1958)
               Jerry Lee Lewis (London:
               1963)
               Swinging Blue Jeans
               (HMV: 1964)
               Little Richard (Creole:
               1977)

Other recordings: Creedence Clearwater Revival (Fantasy); The Everly Brothers (Warner Bros); Screaming Lord Such (HMV); Gene Vincent (Capitol); The Astronauts (RCA); Bruce Springsteen (medley) (Columbia); The Meat Puppets.

See: RIP IT UP for other John Marascalco songs.

GOOD LOVIN'

(Arthur Resnick/Rudy Clark)
The Olympics were a Los Angeles

R&B group whose WESTERN MOVIES (Goldsmith/Smith) was a novelty pop smash in 1958. They cut a number of only moderately successful follow-up singles, except for (BABY) HULLY GULLY (Goldsmith/Smith/Barnum/Clark) which they re-cut themselves as PEANUT BUTTER (Arvee: 1961), though they were billed as The Marathons.

Other people found success covering Olympics' singles: The Kingsmen took BIG BOY PETE (Harris/Terry Jr), reworked the lyrics and called it THE JOLLY GREEN GIANT (Wand: 1965); similarly, GOOD LOVIN' which in its original form couldn't make it into the Top 75, was re-arranged by The Young Rascals whose record topped the American charts less than twelve months later.

The original Rascals single was used on the soundtracks of "The Big Chill" (Columbia: 1983) and "Legal Eagles" (Universal: 1986). Song performed by dance director Kenny Ortega in the musical, "Salsa" (Cannon: 1988).

US HIT: The Young Rascals
            (Atlantic: 1966) Pop

Other recordings: The Grateful Dead (Arista); Bruce Willis (Motown); Bobby McFerrin (EMI); Chain Reaction and The Edwin Hawkins Singers (MCA); Brenton Wood (Brent).

GOOD ROCKIN' TONIGHT
(Roy Brown)
In a 1978 interview with Paul Harris, Roy Brown himself remembered 'When I did GOOD ROCKIN' TONIGHT they called it race records, but when Elvis did it a few months later, they called it Rhythm and Blues; then when Pat Boone did it, they called it rock 'n' roll'.

'Have you heard the news?' ...we certainly have. One of *the* breakthrough R&B songs, written and recorded by Roy Brown in New Orleans in 1947. Brown was a blues shouter and his record rocked and rolled with infectious urgency. Cosimo Matassa, in whose studio GOOD ROCKIN' was recorded, calls the song 'The First Rock 'n' Roll Record!' At the very least, it popularized the word ROCK in rhythm and blues.

US HITS: Roy Brown (DeLuxe:1948)
            Black
            Wynonie Harris (King:
            1948) Black
            Pat Boone (Dot:1959) Pop
            The Honeydrippers
            (EsParanza: 1985)* Pop
UK HITS: Montrose: Medley with
            SPACE STATION NO.
            5 (Warner Bros: 1980)

GOOD ROCKIN' TONIGHT
The late, great Roy Brown was one of New Orleans' most influential singers. His R&B singles for DeLuxe also included LONG ABOUT MIDNIGHT, ROCKIN' AT MIDNIGHT and BOOGIE AT MIDNIGHT plus HARD LUCK BLUES.

Covered by Elvis Presley (amongst many others) on Sun in 1954.

Other recordings: Frankie Lymon (Roulette); Jerry Lee Lewis (Sun); James Brown (King); Buddy Holly (Coral); Carl Perkins, Link Wray (Swan); The Beatles (EMI); Jimmy Witherspoon (Prestige); Rick Nelson (Imperial); Commander Cody and The Lost Planet Airmen (MCA); Merle Kilgore (Starday); P. J. Proby (Liberty).

* Though The Honeydrippers' record is usually credited as a remake of GOOD ROCKIN' TONIGHT, the song is actually Roy Brown's own sequel, ROCKIN' AT MIDNIGHT; however, the two songs are very similar and not mentioning the contemporary record would be an omission.

Sequel records: GOOD MAMBO TONIGHT by Wynonie Harris (King: 1955)
GOOD TWISTIN' TONIGHT by Hank Ballard and The Midnighters (King: 1962).

GOOD VIBRATIONS
(Brian Wilson/Mike Love)
After Phil Spector, Brian Wilson ranks as one of the finest record producers of all time and this is undoubtedly the pinnacle of his work.

A brave cover by Todd Rundgren made it into the US Top 40 in 1976, almost three years after Todd's revival of his own HELLO IT'S ME with which The Nazz had originally charted (SGC: 1969). The version by Psychic TV was a minor UK hit.

US HITS: The Beach Boys (Capitol: 1966) Pop
Todd Rundgren (Bearsville: 1976) Pop
UK HITS: The Beach Boys (Capitol: 1966)
Psychic TV: Medley with ROMAN P. (Temple: 1986)

Other recordings: The Troggs (Atlantic); Hugo Montenegro and His Orchestra (Columbia).

Covers of Beach Boys' hits
Among the Beach Boys hits which were cut by other artists:

BE TRUE TO YOUR SCHOOL (Wilson) by The Ramones
CALIFORNIA GIRLS (Wilson)** by David Lee Roth (Warner Bros: 1985)
DARLIN' : see THINKIN' 'BOUT YOU BABY (below)
DO IT AGAIN (Wilson/Love) by Wall Of Voodoo (I.R.S.: 1987)
DON'T WORRY BABY (Wilson/Christian)** by Bryan Ferry (Island:)
by Keith Moon (Polydor: 1974)
by B. J. Thomas (MCA: 1977)
GOD ONLY KNOWS (Wilson/Asher) by David Bowie (EMI America: 1984)
by Neil Diamond (Columbia: 1977)
by Queen (EMI: 1975)
HELP ME RHONDA (Wilson) by Johnny Rivers (Epic: 1975)
I CAN HEAR MUSIC (Spector/Barry/Greenwich) by Larry Lurex (aka Freddie Mercury) (EMI: 1973)
THINKIN' 'BOUT YOU BABY (Wilson/Love): this song was originally produced by Brian

GOOD VIBRATIONS
The original Beach Boys. *left to right:* Carl, Mike, Brian, Alan and Dennis. Their vibrations had begun spreading in 1962 with SURFIN' and SURFIN' SAFARI (both written by Brian Wilson and Mike Love); BE TRUE TO YOUR SCHOOL was their ninth hit song and featured on the track were the voices of The Honeys, a girl-group closely associated with the Beach Boys; individually The Honeys were Ginger Blake (a girlfriend of producer Gary Usher who himself was a collaborator of Brian's) and her cousins, Marilyn and Diane Rovell. Marilyn later became Mrs Brian Wilson and a few years after The Honeys had broken up, she (Marilyn) and Diane formed the duo, Spring (known overseas as American Spring), cutting one classic album for UA which Brian produced.

Recorded by THE BEACH BOYS on CAPITOL RECORDS

BE TRUE TO YOUR SCHOOL

Words and Music by BRIAN WILSON

SEA OF TUNES PUBLISHING COMPANY

3701 W. 119th St., HAWTHORNE, CALIFORNIA

Sales & Shipping: Suite 611, 1841 Broadway, New York 23, N.Y.

Wilson with Sharon Marie on a Capitol single in 1964; it was later adapted and reconstructed by Brian as DARLIN', a Beach Boys hit of 1968; under its original title song was re-cut by Spring (Marilyn Wilson and her sister, Diane Rovell) for UA in 1972.

GOODNIGHT MY LOVE (PLEASANT DREAMS)

(John Marascalco/George Motola) Wonderfully melodic, slow-paced love song. The original single is a fine example of the late Jesse Belvin's superb vocal ability and provides poignant reason why he was regarded as the west coast's foremost R&B singer of his day. Song was used by DJ Alan Freed as his closing radio theme on WABC in New York.

His original GOODNIGHT MY LOVE master is heard on the soundtrack of "The Big Town" (Columbia: 1987), and Los Lobos performed a new version in "La Bamba" (Columbia: 1987).

US HITS: Jesse Belvin (Modern: 1956) Black
The McGuire Sisters (Coral: 1956) Pop
Ray Peterson (RCA: 1959) Pop
The Fleetwoods (Dolton: 1963) Pop
Paul Anka (RCA: 1969) Pop
Tavares (Capitol: 1977) Black

Other recordings: Gladys Knight and The Pips; Bobby Vinton (Epic); Los Lobos/*La Bamba* soundtrack (Slash/Warner Bros); The Tymes (Parkway); Barry and The Tamerlanes (Warner Bros).

See: RIP IT UP for other John Marascalco songs.

GOODNIGHT, SWEETHEART, GOODNIGHT

(Calvin Carter/James Hudson) Also occasionally known as GOODNIGHT, IT'S TIME TO GO, this ballad was first recorded by doo-wop vocal group The Spaniels, led by James 'Pookie' Hudson. Song regained fame in the 1970s as the closing theme of Sha Na Na's television show.

US HITS: The Spaniels (Vee-Jay:1954) Pop & Black
The McGuire Sisters (Coral: 1954) Pop

Other recordings: Sha Na Na (Buddah).

GOT LOVE IF YOU WANT IT

(Edwin Meadows/Gregg Giuffria) Also known as I GOT LOVE IF YOU WANT IT.

One of the all-time R&B standards so prominent in British groups' repertoires, this swampy blues was originally the B-side of Baton Rouge, Louisiana artist Slim Harpo's classic, I'M A KING BEE (Excello: 1956).

Besides being recorded by Warren Smith (Sun: 1958), The Kinks (Pye: 1964), The Yardbirds (UK Columbia: 1965) and Johnny Winter (Imperial: 1969), it was also musically copped by The Who (under their original name, 'The High Numbers') for their first single, I'M THE FACE (Meaden) (Fontana: 1964) and by The Pretty Things as THIRTEEN CHESTER STREET (Fontana: 1965).

Also recorded by Angel (Casablanca) and John Hammond (Columbia).

Though they never recorded the song, the Rolling Stones used an adaptation of the song's title for a British EP (UK Decca: 1965) and a 'live' album in the US (London: 1966): *Got Live If You Want It.*

GOT MY MOJO WORKING

(McKinley Morganfield)
Many versions of the blues standard are credited to McKinley Morganfield aka Muddy Waters, but his was not the original version. As CBS' Sol Rabinowitz recounted to Arnold Shaw in the latter's R&B tome, "Honkers And Shouters", the first record of the song was cut by Ann Cole for Baton in 1957; the full title was at that time: GOT MY MOJO WORKING (BUT IT JUST WON'T WORK ON YOU). As Rabinowitz remembers, Ann Cole had been touring with Muddy Waters and amongst her repertoire at the time was 'Mojo'. Muddy supposedly loved the song and went to Chess to record it; however, when he arrived at the studio, he couldn't remember all the lyric, so he added some words of his own...and thereby, his version of the song was born. So significant was the song in changing beat groups into R&B bands in Britain, that Kingsize Taylor (of the Dominoes) remarked upon the sudden change of repertoire, when returning from a regular Hamburg stint to his native Liverpool in 1964, that it seemed to be the 'new national anthem'.

In 1966, jazz organist Jimmy Smith released a two-part single of GOT MY MOJO WORKING and it figured on the American Pop and R&B charts.

Other recommended versions of the song: Manfred Mann (HMV); Johnny Rivers (Imperial); Long John Baldry (UA); B. B. King, Muddy Waters and Big Mama Thornton (Intermedia); Paul Butterfield Blues Band (Elektra); Chico Hamilton (Impulse); The Zombies (UK Decca); Professor Longhair (Atlantic); Shadows Of Knight (Dunwich); The Mojos (UK Decca); Janie Fricke (Columbia); The Graham Bond Organisation (UK Columbia); Sam The Sham and The Pharoahs (MGM); Willie Dixon (Pausa); Conway Twitty (MGM); Alexis Korner's Blues Incorporated (UK Decca); Cliff Bennett and the Rebel Rousers (UK Columbia).

GREAT BALLS OF FIRE

(Otis Blackwell/Jack Hammer)
Jerry Lee Lewis (nicknamed 'The Killer') broke through in 1957 with WHOLE LOTTA SHAKIN' GOIN' ON, followed by this legendary song which opens with the accusations: 'You shake my nerves and you rattle my brain!' With his pumping piano accompaniment, Jerry Lee sang GREAT BALLS in one of those rock 'n' roll movies with a cast of seemingly thousands, "Jamboree", which was re-titled "Disc Jockey Jamboree" for England.

Some thirteen years later, he was captured on film in "Keep On Rockin'" (Pennebaker: 1972), still singing GREAT BALLS! He was as spectacular as ever eight years later when he appeared in the Alan Freed story, "American Hot Wax" (Paramount: 1978). His original version was featured on the soundtrack of "Stand By Me" in 1986. Co-writer and fellow pianist Jack Hammer came to London in the 1970s to record, while Otis Blackwell's name is listed on many hit songs including some of Elvis Presley's milestones (see entry on ALL SHOOK UP).

"Great Balls Of Fire!" became the title of the Jerry Lee Lewis biographical movie (Orion: 1989) in which Dennis Quaid 'played' (many critics charge 'overacted') the role of the Killer, lip-synching to Jerry Lee's own re-recordings of his original hits. Polydor released the official soundtrack album.

US HITS: Jerry Lee Lewis (Sun: 1958) Black & Pop
           Tiny Tim (Reprise:1969) Pop
UK HITS: Jerry Lee Lewis (London: 1957)
           Tiny Tim (Reprise: 1969)

GREAT BALLS OF FIRE
Jerry Lee Lewis at his pumping piano during his days on Sam Phillips' legendary Sun label.

A 1969 cover of GREAT BALLS was this single by The Hassles featuring Billy Joel.

Other recordings: Otis Blackwell (Inner City); Dr Feelgood (UA); Billy J. Kramer (Parlophone); Sha Na Na (Buddah); Dolly Parton (RCA); Georgia Gibbs (RCA); Mae West (MGM); Mickey Gilley (Epic); The Hassles (UA); Black Oak Arkansas (MCA); The Kingsmen (Wand).

See: ALL SHOOK UP for other Otis Blackwell songs.

THE GREAT PRETENDER

(Buck Ram)

The Platters were the most popular black vocal group during the early days of rock 'n' roll, dramatically singing love songs which ranged from 1930s chestnuts MY PRAYER (Boulanger/ Kennedy) and SMOKE GETS IN YOUR EYES (Kern/ Harbach) to original ballads like ONLY YOU (AND YOU ALONE), TWILIGHT TIME and THE GREAT PRETENDER, written or co-written by their producer and manager, Buck Ram.

The most famous line-up of the four men/one girl Platters (personnel changed many times over the years) can be seen and heard performing THE GREAT PRETENDER in one of the movies that started it all... "Rock Around The Clock" (Columbia: 1956), and their original Mercury single shines through the soundtrack of "American Graffiti" (Universal: 1973) and, surprisingly, in Rainer Werner Fassbender's "The Bitter Tears Of Petra Von Kant" (Tango/New Yorker: 1972).

US HIT: The Platters (Mercury: 1956) Black & Pop
UK HITS: The Platters (Mercury: 1956)
            Jimmy Parkinson (UK Columbia: 1956)
            Freddie Mercury (Parlophone: 1987)

Other recordings: Rod Stewart (Warner Bros); The Band (Capitol); Sam Cooke (RCA); The Righteous Brothers (Verve); Dolly Parton (RCA); Roy Orbison (Monument); The Stylistics (Amherst).

The Platters' original 1955 Mercury recording of ONLY YOU (Ram) is prominently featured on the soundtrack of the Michael Douglas–Kathleen Turner–Danny DeVito movie, "The War Of The Roses" (20th Century Fox: 1989).

GROOVIN'

(Felix Cavaliere/Eddie Brigati)

'Groovin...on a Sunday afternoon' was written by two of the four Young Rascals, who were later known simply as The Rascals. They actually had three US Number One singles, of which the first was GOOD LOVIN' (Clark/Resnick) (Atlantic: 1966) which was a cover of a record by The Olympics (Loma: 1965); their other chart-topper was PEOPLE GOT TO BE FREE (Atlantic: 1968), again written by Felix and Eddie who, along with fellow-Rascal Gene Cornish, had previously served as members of twisting Joey Dee's Starliters.

Long before they cut GROOVIN, The Olympics hit with WESTERN MOVIES (Goldsmith/Smith) in 1958 and two years later with BIG BOY PETE (Harris/Terry Jr.), the lyric of which was later reworked as JOLLY GREEN GIANT for The Kingsmen (Wand: 1965).

US HITS: The Young Rascals (Atlantic: 1967) Black & Pop
            Booker T. and The M.G's (Stax: 1967) Black & Pop
UK HIT: The Young Rascals (Atlantic: 1967)

Other recordings: Wilson Pickett (Big Tree); Kenny Rankin (Little

David); Brigati (Elektra); Ian Matthews (Columbia); Leif Garrett (Scotti Bros); Aretha Franklin (Atlantic); The Flying Pickets (10).

A GROOVY KIND OF LOVE
(Toni Wine/Carole Bayer)
Long before Phil Collins sat in that cavernous room staring at scenes from "Buster" (in the video for his single) and even before Wayne Fontana's group took the song to the dizzy heights for the first time, it was Patti LaBelle and Her Belles who recorded the original version (Atlantic: 1966). Featured by Phil Collins on the soundtrack of "Buster" (Hemdale: 1988).

US HITS: The Mindbenders
          (Fontana: 1966) Pop
          Phil Collins (Atlantic:
          1988) Pop
UK HITS: The Mindbenders
          (Fontana: 1966)
          Phil Collins (Virgin: 1988)

Other recordings: Sonny and Cher (Atco); Friday Browne (UK Philips); Petula Clark (Warner Bros).

Song was the first success for co-writer Carole Bayer Sager who later wrote MIDNIGHT BLUE and COME IN FROM THE RAIN with Melissa Manchester; WHEN I NEED YOU with Leo Sayer; EVERYTHING OLD IS NEW AGAIN with Peter Allen; NOBODY DOES IT BETTER with Marvin Hamlisch, plus a string of chart records with husband Burt Bacharach, including a hit which Dionne Warwick sang with Elton John, Stevie Wonder and Gladys Knight; titled THAT'S WHAT FRIENDS ARE FOR (Arista: 1985), it was originally written for Rod Stewart to sing on the soundtrack of a forgotten madcap comedy movie called "Night Shift" (Warner Bros: 1982).

H

HALFWAY TO PARADISE
(Gerry Goffin/Carole King)
Years before he was lead singer of Dawn, racking up Number One hits such as KNOCK THREE TIMES (Levine/Brown) (Bell: 1970) and TIE A YELLOW RIBBON ROUND THE OLD OAK TREE (Levine/Brown) (Bell: 1973), Tony Orlando was a solo artist on Epic.

He had two major ballad singles, of which BLESS YOU (Barry Mann/Cynthia Weil) was the more successful; it went Top 10 in the UK

HALFWAY TO PARADISE
Tony Orlando as he looked when he toured Britain in 1962 with Bobby Vee, Clarence 'Frogman' Henry, Jimmy Crawford and The Springfields.

where it was released on Fontana.

Prior to that, Tony cut HALFWAY TO PARADISE, another heartwrenching love song; it was a British cover by early Liverpool artiste Billy Fury which took chart honours. Fury was an emotional singer who somewhat visually resembled Eddie Cochran and whose growling vocals were sometimes reminiscent of Elvis Presley's; he went on to hit with another Goffin/King song, I'D NEVER FIND ANOTHER YOU (UK Decca: 1961) – though it is his pioneering British rockabilly album *Sound of Fury* that remains his ultimately collectable memorial.

US HIT: Tony Orlando (Epic: 1961)
           Pop
UK HIT: Billy Fury (UK Decca: 1961)

Other recordings: Ben E. King (EMI America); Bobby Vinton (Epic); Brian Poole and The Tremeloes (UK Decca).

See: UP ON THE ROOF for other Gerry Goffin and Carole King songs.

HALLELUJAH, I LOVE HER SO
(Ray Charles)
Outstanding gospel-based blues which became a rock 'n' roll classic, primarily after Eddie Cochran's Liberty recording which he performed on what turned out to be his only UK tour. Cochran's studio version had been cut in October 1959 in Hollywood with overdubbed strings which were faithfully re-created the following January at ABC Television's Granada Studios in Manchester when he guested on the Marty Wilde-hosted show, "Boy Meets Girls". Three months later, Eddie's tour of England ended with the tragic car accident which took his life.

US HITS: Ray Charles (Atlantic: 1956) Black
           George Jones and Brenda

Lee (Epic: 1984)
           Country
UK HITS: Eddie Cochran (London: 1960)
           Dick Jordan (Oriole: 1960)

Other recordings: Frank Sinatra (Reprise); Joe Brown (Pye); Humble Pie (A&M); Tony Sheridan (Polydor); The Beatles (Belaphon); Bobby Darin (Atco); The Animals (UK Columbia); Joe Williams (Roulette); Stevie Wonder (Tamla).

Female version: HALLELUJAH, I LOVE HIM SO by Peggy Lee (Capitol: 1959).

HANDY MAN
(Otis Blackwell/Jimmy Jones)
Falsettoed hit song for which James

Jimmy Jones used his falsetto voice to memorable effect on both HANDY MAN and its follow-up, GOOD TIMIN' (Ballard Jr./Tobias).

Taylor pared down the tempo for his 1977 revival.

US HITS: Jimmy Jones (Cub: 1960) Black & Pop
Del Shannon (Amy: 1964) Pop
James Taylor (Columbia: 1977) Pop

UK HITS: Jimmy Jones (MGM: 1960)
Del Shannon (Stateside: 1964)

Other recording: Otis Blackwell (Inner City).

Jimmy Jones' follow-up single was GOOD TIMIN' (Ballard Jr/Tobias) (Cub: 1960); among later releases was a cover of 39-21-40 SHAPE (Johnson) (Bell: 1967), originally by The Showmen (Minit: 1963).

HANG ON SLOOPY
(Bert Russell/Wes Farrell)
This song was first evident in the States when R&B group The Vibrations charted with it as MY GIRL SLOOPY (Atlantic: 1964), but under the revised title of HANG ON SLOOPY, it hit the top of the American charts via The McCoys, with lead singer–guitarist Rick Derringer, who later cut a solo version of the song for Blue Sky in 1978.

An instrumental reading of the tune by pianist Ramsey Lewis was also a huge seller in the States at the same time as The McCoys' version.

US HITS: The McCoys (Bang: 1965) Pop
The Ramsey Lewis Trio (Cadet: 1965) Black & Pop

UK HITS: The McCoys (Immediate: 1965)
The Sandpipers (Satril: 1976)

Other recordings: Downliners Sect (UK Columbia); The Yardbirds (UK Columbia); The Supremes (Motown); The Strangeloves (Bang); Little

Caesar and The Consuls (Mala); Johnny Rivers (UA).

See: TWIST AND SHOUT for other Bert Berns (aka Bert Russell) songs.

HAPPY HAPPY BIRTHDAY BABY
(Margo Sylvia/Gilbert Lopez)
Originally a doo-wop hit for R&B group The Tune Weavers, and written by their lead singer and her brother.

Song was later adapted as MERRY MERRY CHRISTMAS BABY recorded by Dodie Stevens (Dot: 1960) and re-cut in 1988 by Margo Sylvia herself for the Classic Artists label.

In between time, Ronnie Milsap revived HAPPY HAPPY BIRTHDAY BABY in 1986 and it became a Number One country record.

US HITS: The Tune Weavers (Checker: 1957) Black & Pop
Ronnie Milsap (RCA: 1986) Country

Other recordings: The Four Seasons (Vee-Jay); Sandy Posey (Columbia).

HAPPY TOGETHER
(Garry Bonner/Alan Gordon)
The penultimate record by America's Turtles, led by Howard Kaylan and Mark Volman. Messrs Bonner and Gordon also wrote the Turtles' follow-up, SHE'D RATHER BE WITH ME plus YOU KNOW WHAT I MEAN and SHE'S MY GIRL. HAPPY TOGETHER was also recorded by Dawn with Tony Orlando in a medley with Del Shannon's RUNAWAY (Bell) which briefly made the US Charts in 1972.

US HITS: The Turtles (White Whale: 1967) Pop
The Captain and Tennille (Casablanca: 1980) Pop

UK HIT: The Turtles (London: 1967)

Other recordings: Donna Fargo (Warner Bros); T. G. Sheppard (Warner Bros).

Howard Kaylan and Mark Volman, also known as Flo and Eddie, were also one-time members of The Mothers Of Invention with Frank Zappa. They and the other Turtles wrote another of their classic singles, ELENORE, a Top 10 hit on White Whale in 1968.

Other Garry Bonner/Alan Gordon hit songs include CELEBRATE by Three Dog Night (Dunhill: 1970) and THE CAT IN THE WINDOW by Petula Clark (Warner Bros: 1967).

In 1989, Flo And Eddie (aka Messrs. Volman and Kaylan) sued rap group De La Soul claiming that TRANSMITTING LIVE FROM MARS (Huston/Mercer/Jolicoeur/Mason) from the first De La Soul album *3 Feet High And Rising* (Tommy Boy: 1989) contained a portion of a Turtles song, YOU SHOWED ME (McGuinn/Clark), originally on the Turtles' *Battle Of The Bands* LP (White Whale: 1968).

A HARD RAIN'S GONNA FALL
(Bob Dylan)
Bryan Ferry's first solo hit was this Bob Dylan song from the composer's *Freewheelin' Bob Dylan* album (Columbia: 1963).

UK HIT: Bryan Ferry (Island: 1973)

Other recordings: Joan Baez (Vanguard); Leon Russell (MCA).

Ferry's subsequent chart singles included remakes of THE IN CROWD and LET'S STICK TOGETHER (both covered in their individual entries) along with the 1930s' standard, SMOKE GETS IN YOUR EYES (Kern/Harbach), which was revived in the rock era by The Platters (Mercury: 1959).

See: BLOWIN' IN THE WIND for other Bob Dylan songs.

HARLEM SHUFFLE
(Bob Relf/Earl Nelson)
The original Bob and Earl were Bobby Byrd (aka Bobby Day of ROCKIN' ROBIN**) and Earl Nelson, both of the R&B vocal group, the Hollywood Flames. They recorded under that name for Class records in 1958. Byrd was replaced by Bob Relf of The Laurels. After a minor hit on Tempe in 1962, the new Bob and Earl recorded the classic HARLEM SHUFFLE, with a dramatic uptown production by Barry White. Nelson, the lead singer of the Flames, went on to have the hit THE DUCK as Jackie Lee in 1965.

US HITS: Bob and Earl (Marc: 1964)
            Black & Pop
            The Rolling Stones
               (Rolling Stones: 1986)
            Pop
UK HITS: Bob and Earl (Island:
               1969)
            The Rolling Stones
               (Rolling Stones: 1986)

Other recordings: The Traits (Scepter); The Righteous Brothers (Verve); Terry Knight and The Pack (Lucky Eleven); Wayne Cochran (King); The Action (Parlophone).

The Traits, whose version eeked into the backend of Billboard's Hot 100 in '66, were Roy Head's backing group whom we had heard the previous year behind the said Texan singer on his own biggest hit song, TREAT HER RIGHT (Back Beat: 1965).

HAVING A PARTY
(Sam Cooke)
Sam Cooke's follow-up to his TWISTIN' THE NIGHT AWAY hit (RCA: 1962) was a double-sided classic, HAVING A PARTY and BRING IT ON HOME TO ME.

US HITS: Sam Cooke (RCA: 1962)
            Black & Pop
            The Ovations (MGM:
               1973) Black
            The Pointer Sisters (Blue

Thumb: 1977)
Black & Pop
Luther Vandross Medley
with BAD BOY (Epic:
1982) Black & Pop
UK HIT: The Osmonds (MGM:
1975)

Other recordings: Tina Turner
(Capitol); Southside Johnny and The
Asbury Dukes (Epic); Diana Ross
and The Supremes (Motown); Norma
Jean (Bearsville).

See: ONLY SIXTEEN for other Sam
Cooke songs.

A HAZY SHADE OF WINTER

(Paul Simon)
A song from Simon and Garfunkel's
Bookends album (Columbia: 1968).

US HITS: Simon and Garfunkel
(Columbia: 1966) Pop
The Bangles (Def Jam:
1988) Pop

HE AIN'T HEAVY, HE'S MY BROTHER

(Bobby Scott/Bob Russell)
An American ballad which became
a world-wide smash for The Hollies
the first time around in 1970. Their
record happened all over again
eighteen years later when a British
TV commercial for beer re-launched
the song. Ironically at the same time,
after laying dormant for several
years, HE AIN'T HEAVY was also
chosen as the playout song on the
soundtrack of Sylvester Stallone's
movie, "Rambo III" (Tri-Star: 1988),
for which a new version by Bill
Medley was specially recorded.

US HITS: The Hollies (Epic: 1970)
Pop
Neil Diamond (Uni: 1970)
Pop
UK HITS: The Hollies (Parlophone:
1969)
The Hollies (Parlophone:
1988 Re-release)

Other recordings: Cher (MCA);
Cissy Houston (Private Stock); Olivia
Newton-John (MCA); The
Persuasions (in a medley with
Carole King's YOU'VE GOT A
FRIEND) (Capitol); Gerry and The
Pacemakers (UK Columbia); Matt
Monro (Capitol).

Bobby Scott also co-wrote A TASTE
OF HONEY which The Beatles
recorded (see the DIZZY MISS
LIZZY entry).

HE'S A REBEL

(Gene Pitney)
Teen singer Gene Pitney wrote this
song which has become a girl group

HE'S A REBEL
The Blossoms, including Darlene Love (*centre*),
actually provided the vocals on the Crystals
record of HE'S A REBEL. The Blossoms did lots of
session work, and were seen backing up Marvin
Gaye in the filmed "TAMI Show" (aka "Gather No
Moss") (1964).

classic as recorded by The Crystals and produced by Phil Spector; the lead voice on the track is that of Darlene Love, a member of session group, The Blossoms. Philles, the record label formed by and created out of the names of Phil Spector and his partner Lester Sill, beat another version of HE'S A REBEL to the punch, for Liberty Records' staff producer Snuff (Tom) Garrett had cut the song with MOR singer, Vikki Carr.

US HIT: The Crystals (Philles: 1962) Black & Pop
UK HIT: The Crystals (London: 1962)

Other recordings: Elkie Brooks (A&M); Maureen McGovern (Warner Bros); The Orlons (Cameo); Debby Boone (Warner Bros).

HE'S SO FINE
(Ronnie Mack)
Classic girl group song immortalized by R&B vocal quartet The Chiffons whose single topped the Billboard chart in early 1963. George Harrison utilized the melody for his own MY SWEET LORD hit in 1970, a fact which was successfully contested in court by the late Ronnie Mack's lawyer. The other hit versions listed here were very minor successes.

The Chiffons were produced by Bright Tune Productions, aka The Tokens (*see:* THE LION SLEEPS TONIGHT**).

US HITS: The Chiffons (Laurie: 1963) Pop & Black
          Jody Miller (Epic: 1971) Pop & Country
          Kristy and Jimmy McNichol (RCA: 1978) Pop
UK HIT: The Chiffons (Stateside: 1963)

Other recordings: Dee Dee Sharp (Cameo); Jane Olivor (Columbia); Jonathan King (UK Decca); Beverly Warren (B.T. Puppy).

HE'S SO FINE
The doo-lang darlings themselves! The Chiffons were produced by The Tokens and their other big hits were ONE FINE DAY (Goffin/King) and SWEET TALKIN' GUY (Greenberg/Morris/Baer/Schwartz).

HEART FULL OF SOUL
(Graham Gouldman)
The Yardbirds' biggest UK hit (it was Top 10 in the States also) opens with Jeff Beck's memorable simulation of a sitar.

US HIT: The Yardbirds (Epic: (1965) Pop
UK HIT: The Yardbirds (Columbia: 1965)

Other recording: Chris Isaak (Warner Bros).

Graham Gouldman songs
Both this and two other Yardbirds' smashes, FOR YOUR LOVE and EVIL HEARTED YOU (both Columbia: 1965), were written by

Graham Gouldman, a hugely successful British composer who went on to become a member of 10CC and was later to form the duo, Wax, with Andrew Gold whose largest US solo single was his own LONELY BOY (Asylum: 1977).

Among Graham Gouldman's other major hit songs:

BUS STOP* by The Hollies
    (Parlophone: 1966)
LISTEN PEOPLE by Herman's
    Hermits (UK Columbia: 1966)
LOOK THROUGH ANY WINDOW
    by The Hollies (Parlophone: 1965)
NO MILK TODAY by Herman's
    Hermits (UK Columbia: 1966)
PAMELA, PAMELA by Wayne
    Fontana (Fontana: 1966)
TALLYMAN by Jeff Beck (UK
    Columbia: 1967)

Written with Kevin Godley and Lol Creme:

RUBBER BULLETS by 10CC (UK:
    1973)

Written with Eric Stewart:

ART FOR ART'S SAKE by 10CC
    (Mercury: 1975)
DREADLOCK HOLIDAY by 10CC
    (Mercury: 1978)
GOOD MORNING JUDGE by 10CC
    (Mercury: 1977)
I'M NOT IN LOVE by 10CC
    (Mercury: 1975)
THE THINGS WE DO FOR LOVE by
    10CC (Mercury: 1976)
WALL STREET SHUFFLE by 10CC
    (UK: 1974)

* After The Hollies scored with his BUS STOP,
  Graham Gouldman returned the compliment
  by recording a version of their STOP, STOP,
  STOP (Clarke/Nash/Hicks) on a UK Decca
  single.

HEARTBREAK HOTEL
(Mae Boren Axton/Tommy Durden/
Elvis Presley)
Co-written by Mae Axton, mother of country singer–songwriter and actor Hoyt Axton, HEARTBREAK HOTEL

was Elvis' first Number One single in the States. He is seen performing the song in the documentary, "Elvis – That's The Way It Is" (MGM: 1970), but a far more powerful performance is his 1957 television appearance on the Dorsey Brothers' TV "Stage Show", as included now in the compilation film, "This Is Elvis" (Warner Bros: 1981).
    A number of artists have attempted to repeat Elvis' success with the song, but even the single by Frijid Pink who'd previously hit Top Ten status with a revival of HOUSE OF THE RISING SUN, barely cracked the Top 75.

US HITS: Elvis Presley (RCA: 1956)
                Pop, Black & Country
                Frijid Pink (Parrot: 1970)
                Pop
UK HITS: Elvis Presley (HMV: 1956)
                Stan Freberg (Capitol:
                1956)
                Elvis Presley (RCA: 1971
                Re-release)

Other recordings: Delaney and Bonnie (Atco); Roger Miller (Smash); Conway Twitty (MGM); The Cadets (Modern); Chet Atkins (RCA); Pat Boone (Dot); Connie Francis (MGM); Ann-Margret (RCA); Willie Nelson and Leon Russell (Columbia).

Parody records: HEARTBREAK HOTEL by Stan Freberg (Capitol: 1956)
HEART BROKE MOTEL by Homer and Jethro (RCA: 1956)

HEARTS OF STONE
(Rudolph Jackson/Edward Ray)
Excellent example of the versatility of a great pop song. Originally recorded by The Jewels (Original Sound and R&B labels: 1954), it was covered by The Charms led by Otis Williams. The Fontane Sisters, the white girl trio who covered many black hits, successfully re-cut it as well, and Kentucky's Red Foley scored with a country version. After

HELLO MARY LOU

Ricky Nelson was the consummate all-American teenage idol. He grew up on his parents' TV series, "The Adventures of Ozzie And Harriet", began making records, briefly for Verve and then settled in to a long stint with Imperial, where he worked with The Jordanaires and a crew of legendary session players, including guitarists James Burton and Barney Kessell along with James Kirkland on bass. Most of his British hits had been successful for him at home, with the exception of SOMEDAY (YOU'LL WANT ME TO WANT YOU) (Hodges), an old 1946 song which was revived in '58 in America by Jodie Sands and, two years later, by both Della Reese and by Brook Benton; Ricky's version took off in England and made it into the Top 10 towards the end of 1958.

Creedence Clearwater Revival disbanded, John Fogerty recorded as the Blue Ridge Rangers and revived HEARTS OF STONE.

US HITS: The Charms (DeLuxe: 1954) Black & Pop
Red Foley (Decca: 1954) Country
The Fontane Sisters (Dot: 1955) Pop
Bill Black's Combo (Hi: 1961) Black & Pop

Blue Ridge Rangers (Fantasy: 1973) Pop

Other recordings: Johnny Preston (Mercury); Connie Francis (MGM); Sandy Nelson (Imperial); Stoneground (Warner Bros); Al Caiola (UA).

Sequel record: HEARTS CAN BE BROKEN (Torrance) by The Jewels (Imperial: 1955)

HELLO MARY LOU

(Gene Pitney)
Written by teen ballad singer Gene Pitney, who also wrote HE'S A REBEL (a 1962 hit for The Crystals). I WANNA LOVE MY LIFE AWAY (Gene's own first hit on Musicor in 1961) and RUBBER BALL which scored for Bobby Vee on Liberty that same year and which was successfully covered in England by both Marty Wilde (Philips: 1961) and The Avons (UK Columbia: 1961). Incidentally, Ricky Nelson's was not the first version of HELLO MARY LOU as it had been previously

recorded by country singer Johnny
Duncan (Leader).

US HITS: Ricky Nelson
(Imperial:1961) Pop
Bobby Lewis (UA: 1970)
Country
The Statler Brothers
(Mercury: 1985)
Country
UK HIT: Ricky Nelson (London:
1961)

Other recordings: Johnny Hallyday
(Phillips); Gene Pitney (Musicor);
Loggins and Messina (Columbia);
Creedence Clearwater Revival
(Fantasy); New Riders Of The Purple
Sage (Columbia).

HEY! BABY
(Margaret Cobb/Bruce Channel)
Country-flavoured, million-selling
pop hit by Texan Bruce Channel
with probably the most memorable
harmonica intro in rock 'n' roll
history, played by Delbert
McClinton, who scored with his own
Top Ten hit GIVING IT UP FOR
YOUR LOVE on Capitol in 1980.
Song has been revived a number of
times and two versions, by Jose
Feliciano (RCA: 1969) and Ringo
Starr (Atlantic: 1977), were minor
pop charters. Anne Murray's country
hit in 1982 made their Top 10 listings.
   The original hit record of HEY
BABY has been featured on several
movie soundtracks including "The
Hollywood Knights" (Columbia: 1980)
and "Dirty Dancing" (Vestron: 1987).

US HITS: Bruce Channel (Smash:
1962) Black & Pop
Anne Murray (Capitol:
1982) Country
UK HIT: Bruce Channel (Mercury:
1962)

Other recordings: Juice Newton
(Capitol); Joe Stampley (Epic); Brian
Poole and The Tremeloes (UK
Decca).

HEY GIRL
(Gerry Goffin/Carole King)
Freddie Scott was a writer for the
Columbia music publishing
company, who recorded a demo of
Carole King and Gerry Goffin's HEY
GIRL which was so good that it was
released. It became a Top Ten hit,
but Freddie wouldn't have another
major hit until ARE YOU LONELY
FOR ME (Shout: 1966), something of
a re-write of Bobby Moore and The
Rhythm Aces' SEARCHING FOR MY
LOVE. In retrospect, HEY GIRL was
a forerunner of the sound of the
Righteous Brothers, who recorded it
on their *Soul And Inspiration* album
(Verve: 1966).

HEY, GIRL
Freddie Scott, who first sang HEY, GIRL, also cut
the original of ARE YOU LONELY FOR ME BABY
(Berns), which was an R&B hit for Chuck Jackson
(Motown: 1969).

US HITS: Freddie Scott (Colpix: 1963) Black & Pop
Bobby Vee:Medley with MY GIRL (Robinson/White) (Liberty: 1968) Pop
Donny Osmond (MGM: 1971) Pop

Other recordings: Carole King (Capitol); Isaac Hayes (Columbia); George Benson (Warner Bros).

See: UP ON THE ROOF for other Gerry Goffin and Carole King songs.

HEY JOE

(Billy Roberts)
A shocking tale of infidelity and crime of passion, this punk/psychedlic standard was played by seemingly every rock band in the late 1960s after it was first popularized in the Los Angeles area; L.A. band The Leaves had the first hit of the song under the title, HEY JOE, WHERE ARE YOU GONNA GO? Following cover versions by other local groups Love (Elektra: 1966), The Byrds (Columbia: 1966), The Enemies (with Cory Wells of Three Dog Night) (MGM: 1966), The Standells (Tower: 1966) and The Music Machine (Original Sound: 1966), Tim Rose gave the song the slow arrangement (Columbia: 1967) that became famed in Jimi Hendrix's debut hit.

Although the song has been variously credited to Dino Valenti (or his pseudonym 'Chester Powers'), Billy Cox *and* Billy Roberts, HEY JOE historian Giuseppe St Joseph asserted in a fine "Goldmine" article (January 15, 1988), that the latter obscure folk writer composed the song and then disappeared... perhaps to Mexico?

HEY JOE is featured in the movies "Popcorn" (Sherpix: 1970), "Jimi Hendrix" (Warner Bros: 1973) and "Rock City" (Columbia: 1973).

US HITS: The Leaves (Mira: 1966) Pop
Wilson Pickett (Atlantic: 1969) Black & Pop
UK HIT: The Jimi Hendrix Experience (Polydor: 1967)

Other recordings: Roy Buchanan (Polydor); Cher (Imperial); The Shadows Of Knight (Dunwich); The Cryan' Shames (Columbia); Santa Esmerelda (Casablanca); Creation (Planet); Marmalade (CBS); Sandy Nelson (Imperial); Deep Purple (Harvest).

HEY JUDE

(John Lennon/Paul McCartney)
One of the most enduring Beatle ballads, it was inspired by Julian Lennon. Sung by Paul on the first Beatles single on their own Apple label. Recorded two ways by Elvis Presley, firstly for the *Elvis Now* album (RCA: 1972) and secondly in a medley with YESTERDAY (Lennon/McCartney) which was initially recorded in 1969 and released on the *On Stage* album (RCA: 1970). Performed by The Brothers Johnson on the soundtrack album, *All This And World War II* (20th Century Records: 1976).

The Beatles' original record was heard on the soundtrack of the Jane Fonda/Jon Voight movie, "Coming Home" (UA: 1978) and the song was also featured in Robert Redford's movie, "Ordinary People" (Paramount: 1980), the John Candy comedy "Going Berserk" (Universal: 1983), and John Hughes' masterful teen drama, "Sixteen Candles" (Paramount: 1984).

UK HITS: The Beatles (Apple: 1968)
Wilson Pickett (Atlantic: 1969)
US HITS: The Beatles (Apple: 1968) Pop
Wilson Pickett (Atlantic: 1969) Black & Pop

Other recordings: The Temptations (Motown); Sonny and Cher (MCA); Duane Allman (Capricorn); The Bar-Kays (Volt); Ella Fitzgerald (Prestige); Bill Medley (MGM); The Jazz Crusaders (Liberty); The Everly Brothers (Warner Bros); Yusef Lateef (Atlantic); Tom Jones (UK Decca); Jessi Colter (Capitol); The Ventures (Liberty); Jose Feliciano (RCA); "Beatlemania" Original cast (Arista); Sarah Vaughan (Atlantic); Charlie Whitehead (Wiz); The Supremes (Motown).

Apple was the most famous of all record labels formed by artists. However, despite its initial successes, which also included Mary Hopkin's huge seller THOSE WERE THE DAYS (Raskin) (1968), the company did not live up to its obvious expectations.

The formidable Lennon/ McCartney list of hit songs includes many other significant ballads, of which YESTERDAY stands out as the most recorded of all Beatle songs. Not all Beatles' records were released in the same sequence in different countries and YESTERDAY is a prime example of this, for it was a Number One single in America back in 1965; however, in Britain it remained an album track (on the *Help!* soundtrack) until it was finally released as a UK single in March 1976.

See: WITH A LITTLE HELP FROM MY FRIENDS for other John Lennon and Paul McCartney songs.

HEY THERE LONELY BOY/HEY THERE LONELY GIRL
(Earl Shuman/Leon Carr)
Gently rhythmic R&B love song which started out as HEY THERE LONELY BOY when it was recorded by Ruby and The Romantics; their version made it into the US Top 30 in 1963, but Eddie Holman's re-make titled HEY THERE LONELY GIRL was a Top 5 record seven years later.

US HITS:	Ruby and The Romantics (Kapp: 1963) Pop
	Eddie Holman (ABC: 1970) Black & Pop
	Robert John (EMI America: 1980) Pop
	Gerry Woo (Polydor: 1987) Black
UK HIT:	Eddie Holman (ABC: 1974)

Other recordings: Shaun Cassidy (Warner Bros); Stacy Lattisaw (Cotillion); Mark Dalton (MCA); Flakes (Salsoul).

Gender changes in rock and pop songs are commonplace. Other key examples include Tracey Ullman's hit MY GUY (Barson) (Stiff: 1984) which was originally recorded as MY GIRL by Madness (Stiff: 1980).

HI-HEEL SNEAKERS
(Robert Higgenbotham)
The late Tommy Tucker's classic of R&B, the staple of just about every burgeoning blues band – usually white – on both sides of the Atlantic. The composer clearly felt a change of name more appropriate for the performance. Also performed by Cross Section on the soundtrack of "Quadrophenia" (Who Films: 1979).

US HITS:	Tommy Tucker (Checker: 1964) Black & Pop
	Stevie Wonder (Tamla: 1965) Pop
	Jose Feliciano (RCA: 1968) Black & Pop
UK HIT:	Tommy Tucker (Pye: 1964)

Other recordings: The Graham Bond Organisation (UK Decca); Jerry Lee Lewis (Smash); The Chambers Brothers (Fantasy); Tom Jones (UK Decca); Elvis Presley (RCA); Rufus Thomas (Stax); Bill Haley and His Comets (Sonet); Ramsey Lewis (Columbia); The Everly Brothers (Warner Bros); Ronnie Milsap (RCA); The McCoys (Bang); Boots Randolph (Monument); Felix

Pappalardi (A&M); Roland Kirk (Atlantic); Cleo Laine (RCA); Georgie Fame (UK Columbia); Johnny Otis (Kent); The Searchers (Pye).

Answer record: SLIP-IN MULES (NO HI-HEEL SNEAKERS) by Sugar Pie DeSanto (Checker: 1964).

HIGHER AND HIGHER

See: (YOUR LOVE KEEPS LIFTING ME) HIGHER AND HIGHER.

THE HIPPY HIPPY SHAKE

(Chan Romero)
Latin rocker Chan Romero's single claim to fame was this song of which Romero himself cut the original version (Del-Fi: 1960). The Swinging Blue Jeans originally covered the song successfully in Britain and their version was recently re-released when HIPPY HIPPY SHAKE was used on the soundtrack of the Tom Cruise movie, "Cocktail" (Touchstone: 1988). In the film, Cruise and co-star Bryan Brown juggle liquor bottles in the air to the strains of the Georgia Satellites' version of SHAKE.

In a 1989 interview with dee-jay Steve Propes, Chan Romero revealed that his inspiration for the opening line of this song was actress Nancy Kwan and the memorable way in which she said 'For goodness sake' in the motion picture "The World Of Suzie Wong" (Paramount: 1960).

US HITS: The Swinging Blue Jeans
            (Imperial: 1964) Pop
            The Georgia Satellites
            (Elektra: 1988) Pop
UK HIT: The Swinging Blue Jeans
            (HMV: 1963)

Other recordings: The Rattles (Philips); Kingsize Taylor and The Dominoes (Polydor); The Beatles (Bellaphon).

HIT THE ROAD JACK

(Percy Mayfield)
Percy Mayfield, whose PLEASE SEND ME SOMEONE TO LOVE** had lit up the R&B skyline in 1950, wrote a slew of songs for Ray Charles in the early 1960s in addition to recording for Ray's own label, Tangerine. HIT THE ROAD JACK was the cream of Percy's crop which also included AT THE CLUB (not The Drifters' song), HIDE NOR HAIR, BUT ON THE OTHER HAND BABY and MY BABY DON'T DIG ME, all best-selling R&B singles for Mr Charles.

US HIT: Ray Charles
           (ABC/Paramount: 1961)
           Black & Pop
UK HIT: Ray Charles (HMV: 1961)

Other recordings: Jerry Lee Lewis (Smash); The Animals (MGM); Conway Twitty and Loretta Lynn (MCA); Suzi Quatro (Bell); Helen Reddy (Capitol); Buster Poindexter (RCA).

Answer records: I CHANGED MY MIND JACK by Jo Ann Campbell (ABC/Paramount: 1962) WELL, I TOLD YOU by The Chantels (Carlton: 1961).

HOLD ON, I'M COMIN'

(Isaac Hayes/David Porter)
Also known as: HOLD ON, I'M A-COMIN'.

Standout song from the mid-1960s soul wave, sung originally by Sam (Moore) and Dave (Prater). It typified the output of the now-legendary Stax Record company of Memphis, Tennessee.

Written by Isaac Hayes (before his 1971 smash THEME FROM SHAFT) and David Porter who were one of the hottest composing teams of their day; among their other songs: SOUL MAN (also for Sam and Dave, the year after HOLD ON, B-A-B-Y by Carla Thomas (Stax: 1966), 60 MINUTES OF YOUR LOVE cut by

Homer Banks (Minit: 1966), and YOUR GOOD THING (IS ABOUT TO END) initially by Mable John (Little Willie's sister) (Stax: 1966) and later, by Lou Rawls (Capitol: 1969).

US HIT: Sam and Dave (Stax: 1966) Black & Pop

Other recordings: Aretha Franklin (Arista); The Soul Children (Stax); Erma Franklin (Brunswick); George Benson (CTI); Solomon Burke (Infinity); Tom Jones (UK Decca); Bryan Ferry (Atlantic); Jon and Robin (Abnak); Burton Cummings (Portrait); Waylon Jennings and Jerry Reed (RCA); Chuck Jackson and Maxine Brown (Wand); Geno Washington (Piccadilly); Jerry Lee Lewis (Mercury).

On her 1989 album, *Cry Like A Rainbow – Howl Like The Wind*, Linda Ronstadt included a remake of another Sam & Dave oldie which was written by Hayes & Porter, namely WHEN SOMETHING IS WRONG WITH MY BABY. In turn, the latter was Sam & Dave's 1967 follow-up to their YOU GOT ME HUMMIN' classic (also Hayes/Porter) which itself was covered by an east-coast band called The Hassles (UA: 1967), of whom Billy Joel was a member.

HONEY HUSH

(Lou Willie Turner)
'Hi! Yo! Hi! Yo! Silver!' From out of the past, Big Joe Turner rides again in this galloping, seminal R&B classic! Joe Turner recorded HONEY HUSH in New Orleans in 1953 with Edgar Blanchard's band. It became a massive R&B hit that year and laid the groundwork for Turner's classic SHAKE, RATTLE AND ROLL** the next year.
    The Johnny Burnette Trio version (Coral: 1956) with raw guitar chords by Paul Burlison, popularized the song with a whole different audience, as did the 1970s version by US-based British band Foghat (Bearsville).

US HIT: Joe Turner (Atlantic: 1953) Black & Pop

Other recordings: Elvis Costello (Columbia); Count Basie and Joe Turner (Pablo); Roomful Of Blues (Island); The Outlaws (Warner Bros); Jerry Lee Lewis (Sun); P. J. Proby (Liberty); Clyde McPhatter (Atlantic).

HONKY TONK WOMEN

(Mick Jagger/Keith Richards)
Perennial Stones classic of which they also recorded a country version called COUNTRY HONK on their *Let It Bleed* album (UK Decca: 1969). A number of country artists actually recorded HONKY TONK WOMEN in its original form, including Texas' own Charlie Walker for whom (in 1970) it became the third honky tonk-themed hit of his career, after CLOSE ALL THE HONKY TONKS (Simpson) (Epic: 1964) and HONKY-TONK SEASON (Frazier) (Epic: 1969).

UK HIT: The Rolling Stones (Decca: 1969)
US HIT: The Rolling Stones (London: 1969) Pop

Other recordings: Ike and Tina Turner (Minit/Liberty); Elton John (DJM); Humble Pie (A&M); Waylon Jennings (RCA); Rick Nelson and The Stone Country Band (Decca); Joe Cocker (A&M); Gram Parsons and The Flying Burrito Bros (A&M); The Meters (Reprise); LaCosta (Capitol); Ronnie Milsap (RCA); Charlie Walker (Epic).

See: PAINT IT BLACK for other Mick Jagger and Keith Richard songs.

HOOCHIE COOCHIE MAN

See: I'M YOUR HOOCHIE COOCHIE MAN.

HOOKED ON A FEELING

(Mark James)
First-rate pop song by Mark James
(who also wrote ALWAYS ON MY
MIND) with startling analogies
between love and drug addiction.
The original version by Texas pop
singer B. J. Thomas featured one of
the most interesting uses of a sitar on
a major hit; that single made the US
Top Five and then the revival by
Swedish group Blue Suede went all
the way to Number One.

UK pop 'wunderkind' Jonathan
King coincidentally recorded a
grunting version of the same song.

US HITS: B. J. Thomas (Scepter:
           1969) Pop
           Blue Suede (EMI: 1974)
           Pop
UK HIT: Jonathan King (UK Decca:
           1971)

Other recording: Louise Mandrell
and R. C. Bannon (Epic).

HOT ROD LINCOLN

(Charles Ryan/W.S. Stevenson)
Charlie Ryan originally recorded
HOT ROD LINCOLN for the
Souvenir label in Spokane,
Washington, in 1955. The single
featured tough steel guitar sound
effects by Neal Livingston. Five
years later, he re-cut the song for
Gene Autry's Four Star label and had
a country and pop hit, covered for
more sales that year by Johnny Bond
and, in 1972, by a group that Gene
'Phantom Empire' Autry would have
surely approved...Commander Cody
and His Los Planet Airmen.

HOT ROD LINCOLN was
essentially a re-write of the 1951
country hit, HOT ROD RACE
(Wilson), which was recorded by
Red Foley (Decca), Ramblin' Jimmie
Dolan (Capitol) and Tiny Hill
(Mercury). As such, HOT ROD
LINCOLN is by far the best known
pure example of hillbilly boogie in
the rock 'n' roll era, unless you want
to count WHOLE LOTTA SHAKIN'
GOIN' ON**.

US HITS: Johnny Bond (Republic:
            1960) Pop
            Charlie Ryan (Four Star:
            1960) Pop & Country
            Commander Cody and
            His Lost Planet Airmen
            (Paramount: 1972) Pop

Other recording: Asleep At The
Wheel (Epic).

See: MAYBELLENE for other car
songs.

HOUND DOG

(Jerry Leiber/Mike Stoller)
A cornerstone of early rock 'n' roll
history, and one of Elvis Presley's
breakthrough songs, though not
originally recorded by him.

A full three years before 'the King'
performed it on the Milton Berle,
Steve Allen and Ed Sullivan TV
shows (when producers tried to
mask his gyrations by shooting him
only from the waist-up), Willie Mae
Thornton gave what "Cash Box"
magazine described as a frenzied
performance on her original single
version. Leiber and Stoller's song
thus began life as a gutsy Delta
blues.

US HITS: Willie Mae 'Big Mama'
            Thornton (Peacock:
            1953) Black
            Elvis Presley (RCA:1956)
            Black & Pop
UK HITS: Elvis Presley (HMV: 1956)
            Elvis Presley (RCA: 1971
            Re-release)

Other recordings: Little Richard
(Vee-Jay); Jerry Lee Lewis (Smash);
Conway Twitty (Polydor); Uriah
Heep (Bronze); Odetta (Vanguard);
John Entwhistle (Track); Little Esther
(Federal); Sha Na Na (Buddah);
Scotty Moore (Columbia); Betty
Everett (Vee-Jay); The Scorpions
(RCA); The Everly Brothers (Warner
Bros); Ian Whitcomb (Tower); The
Spinners (Atco); Albert King (Stax);
Billy 'Crash' Craddock (ABC/Dot);
101 Strings (Alshire); The Easybeats

(UA); The Osmonds (MGM); Chris Farlowe and The Thunderbirds (UK Columbia); Freddie Bell and The Bellboys (Mercury).

Billy Vera tells a story about Freddie Bell & The Bellboys, the white group who had a major early UK rock hit with GIDDY UP A DING DONG released on Mercury in 1956. Apparently Freddie Bell, who has been a lounge act in Las Vegas for many years, announces on stage that Elvis was inspired to cut "Hound Dog" after seeing he and The Bellboys sing it live.

Answer records: BEAR CAT (Phillips) by Rufus 'Hound Dog' Thomas, Jr (Sun: 1953) GO 'WAY HOUND DOG by Cliff Johnson (Columbia: 1957).

Parody record: HOUN' DAWG by Homer and Jethro (RCA: 1956)

(HOUND DOG was one of six Elvis originals, extracts of which were edited together to comprise THE ELVIS MEDLEY single that charted briefly in 1985. The other clips were from JAILHOUSE ROCK,DON'T BE CRUEL, TEDDY BEAR, BURNING LOVE and SUSPICIOUS MINDS. Similar concepts were put together by EMI using masters of The Beach Boys and also of The Beatles, the latter titled THE BEATLES MOVIE MEDLEY.)

See: JAILHOUSE ROCK for other Jerry Leiber and Mike Stoller songs.

See: ROCK AROUND THE CLOCK for the SWING THE MOOD record.

THE HOUSE OF THE RISING SUN
(Traditional)
Traditional blues with a storyline about a prostitute which was popularized in the rock era by The Animals, who got it from Bob Dylan's first album, *Bob Dylan* (Columbia: 1962). The Animals' version altered the storyline somewhat and, with a magnificent arrangement by organist

Alan Price (to whom their record gives writer credit), it became a world-wide smash. Price's instrumentation together with Eric Burdon's deep, black vocal is said to have influenced Dylan to 'go electric', thus creating folk rock.
    The Animals performed HOUSE OF THE RISING SUN in the British music film, "Pop Gear" (US Title: "Go Go Mania!") in 1965.
    Later versions by both Santa Esmerelda and Dolly Parton made indents on the back end of the pop charts in America.

UK HITS:	The Animals (Columbia: 1964)	
	Frijid Pink (Deram: 1970)	
US HITS:	The Animals (MGM: 1964) Pop	
	Frijid Pink (Parrot: 1970) Pop	

Other recordings: Joan Baez (Vanguard); Waylon Jennings (RCA); The Everly Brothers (Warner Bros); The Chambers Brothers (Fantasy); Santa Esmerelda (Casablanca); The Supremes (Motown); Marianne Faithfull (UK Decca); Chas McDevitt and Shirley Douglas (UK Columbia); The Weavers (Decca); Ramblin' Jack Elliot.

HOW SWEET IT IS (TO BE LOVED BY YOU)
(Brian Holland/Lamont Dozier/Eddie Holland)
Marvin Gaye's song received a fast second lease on life when Motown session sax player Jr Walker cut his own version as the follow-up to his (I'M A) ROAD RUNNER hit (Soul: 1966) which was also from the collective pens of Holland, Dozier and Holland.

US HITS:	Marvin Gaye (Tamla: 1965) Black & Pop
	Jr Walker and The All Stars (Soul: 1966) Black & Pop
	James Taylor (Warner Bros: 1975) Pop

Recorded by Marvin Gaye on Tamla Records

HOW SWEET IT IS
(TO BE LOVED BY YOU)
By EDDIE HOLLAND, BRIAN HOLLAND and LAMONT DOZIER

Jobete Music Co., Inc.

75¢

The late Marvin Gaye was the first artist to chart with HOW SWEET IT IS. Aside from his duets with Mary Wells, Kim Weston and Tammi Terrell, Marvin's other early hits ranged from CAN I GET A WITNESS (Holland/Dozier/Holland) and HITCH HIKE (Gaye/Paul/Stevenson), both of which were included on albums by The Rolling Stones.

Tyrone Davis (Columbia: 1980) Black

UK HITS: Marvin Gaye (Stateside: 1964)
Jr Walker and The All Stars (Tamla Motown: 1966)

Other recordings: Earl Van Dyke and The Soul Brothers (Soul); The Elgins (V.I.P.); Joe Williams with Thad Jones and Mel Lewis (Solid State).

See: DEVIL WITH A BLUE DRESS for other Motown hits.

Holland/Dozier/Holland songs
Brian Holland, Lamont Dozier and Eddie Holland were the Lennon/McCartney of Motown Records in the 1960s. Their earliest hits were LOCKING UP MY HEART by The Marvelettes, and COME AND GET THESE MEMORIES by Martha and The Vandellas in 1963.

They were the ideal Motor City writing team, as together they produced production line hits with interchangeable parts which have stood the test of time.

Among their accomplishments are an awesome ten US Number One hits by The Supremes. In 1968 the team left Motown and formed the Invictus and Hot Wax labels, where they wrote under pseudonyms due to legal entanglements with Motown, though they returned to the fold in the 1980s to produce a Four Tops album.

The following are some of Holland/Dozier/Holland's most enduring hits:

BABY I NEED YOUR LOVING** by The Four Tops (Motown: 1964)
by Johnny Rivers (Imperial: 1967)
BABY LOVE by The Supremes (Motown: 1964)
BACK IN MY ARMS AGAIN by The Supremes (Motown: 1965)
BERNADETTE by The Four Tops (Motown: 1967)
CAN I GET A WITNESS** by Marvin Gaye (Tamla: 1963) by Lee Michaels (A&M: 1971)
by Jr Walker and The All Stars (Soul: 1967)
GIVE ME JUST A LITTLE MORE TIME by The Chairmen Of The Board (Invictus: 1970)
THE HAPPENING (with Frank DeVol) by The Supremes (Motown: 1967)
by Herb Alpert (A&M: 1967)
HEATWAVE by Martha and The Vandellas (Gordy: 1963)
by Linda Ronstadt (Asylum: 1975)
HEAVEN MUST HAVE SENT YOU by The Elgins (V.I.P.: 1966)
by Bonnie Pointer (Motown: 1979)

The original Supremes. *Left to right:* Florence Ballard, Mary Wilson, Diana Ross, performing at Santa Monica Civic Auditorium before the cameras for what became the movie known as "The TAMI Show" but released in Britain as "Gather No Moss" (Grand National: 1964).

HOW SWEET IT IS (TO BE LOVED BY YOU)** by Marvin Gaye (Tamla: 1964)
by James Taylor (Warner Bros: 1975)
I CAN'T HELP MYSELF (SUGAR PIE, HONEY BUNCH)** by The Four Tops (Motown: 1965)
by Donnie Elbert (Avco:1971)
I HEAR A SYMPHONY by The Supremes (Motown: 1965)

IT'S THE SAME OLD SONG by The Four Tops (Motown: 1965)
by K.C. and The Sunshine Band (TK: 1978)
JIMMY MACK by Martha and The Vandellas (Gordy: 1967)
LOVE IS HERE AND NOW YOU'RE GONE by The Supremes (Motown: 1967)
MICKEY'S MONKEY by The Miracles (Tamla: 1963)
MY WORLD IS EMPTY WITHOUT YOU by The Supremes (Motown: 1965)
NOWHERE TO RUN by Martha and The Vandellas (Gordy: 1965)
REACH OUT AND I'LL BE THERE** by The Four Tops (Motown: 1965)
REFLECTIONS by The Supremes (Motown: 1967)

STANDING IN THE SHADOWS OF
LOVE by The Four Tops
(Motown: 1966)
STOP! IN THE NAME OF LOVE by
The Supremes (Motown: 1964)
by The Hollies (Atlantic: 1983)
TAKE ME IN YOUR ARMS by Kim
Weston (Gordy: 1965)
by The Doobie Brothers (Warner
Bros: 1975)
THIS OLD HEART OF MINE by The
Isley Brothers (Tamla: 1966)
WHERE DID OUR LOVE GO by The
Supremes (Motown: 1964)
by Donnie Elbert (All Platinum:
1971)
YOU CAN'T HURRY LOVE** by The
Supremes (Motown: 1966)
by Phil Collins (Atlantic: 1983)
YOU KEEP ME HANGIN' ON** by
The Supremes (Motown: 1966)
by Vanilla Fudge (Atco: 1968)

Brian, Lamont and Eddie were also
co-writers, along with John Madara,
David White and Leonard Borisoff, of
1-2-3, a major hit for Len Barry
(Decca: 1965), released in the UK on
Brunswick.

HURT SO BAD
(Teddy Randazzo/Bobby Hart/Bobby
Wilding)
Teddy Randazzo was a member of
The Three Chuckles (they sang
CINNAMON SINNER (Chase) in
"The Girl Can't Help It" (20th Century
Fox: 1956). He was a solo artist on
various labels, including Don Costa's
DCP around the time that Little
Anthony and The Imperials switched
from End to the UA-distributed DCP.

Randazzo wrote or co-wrote and
produced the following Little
Anthony hits: I'M ON THE OUTSIDE
(LOOKING IN) (1964), GOIN' OUT
OF MY HEAD**(1964) and TAKE
ME BACK (1965) plus HURT SO
BAD, revived fifteen years later by
Linda Ronstadt.

US HITS: Little Anthony and The
Imperials (DCP: 1965)
Black & Pop
Linda Ronstadt (Asylum:
1980) Pop

Other recordings: Arthur Prysock
(Old Town); The Philly Devotions
(Columbia); David Cassidy (MCA).

One of Little Anthony's earlier hits,
SHIMMY, SHIMMY, KO-KO-BOP
(End: 1960), was first recorded by
The El Capris as KO KO WOP
(Bullseye: 1956). Song was written by
Robert T. Smith and was recently
revived by The Idolls (Downstairs:
1989).

HUSH
(Joe South)
Written by singer–songwriter Joe
South, who himself scored big with
his GAMES PEOPLE PLAY (Capitol:
1969).

In 1965, Billy Joe Royal had taken
South's DOWN IN THE BOONDOCKS
into the American Top 10 and, two
years later, charted with HUSH.

British band Deep Purple racked
up their first US hit single with their
version of HUSH; in fact, their initial
three singles to sell in the States
were covers of significant pop songs,
the other two being Neil Diamond's
KENTUCKY WOMAN
(Tetragrammaton: 1968) and the Ike
and Tina Turner soulster, RIVER
DEEP MOUNTAIN HIGH (Spector/
Greenwich/Barry)**
(Tetragrammaton: 1969).

HUSH was also included in a
medley single with The Hollies' hit
tune I'M ALIVE (Ballard) by
European group Blue Suede (EMI:
1975), which charted for them in
America.

US HITS: Billy Joe Royal (Columbia:
1967) Pop
Deep Purple
(Tetragrammaton:
1968) Pop

Other recordings: Gladys Knight and The Pips (Soul)

Joe South's other hit songs include UNTIE ME by The Tams (Arlen: 1962), BE YOUNG, BE FOOLISH, BE HAPPY by The Tams (ABC: 1968), ROSE GARDEN by Lynn Anderson (Columbia: 1970) and I KNEW YOU WHEN, a hit twice for Billy Joe Royal (Columbia: 1965) and then by Linda Ronstadt (Asylum: 1983).

I

I ALMOST LOST MY MIND
(Ivory Joe Hunter)
Singer–songwriter Ivory Joe Hunter's 12-bar blues-based I ALMOST LOST MY MIND was one of his most enduring songs, along with SINCE I MET YOU BABY** and two of Elvis Presley's hits: MY WISH CAME TRUE (RCA: 1959) and AIN'T THAT LOVIN' YOU BABY (RCA: 1964).

US HITS:	Ivory Joe Hunter (MGM: 1950) Black
	Nat 'King' Cole (Capitol: 1950) Black
	Pat Boone (Dot: 1956) Pop
UK HIT:	Pat Boone (London: 1956)

Other recordings: Floyd Tillman (Columbia); Duane Eddy (Jamie); Willie Nelson and Hank Snow (Columbia); Fats Domino (Silver Eagle); The Everly Brothers (Warner Bros).

I CAN SEE CLEARLY NOW
(Johnny Nash)
Actor–singer Johnny Nash cut a number of reggae-based singles, some of which he recorded in Kingston, Jamaica. These included his own song, HOLD ME TIGHT (Jad: 1968), CUPID**, Bob Marley's

composition STIR IT UP (Epic: 1973), and this song, which became the first Number One single in American chart history with a prominent reggae beat.

US HITS:	Johnny Nash (Epic: 1972) Black & Pop
	Ray Charles (Atlantic: 1978) Black
UK HIT:	Johnny Nash (CBS: 1972)

Other recordings: Gladys Knight and The Pips (Buddah); Roger Whittaker (RCA); Dobie Gray (Infinity).

Another Nash song, WHAT KIND OF LOVE IS THIS was a hit for Joey Dee and The Starliters (Roulette: 1962) which they featured in the movie, "Two Tickets To Paris" (Columbia: 1962).

(I CAN'T GET NO) SATISFACTION
(Mick Jagger/Keith Richards)
Sensational Rolling Stones original, led in by one of the most identifiable guitar intros in rock 'n' roll history. Recorded in the States, it hit the Number One slot on both sides of the Atlantic. Revived almost a decade later in the UK by Jonathan King using one of his *noms de plume*, Bubblerock.

Performed by Justine Bateman and Mystery in the motion picture, "Satisfaction" (20th Century Fox: 1988). SATISFACTION was also used

as a significant theme in Francis Coppola's "Apocalypse Now" (UA: 1979).

UK HITS: The Rolling Stones
                (Decca: 1965)
                Bubblerock (UK: 1974)
US HITS: The Rolling Stones
                (London: 1965) Black &
                Pop
                Otis Redding (Volt: 1966)
                Black & Pop

Other recordings: Devo (Warner Bros); Mary Wells (Atco); Billy Preston (Capitol); Jose Feliciano (RCA); The Strangeloves (Bang); Aretha Franklin (Atlantic); Blue Cheer (Philips); Manfred Mann (HMV); Sandie Shaw (Pye); Herbie Goins and The Night Timers (Parlophone); Chris Farlowe (Immediate); Samantha Fox (Jive), George Burns (Buddah).

I CAN'T HELP MYSELF
(Brian Holland/Lamont Dozier/Eddie Holland)
Sub-titled SUGAR PIE, HONEY BUNCH, this was the Four Tops' first American Number One and their initial song to register on the British charts. The Tops' original single was featured on the soundtrack of "Where The Buffalo Roam" (Universal: 1980).

US HITS: The Four Tops (Motown:
                1965) Black & Pop
                Donnie Elbert (Avco:
                1972) Black & Pop
                Bonnie Pointer (Motown:
                1980) Black & Pop
UK HITS: The Four Tops (Tamla
                Motown: 1965)
                Donnie Elbert (Avco:
                1972)
                The Four Tops (Tamla
                Motown: 1970 Re-
                release)

Other recordings: Diana Ross and The Supremes (Motown); Dolly Parton (RCA); Axe (MCA); Gene Ammons (Prestige).

I FEEL LOVE
(Donna Summer/Giorgio Moroder/ Pete Bellotte)

US HIT: Donna Summer
                (Casablanca: 1977) Pop
UK HITS: Donna Summer (GTO:
                1977)
                Bronski Beat and Mark
                Almond (Forbidden
                Fruit: 1985)

I FOUGHT THE LAW
(Sonny Curtis)
Bobby Fuller was a Texan who idolized Buddy Holly and he, too, died tragically and mysteriously of asphyxiation, but not before having US hits with the post-Holly Crickets' song, I FOUGHT THE LAW, and Buddy's own LOVE'S MADE A FOOL OF YOU.

I FOUGHT THE LAW
Sonny Curtis' song was a hit for The Bobby Fuller Four led by the late Bobby Fuller (*third from left*). A Texas band, they also cut a fine version of Buddy Holly's LOVE'S MADE A FOOL OF YOU (Mustang: 1966).

US HIT: The Bobby Fuller Four
                (Mustang: 1966) Pop
UK HIT: The Bobby Fuller Four
                (London: 1966)

Other recordings: The Crickets

(Liberty); Hank Williams Jr (Warner Bros); Sonny Curtis (Elektra); Kris Kristofferson and Rita Coolidge (A&M); The Clash (CBS); The Stray Cats (EMI).

I GOT A WOMAN
(Ray Charles)
Ray Charles recorded I GOT A WOMAN (aka I'VE GOT A WOMAN) in 1954 and it became his first Number One R&B single. The first instrumental cover was a two-parter single by organist Jimmy McGriff. The versions by Freddie Scott and Rick Nelson were significantly less successful, each just making it inside the US Top 50.

US HITS: Ray Charles (Atlantic: 1955) Black
Jimmy McGriff (Sue: 1962) Black & Pop
Freddie Scott (Colpix: 1963) Pop
Rick Nelson (Decca: 1963) Pop

Other recordings: Elvis Presley (RCA); Sonny Terry and Brownie McGhee (Fantasy); Delaney and Bonnie (Atco); Bill Haley and His Comets (Sun); Jimmy Smith (Blue Note); The Everly Brothers (Warner Bros); Jerry Lee Lewis (Smash); Them featuring Van Morrison (UK Decca); Carl Perkins (Columbia); Bobby Darin (Atco); Conway Twitty (MGM); Adam Faith (Parlophone); Chet Atkins (RCA); The Monkees (Rhino); George Benson (A&M); The Honeydrippers (Es Paranza); Big Jay McNeely (Big Jay).

Answer record: YOU SAID YOU HAD A WOMAN by Geneva Vallier.

I GOT MY MOJO WORKING
See: GOT MY MOJO WORKING.

I GOT YOU BABE
(Salvatore Bono)
One of the great Sonny and Cher duets successfully revived by Birmingham band UB40 with guest singer Chrissie Hynde.

It was Sonny and Cher's breakthrough single which topped the US charts in August 1965; dressed in their outlandish hippy styles, they became rock's favourite couple. Song was featured in Sonny and Cher's movie, "Good Times" (Columbia: 1967) and then sung by Tiny Tim in the 1968 rockumentary film, "You Are What You Eat".

US HITS: Sonny and Cher (Atco: 1965) Pop & Black
Etta James (Cadet: 1968) Pop & Black
UB40 with Chrissie Hynde (A&M:1985) Pop
UK HITS: Sonny and Cher (Atlantic: 1965)
UB40 with Chrissie Hynde (Dep International: 1985)

Other recordings: Manfred Mann (HMV); The Dictators (Asylum).

I GOT YOU (I FEEL GOOD)
(James Brown)
With a scream that must have launched a thousand thrills, soul music's brother number one opens this, one of his greatest singles...a song which should really be known by its sub-title, as I FEEL GOOD is the opening and most memorable line – and just listen to that bass pattern.

James Brown's original single is heard on the soundtrack of "Good Morning Vietnam" (Touchstone: 1987).

US HIT: James Brown and The Famous Flames (King: 1965) Black & Pop
UK HIT: James Brown and The Famous Flames (Pye International: 1966)

Other recordings: Mitch Ryder and The Detroit Wheels (New Voice); Quincy Jones (Mercury).

I HEAR YOU KNOCKING

(Dave Bartholomew/Pearl King)
Rock 'n' roll classic which started out when it was written for R&B artist, Smiley Lewis; his record was a major hit on what were then called the 'race music' charts (the equivalent of R&B and Black music charts), but it was a cover record by white actress–singer, Gale Storm, which climbed to the top of the mainstream hit parade. Fats Domino cut it six years later, but it was

Welsh rock 'n' roller Dave Edmunds who really brought the song back in both America and in Britain where it was a Number One single.

US HITS: Smiley Lewis (Imperial: 1955) Black
Gale Storm (Dot: 1955) Pop
Fats Domino (Imperial: 1961) Pop
Dave Edmunds (MAM: 1971) Pop

UK HIT: Dave Edmunds (MAM: 1970)

Other recordings: Connie Francis (MGM); Mac Wiseman (Dot); Joe Turner (Intermedia); Ernie Freeman (Imperial).

Dave Bartholomew songs

In the 1940s and 1950s, trumpeter–bandleader–composer–producer Dave Bartholomew was one of the key people responsible for what became known the world over as the New Orleans sound. He co-wrote many of Fats Domino's many hits as well as having his own catalogue of successful songs.

Among the hit recordings of Dave Bartholomew's songs:

AIN'T THAT A SHAME (with Antoine Domino)** by Fats Domino (Imperial: 1955)
by The Four Seasons (Vee-Jay: 1963)
by Cheap Trick (Epic: 1979)
THE BELLS ARE RINGING (with Overton Lemon) by Smiley Lewis (Imperial: 1952)
BLUE MONDAY (with Antoine Domino)** by Fats Domino (Imperial: 1956)
THE FAT MAN (with Antoine Domino) by Fats Domino (Imperial: 1950)
GOIN' TO THE RIVER (with Antoine Domino) by Fats Domino (Imperial: 1953)
I'M GONNA BE A WHEEL SOMEDAY (with Roy Hayes and Antoine Domino)** by Fats

I HEAR YOU KNOCKING

Trumpeter–bandleader–artist–composer–producer Dave Bartholomew is among a handful of people responsible for the sound of New Orleans-originated R&B. In addition to I HEAR YOU KNOCKING and the long line of hits which he co-wrote with Fats Domino, Dave also penned ONE NIGHT and WITCHCRAFT which were originally recorded by Smiley Lewis (Imperial: 1955) and The Spiders (Imperial: 1955) respectively; both tunes were later successfully covered by Elvis Presley for RCA in 1958 and 1963. The album pictured here is one of three compilations released by French EMI (Pathe Marconi), containing Batholomew's solo Imperial output including the original of THE MONKEY, his 'spoken' vocal recently re-recorded by The Fabulous Thunderbirds.

One of New Orleans' few R&B vocal groups, The Spiders, was built around two brothers namely Chick and Chuck Carbo. Their big songs were YOU'RE THE ONE and I DIDN'T WANT TO DO IT, both written by Adolph Smith; and then there was Dave Bartholomew's memorable WITCHCRAFT, first recorded by The Spiders on August 27th, 1955 and revived by Elvis Presley at a Nashville session 7 years, 9 months and 31 days later!

Domino (Imperial: 1959)
LET THE FOUR WINDS BLOW (with Antoine Domino) by Roy Brown (Imperial: 1957)
MY GIRL JOSEPHINE (with Antoine Domino) by Fats Domino (Imperial: 1960)
by the Applejacks (UK Decca: 1964)
ONE NIGHT (with Pearl King)** by Elvis Presley (RCA: 1958)
SICK AND TIRED (with Chris Kenner)** by Chris Kenner (Imperial: 1957)
by Fats Domino (Imperial: 1958)
THREE TIMES SEVEN EQUALS TWENTY-ONE by Jewel King (Imperial: 1950)
TRY ROCK AND ROLL by Bobby Mitchell (Imperial: 1956)
WALKING TO NEW ORLEANS (with Antoine Domino and Robert Guidry) by Fats Domino (Imperial: 1960)
WITCHCRAFT by The Spiders (Imperial: 1956)
by Elvis Presley (RCA: 1963)

One other significant Bartholomew song is THE MONKEY, a social commentary comparing mankind's morals to the law of the jungle. Dave recorded this, a narrative set to a laid-back shuffle rhythm, for Imperial in 1957 and it was revived by The Fabulous Thunderbirds on their 1982 Chrysalis album *T-Bird Rhythm.*

I HEARD IT THROUGH THE GRAPEVINE
(Norman Whitfield/Barrett Strong)
All-time Motown classic, initially recorded by Gladys Knight and The Pips. They performed it in-concert in "Save The Children" (Paramount: 1973).

The British reissue in 1986 of the Marvin Gaye version was triggered by the use of a soundalike version on a TV ad for Levi's jeans. In the States, a similar resurgence of the song's popularity came about after the birth of the 'California Raisins', singing cartoon characters decked out in brightly coloured sneakers and white gloves; these little figures became instantly successful pitchmen for the California Raisin Advisory Board and were the invention of a new process called Claymation; singer and legendary session drummer Buddy Miles was the voice on the soundbeds singing GRAPEVINE.

Creedence Clearwater's version of I HEARD IT THROUGH THE GRAPEVINE was heard on the soundtrack of the Bill Murray comedy, "Where The Buffalo Roam" (Universal: 1980), while the Glenn Close drama, "The Big Chill" (Columbia: 1983), used Marvin Gaye's chart recording to great effect.

US HITS: Gladys Knight and The Pips (Soul: 1967) Black & Pop
Marvin Gaye (Tamla: 1968) Black & Pop
Creedence Clearwater

Revival (Fantasy: 1976)
Pop
Roger (Warner Bros:
1981) Black & Pop
The California Raisins
(Priority: 1988) Pop
UK HITS: Gladys Knight and The
Pips (Tamla Motown:
1967)
Marvin Gaye (Tamla
Motown: 1969)
The Slits: Medley with
Typical Girls (Island:
1979)
Marvin Gaye (Tamla
Motown: 1986 Re-
release)

Other recordings: Smokey Robinson
and The Miracles (Tamla); Ike and
Tina Turner (UA); Kris Kristoffersen
and Rita Coolidge (A&M); The
Temptations (Gordy); Ronnie Milsap
(RCA); Bobby Taylor and The
Vancouvers (Gordy); King Curtis
(Atco); The Isley Brothers (Tamla);
Ella Fitzgerald (Reprise).

See: REET PETITE for further details
of the use of I HEARD IT THROUGH
THE GRAPEVINE in the 1986
advertisement.

See: DEVIL WITH A BLUE DRESS
ON for other Motown hits.

GRAPEVINE co-writer Norman
Whitfield was an extremely
successful Motown producer with
acts like The Temptations, Marvin
Gaye and Edwin Starr. Many of his
hits with The Temps and Starr were
almost torn from newspaper
headlines, although JUST MY
IMAGINATION (RUNNING AWAY
WITH ME) (Whitfield/Strong) was as
sublime a Smokey Robinson-style
ballad as one could ask for.

Other songs by Whitfield with his
major collaborator, Barrett Strong of
MONEY** fame, include CLOUD
NINE, I CAN'T GET NEXT TO YOU,
PSYCHEDLIC SHACK, BALL OF
CONFUSION and PAPA WAS A
ROLLING STONE, all originally by

The Temptations; WAR by Edwin
Starr and SMILING FACES
SOMETIMES by The Undisputed
Truth. See also: AIN'T TOO PROUD
TO BEG** and I WISH IT WOULD
RAIN.**

I KNOW (YOU DON'T LOVE ME NO MORE)
(Barbara George)
Milestone female R&B love song,
written and first recorded by
Louisiana's Barbara George, with
one of the punchiest trumpet solos in
rock 'n' roll.
    Performed by Marisela in the
musical movie, "Salsa" (Cannon:
1988).

US HIT: Barbara George (AFO:
           1961) Black & Pop

Other recordings: Cher (MCA); The
Newbeats (Hickory); Fats Domino
(Reprise); Gloria Jones (Minit); Rod
Taylor (Asylum); Ike and Tina
Turner (UA); Anne Murray (Capitol);
Bonnie Raitt (Warner Bros); Billy J.
Kramer and The Dakotas (Parlophone).

I LIKE IT LIKE THAT (PART 1)
(Chris Kenner)
'Come on, let me show where it's at'
invites New Orleans singer Chris
Kenner on this, his huge danceable
R&B seller of 1961. He also wrote
LAND OF 1000 DANCES** as well
as SICK AND TIRED (originally
called OH, BABE) with which Fats
Domino had charted in 1958.
    The Chris Kenner record was
heard on the soundtrack of Stanley
Kubrick's Vietnam war movie, "Full
Metal Jacket" (Warner Bros: 1987).

US HIT: Chris Kenner (Instant:
           1961) Pop & Black
           The Dave Clark Five
           (Epic: 1965) Pop

Other recordings: The Nashville
Teens (UK Decca); Loggins and
Messina (Columbia); Jerry Lee
Lewis (Elektra); The Ventures

(Liberty); Them featuring Van
Morrison (UK Decca); Brinsley
Schwarz (UA).

Answer record: I DON'T LIKE IT
LIKE THAT by The Bobbettes
(Gone: 1961).

I ONLY WANT TO BE WITH YOU

(Mike Hawker/Ivor Raymonde)
A fine, soaring ballad by two local
songwriters which became the first
solo hit for Dusty Springfield,
Britain's most successful girl singer
of the 1960s, who had previously
been one third of the folksinging
Springfields, with her brother Tom
and Mike Hurst. The song was
revived thirteen years later by The
Bay City Rollers (as I ONLY
WANNA BE WITH YOU) and then
by The Tourists, whose lead singer
was Annie Lennox. It was the
biggest of five best-selling singles
that The Tourists clocked up before
Annie and Dave Stewart left to form
Eurythmics in 1981.

Samantha Fox's 1989 revival,
produced by the ubiquitous late '80s
team of Stock/Aitken/Waterman,
used slightly the revised version of
the song's title, I ONLY WANNA BE
WITH YOU.

US HITS: Dusty Springfield (Philips:
           1964) Pop
           Bay City Rollers
           (Arista:1976) Pop
           The Tourists (Epic: 1980)
           Pop
           Nicolette Larson (Warner
           Bros:1982) Pop
UK HITS: Dusty Springfield (Philips:
           1963)
           Bay City Rollers (Bell:
           1976)
           The Tourists (Logo: 1979)

Other recording: Southside Johnny
and The Jukes (Atlantic).

See: SON OF A PREACHER MAN
for other Dusty Springfield hits.

I PUT A SPELL ON YOU

(Jay Hawkins)
Listen to Nina Simone's sultry version
of I PUT A SPELL ON YOU and it
may be difficult to believe that it was
written by an R&B singer with fire in
his eyes and a penchant for opening
his stage-act by climbing out of a
coffin, carrying a human skull!

As Jay tells it, he first recorded it
as a soft romantic ballad himself, but
his most famous version was cut for
Columbia's Okeh label in 1956;
famous, not just because it became
the definitive record of the song, but
because everyone on the session,
including players like Mickey
'Guitar' Baker and Sam 'The Man'
Taylor were totally drunk! A few

I PUT A SPELL ON YOU
The wild man himself, Screamin' Jay Hawkins,
whose I PUT A SPELL ON YOU has become a
R&B standard, a soulful ballad and even a
Halloween favourite!

years later, The Animals' former organist Alan Price revived it in England as his first Alan Price Set single.

It has had a movie life too, for the song is played memorably on a radio in Jim Jarmush's black-and-white cult film, "Stranger In Paradise" (1984) and Screamin' Jay performs it himself on-stage in Floyd Mutrux's Alan Freed biopic, "American Hot Wax" (Paramount: 1978), though regrettably, most of Jay's performance ended up on the cutting-room floor.

US HITS: Nina Simone (Philips: 1965) Black
Creedence Clearwater Revival (Fantasy: 1968) Pop
UK HITS: Nina Simone (Philips: 1965)
The Alan Price Set (UK Decca: 1966)
Nina Simone (Philips: 1969 Re-release)

Other recordings: Pete Townshend (Atco); The Animals (Polydor); The Crazy World Of Arthur Brown (Track); Audience (Elektra); Them (UK Decca); John Mayall.

Alan Price had a huge British seller with SIMON SMITH AND HIS AMAZING DANCING BEAR (UK Decca: 1967), an early success in the career of songwriter Randy Newman; Manfred Mann cut his SO LONG DAD later that same year (Fontana) and Jackie DeShannon with whom he also co-wrote, had recorded his DID HE CALL TODAY, MAMA? on the B-side of her NEEDLES AND PINS (Liberty: 1963). Randy Newman's first song to crest the American charts was MAMA TOLD ME (NOT TO COME) recorded by Three Dog Night (Dunhill: 1970) which was produced by Richard Podolor; Podolor was himself a composer, getting co-writing credit with drummer Sandy Nelson on his hit LET THERE BE

DRUMS in 1961 on Imperial, the label for which Podolor recorded under the pseudonym, Richie Allen.

I SAW HER STANDING THERE/I SAW HIM STANDING THERE
(John Lennon/Paul McCartney)
Sung by Paul McCartney on the first Beatles' album, *Please Please Me* (Parlophone: 1963). John Lennon later recorded it with Elton John 'live' at Madison Square Garden in New York.

Later revived by Tiffany as I SAW HIM STANDING THERE.

UK HITS: The Elton John Band Featuring John Lennon (DJM: 1981)
Tiffany (MCA: 1988)
US HITS: The Beatles (Capitol: 1964) Pop
Tiffany (MCA: 1988) Pop

Other recordings: The Tubes (A&M); Anthony Newley (UK Decca); Jerry Garcia (Arista); Duffy Power (Parlophone); Little Richard (Reprise).

This was not the only Beatle song to be recorded with a change of gender; AND I LOVE HIM (Lennon/McCartney) charted for Esther Phillips (the former 'Little Esther') on Atlantic in 1965.

See: WITH A LITTLE HELP FROM MY FRIENDS for other John Lennon and Paul McCartney songs.

I SAY A LITTLE PRAYER
(Burt Bacharach/Hal David)
One of the Bacharach/David series of hits written for Dionne Warwick. Song also recorded successfully as a duet, particularly by Isaac Hayes and Dionne Warwick who utilized it in a medley with BY THE TIME I GET TO PHOENIX (ABC: 1977), which made the Top 75 R&B chart.

US HITS: Dionne Warwick (Scepter: 1967) Black & Pop

Aretha Franklin (Atlantic:
1968) Black & Pop

UK HITS: Aretha Franklin (Atlantic:
1968)
Bomb The Bass Featuring
Maureen (Rhythm
King: 1988)

Other recordings: Burt Bacharach
(A&M); Martha Reeves and The
Vandellas (Gordy); Glen Campbell
and Anne Murray (Capitol).

See: MAKE IT EASY ON YOURSELF
for other Burt Bacharach and Hal
David songs.

I SHOT THE SHERIFF
(Bob Marley)
Bob Marley and The Wailers were
the foremost exponents of reggae
music; Island Records promoted the
Jamaican band heavily in Britain,
where six of their singles made the
Top 10 charts, namely JAMMING/
PUNKY REGGAE PARTY (1977), IS
THIS LOVE (1978), COULD YOU BE
LOVED (1980), NO WOMAN NO
CRY (1981), BUFFALO SOLDIER
(1983) and ONE LOVE/PEOPLE GET
READY (1984).
   British guitarist Eric Clapton
recorded his version of I SHOT THE
SHERIFF for his *461 Ocean
Boulevard* album and the single
went to Number One in the States
and cracked the Top 10 in Britain.

US HIT: Eric Clapton (RSO: 1974)
Black & Pop
UK HIT: Eric Clapton (RSO: 1974)

Other recordings: Deodato (MCA);
Redd Holt Unlimited (Paula).

Incidentally, one of the two
background singers on Eric
Clapton's record was Yvonne
Elliman, who herself had charted
two years earlier with I DON'T
KNOW HOW TO LOVE HIM (Lloyd
Webber/Rice), the showstopper
from the musical, "Jesus Christ
Superstar" (MCA: 1972); Yvonne
later racked up two UK Top 10

records, firstly with Barry and Robin
Gibb's LOVE ME (RSO: 1976) and
later with IF I CAN'T HAVE YOU
(RSO: 1978) which all three Bee
Gees wrote for her to sing on the
soundtrack of "Saturday Night Fever"
(Paramount: 1977).

Reggae songs
Other memorable reggae hits to
cross over into the pop charts
(including early British ska and blue-
beat records):

BREAKFAST IN BED (Fritts/
Hinton)** by UB40 With Chrissie
Hynde (Dep International: 1988)
DOUBLE BARREL (Riley) by Dave
and Ansil Collins (Technique:
1971)
EVERYTHING I OWN (Gates) by
Ken Boothe (Trojan: 1974)
I CAN SEE CLEARLY NOW
(Nash)** by Johnny Nash (Epic:
1972)
ISRAELITES (Dacres/Kong) by
Desmond Dekker and The Aces
(Pyramid: 1969)
IT MEK (Dacres/Kong) by Desmond
Dekker and The Aces (Pyramid:
1969)
LIQUIDATOR (Johnson) by Harry J.
All Stars (Trojan: 1969)
LOVE OF THE COMMON PEOPLE
(Hurley/Wilkins) by Nicky Thomas
(Trojan: 1970)
MANY RIVERS TO CROSS (Cliff)**
by UB40 (Dep International: 1983)
MONKEY MAN (Hibbert) by The
Maytals (Trojan: 1970)
MONKEY SPANNER (Riley) by
Dave and Ansil Collins
(Technique: 1971)
MY BOY LOLLIPOP (Roberts/
Levy)** by Millie (Fontana: 1964)
RED, RED WINE (Diamond)** by
Jimmy James and The Vagabonds
(Pye: 1968)
by Tony Tribe (Downtown: 1969)
by UB40 (Dep International: 1983)
SHOTGUN WEDDING (Hammond)
by Roy C (Island: 1966)
STIR IT UP (Marley) by Johnny Nash

(CBS: 1972)
WHY CAN'T WE BE FRIENDS
(Allen/Brown/Dickerson/
Goldstein/Jordan/Miller/Oskar/
Scott) by War (UA: 1975)
WILD WORLD (Stevens)** by Maxi
Priest (Ten: 1988)
WONDERFUL WORLD, BEAUTIFUL
PEOPLE (Cliff) by Jimmy Cliff
(Trojan: 1969)
YOU CAN GET IT IF YOU REALLY
WANT (Cliff)** by Desmond
Dekker and The Aces (Trojan:
1970)
YOUNG, GIFTED AND BLACK
(Simone/Irvine)** by Bob and
Marcia (Harry J: 1970)

I THINK WE'RE ALONE NOW
(Ritchie Cordell)
One of two Tommy James' hits
revived in 1987 and both of them
reached Number One in America
the second time around! To give you
an idea of the time-lapse between
the two versions, the original Tommy
James single of I THINK WE'RE
ALONE NOW climbed the US charts
four years before Tiffany was born!
(See also: MONY, MONY.)

US HITS: Tommy James and The
           Shondells (Roulette:
           1967) Pop
           Tiffany (MCA: 1987) Pop
UK HIT: Tiffany (MCA: 1987)

Other recordings: The Rubinoos
(Beserkley); Lene Lovich (Stiff).

I WANT CANDY
(Robert Feldman/Gerald Goldstein/
Richard Gottehrer/Bert Berns)

US HITS: The Strangeloves (Bang:
           1965) Pop
           Bow Wow Wow (RCA:
           1982) Pop

See: TWIST AND SHOUT for other
Bert Berns songs.

I'D RATHER GO BLIND
(Bill Foster/Ellington Jordan)
Strangely, this song has never been
a hit in America, but that is a mere
oversight, because its definitive
interpretation was by Etta James,
recorded during her stellar years at
Chess.

UK HITS: Chicken Shack (Christine
           McVie's vocal) (Blue
           Horizon: 1969)
           Ruby Turner (Jive: 1987)

Other recordings: Rod Stewart
(Mercury); Christine McVie (Sire)

Etta has a glorious blues-tinged
voice with which she effortlessly
turns to gospel or R&B or rock 'n'
roll, or simply and gratifyingly, the
blues itself. Her range is further
exemplified by diverse hits such as
THE WALLFLOWER (WORK WITH
ME ANNIE**) (Modern: 1955) as
contrasted with her reading of the
1940s movie song, AT LAST
(Warren/Gordon), which has
ironically gone full circle now that
the soundtrack of Dustin Hoffman
and Tom Cruise's movie "Rain Man"
(UA: 1988) has included Etta's 1961
hit recording (Argo) on its
soundtrack.

I'M A BELIEVER
(Neil Diamond)
One of three songs to top the
American charts for The Monkees,
the foursome gathered together for
the zany half-hour TV series. The
boys' other Number Ones were
LAST TRAIN TO CLARKSVILLE
(Colgems: 1966), written by Tommy
Boyce and Bobby Hart (who were
also artists in their own right as a
duo).
  Neil Diamond's marginal hit
version of the song was a reissue on
Bang records, his first label for
whom he had cut the song in 1966.

US HITS: The Monkees (Colgems:
           1966) Pop

Neil Diamond (Bang:
1971) Pop
UK HITS: The Monkees (RCA: 1967)
Robert Wyatt (Virgin:
1974)

Other recordings: Bram Tchaikovsky
(Radar); Barbara Mandrell (MCA);
Davy Jones, Mickey Dolenz and
Peter Tork (Rhino); Neil Diamond
(Columbia).

Another of The Monkees' major hit
songs, DAYDREAM BELIEVER, was
written by John Stewart who was a
former member of folk group The
Kingston Trio; Stewart had his own
Top single in the States in 1979
called GOLD (Stewart), on which he
was joined by Stevie Nicks and
Lindsey Buckingham.

Neil Diamond songs
The Monkees also scored with a
second Neil Diamond tune... A
LITTLE BIT ME, A LITTLE BIT YOU
(Colgems: 1967), a huge hit on both
sides of the Atlantic. Other key
recordings of Neil Diamond songs
by artists other than Neil himself
include:

THE BOAT THAT I ROW by Lulu
(UK Columbia: 1967)
KENTUCKY WOMAN by Deep
Purple (Tetragrammaton: 1968)
RED, RED WINE** by Jimmy James
and the Vagabonds (Piccadilly:
1969)
by UB40 (Dep International: 1983)
SUNDAY AND ME by Jay and The
Americans (UA: 1965)

I'M A MAN
(Ellas McDaniel)
This is Bo Diddley's macho
masterpiece that was half of perhaps
the most influential two-sided R&B
hit of all time (the coupling was his
self-titled BO DIDDLEY). Chess
Records maximized their money by
having Muddy Waters record

basically the same song under the
title MANNISH BOY a few months
later for another chart hit! It was
fitting, though, as Bo wrote the song
as something of a tribute to Muddy.
The Rolling Stones, who idolized Bo
Diddley and were named after a
Muddy Waters song, later recorded
MANNISH BOY (McDaniel/London/
Morganfield) (Rolling Stones: 1977).
And probably the strangest use of
the song to date, Muddy's later
version with Johhny Winter, was on
the sound-track of a Levi Jeans TV
commercial in Britain in 1988 –
making it a hit again!
Bo Diddley's original of I'M A
MAN was released on Checker in
1955. (The flipside, BO DIDDLEY,
made Number One on the race
charts.)

Other recordings: The Yardbirds
(UK Columbia); The Who
(Brunswick); Jimi Hendrix.

Sequel record: I'M BAD by Bo
Diddley (Checker: 1956).

Answer records: W–O–M–A–N by
Etta James (Modern: 1955)
I'M A WOMAN (Leiber/Stoller) by
Christine Kitrell (Vee-Jay: 1961)
by Peggy Lee (Capitol: 1963)
by Maria Muldaur (Reprise: 1974).

See: BO DIDDLEY for other Bo
Diddley songs.

**I'M GONNA BE A WHEEL
SOMEDAY**
(Roy Hayes/Dave Bartholomew/
Antoine Domino)
When Roy Hayes, from Baton Rouge,
Louisiana, sent Imperial A&R chief
Dave Bartholomew a tape of this
song, Dave instinctively knew that
the song was a hit.
He booked a studio and musicians,
and stood Roy Hayes in front of the
microphone. But, as Bartholomew
recalls, he couldn't sing it!
So Dave said, 'How could you
make a tape like this, send it to me,
and when you get to the studio, you

can't sing?' Hayes replied: 'Dave, I just sang the song at home, beating on a chair, but I never really sang with a band.'

Imperial gave the song to Bobby Mitchell who sold 300,000 copies, and two years later, Fats Domino released his version and the song became a million-seller.

Song performed by Los Lobos on the soundtrack of the comedy movie, "A Fine Mess" (Columbia: 1986).

US HIT: Fats Domino
           (Imperial:1959) Pop &
           Black

Other recordings: Wayne Fontana (Fontana); Asleep At The Wheel (Epic); Sandy Nelson (Imperial); Clyde McPhatter (Mercury); 'A Fine Mess' soundtrack (Motown); Paul McCartney (EMI).

Sequel record: I DON'T WANT TO BE A WHEEL NO MORE (Dave Bartholomew) by Bobby Mitchell (Imperial: 1963)

See: I HEAR YOU KNOCKING for other Dave Bartholomew songs.

I'M GONNA MAKE YOU LOVE ME

(Jerry Ross/Jerry A.Williams/Kenneth Gamble)
First version of this R&B love song was by Dee Dee (sister of Dionne) Warwick, followed by a version from British resident Madeleine Bell who formed UK group Blue Mink in the late 1960s. The third and most successful version of the song was by the combined efforts of Diana Ross and The Supremes *and* The Temptations!

US HITS: Dee Dee Warwick
           (Mercury: 1967) Black
           Madeleine Bell (Philips:
           1968) Black & Pop
           Diana Ross and The
           Supremes and The
           Temptations (Motown:
           1969) Black & Pop
UK HIT: Diana Ross and The

Supremes and The Temptations (Tamla Motown: 1969)

I'M INTO SOMETHING GOOD

(Gerry Goffin/Carole King)
This was the song which gave Herman's Hermits their first hit and their only British Number One. It was originally recorded by Earl-Jean, a member of The Cookies, who cut the first version of CHAINS**.

Other Herman's Hermits covers included SILHOUETTES** and WONDERFUL WORLD** and I CAN TAKE OR LEAVE YOUR LOVING (Jones) which had originally been recorded by another British group, The Foundations (Pye: 1967).

Ironically, Herman's two biggest US hits were British songs, neither of which charted for him in his home country. MRS BROWN YOU'VE GOT A LOVELY DAUGHTER (Peacock) took America by storm, while equal success came for I'M HENRY VIII, I AM (Weston/Murray), an old British music-hall song which Herman and his group featured in their MGM movie, "Hold On!" (MGM:1966).

Also in the same movie was the old George Formby favourite, LEANING ON THE LAMP POST (Gay); this too made it into the Top 10 for Herman in America, where more recently, the song has been performed on stage by Tim Curry in a revival of the Broadway and London smash-hit musical show, "Me And My Girl".

Herman's Hermits performed I'M INTO SOMETHING GOOD in the British movie, "Pop Gear" (US Title: "Go Go Mania!") (1965) and in their own starring vehicle, "Mrs Brown You've Got A Lovely Daughter" (MGM: 1968). Most recently, Peter Noone re-cut the song for the soundtrack of the Leslie Nielsen/Priscilla Presley comedy spoof "The Naked Gun" (Paramount: 1988).

US HITS: Earl-Jean (Colpix: 1964)
           Pop
           Herman's Hermits (MGM:
           1964) Pop
UK HIT: Herman's Hermits (UK
           Columbia: 1964)

See: UP ON THE ROOF for other
Gerry Goffin and Carole King songs.

I'M LEAVING IT ALL UP TO YOU
(Don Harris/Dewey Terry Jr)
A song that has been a hit in all
three major genres...black, pop and
country, the latter represented by
Freddy Fender's charted version
(ABC: 1978). Written by guitarist Don
'Sugarcane' Harris and pianist
Dewey Terry Jr who are also known
as Don and Dewey; as recording
artists, they cut the original versions
of songs which they wrote and which
were hits for other artists, including
BIG BOY PETE by The Olympics
(Arvee: 1960), FARMER JOHN by
The Premiers (Warner Bros: 1964),
THE LETTER by Sonny and Cher
(Vault: 1965) and JUSTINE by The
Righteous Brothers (Moonglow:
1965). They also cut this tune which
is alternatively known as LEAVIN' IT
ALL UP TO YOU.

US HITS: Dale and Grace (Montel:
           1963) Black & Pop
           Donny and Marie
           Osmond (MGM: 1974)
           Pop

Other recordings: Linda Ronstadt
(Capitol); Don and Dewey
(Specialty); Ike Turner (UA); The
Righteous Brothers (Verve); Sonny
and Cher (Atlantic); Johnny and
Jonie Mosby (Capitol); Bill Anderson
and Jan Howard (Decca).

I'M MOVIN' ON
(Clarence E. Snow)
Canadian country star Hank Snow
wrote and originally recorded this
song which has defied musical
barriers; a genuine crossover hit in

all senses of the word. One recent
revival was by John Kay of
Steppenwolf.

US HITS: Hank Snow (RCA: 1950)
           Country
           Don Gibson (RCA: 1959)
           Country
           Ray Charles (Atlantic:
           1959) Black & Pop
           Matt Lucas (Smash: 1963)
           Pop
           John Kay (Dunhill: 1972)
           Pop
           Emmylou Harris (Warner
           Bros: 1983) Country

Other recordings: The Rolling Stones
(UK Decca); The Everly Brothers
(Warner Bros); The Box Tops (Mala);
George Thorogood (EMI); Willie
Nelson (Columbia); Elvis Presley
(RCA); Hank Thompson (Dot).

I'M WALKIN'
(Antoine Domino/Dave
Bartholomew)
Among Fats Domino's biggest
crossover successes was I'M
WALKIN' which was covered by a
young Ricky Nelson.
   In 1986, both Fats and this song
were used in a national American
advertising campaign for (what
else?!) the "Walking Magazine". The
ad-line read: 'In the fifties, Fats
Domino sang about walking. Now
he's doing it, with the help of our
magazine. He's passing up the
blueberry pie and walking up
blueberry hill.'
   Song was performed by Fats
Domino in the rock movie, "The Big
Beat" (Universal: 1958) and, much
more recently, Steve Martin sang a
few bars in his comedy, "Roxanne"
(Columbia: 1987).
   Fats's original recording has
cropped up on various movie
soundtracks including "The Blues
Brothers" (Universal: 1980) and the
romantic comedy, "Nobody's Fool"
(Island: 1986).

US HITS: Fats Domino (Imperial:
          1957) Black & Pop
          Ricky Nelson (Verve:
          1957) Pop
UK HIT: Fats Domino (London: 1957)

Other recordings: Cliff Richard
(Columbia); Connie Francis (MGM);
Dave Bartholomew (Imperial); Doug
Kershaw (Warner Bros); Nancy
Sinatra (Reprise); Bill Haley and His
Comets (Accord); Paul Evans
(Guaranteed); Shorty Long
(Motown); Rosie Flores (Reprise);
Duane Eddy (Jamie); Chubby
Checker (Parkway); Jerry Lee Lewis
(Mercury); Rocking Dopsie and The
Cajun Twisters.

See: I HEAR YOU KNOCKING for
other Dave Bartholomew songs.

I'M YOUR HOOCHIE COOCHIE MAN

(Willie Dixon)
Also known as HOOCHIE COOCHIE
MAN (spelt various ways), this is
probably bluesman Willie Dixon's
finest statement, alongside his YOU
CAN'T JUDGE A BOOK BY THE
COVER.** Another staple of every
British blues group repertoine of the
1960s onwards.
    A regional hit in 1971 for New
Orleans' artist, Skip Easterling
(Instant), arranged by R&B legend
Huey 'Piano' Smith.
    Song performed by Fear on the
soundtrack of the rock music
comedy "Get Crazy" (Embassy: 1983).

US HIT: Muddy Waters (Chess:
          1954) Black

Other recordings: The Allman
Brothers (Capricorn); John Mayall
(UK Decca); Steppenwolf (Dunhill);
Dion (Columbia); Junior Wells
(Vanguard); Jimmy Smith (Verve);
Chuck Berry (Chess); Manfred Mann
(HMV); Sam The Sham and The
Pharoahs (MGM); Jimi Hendrix
(Rykodisc); Tim Hardin, Long John
Baldry (UA); Wayne Fontana and
The Mindbenders (Fontana); Alexis
Korner (UK Decca).

Willie Dixon songs
Other versions of Willie Dixon songs
include:

DONCHA' THINK IT'S TIME (written
with Clyde Otis) by Elvis Presley
(RCA: 1958)
I AIN'T SUPERSTITIOUS by The
Savoy Brown Blues Band (UK
Decca: 1969)
by The Jeff Beck Group (UK
Columbia: 1975)
I JUST WANT TO MAKE LOVE TO
YOU by Chuck Berry (Chess: 1959)
by The Rolling Stones (UK Decca:
1964)
by Foghat (Bearsville: 1972 and
1977)
LITTLE RED ROOSTER** by the
Rolling Stones (UK Decca: 1964)
by Sam Cooke (RCA: 1963)
SEVENTH SON** by Johnny Rivers
(Imperial: 1965)
SPOONFUL by The Allman Joys
(Dial: 1966)
by Cream (Polydor: 1966)
by the Paul Butterfield Blues Band
(Elektra: 1966)
WANG DANG DOODLE by Howlin'
Wolf (Chess: 1963)
by Love Sculpture with Dave
Edmunds (Harvest: 1968)
by The Pointer Sisters (Blue
Thumb: 1973)
by Koko Taylor (Checker: 1966)
YOU SHOOK ME by Led Zeppelin
(Atlantic: 1969)

I'VE BEEN LOVING YOU TOO LONG

(Otis Redding/Jerry Butler)
Definitive deep soul ballad, of which
there are at least two heart-stopping
versions: by Otis himself, and by
Tina Turner, whose performance of
the song in the Rolling Stones'
concert movie, "Gimme Shelter"
(Cinema V: 1971), almost sets the
celluloid on fire! I'VE BEEN LOVING
YOU was also the highspot of Ike
and Tina's *Outta Season* album (Blue
Thumb: 1969).

Performed by Otis Redding in "Monterey Pop" (Leacock/ Pennebaker: 1968) and by Joe Cocker in "Mad Dogs and Englishmen" (MGM: 1971).

US HITS: Otis Redding (Volt: 1965) Black & Pop
            Ike and Tina Turner (Blue Thumb: 1969) Black & Pop

Other recordings: Irma Thomas (Chess); The Rolling Stones (UK Decca); James and Bobby Purify (Bell); Chris Farlowe (Immediate); Cindy Scott (Veep); Billy Vera (Atlantic); Lillo Thomas (Capitol); Joe Cocker (A&M).

I'VE BEEN LOVING YOU was also a country hit for Barbara Mandrell (Columbia: 1966); in fact, the Houston-born country singer cut a number of covers of R&B songs including THE TEN COMMANDMENTS OF LOVE (Paul/Woods) (Epic: 1974) which was originally by Harvey and The Moonglows (Chess: 1958), (IF LOVING YOU IS WRONG) I DON'T WANT TO BE RIGHT (Banks/Jackson/Hampton)(ABC: 1979) with which Luther Ingram had initially scored (KoKo: 1972), DO RIGHT WOMAN-DO RIGHT MAN (Penn/Moman) (Columbia: 1971) which she borrowed from Aretha Franklin (Atlantic: 1967) plus WOMAN TO WOMAN (Banks/Marion/Thigpen) (ABC: 1978) which had been an R&B Number One for Shirley Brown (Truth: 1974).

I'VE GOT MY MOJO WORKING
See: GOT MY MOJO WORKING.

IF I WERE A CARPENTER
(Tim Hardin)
Wistful love song by folksinger, the late Tim Hardin, who cut it on his *Tim Hardin – Volume II* album (Verve: 1966).

US HITS: Bobby Darin (Atlantic: 1966) Pop
            The Four Tops (Motown: 1968) Black & Pop
            Johnny Cash and June Carter (Columbia: 1970) Pop & Country
            Bob Seger (Palladium: 1972) Pop
            Leon Russell (Shelter: 1974) Pop
UK HITS: Bobby Darin (Atlantic: 1966)
            The Four Tops (Tamla Motown: 1968)

Other recordings: Joan Baez (Vanguard); The Swinging Blue Jeans (Sonet); The Everly Brothers (Warner Bros).

Answer records (with just the genders changed throughout): IF YOU WERE A CARPENTER by Tippi Hedren (Challenge: 1966) by Jody Miller (Capitol: 1966).

IF YOU GOTTA MAKE A FOOL OF SOMEBODY
(Rudy Clark)
Known for his zany humour and a habit of leaping about on stage (around which a dance-step was briefly created in America!), Freddie Garrity and his Manchester group The Dreamers, found success in the early days of the Beatle boom with some original songs, including I'M TELLING YOU NOW (Garrity/ Murray) and YOU WERE MADE FOR ME (Mitch Murray).

However, their first UK hit was a cover of IF YOU GOTTA MAKE A FOOL OF SOMEBODY, an American R&B record by James Ray. It was the same James Ray who cut the original version of GOT MY MIND SET ON YOU (another Rudy Clark composition) which was a huge hit for George Harrison on Dark Horse in 1987.

Incidentally, R&B songstress Maxine Brown, whose 1964 Wand hit OH NO, NOT MY BABY (Carole

King/Gerry Goffin) was revived in 1973 by both Rod Stewart (on Mercury) and Merry Clayton (for Ode), also charted in the States with a version of IF YOU GOTTA MAKE A FOOL (Wand: 1966), but the James Ray original has never been surpassed.

US HIT: James Ray (Caprice: 1962) Black & Pop
UK HIT: Freddie and The Dreamers (UK Columbia: 1963)

Other recordings: Timi Yuro (Liberty); Bonnie Raitt (Warner Bros); Amazing Rhythm Aces (ABC); Eddie Floyd (Stax); Labelle (Warner Bros); Calvin Grayson (Capitol); Jackie DeShannon (Imperial); The Artwoods (UK Decca); Night (Planet); Brian Poole and The Tremeloes (UK Decca).

IF YOU WANNA BE HAPPY
(Frank Guida/Carmela Guida/Joseph Royster)
Calypso-based R&B song with which Jimmy Soul topped the American charts in mid-1963. Based on a traditional calypso song called UGLY WOMAN, this was produced by Frank Guida who is known for his SONIC MUD productions on Gary US Bonds' hits.

The song was later a minimal UK hit for Rocky Sharpe and The Replays who had previously racked up significant sellers with their revivals of RAMA LAMA DING DONG (Jones Jr) originally by The Edsels (Twin: 1961) and SHOUT SHOUT (KNOCK YOURSELF OUT), which first charted for its composer, Ernie Maresca (Seville: 1962).

US HIT: Jimmy Soul (SPQR: 1963) Black & Pop
UK HITS: Jimmy Soul (Stateside: 1963)
          Rocky Sharpe and The Replays (Polydor: 1983)

Other recordings: The Rolling Stones (Rolling Stones); Randy Meisner (Asylum).

IKO IKO
(James 'Sugar Boy' Crawford)
To many, IKO IKO by The Dixie Cups was a new song when their single first came out in 1965. It was actually composed as JOCK-O-MO by New Orleans R&B writer–singer James 'Sugar Boy' Crawford, who based it on two Mardi Gras Indian chants; he recorded his song on Checker in 1954 and it became a huge New Orleans hit.

Performed by The Dixie Cups on the soundtrack of "The Big Easy" (Kings Road: 1986) and by The Belle Stars in "Rain Man" (UA: 1988).

Though not all the recorded versions of IKO IKO credit Sugar Boy, they are all variations on his theme, so I list some of them below as if they were one and the same.

US HITS: The Dixie Cups (Red Bird: 1965) Black & Pop
          Dr John (Atco: 1972) Pop
UK HITS: The Dixie Cups (Red Bird:1965)
          Natasha (Towerbell: 1982)
          The Belle Stars (Stiff: 1982)

Other recordings: Cyndi Lauper (Portrait); Rolf Harris (UK Columbia); The Neville Brothers (A&M); Long John Baldry (Pye); The Four Pennies (Philips); The Pennies (UA/Rockfield).

IMAGINE
(John Lennon)
Title song from John Lennon's second solo album, *Imagine* was inspired by a Yoko Ono poem. Lennon's own sparse piano intro sets the scene for this parable to the perfect world.

Single was re-released due to overwhelming public demand following his tragic death in December 1980, after which the song became his unofficial tribute. Ironically, in Britain, the reissued 45 nudged John's then-current single, JUST LIKE STARTING OVER (Lennon) (Geffen: 1980), out of the Number One slot.

American female R&B singer Randy Crawford's remake made a brief appearance on the backend of the charts, in the UK in '82 and in the US the following year (Warner Bros).

In 1988, the song gave its title to the movie, "Imagine: John Lennon" (Warner Bros) which traced his life and times in original footage and music. EMI released a corresponding album which included two versions of the song, one of which was a previously unreleased rehearsal take.

UK HITS: John Lennon (Apple: 1975)
            John Lennon (Apple: 1980 Re-release)
US HIT: John Lennon/Plastic Ono Band (Apple: 1971) Pop

Other recordings: Joan Baez (A&M); Tracie Spencer (Capitol); Average White Band and Ben E. King (Atlantic); Sarah Vaughan (Mainstream); Mark Knopfler and Chet Atkins (Virgin).

See: WITH A LITTLE HELP FROM MY FRIENDS for songs by John Lennon and Paul McCartney.

THE IN CROWD

(Billy Page)
Major dance song which provided the mid-sixties with a full-blown status moniker. Song was revived almost a decade later by the heart and soul of Roxy Music.

US HITS: Dobie Gray (Charger: 1965) Black & Pop
            The Ramsey Lewis Trio (Argo: 1965) Black & Pop
UK HITS: Dobie Gray (London: 1965)
            Bryan Ferry (Island: 1974)

Other recordings: The Chipmunks (Liberty); Pete Fountain (MCA); The Mamas and The Papas (Dunhill).

In 1973, Dobie Gray staged a successful chart comeback, spearheaded by the song DRIFT AWAY (Decca: 1973), written and produced by Mentor Williams.

IN THE MIDNIGHT HOUR

(Steve Cropper/Wilson Pickett)
Spectacular, classic song from the soul sixties, delivered by the 'wicked Pickett' whose mischievous voice was perfect for the sexual promises which the lyric makes.

Song performed by B. B. King on the soundtrack of the underworld thriller, "Into The Night" (Universal: 1985).

US HIT: Wilson Pickett (Atlantic: 1965) Pop & Black
            Little Mac and The Boss Sounds (Atlantic: 1965) Black

The Mirettes (Revue:
    1968) Pop & Black
Cross Country (Atco: 1973
    Pop
Razzy Bailey (RCA: 1984)
    Country
UK HIT: Wilson Pickett (Atlantic:
    1965)

Other recordings: Jon and Robin
(Abnak); Samantha Sang (UA); Jam
(Polydor); Roxy Music (Polydor);
Delbert McClinton (Capitol); Billy
Preston (Capitol); Tina Turner
(Capitol); B. B. King (ABC); The
Rascals (Atlantic); Wilson Pickett
(Manhattan); Chris Farlowe
(Immediate); The Elgins (V.I.P.);
Mitch Ryder and The Detroit Wheels
(New Voice).

Answer record: YOU CAN'T LOVE
ME (IN THE MIDNIGHT HOUR)
by Ann Mason (Atlantic: 1965)

IN THE STILL OF THE NITE
(Fred Parris)
Actually titled (I'LL REMEMBER) IN
THE STILL OF THE NITE, Fred
Parris was in the US Army when he
was inspired by guard duty at three
o'clock in the morning to write this
all-time doo-wop classic.
Unfortunately, he was still in the
Army and abroad in Japan when the
song became a hit! He later
returned, however, to lead the group
for many years.
    Both The Five Satins (with Fred
Parris) and this song were featured
in the concert documentary film, "Let
The Good Times Roll" (Columbia:
1973). More recently, the original
Five Satins record was heard on the
soundtrack of "Dirty Dancing"
(Vestron: 1987). Song is also
performed by Debbie Gibson in her
recent "Live In Concert/The 'Out Of
The Blue Tour'" (Atlantic Video).
    Both the revivals by Paul Anka
and by instrumentalists Santo and
Johnny achieved the lower regions
of the US Top 75.

IN THE STILL OF THE NIGHT
The Five Satins were originally called The
Scarletts. Formed by Fred Parris, who wrote and
originally sang IN THE STILL OF THE NIGHT,
though he doesn't appear on all Five Satins
records.

US HITS: The Five Satins (Ember:
    1956) Black & Pop
    Santo and Johnny
    (Canadian-American:
    1964) Pop
    Paul Anka (RCA: 1969)
    Pop

Other recordings: The Beach Boys
(Brother/Reprise); The Del Vikings
(Dot); John Sebastian (Reprise);
Ronnie Milsap, in a medley called
LOST IN THE FIFTIES (RCA); Donna
and The Persuasions (Blue Sky);
Johnny Mathis and Take 6
(Colombia).

Not to be confused with the 1937
Cole Porter standard, IN THE STILL

OF THE NIGHT which Dion and The Belmonts successfully revived on Laurie in 1960.

IT AIN'T ME BABE
(Bob Dylan)
Among Bob Dylan's more personal songs, it was included in his fourth album, *Another Side Of Bob Dylan*, released in mid-1964. Performed by Dylan in his movie, "Renaldo and Clara" (1978).

US HITS: Johnny Cash (Columbia: 1964) Pop
              The Turtles (White Whale: 1965) Pop
UK HIT: Johnny Cash (CBS: 1965)

Other recordings: Bryan Ferry (Atlantic); Joan Baez (Vanguard); Maxine Weldon (Mainstream); Johnny Cash and June Carter (Columbia); Lester Flatt and Earl Scruggs (Columbia); The Surfaris (Decca); Dino, Desi and Billy (Reprise); Davy Jones (Colpix).

See: BLOWIN' IN THE WIND for other Bob Dylan songs.

IT DOESN'T MATTER ANYMORE
(Paul Anka)
Paul Anka and the late Buddy Holly toured Australia together in 1958. Paul thought that this song would be perfect for Buddy, even though many of Holly's hits until then had been self-written or co-composed with producer/manager Norman Petty. It was the first Holly record to feature a string section, and the title became somewhat ironic in light of Buddy's death, while it was climbing the charts.

Naturally, Anka wrote most of his huge teen hits himself, including DIANA (ABC/Paramount: 1957), YOU ARE MY DESTINY (ABC: 1958), LONELY BOY (ABC: 1959), PUT YOUR HEAD ON MY SHOULDER (ABC: 1959), PUPPY LOVE (ABC: 1960), and (YOU'RE) HAVING MY BABY (UA: 1974).

US HITS: Buddy Holly (Coral: 1959) Pop
              Linda Ronstadt (Capitol: 1975) Pop
UK HIT: Buddy Holly (Coral: 1959)

Other recordings: Don McLean (Arista); Paul Anka (RCA); Daryl Hall and John Oates (RCA); Freddie and The Dreamers (UK Columbia); Wanda Jackson (Capitol).

See: LOVE'S MADE A FOOL OF YOU for other Buddy Holly songs.

IT WILL STAND
(Norman Johnson)
'Rock and roll forever will stand' is the message of this, one of the all-time beach music favourites. Written by Norman Johnson, the then-lead singer of The Showmen, and later, leader of The Chairmen Of The Board whose big song was GIVE ME JUST A LITTLE MORE TIME (Invictus: 1970). Although a classic of its kind, the original Showmen single was never a major hit. It was originally released on Minit in 1961 and later reissued on Imperial and UA.

Track was used as the linking theme of the TV documentary "Heroes Of Rock 'N' Roll", first shown on the ABC network in 1979.

The Showmen's original record is heard on the soundtrack of the movie "Shag" (Palace: 1988).

US HIT: The Showmen (Minit: 1961) Pop

Other recordings: Jonathan Richman (Beserkley); The Charlie Underwood Band (Loma).

IT'S A MAN'S MAN'S MAN'S WORLD (BUT IT WOULDN'T BE NOTHING WITHOUT A WOMAN OR GIRL)
(James Brown/Betty Newsome)

US HIT: James Brown and The Famous Flames (King: 1966) Black & Pop

Other recordings: Tom Jones (UK Decca); Brilliant (Atlantic).

Answer record: IT'S A MAN'S WOMAN'S WORLD (Jones/Jones) by Irma Thomas (Imperial: 1966) (produced by James Brown himself).

See: PLEASE, PLEASE, PLEASE for other James Brown hits.

IT'S ALL OVER NOW
(Bobby Womack)
One of the key songs which established The Rolling Stones, IT'S ALL OVER NOW was originally recorded by The Valentinos, who had evolved out of the Womack Brothers' gospel group. The five brothers were Bobby, Curtis, Harris,

IT'S ALL OVER NOW
A 1960s publicity shot of Bobby Womack when, after doing session work, he signed with Minit Records and went to Memphis and cut his FLY ME TO THE MOON (Minit: 1968) album with producer Chips Moman.

Friendly Jr and Cecil, the latter most recently recording with his wife Linda (daughter of the late Sam Cooke) under the name 'Womack and Womack'. IT'S ALL OVER NOW was in fact the Stones' third US hit and in later years, Bobby worked with the group on record.

Among his other song writing successes were two Wilson Pickett best-sellers, I'M A MIDNIGHT MOVER and I'M IN LOVE. The young Bobby had played guitar in Sam Cooke's band and The Valentinos were signed to Cooke's Sar label; another of the songs they cut was LOOKIN' FOR A LOVE (J.W. Alexander/Zelda Samuels) which was later revived by The J. Geils Band (their first US hit, on Atlantic in 1971) and subsequently, successfully re-cut by Bobby himself (UA: 1974).

US HITS: The Valentinos (Sar: 1964) Black & Pop
The Rolling Stones (London: 1964) Pop
UK HITS The Rolling Stones (UK Decca: 1964)

Other recordings: Bobby Womack and Bill Withers (UA); Rod Stewart (Mercury); The Swinging Blue Jeans (HMV); John Anderson (Warner Bros); Charlie Rich (RCA); Ducks DeLuxe (RCA).

IT'S GONNA TAKE A MIRACLE
(Teddy Randazzo/Bobby Weinstein/ Lou Stallman)
Song which, first time out, became a mini girl-group classic.

US HITS: The Royalettes (MGM: 1965) Black & Pop
Deniece Williams (ARC: 1982) Black & Pop

Other recording: Laura Nyro and Labelle (Columbia)

IT'S IN HIS KISS
See: THE SHOOP SHOOP SONG.

IT'S LATE

(Dorsey Burnette)

An early smash-hit for young Ricky Nelson, it was originally recorded by Dorsey Burnette himself for the same label, but his track was never released until years later. It was originally 'covered' in Britain by local singer, Vince Eager (Parlophone), who was closely modelled on America's teen sensation, Fabian. Dorsey and his brother Johnny co-wrote a couple of other Ricky Nelson hits including WAITIN' IN SCHOOL (Imperial: 1957) and BELIEVE WHAT YOU SAY (Imperial: 1958).

US HITS: Ricky Nelson (Imperial:
            1959) Pop
UK HITS: Ricky Nelson (London:
            1959)
            Shakin' Stevens (Epic:
            1983)

Dorsey Burnette's biggest hit record as an artist was his own TALL OAK TREE (Era: 1960); he wrote several other songs which Ricky recorded, both on Imperial and Decca, and then his career as a solo artist resumed with a series of country hits between 1972 and 1977 on Capitol, Melodyland and Calliope. He died in 1979, a year before his son Billy started making a name as a rock artist. See also under: YOU'RE SIXTEEN.

IT'S MY PARTY

(Herb Weiner/John Gluck Jr/Wally Gold)

Among the best American teen girl records of the early 1960s was this song recorded by 17-year-old Lesley Gore. It was Lesley's initial record and also marked Quincy Jones' first as a producer.

US HIT: Lesley Gore (Mercury:
            1963) Pop
UK HITS: Lesley Gore (Mercury:
            1963)
            Dave Stewart with
              Barbara Gaskin (Stiff/
              Broken: 1981)

Other recordings: Bryan Ferry (Island); The Chiffons (Laurie); Helen Shapiro (UK Columbia).

Lesley's next three singles all went Top 10 including JUDY'S TURN TO CRY (listed below), SHE'S A FOOL (Raleigh/Barkan), and YOU DON'T OWN ME (Madara/White); another A-side down the line was MAYBE I KNOW (Barry/Greenwich) and in 1965, an early Marvin Hamlisch song (co-written with Howard Liebling) called SUNSHINE, LOLLIPOPS AND RAINBOWS (Mercury: 1965) charted for her following her on-screen

The late Dorsey Burnette who, with his brother Johnny, wrote such hits as BELIEVE WHAT YOU SAY, another major Ricky Nelson US hit (Imperial: 1958).

performance of the song in the movie "Ski Party" (American International: 1965).

In later years, Lesley Gore cut a couple of memorable duet records; one was with Oliver, the hit recording artist of GOOD MORNING STARSHINE (Rado/Ragni/MacDermot) (Jubilee: 1969); under the name 'Billy 'n' Sue', they released a revival of COME SOFTLY TO ME ('Troxel/Christopher/Ellis) on Crewe in 1970. Lesley's most recent vinyl partnership was with Lou Christie for a duet medley of SINCE I DON'T HAVE YOU (Beaumont/Vogel/Verscharen/ Lester/Taylor/Rock/ Martin) and IT'S ONLY MAKE BELIEVE (Twitty/ Nance)** on Manhattan in 1987.

Lesley wrote or co-wrote all the songs on her album *Someplace Else Now* (Mowest: 1972) and eight years later, contributed to two songs in the movie "Fame" (MGM: 1980) for which her brother Michael won an Oscar for the title song sung by Irene Cara.

Sequel record: JUDY'S TURN TO CRY (Ross/Lewis) by Lesley Gore (Mercury: 1963)

Although by different composers, this song continued the storyline of Judy and Johnny, whom Lesley Gore sang about in IT'S MY PARTY.

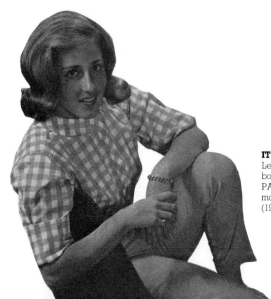

Sequel songs

The idea of continuing the same narrative from record to record has often been used in rock 'n' roll, particularly by Chuck Berry. For example, his BYE BYE JOHNNY (Chess: 1960) is a sequel to JOHNNY B. GOODE (Chess: 1958), while LITTLE MARIE (Chess: 1964) was a continuance of the storyline of his own MEMPHIS (Chess: 1958).

Similarly, LaVern Baker's rousing tale of JIM DANDY, written by Lincoln Chase and released by Atlantic in 1956, bore a sequel song called JIM DANDY GOT MARRIED which became another LaVern Baker R&B crossover record (Atlantic: 1957).

The teenage R&B duo of Shirley and Lee (see also under LET THE GOOD TIMES ROLL) were known as the 'Sweethearts Of The Blues' and their mythical on-off romantic relationship was kept alive by a succession of songs: I'M GONE (Lee/Bartholomew), SHIRLEY COME BACK TO ME (Goodman/Lee), SHIRLEY'S BACK (Goodman/Lee), SO IN LOVE (Goodman/Lee), THE PROPOSAL (Lee), TWO HAPPY PEOPLE (Lee), LEE GOOFED (Lee), FEEL SO FINE (Lee), LEE'S DREAM (Lee)...a rhythm and blues running soap opera.

One more couple who appeared lost in love were Paul and Paula; their record HEY PAULA (Hildebrand) (Philips: 1962) became one of the first US Number Ones of 1963; it had been originally released under their real names, Jill and Ray (Ray was Ray Hildebrand, its composer) and following HEY PAULA's success, the saga of their courtship continued with YOUNG

IT'S MY PARTY
Lesley Gore, who in later years had releases on both Motown and A&M; performed both IT'S MY PARTY and MAYBE I KNOW in the rock concert movie, 'The TAMI Show' aka "Gather No Moss" (1964).

LOVERS and FIRST QUARREL; however, the novelty soon wore off and after a further song, FIRST DAY BACK AT SCHOOL (Philips: 1963), they disappeared from sight. (In Britain, HEY PAULA was covered by both Elaine and Derek for Pye Piccadilly and The Avons for Decca.)

For other key R&B/R&R sequel songs, see the following entries: PAPA-OOM-MOW-MOW**, PLEASE MR POSTMAN** and WORK WITH ME ANNIE**.

IT'S NOW OR NEVER

(Wally Gold/Aaron Schroeder)
The dramatic Italian love song, O SOLE MIO (Capurro/di Capua), had been transposed into English several times. Movie and radio singer Tony Martin had a big seller with one such adaptation, THERE'S NO TOMORROW (Hoffman/Corday/Carr) (RCA: 1951), which he sang in the movie musical, "Two Tickets To Broadway" (RKO: 1951).

A new version of the old song was written specially for Elvis Presley and this same adaptation was covered over twenty years later by John Schneider, who at that time (1981) was co-star of one of TV's hottest shows, "The Dukes Of Hazzard" (CBS).

IT'S NOW OR NEVER remains one of Elvis' best-ever selling UK singles and it climbed the charts there again in 1977, when a re-released version lodged inside the British Top 50.

US HITS: Elvis Presley (RCA: 1960)
          Black & Pop
          John Schneider (Scotti
          Brothers: 1981) Pop
UK HITS: Elvis Presley (RCA: 1960)

Based on the classics

Many rock era songs and instrumentals* have been based on classical melodies. The following is a selective list:

ALONE AT LAST (Lehmann) based on Tchaikovsky's Piano Concerto No.1 in B flat minor recorded by Jackie Wilson (Brunswick: 1960)

ASIA MINOR*(Wisner) based on Grieg's Piano Concerto by Kokomo (aka Jimmy Wisner) (Felsted: 1961)

BUMBLE BOOGIE* (Fina) based on Rimsky-Korsakov's 'Flight Of The Bumble Bee' by B. Bumble and The Stingers (Rendevous: 1961)

CAN'T HELP FALLING IN LOVE (Peretti/Creatore/Weiss) based on Martini's PLAISIR D'AMOUR by Elvis Presley (RCA: 1961)

COULD IT BE MAGIC (Manilow/Anderson) based on Chopin's Prelude in C minor by Barry Manilow (Arista: 1975)

DAWNING (Leiber/Stoller) based on Grieg's Peer Gynt Suite by Jay and The Americans (UA: 1962)

DON'T YOU KNOW (Worth) based on Musetta's Waltz from Puccini's "La Bohème" by Della Reese (RCA: 1959)

A FIFTH OF BEETHOVEN* (Murphy) based on Beethoven's 5th Symphony by Walter Carlos and The Big Apple Band (Private Stock: 1976)

HELLO MUDDAH, HELLO FADDUH! (A LETTER FROM CAMP) (Sherman/Busch) based on Dance Of The Hours from Ponchielli's "La Gioconda" by Allan Sherman (Warner Bros: 1963)

HOOKED ON CLASSICS*, a medley of themes by Tchaikovsky, Rimsky-Korsakov, Grieg, Mozart, Sibelius, Handel, Clarke, Bizet and even Gershwin by Louis Clark and The Royal Philharmonic Orchestra (RCA: 1981)

IF I HAD WORDS (Hodge) based on a theme from Saint-Saens' 3rd Symphony, Opus 78 by Scott Fitzgerald and Yvonne Keeley (Pepper: 1978)

A LOVER'S CONCERTO was created for The Toys and earned them an international hit. Among the trio's later singles was their own revival of Brian Hyland's 1962 smash, SEALED WITH A KISS (Geld/Udell).

A LOVER'S CONCERTO (Randell/ Linzer) based on Bach's Minuet in G by The Toys (Dynovoice: 1965)
LULLABY OF LOVE (Sherrill/Butler) based on Brahms' 'Lullaby' by The Poppies (Epic: 1966)
MADAM BUTTERFLY (UN BEL DI VEDREMO) (McLaren/Hague/ Turbitt) based on Puccini's "Madame Butterfly" by Malcolm McLaren (Virgin: 1984)
MY CLAIRE DE LUNE (Arr: Leiber/ Stoller) based on Debussy's 'Clair de Lune' from "Suite Bergamasque" by Steve Lawrence (UA: 1961)
NIGHT OF FEAR (Wood) based on Tchaikovsky's "1812 Overture" by The Move (Deram: 1967)

NUT ROCKER*(Fowley) based on Tchaikovsky's "Nutcracker Suite" by B. Bumble and The Stingers (Rendevous: 1962)
PAINTER (Christie/Herbert) based on 'One Fine Day' from Puccini's "Madame Butterfly" by Lou Christie (MGM: 1966)
A SONG OF JOY (Orbe/De Los Rios/Parker) based on Beethoven's Symphony No.9 by Miguel Rios (A&M: 1970)

IT'S ONLY MAKE BELIEVE
(Conway Twitty/Jack Nance)
The song which really put Harold Jenkins (aka Conway Twitty) on the universal music map. Conway's original singing style was in part a sobbing, throbbing vocal reminiscent of Elvis Presley's. Born in Mississippi, he began with a string of pop hits including LONELY BLUE BOY, actually written by two of Elvis' movie songsmiths Fred Wise and Ben Weisman, and revivals of the traditional DANNY BOY plus the old Nat 'King' Cole success, MONA LISA (Livingston/Evans); then, as time went by and he switched labels, Conway Twitty became firmly entrenched in a lucratively successful country music career and he's still making big sellers today.

US HITS: Conway Twitty (MGM: 1958) Black & Pop
           Glen Campbell (Capitol: 1970) Pop
UK HITS: Conway Twitty (MGM: 1958)
           Billy Fury (UK Decca: 1964)
           Glen Campbell (Capitol: 1970)
           Child (Ariola: 1978)

Other recordings: Connie Francis (MGM); Robert Gordon (RCA); Loretta Lynn and Conway Twitty (MCA).

IT'S YOUR THING

(Rudolph Isley/Randolph Isley/
O'Kelly Isley)
From over two decades of R&B hits
from The Isley Brothers, IT'S YOUR
THING is one of the milestones. It
was the trio's first success on their
own T-Neck label and years later,
another trio revived it under the title:
SHAKE YOUR THANG ...only this
time, the trio were girls, and rappers
as well!

US HIT: The Isley Brothers
             (T-Neck: 1969)
             Black & Pop
UK HITS: The Isley Brothers (Major
             Minor: 1969)
             Salt 'N' Pepa: billed as
             SHAKE YOUR THANG
             (ffrr/London: 1989)

Other recordings: Ann Peebles (Hi);
Dyke and The Blazers (Original
Sound).

Answer record: IT'S MY THING
(YOU CAN'T TELL ME WHO TO
SOCK IT TO) (Brown) by Marva
Whitney (King: 1969)

J

JAILHOUSE ROCK

(Jerry Leiber/Mike Stoller)
A major Elvis Presley tune, and one
of the most electrifying numbers in
musical movie history. Elvis
reportedly choreographed the
routine himself and it virtually set the
screen on fire wherever "Jailhouse
Rock" (MGM: 1957) was shown.

US HIT: Elvis Presley (RCA: 1957)
             Black & Pop
UK HIT: Elvis Presley (RCA: 1958)

The RCA single has been
successfully re-released in England

on two occasions, in 1971 and 1977.

Other recordings: Billy 'Crash'
Craddock (Capitol); ZZ Top (Warner
Bros); Merle Haggard (MCA); Jerry
Lee Lewis (Sun); Johnny Cougar
(MCA); Sha Na Na (Kama Sutra);
Johnny and Edgar Winter (Blue Sky);
Albert King (Stax); David Cassidy
(Bell); The Osmonds (MGM); Sandy
Nelson (Imperial); The Blues
Brothers (Atlantic).

Leiber and Stoller songs

Probably the most successful R&B/
R&R writing team to date, Jerry
Leiber and Mike Stoller were two
white guys who wrote sensational
songs for black artists, including a
string of hits for The Drifters and The
Coasters and, after Elvis Presley
scored with their HOUND DOG, they
wrote for him also.

Among the hit records of other
Leiber and Stoller songs:

ALONG CAME JONES** by The
    Coasters (Atco: 1959)
BOSSA NOVA BABY by Elvis
    Presley (RCA: 1963)
CHARLIE BROWN by The Coasters
    (Atco: 1959)
DANCE WITH ME (written with
    George Treadwell, Irv Nahan and
    Louis Lebish) by The Drifters
    (Atlantic: 1959)
DRIP DROP** by The Drifters
    (Atlantic: 1958)
FRAMED by The Robins (Spark:
    1954)
HOUND DOG** by Elvis Presley
    (RCA: 1956)
I KEEP FORGETTIN' by Chuck
    Jackson (Wand: 1962)
    by Michael McDonald (Warner
    Bros: 1982)
I'M A WOMAN by Peggy Lee
    (Capitol: 1963)
I (WHO HAVE NOTHING) by Ben E.
    King (Atco: 1963)
    by Shirley Bassey (UK Columbia:
    1963)
    by Tom Jones (UK Decca: 1970)

ELVIS PRESLEY
AT HIS GREATEST!

7 NEW SONGS!

IN HIS FIRST BIG DRAMATIC SINGING ROLE!

M-G-M PRESENTS

Jailhouse Rock

in CinemaScope
An Avon Production

CO STARRING
Judy Tyler · WITH Mickey Shaughnessy · Dean Jones · Jennifer Holden

SCREEN PLAY BY   DIRECTED BY   PRODUCED BY
Guy Trosper · Richard Thorpe · Pandro S. Berman

'A'

Singing! Fighting!
Dancing! Romancing!

By far the most successful rock star in movie history, Elvis Presley had some outstanding title songs – LOVE ME TENDER (Matson/Presley), LOVING YOU (Leiber/Stoller), KING CREOLE (Leiber/Stoller), G.I. BLUES (Tepper/Bennett), WILD IN THE COUNTRY (Peretti/Creatore/Weiss) and this, from his third motion picture.

by Sylvester (Fantasy: 1979)
IS THAT ALL THERE IS? by Peggy Lee (Capitol: 1969)
KANSAS CITY** by Wilbert Harrison (Fury: 1959)
LITTLE EGYPT** by The Coasters (Atco: 1961)

LOVE ME by Elvis Presley
(RCA: 1957)
LOVE POTION NUMBER NINE** by
The Clovers (UA: 1959)
LOVING YOU by Elvis Presley
(RCA: 1957)
LUCKY LIPS by Ruth Brown
(Atlantic: 1957)
by Cliff Richard (UK Columbia:
1963)
(MARIE'S THE NAME) HIS LATEST
FLAME by Elvis Presley
(RCA: 1961)

BLACK DENIM TROUSERS was *another* Leiber
and Stoller American hit (it went Top 10 in 1955);
one of the three members of The Cheers was Bert
Convy, who today is a successful host of a TV-
game show.

ON BROADWAY** (with Barry
Mann and Cynthia Weil)** by The
Drifters (Atlantic: 1963)
ONLY IN AMERICA (with Barry
Mann & Cynthia Weil) by Jay and

The Americans
(UA: 1963)
POISON IVY** by The Coasters
(Atco: 1959)
RIOT IN CELL BLOCK #9** by The
Robins (Spark: 1954)
RUBY BABY** by Dion
(Columbia: 1963)
SAVED by LaVern Baker
(Atlantic: 1961)
SEARCHIN'** by The Coasters
(Atco: 1957)
SHE'S NOT YOU (with Doc Pomus)
by Elvis Presley (RCA: 1962)
SOME OTHER GUY (with Richard
Barrett)** by The Big Three (UK
Decca: 1963)
STAND BY ME (with Ben E. King)**
by Ben E. King (Atco: 1961)
THERE GOES MY BABY (with
George Treadwell, Benjamin
Nelson and Lover Patterson) by
The Drifters (Atlantic: 1959)
TREAT ME NICE by Elvis Presley
(RCA: 1957)
YAKETY YAK** by The Coasters
(Atco: 1958)
YOUNG BLOOD (with Doc Pomus)
by The Coasters (Atco: 1957)

Jerry Leiber wrote SPANISH
HARLEM with Phil Spector.

JAMBALAYA (ON THE BAYOU)
(Hank Williams)
All-time classic, written and first
recorded by the late Hank Williams
on a Number One country record on
MGM in 1952. The big pop cover
that year was by Jo Stafford on
Columbia. Virtually no country band
or solo artist has failed to feature the
song.

US ROCK ERA HITS:	Fats Domino (Imperial: 1962) Pop
	The Blue Ridge Rangers (aka John Fogerty) (Fantasy: 1973) Pop
UK ROCK ERA HITS:	Fats Domino (London: 1962)
	The Carpenters (A&M: 1974)

Other recordings: The Nitty Gritty Dirt Band (UA); Freddy Fender (MCA); Jerry Lee Lewis (Sun); Gerry and The Pacemakers (UK Columbia); Bobby Comstock (Atlantic); Brenda Lee (Decca); Jesse Colin Young (Warner Bros); Jo-El Sonnier (Eagle Int'l); Doug Kershaw (Warner Bros); Wanda Jackson (Capitol); Emmylou Harris (Reprise); Rusty Draper (Mercury); Hank Locklin (RCA); Johnny Duncan (UK Columbia); Tony Sheridan (Polydor); and many, many others.

JENNY, JENNY
(Enotris Johnson/Richard Penniman)
A Little Richard rock 'n' roll classic which he performed in the concert movies, "Sweet Toronto" (Pennebaker: 1971) and "The London Rock 'N' Roll Show" (Clifton Films: 1974).

US HIT: Little Richard (Specialty: 1957) Black & Pop
UK HIT: Little Richard (London: 1957)

Other recordings: Delaney and Bonnie with Eric Clapton (Atco); Jerry Lee Lewis (Mercury); Carl Perkins (Columbia); David Cassidy (Bell); Bill Haley and His Comets.

See also: JENNY TAKE A RIDE.

JENNY TAKE A RIDE
(Enotris Johnson/Richard Penniman/ Bob Crewe)
A medley of Little Richard's JENNY JENNY song and the traditional C. C. RIDER, put together by songwriter– producer–artist Bob Crewe, specifically for Mitch Ryder.
    Performed by Mitch Ryder and The Detroit Wheels on the soundtrack of the Martin Scorsese movie, "Who's That Knocking At My Door?" (Trimrod: 1968).

US HIT: Mitch Ryder and The Detroit Wheels (New Voice: 1966) Pop

UK HIT: Mitch Ryder and The Detroit Wheels (Stateside: 1966)

Other recording: Johnny and Edgar Winter (Blue Sky).

See also: SEE SEE RIDER.

JOHNNY B.GOODE
(Chuck Berry)
Quintessential motor-mouth lyric and *that* guitar introduction make up one of Chuck Berry's finest. The master performed it himself in "Go Johnny Go" (Hal Roach: 1959) and in "The TAMI Show" (UK original titles: "Teenage Command Performance" and "Gather No Moss") (AIP:1965).
    Hendrix performed it in "Jimi Plays Berkeley" (1971), Johnny Winter did it in the "Sound Of The Seventies" shot that same year, Presley sang it in "Elvis On Tour" (MGM: 1972), The Sex Pistols' version is in "The Great Rock And Roll Swindle" (Virgin: 1980) and Judas Priest perform it on the soundtrack of the teen comedy "Johnny Be Good" (Orion: 1988). In the Chuck Berry bio-concert movie, "Hail! Hail! Rock 'N' Roll" (Universal: 1987), it was performed by Julian Lennon.

US HIT: Chuck Berry (Chess: 1958) Black & Pop
UK HITS: The Jimi Hendrix Experience (Polydor: 1972)
            Peter Tosh (EMI: 1983)
            Judas Priest (Atlantic: 1988)

Other recordings: The Beach Boys (Capitol); The Grateful Dead (Warner Bros); Bill Black's Combo (Hi); Dion DiMucci (Columbia); Freddie and The Dreamers (UK Columbia); Jerry Lee Lewis (Smash); Frank Marino and Mahogany Rush (Columbia); Jimi Hendrix (Capitol); James Burton ; Johnny Winter (Columbia); The Shadows (UK Columbia).

Sequel record: BYE BYE JOHNNY (Berry) by Chuck Berry (Chess: 1960) covered by The Rolling Stones (UK Decca: 1964).

See: MEMPHIS for other Chuck Berry songs.

JOHNNY REMEMBER ME
(Geoffrey Goddard)
One of the milestones of British pop... JOHNNY REMEMBER ME was in the tradition of America's TELL LAURA I LOVE HER ...a death song full of teen passion and lust. Served up as a vehicle for the actor John Leyton who, ironically, had covered TELL LAURA himself. Leyton was all over the front pages...a brooding, blond star of a popular British TV soap opera, "Harper's West One". Produced by the late Joe Meek.

UK HITS: John Leyton (Top Rank: 1961)
The Meteors (I.D. 1983)
Bronski Beat and Marc Almond: Medley with I FEEL LOVE (Summer/Moroder/Bellotte) and LOVE TO YOU BABY (Moroder/Bellotte) (Forbidden Fruit: 1985)

Other recording: Showaddywaddy (Bell/Arista).

Joe Meek classics
Joe Meek was the first of the great independent British record producers. Operating with relatively crude equipment three floors above a leather goods store in the Holloway Road, North London, he put his indelible stamp on a series of singles which were far ahead of their time. His biggest claim to fame was The Tornados' atmospheric TELSTAR, a world wide Number One instrumental smash, which Meek himself wrote. Yet his John Leyton records, cut when the young actor was the hearthrob of British televsion, are his real legacy; full of pulsating rhythms, echoing sound effects and angelic voices, Meek's records were as artistically astounding as Phil Spector's productions a few thousand miles away. Sadly, Joe's untimely death robbed us of knowing how widespread his influence would have become on the British record industry. The following is a list of some of his best work, released both on his own 'Triumph' label and the major UK companies of the day to whom he licensed his 'RGM' productions:

ALONG CAME CAROLINE (Cox/Stephens/McGrath/Steel) by Michael Cox (HMV: 1960)
ANGELA JONES (Loudermilk) by Michael Cox (Triumph: 1960)
CAN'T YOU HEAR THE BEAT OF A BROKEN HEART (Duke) by Iain Gregory (Pye: 1962)
GREEN JEANS (Alexander) by The Flee-Rekkers (Triumph: 1960)
HAVE I THE RIGHT (Blaikley) by The Honeycombs (Pye: 1964)
JUST LIKE EDDIE (Goddard) by Heinz (UK Decca: 1963)
ONLY THE HEARTACHES (Walker) by Houston Wells and the Marksmen (Parlophone: 1963)
PLEASE STAY (Bacharach/Hilliard) by The Cryin' Shames (UK Decca: 1966)
SEVENTEEN COME SUNDAY (Goddard) by Gerry Temple (HMV: 1961)
SON THIS IS SHE (Goddard) by John Leyton (HMV: 1962)
TELSTAR (Meek) by The Tornados (UK Decca: 1962)
WILD WIND (Goddard) by John Leyton (Top Rank: 1961)

See: TELL LAURA I LOVE HER for other death songs.

JUMPIN' JACK FLASH

(Mick Jagger/Keith Richards)
Classic Stones song from their early
days which they performed in the
legendary Altamont concert, and
which was subsequently included in
the Maysles Brothers film of that
event, "Gimme Shelter" (1970).

Aretha Franklin's first-rate revival
in 1986 was produced by Keith
Richards and featured on the
soundtrack of Whoopi Goldberg's
comedy movie, "Jumpin' Jack Flash"
(20th Century Fox: 1986).

US HITS: The Rolling Stones
          (London: 1968) Pop
          Aretha Franklin (Arista:
          1986) Pop
UK HITS: The Rolling Stones (UK
          Decca: 1968)

Other recordings: Geno Washington
(Pye); Johnny Winter (Columbia);
Leon Russell (Shelter); Peter
Frampton (A&M); Ike and Tina
Turner (UA); Thelma Houston
(Dunhill).

JUST DON'T WANT TO BE LONELY TONIGHT

(Vinnie Barrett/Bobby Eli/John C.
Freeman)

US HITS: Ronnie Dyson (Columbia:
          1973) Black & Pop
          The Main Ingredient
          (RCA: 1974) Black &
          Pop
UK HITS: The Main Ingredient
          (RCA: 1974)
          Freddie McGregor
          (Germain: 1987)

JUST ONE LOOK

(Doris Troy/Gregory Carroll)
R&B singer–songwriter Doris Troy
enjoyed the initial hit of her song in
1963 and, though that single didn't
make the British charts, it was a club
favourite; The Hollies covered it the
following year and it has since been
used in TV car commercials. In 1984

Doris Troy herself introduced JUST
ONE LOOK in "Mama, I Want To
Sing", the stage musical based on
Doris' upbringing in the church and
written by her sister and brother-in-
law.

US HITS: Doris Troy (Atlantic: 1963)
          Black & Pop
          The Hollies (Imperial:
          1967) Pop
          Linda Ronstadt (Asylum:
          1979) Pop
UK HITS: The Hollies (Parlophone:
          1964)
          Faith, Hope and Charity
          (RCA: 1976)

Other recordings: Anne Murray
(Capitol); Gerry and The
Pacemakers (UK Columbia); Rick
Springfield (Mercury); Martha and
The Vandellas (Motown); Lulu and
the Luvvers (UK Decca).

Sequel record: ANOTHER LOOK by
Doris Troy.

Incidentally, The Hollies also
recorded another of Doris Troy's
songs, WHATCHA GONNA DO
'BOUT IT (Payne/Carroll)
(Parlophone: 1964).

KANSAS CITY

(Jerry Leiber/Mike Stoller)
Originally released as K. C. LOVIN'
and recorded by Little Willie
Littlefield (Federal: 1952), it was
re-cut under the title KANSAS CITY
by Wilbert Harrison. A decade later,
Wilbert recorded the original of
LET'S WORK TOGETHER**.

In 1964, The Beatles recorded a
medley combining KANSAS CITY
and Little Richard's HEY, HEY, HEY,
HEY (GOING BACK TO

BIRMINGHAM) on their *Beatles For Sale* album for Parlophone, and performed it in the rockumentary, "Let It Be" (UA: 1970).

US HITS: Wilbert Harrison (Fury: 1959) Black & Pop
Hank Ballard and The Midnighters (King: 1959) Black
Trini Lopez (Reprise: 1964) Pop
James Brown and The Famous Flames (King: 1967) Black
UK HITS: Little Richard (London: 1959)
Trini Lopez (Reprise: 1963)

Other recordings: Fats Domino (ABC/Paramount); Jimmy Witherspoon (Prestige); H. B. Barnum (Imperial); Brenda Lee (Decca); T-Bone Walker (Reprise); The Coasters (Atco); Peggy Lee (Capitol); David Bromberg (Columbia); Little Richard (Specialty); Wanda Jackson (Capitol); Clyde McPhatter (Mercury); Johnny Rivers (MCA); Little Milton (Checker); Lou Rawls (Capitol); Jay and The Americans (UA); Libby Titus (Columbia); Pete Best (Cameo); Ace Cannon (Hi); Bill Haley and His Comets (Warner Bros); Bob Wills (Kapp); Scatman Crothers (Motown); Pat Boone (Dot); Alexis Korner (UK Decca); The Everly Brothers (Warner Bros); Freddie and The Dreamers (UK Columbia).

Sequel record (to K.C. LOVIN'): MISS K.C.'S FINE by Little Willie Littlefield (Federal: 1953).

See: JAILHOUSE ROCK for other Jerry Leiber and Mike Stoller songs.

KEEP A-KNOCKIN'
(Richard Penniman/Bert Mays/J.Mayo Williams)
Classic Little Richard rocker which he himself performed in the Alan Freed movie, "Mister Rock and Roll" (Paramount: 1957). His original record used to great effect in John Carpenter's movie of Stephen King's "Christine" (Columbia: 1983).

US HIT: Little Richard (Specialty: 1957) Black & Pop
UK HIT: Little Richard (London: 1957)

Other recordings: Mott The Hoople (Atlantic); The Everly Brothers (Cadence); The Flamin' Groovies (Buddah); Wet Willie (Warner Bros); Suzi Quatro (Bell); The Blasters (Slash); Jimi Hendrix (Pickwick); The Dave Clark Five (UK Columbia); Johnny Rivers (Imperial).

KEEP ON DANCING
(Willie David Young)
The Gentrys were a dance band from Memphis, Tennessee, when they recorded KEEP ON DANCING a cheesy one-note hit, which featured the irritating and cheap, but nonetheless wonderful Farfisa organ sound also heard on fellow Memphians Sam The Sham and The Pharoahs' WOOLY BULLY. The Gentrys had no comparable success, but their song was revived by another cheesy group, The Bay City Rollers. Larry Raspberry, the Gentrys' lead vocalist later formed his own group, Larry Raspberry and The High Steppers. Original version was by The Avantis (Argo: 1963).

US HIT: The Gentrys (MGM: 1965) Pop
UK HIT: The Bay City Rollers (UK Bell: 1971)

KILLING ME SOFTLY WITH HIS SONG
(Charles Fox/Norman Gimbel)
Roberta Flack, whose THE FIRST TIME EVER I SAW YOUR FACE (MacColl) topped the US charts in the spring of 1972, first heard KILLING ME SOFTLY as the original version by Lori Lieberman played

Roberta Flack is seen here performing KILLING ME SOFTLY WITH HIS SONG in the charity concert movie, 'Save The Children' (Paramount: 1973). Audiences became aware of her when her record of THE FIRST TIME EVER I SAW YOUR FACE was used on the soundtrack of Clint Eastwood's picture, "Play Misty For Me" (Universal: 1971); the single was released before the movie came out, but after the film's opening, Roberta's record took off like wildfire.

KILLING ME SOFTLY WITH HIS SONG
It was Lori Lieberman's account of seeing Don McLean in concert that inspired Norman Gimbel and Charles Fox to write KILLING ME SOFTLY WITH HIS SONG.

over the radio. The song was actually inspired by folk singer–songwriter Don McLean whose concert Lieberman had attended; she was knocked out by McLean's performance and described her enthusiasm to Charles Fox and Norman Gimbel who were writing songs for her forthcoming album on Capitol.

Lori Lieberman's version was released as a single but the song may never have enjoyed huge hit status had Roberta Flack not had a sixth sense that this was the tune for her.

US HIT: Roberta Flack (Atlantic: 1973) Black & Pop
UK HIT: Roberta Flack (Atlantic: 1973)

One of the more recent versions, by Al B. Sure! (Warner Bros), was on the American pop charts in 1988.

Other recordings: Van McCoy (Arco); Tim Weisberg (A&M); Johnny Mathis (Columbia); Anne Murray (Capitol); Eric Gale (Kudu); Lynn Anderson (Columbia); Perry Como (RCA).

KNOCK ON WOOD
(Eddie Floyd/Steve Cropper)
Classic soul power from Eddie Floyd, originally from the Falcons, a Detroit group of which Wilson Pickett was later also a member. Floyd's original was an R&B Number

One whereas Amii Stewart's atmospheric disco version (which really played with the 'thunder' and 'lightning' references) topped the American pop charts.

US HITS: Eddie Floyd (Stax: 1966)
                  Black & Pop
               Otis Redding and Carla
                  Thomas (Stax: 1967)
                  Black & Pop
               Amii Stewart (Ariola:
                  1979) Black & Pop
UK HITS: Eddie Floyd (Atlantic: 1967)
               Otis Redding and Carla
                  Thomas (Stax: 1967)
               David Bowie (RCA: 1974)
               Amii Stewart (Atlantic:
                  1979)
               Amii Stewart (Sedition:
                  1985 Re-release)

Other recordings: Toots and The Maytals (Island); King Curtis (Atco); Buddy Guy (Vanguard); The Mar-Keys (Stax); Georgie Fame (UK Columbia); Harpers Bizarre (Warner Bros); The Sweet Inspirations (Atlantic); James and Bobby Purify (Bell); The Senate (UA); Herbie Goins and The Night Timers (Parlophone); Count Basie (MCA).

KO KO MO (I LOVE YOU SO)

(Forest Wilson/Jake Porter/Eunice Levy)
Song which started out as an R&B duet between its writers (Forest) Gene (Wilson) and Eunice (Levy), who became man and wife. They cut an almost identical version for Aladdin Records while the Combo single was on the charts.

US HITS: Gene and Eunice
                  (Combo: 1955) Black
               Perry Como (RCA: 1955)
                  Pop
               The Crew-Cuts (Mercury:
                  1955) Pop

Other recordings: The Charms (De Luxe); Tony Bennett (Columbia); The Flamingos (Checker); Marvin and Johnny.

KO KO MO
R&B duo Gene and Eunice recorded their KO KO MO hit twice and TV singing star Perry Como was among the first to 'cover' it!

Sequel record: GO ON KO KO MO by Gene and Eunice (Case: 1958).

LA BAMBA

(Ritchie Valens)
Probably now the best-remembered of the late Ritchie Valens' songs, but never a chart-topper until the movie on his life came out in 1987.
   A US Top 30 single in early 1959, it was originally the flipside of DONNA, the love song with which Valens had the most success.
   Besides being the biopic's title

song, LA BAMBA also shows off the Latin rock beat so associated with Tex-Mex star Valens, which was also evident on his debut hit, COME ON, LET'S GO (Del-Fi: 1958), although a bigger song for The McCoys (Bang: 1966). LA BAMBA was also revived by Los Lobos, a five-man band from Los Angeles, led by Cesar Rosas.

The folk roots of LA BAMBA stretch way back to a Spanish wedding song.

US HITS: Ritchie Valens (Del-Fi: 1958) Pop
            Los Lobos (Slash: 1987) Pop
UK HITS: The Crickets (Liberty: 1964)*
            Los Lobos (Slash: 1987)

* The full title of the Crickets' version is (THEY CALL HER) LA BAMBA and it was arranged by Leon Russell.

Other recordings: Neil Diamond (Bang); Jose Feliciano (RCA); Shirley Bassey (UA); New Riders Of The Purple Sage (Columbia); The Ventures (Dolton); Unit Four Plus Two (UK Decca); The Sandpipers (A&M).

In 1988, Rhino Records released *The Best Of La Bamba*, a collection of ten contrasting versions, including interpretations by Conjunto Medellin De Lino Chavez, The Mormon Tabernacle Choir, Tonio K. and the doo-wop parody group, Big Daddy.

LAND OF 1000 DANCES

(Chris Kenner/Antoine Domino)
An R&B anthem celebrating all the key dance tunes which were in vogue in the early sixties, from the Twist, the Pony, and the Mashed Potato, to the Watusi and the Popeye. Adapted by New Orleans-born singer–songwriter Chris Kenner from an old spiritual called CHILDREN, GO WHERE I SEND YOU.

As he told Tad Jones: 'I just sat down and listened...I got an idea and went to work on it.' The first four lines of the song, which were recorded in Chris' original session for Instant in 1962, were edited out of the released master and remained unheard until Charly Records rescued the complete take for their I LIKE IT LIKE THAT collection of Kenner tunes in 1987. Later versions, such as Wilson Pickett's, also contain the chant, NAA,NA-NA-NA-NAA which first Wilson sings, followed by the back-up chorus.

Ironically, the opening seconds of the Cannibal and The Headhunters' record was also excised prior to release and LAND OF 1000 DANCES remains one of a group of rock history classics in which the exact title never appears in the actual lyrics.

US HITS: Chris Kenner (Instant: 1963) Pop
            Cannibal and The Headhunters (Rampart:1965) Pop
            Thee Midniters (Chattahoochee: 1965) Pop
            Wilson Pickett (Atlantic: 1966) Pop & Black
            The J. Geils Band (EMI America: 1983) Pop
UK HIT: Wilson Pickett (Atlantic: 1966)

Other recordings: Fantastic Johnny C (Phil L.A. of Soul); The Miracles (Tamla); The Electric Indian (UA); Steve Cropper (Stax); Tom Jones (UK Decca); The Kingsmen (Wand); The Action (Parlophone); Fats Domino (ABC); Major Lance (Okeh); Rufus Thomas (Stax); The Flames (Page One), Ted Nugent (Epic); Little Richard (Okeh); The Walker Brothers (Philips); Etta James (Argo); Bill Haley (Orfeon); The Young Rascals (Atlantic); The Wrestlers (Epic); The Elwood Blues Revue with Wilson Pickett (Atlantic); Ike and Tina Turner (UA); Jimi Hendrix.

LAWDY MISS CLAWDY

(Lloyd Price)
Highly influential song in rock 'n' roll history....a blues shouter performed by such as The Beatles, in their "Let It Be" movie (Apple: 1970), and Elvis Presley (RCA: 1956).

Lloyd Price's original single, which went to Number One on the R&B charts, was one of the first black records to sell to whites in significant numbers; it was recorded with Dave Bartholomew's Band and Fats Domino played piano.

In the hall of fame of New Orleans' home-grown R&B classics, they don't come much greater than this! Song has naturally been revived many times, particularly in 1976, when Mickey Gilley stormed the country charts with his version on Playboy.

US HITS: Lloyd Price (Specialty: 1952) Black
            Gary Stites (Carlton: 1960) Pop
            The Buckinghams (USA:1967) Pop
            Mickey Gilley (Playboy: 1976) Country
UK HIT: Elvis Presley (HMV: 1957)

Other recordings: Joe Cocker (A&M); Solomon Burke (Atlantic); Ike Turner (UA); Bill Haley and His Comets (Sonet); The Swinging Blue Jeans (HMV); The Dave Clark Five (UK Columbia); Larry Williams (Specialty); Tommy Roe (ABC); The Hollies (Imperial); Ronnie Hawkins (Monument); Fats Domino (Reprise); Mitch Ryder and The Detroit Wheels (New Voice); Little Richard.

Sequel record: FORGIVE ME, CLAWDY (Price) by Lloyd Price (Specialty: 1956)

LAWDY MISS CLAWDY
Lloyd Price recorded LAWDY MISS CLAWDY for Specialty Records in 1952 and, following a stint in the Army, cut a series of hits for ABC/Paramount including JUST BECAUSE (1957), STAGGER LEE (1958), PERSONALITY (1959) and I'M GONNA GET MARRIED (1959). He also formed two labels of his own, one of which was the Liberty-distributed Double-L, in which his partner was STAGGER LEE co-writer Harold Logan; one of their first singles in 1963 was Lloyd's own version of the jazz standard, MISTY (Garner/Burke).

LEADER OF THE PACK

(George Morton/Jeff Barry/Ellie Greenwich)
Full of teenage angst, this melodramatic love-on-wheels classic was a major international hit, far out-stripping The Shangri-Las' previous single, (REMEMBER) WALKIN' IN THE SAND. Complete with motorcycle noises and other atmospherics, the song is the story of Betty's boyfriend Jimmy; 'Is she really going out with him' they ask at the beginning, and the story unfolds from there.

Performed by Bette Midler in "Divine Madness" (Warner Bros: 1980).

US HITS: The Shangri-Las (Red Bird: 1964) Pop
            UTFO (Select: 1985) Black
            Twisted Sister (Atlantic: 1985) Pop

UK HITS: The Shangri-Las (Red
Bird: 1965)
The Shangri-Las (Kama
Sutra: 1972 Re-release)
The Shangri-Las (Charly/
Contempo: 1976 Re-
release)
Twisted Sister (Atlantic:
1986)

Parody record: LEADER OF THE
LAUNDROMAT (Vance/Pockriss) by
The Detergents (Roulette: 1964)

See: SEA CRUISE for more sound
effects in rock 'n' roll.

LEADER OF THE PACK

The Shangri-Las were on Leiber and Stoller's Red
Bird label and their two mini-melodramas,
REMEMBER (WALKIN' IN THE SAND) (Morton)
and LEADER OF THE PACK were major hits.
Mixing sound effects, spoken dialogue, as well as
the songs themselves, resulted in the most
atmospheric records of their day.

LEAN ON ME
(Bill Withers)
Soul singer Bill Withers topped the American charts with this gospel-styled ballad. Performed by Sandra Reaves-Phillips in the movie itself, and by Thelma Houston and The Winans on the soundtrack of John Avildsen's movie "Lean On Me" (Warner Bros: 1989).

Bill Withers accepting his 1972 Grammy Award for AIN'T NO SUNSHINE which he wrote and which had just been voted 'Best R&B Song'.

Sandra Reaves-Phillips, who also sang in the movie "Round Midnight" (Warner Bros: 1986), cut some R&B singles for Juggy Murray's Broadway label some two decades earlier.

US HITS: Bill Withers (Sussex: 1972)
          Black & Pop
          Melba Moore (Buddah: 1976) Black
          Club Nouveau (Warner Bros) 1987 Black & Pop
UK HITS: Bill Withers (A&M: 1972)
          Club Nouveau (King Jay/Warner Bros: 1987)

Other recordings: Nilsson (RCA); Vikki Carr (Columbia); Crystal Gayle (Columbia).

Bill Withers' surprise UK hit of 1988 was the 'sunshine mix' of his 1978 Columbia hit, LOVELY DAY, a song he wrote himself.

LET IT BE
(John Lennon/Paul McCartney)
From The Beatles' movie, "Let It Be" (Apple: 1970). Performed by Leo Sayer on the soundtrack of "All This and World War II" (20th Century Fox: 1976). Featured by Paul McCartney and Wings on their 'live' album, *Concerts For The People Of Kampuchea* (Atlantic: 1981).

UK HITS: The Beatles (Apple: 1970)
          Ferry Aid (The Sun/ Zeebrugge: 1987)
US HITS: The Beatles (Apple: 1970) Pop
          Joan Baez (Vanguard: 1971) Pop

Other recordings: Aretha Franklin (Atlantic); Ike and Tina Turner (Liberty); John Denver (RCA); Gladys Knight and The Pips (Soul); "Beatlemania" cast (Arista); Tennessee Ernie Ford (Capitol); Bill Withers (Columbia); The Beach Boys (Capitol); "All This And World War II" soundtrack (20th Century).

See: WITH A LITTLE HELP FROM MY FRIENDS for other John Lennon and Paul McCartney songs.

LET THE FOUR WINDS BLOW
(Dave Bartholomew /Antoine Domino)

LET IT BE
Former Ikette Claudia Linnear performing LET IT
BE in the movie version of Joe Cocker's 1970
American tour, "Mad Dogs and Englishmen"
(MGM: 1971).

R&B classic, originally written and
recorded by Dave Bartholomew as
FOUR WINDS (Imperial: 1955).

US HITS: Roy Brown (Imperial:
                1957) Pop
                Fats Domino (Imperial:
                1961) Black & Pop

Other recordings: Bobby Charles
(Imperial); Millie (Island); Brenda
Lee (Decca); Snooks Eaglin
(Crescendo); Trini Lopez (Reprise);
Bobby Vee (Liberty); Sandy Nelson
(Imperial).

See: I HEAR YOU KNOCKING for
other Dave Bartholomew songs.

LET THE GOOD TIMES ROLL
(Leonard Lee/Shirley Goodman)
Probably the finest of rock's early
anthems, recorded by Shirley and
Lee, two New Orleans teenagers

who were dubbed 'The Sweethearts Of The Blues'. The song was heard on the soundtrack of the concert film retrospective "Let The Good Times Roll" (Columbia: 1973). In 1987, some years after (Leonard) Lee's death, Shirley (Goodman) successfully went to court to prove that she co-wrote the song which had previously been credited only to her partner.

US HITS: Shirley and Lee
(Aladdin: 1956)
Pop & Black
Shirley and Lee
(Warwick
re-recording: 1960) Pop
Bunny Sigler: Medley
with Leonard Lee's

FEEL SO GOOD
(Parkway: 1967) Pop &
Black (also covered by
Amen Corner in the UK
on Immediate).

Other recordings: Ray Charles (Atlantic); Barbra Streisand (Columbia); Roy Orbison (Monument); The Animals (UK Columbia); The Righteous Brothers (Moonglow); The Searchers (Pye); The Kingsmen (Wand); Dale and Grace (Montel); Betty Everett and Jerry Butler (Vee-Jay); Johnny Preston (Imperial); Nilsson (RCA), Caesar and Cleo (aka Sonny and Cher) (Reprise); Georgie Fame (UK Columbia); Jimmy Gilmer.

LET'S GO, LET'S GO, LET'S GO
(Hank Ballard)
Also known as THRILL ON THE HILL, Hank Ballard's original record was heard on the soundtrack of Tim Hunter's dark youth drama, "River's Edge" (Hemdale: 1986). Hank always refers to Fats Domino when introducing this song on stage, between the Fat Man's trip up 'Blueberry Hill' and Hank's own 'thrill' on that very same hill!

Performed by John Fogerty in his 1985 concert show at A&M Studios in Hollywood and shown as a cable special on "Showtime".

US HIT: Hank Ballard and The
Midnighters (King:
1960) Pop & Black

Other recordings: The Isley Brothers (UA); Betty LaVette and Hank Ballard (Sun).

Also on Hank Ballard and the Midnighters' UK Charly double album recorded live just before Christmas 1987 at London's Hammersmith Palais.

See: THE TWIST for other Hank Ballard songs.

LET THE GOOD TIMES ROLL
Shirley and Lee were just fourteen and fifteen respectively, when their first record was released in 1950. Aladdin Records billed them as 'The Sweethearts Of The Blues' but they were never linked romantically. Yet on record they sang of adolescent love and heartbreak! Lee went on to make solo singles for Imperial under the name 'Mr. Lee' in 1963, and years later Shirley had a major hit record called SHAME, SHAME, SHAME (Vibration: 1975), credited to 'Shirley and Company'; it was written and produced by Sylvia Robinson, one half of another legendary duo, Mickey and Sylvia (see LOVE IS STRANGE).

LET'S STAY TOGETHER
(Al Green/Willie Mitchell/Al Jackson)
The Reverend Al Green, once described as the George Jones of gospel and soul, wrote this R&B ballad to which Tina Turner added her sultry touch twelve years after his original.
    Another Al Green composition to be reworked was TAKE ME TO THE RIVER, recorded by Talking Heads (Sire: 1978).

US HITS: Al Green (Hi: 1972) Black & Pop
    Isaac Hayes (Enterprise: 1972) Black & Pop
    Tina Turner (Capitol: 1984) Black & Pop
UK HITS: Al Green (London: 1972)
    Jean Carn (Gordy: 1983)
    Tina Turner (Capitol: 1983)

Other recordings: Herbie Mann (Atlantic); Margie Joseph (Atlantic); Little Beaver (Cat).

LET'S STICK TOGETHER
See: LET'S WORK TOGETHER.

LET'S WORK TOGETHER
(Wilbert Harrison)
Originally cut by Wilbert Harrison, recorded as LET'S STICK by Bryan Ferry. A television ad utilizing the Ferry record sparked a revival of the song's popularity and a release of the single.

US HITS: Wilbert Harrison (Sue: 1970) Pop
    Canned Heat (Liberty: 1970) Pop
UK HITS: Canned Heat (Liberty: 1970)
    Bryan Ferry (billed as LET'S STICK TOGETHER) (Island: 1976)
    Bryan Ferry (E.G.: 1988 Re-release)

Other recordings: The Climax Blues Band (Sire); Blue Mink and The Morgan Superstars (Philips).

THE LETTER
(Wayne Carson)
'Give me a ticket for an aeroplane...'
The first of two smash hits for the five-man American group, The Box Tops; their second success was with CRY LIKE A BABY (Penn/Oldham) (Mala: 1968).
    Performed by Joe Cocker with Leon Russell in "Mad Dogs And Englishmen" (MGM: 1970).

US HITS: The Box Tops (Mala: 1967) Black & Pop
    The Arbors (Date: 1969) Pop

LET'S WORK TOGETHER
Bryan Ferry successfully re-cut Wilbert Harrison's own LET'S WORK TOGETHER, re-titling it LET'S STICK TOGETHER. In addition to other solo recordings of classic songs, Ferry has cut some covers over the years with Roxy Music, including versions of the Byrds' milestone, EIGHT MILES HIGH (Clark/Crosby/McGuinn), and Wilson Pickett's soul classic, IN THE MIDNIGHT HOUR (Cropper/Pickett).

Joe Cocker (A&M: 1970)
Pop

UK HITS: The Box Tops
(Stateside: 1967)
The Mindbenders
(Fontana: 1967)
Joe Cocker
(Regal/Zonophone:
1970)

Other recordings: The Pretty Things (Harvest); Bobby Darin (Motown); Dionne Warwick (Arista); Amii Stewart (Ariola); The Beach Boys (Capitol); Ellie Greenwich (UA); Billy Burnette (MCA); The Tams (MCA).

Parody record: VANNA, PICK ME A LETTER by Dr Dave (TSR: 1987) based around the popularity of Vanna White, who, on the American television game show "Wheel Of Fortune", turns the appropriate letters on a giant board.

Wayne Carson Thompson wrote other best sellers by The Box Tops, including SOUL DEEP (Mala: 1969) and NEON RAINBOW (Mala: 1967), but his other major claim to fame is that he co-wrote ALWAYS ON MY MIND★★, a major hit over the years for Willie Nelson, Elvis Presley and The Pet Shop Boys.

LIGHT MY FIRE
(Jim Morrison/John Densmore/Robert Krieger/Raymond Manzarek)
First of two songs to top the US charts (the other was HELLO, I LOVE YOU in '68) for avant-garde west coast-based rock quartet The Doors, led by the late and much-lamented Jim Morrison. LIGHT MY FIRE was edited down from one of the cuts on their first album, *The Doors* (Elektra: 1967). They had literally created the number during their legendary stand at L.A.'s Whiskey A Go-Go club.

Blind singer-guitarist Jose Feliciano began his chart-making career with a FIRE revival, while one of American disco singer Amii

Stewart's singles following her version of Eddie Floyd's KNOCK ON WOOD★★ was a medley including the Doors' classic; her single was a minor US success but a huge hit in England.

US HITS: The Doors (Elektra: 1967)
Pop
Jose Feliciano (RCA:
1968) Pop

UK HITS: The Doors (Elektra: 1967)
Jose Feliciano (RCA:
1968)
Amii Stewart: Medley
with 137 DISCO
HEAVEN (Hansa: 1979)

Other recordings: Jackie Wilson (Brunswick); Minnie Ripperton (Capitol); Mae West (Tower); Young Holt Unlimited (Brunswick); Isaac Hayes (Stax); Stevie Wonder (Tamla); The Four Tops (Motown); Booker T. and The M.G.'s (Stax); Shirley Bassey (UA); Chet Atkins (RCA); The Watts 103rd Street Rhythm Band (Warner Bros); Julie Driscoll with Brian Auger and The Trinity (Marmalade).

Billy Idol's remake of another Doors' classis, L.A. WOMAN (The Doors), was heard on the soundtrack of Michael Mann's 1989 TV movie, *L.A. Takedown.*

LIKE A ROLLING STONE
(Bob Dylan)
Inspired by Alan Price's swirling organ sound in The Animals' THE HOUSE OF THE RISING SUN★★, Bob Dylan got Al Kooper to play organ on LIKE A ROLLING STONE, yet another Dylan diatribe to a socialite girlfriend. The record was revolutionary, not only as a folk–rock landmark, but also in that a six-minute song with obscure lyrics shouted in Dylan's raspy voice topped the US pop charts.

Performed in the rockumentary, "Jimi Hendrix" (Warner Bros: 1973).

US HIT: Bob Dylan (Columbia:
           1965) Pop
UK HIT: Bob Dylan (CBS: 1965)

Other recordings: Cher (Imperial);
The Four Seasons (Philips); The
Creation (Hilton); Lester Flatt and
Earl Scruggs (Columbia); The Young
Rascals (Atlantic); Dino, Desi and
Billy (Reprise); The Surfaris.

See: BLOWIN' IN THE WIND for
other Bob Dylan songs.

THE LION SLEEPS TONIGHT
(Hugo Peretti/Luigi Creatore/George
Weiss)
Based on a South African song, this
hit Number One in the States for The
Tokens, an east coast group founded
by Neil Sedaka, and when fellow-
member Hank Medress played him
the LION SLEEPS TONIGHT record,
Neil dismissed its chances.

But it had a haunting melody line
which folk group The Weavers had
themselves transposed from the
original Zulu song a decade earlier.

Concurrently with The Tokens'
record, Scottish singer Karl Denver
was charting high in the British
charts with a similar adaptation
under the title WIMOWEH.

US HITS: The Tokens (RCA: 1961)
           Pop
           Robert John (Atlantic:
           1972) Pop
UK HITS: The Tokens (RCA: 1961)
           The Karl Denver Trio
           (billed as WIMOWEH)
           (UK Decca: 1962)
           Dave Newman (Pye:
           1972)
           Tight Fit (Jive: 1982)

Other recordings: The Nylons (Open
Air); Rod Erickson (Crescendo);
Boys On The Block (Fantasy).

LITTLE BITTY PRETTY ONE
(Robert Byrd)
Robert Byrd, under his professional

name, Bobby Day, recorded the first
version of LITTLE BITTY with his
group, The Satellites.

Thurston Harris cut a cover
version with his group, The Sharps,
and beat Bobby to the punch...
Thurston reaching Number Six in
Billboard, while the Day record
didn't even break into the Top 50.
The Harris hit version is featured on
the soundtrack of the 1983 movie
"Christine" (Columbia: 1983). LITTLE
BITTY PRETTY ONE was notably
the last hit for two R&B legends of
the 1950s, both of whom tragically
died young: Frankie Lymon and
Clyde McPhatter.

US HITS: Bobby Day (Class: 1957)
           Pop
           Thurston Harris and The
           Sharps (Aladdin: 1957)
           Black & Pop
           Frankie Lymon (Roulette:
           1960) Pop
           Clyde McPhatter
           (Mercury: 1962) Pop
           The Jackson 5 (Motown:
           1972) Black & Pop

Other recordings: The Paramounts
(Parlophone); Jewel Akens.

In 1972 Michael Jackson found solo
success with another rocker which had
been originally recorded by Bobby
Day, namely ROCKIN' ROBIN**.

LITTLE DARLIN'
(Maurice Williams)
A rare example of a white cover of a
black record being generally
recognized as the artistically
superior version. The Gladiolas were
from South Carolina and LITTLE
DARLIN' was written by their lead
singer, Maurice Williams. It was
covered by a group from Canada
whose production of the song
overshadowed the performance of
the original on all charts, even
including the R&B listings! The
Diamonds' record remains an
archetypal group sound of the

period and was featured on the soundtrack of the evocative "American Graffiti" (Universal: 1973).

The Gladiolas later changed their name to Maurice Williams and The Zodiacs and left their immortal stamp on the song STAY**.

US HITS: The Gladiolas (Excello: 1957) Black & Pop
            The Diamonds (Mercury: 1957) Black & Pop
UK HIT: The Diamonds (Mercury: 1957)

LITTLE EGYPT
(Jerry Leiber/Mike Stoller)
Originally recorded by The Coasters, it was performed by Elvis Presley in his movie, "Roustabout" (Paramount: 1964).

US HIT: The Coasters (Atco:1961) Pop & Black

Other recordings: Downliners Sect (UK Columbia); Ray Stevens (Barnaby).

See: JAILHOUSE ROCK for other Jerry Leiber and Mike Stoller songs.

LITTLE LATIN LUPE LU
(Bill Medley)
Bill Medley and Bobby Hatfield were a singing duo originally known as The Paramours, who changed their name because of their 'righteous', 'blue-eyed soul brother' sound. Their first hit, LITTLE LATIN LUPE LU was unique in that it was the only one that was self-penned. The song later made much more noise as the second hit for another great blue-eyed soul band, Mitch Ryder and The Detroit Wheels.

US HITS: The Righteous Brothers (Moonglow: 1963) Pop
            The Kingsmen (Wand: 1964) Black & Pop
            Mitch Ryder and The Detroit Wheels (New Voice: 1966) Pop

LITTLE SISTER
(Doc Pomus/Mort Shuman)
Originally the B-side song to (MARIE'S THE NAME) HIS LATEST FLAME, Elvis Presley's RCA hit of 1961, LITTLE SISTER became a Top 10 country hit in 1987 via a version by Dwight Yoakam.

The song was performed by Ry Cooder in the 1980 rockumentary "No Nukes". It was also re-popularized by Robert Plant and Rockpile on the *Concert For The People Of Kampuchea* album (Atlantic: 1981).

US HITS: Elvis Presley (RCA: 1961) Pop
            Dwight Yoakam (Reprise: 1987) Country

Other recordings: Ry Cooder (Warner Bros); Del Shannon (Big Top).

Answer record: HEY MEMPHIS by LaVern Baker (Atlantic: 1961).

LIVING DOLL
(Lionel Bart)
It took just seven bass notes to introduce LIVING DOLL, Cliff Richard's first Number One. Cliff, along with his back-up band, The Shadows (formerly The Drifters, who changed their name so as not to conflict with the American R&B group), was, at 18 years old, Britain's biggest pop star. LIVING DOLL was written by cockney Lionel Bart...the composer of such smash-hit musicals as "Oliver" and "Fings Ain't What They Used To Be", and it was sung by Cliff in the 1959 film "Serious Charge" directed by Terence Young who later helmed three of the James Bond movies.

Rarely do Number One pop songs get a second chance to hit the top...Even more obscure are instances where the same recording artist repeats the feat, but in 1986, Cliff Richard was back topping the best-seller lists with a new version of LIVING DOLL recorded with the stars of the BBC TV series "The Young Ones" (which took its name from another Cliff hit!). Put that in the record books!

UK HITS: Cliff Richard (Columbia: 1959)
Cliff Richard and The Young Ones (WEA: 1986)

THE LOCO-MOTION
(Gerry Goffin/Carole King)
Carole King and her then-husband Gerry Goffin wrote this classic dance invitation ('Come on baby') for their teenage babysitter, Eva Boyd. Todd Rundgren produced Grand Funk's Number One version twelve years later, and the late 1980s revival was by Australian Kylie Minogue, produced by the British production team of Stock, Aitken and Waterman.

   Song was originally covered in England by The Vernons Girls (UK Decca: 1962) and a remake by Dave Stewart (not Dave Stewart of Eurythmics) with Barbara Gaskin charted briefly in 1986 on Broken.

US HITS: Little Eva (Dimension: 1962) Black & Pop
Grand Funk Railroad (Capitol: 1974) Pop
Kylie Minogue (Geffen: 1988) Pop
UK HITS: Little Eva (London: 1962)
Kylie Minogue (PWL: 1988)

Other recordings: Brian Poole (UK Decca); The Chiffons (Laurie); Carole King (Capitol); The Ventures (Liberty); Sandy Denny (A&M); The Human Beinz (Capitol).

Eva Boyd's popularity even produced a song called LITTLE EVA recorded by a group calling themselves The Locomotions (Gone: 1962)!

Sequel record: DANCE TO THE LOCOMOTION by Teddy Randazzo (ABC Paramount: 1962).

See: UP ON THE ROOF for other Gerry Goffin and Carole King songs.

LONG TALL SALLY
(Enotris Johnson/Robert Blackwell/ Richard Penniman)
Though Chuck Berry wrote and sang about MAYBELLENE** (Chess: 1954) and NADINE (1964), Little Richard appeared to corner the market in R&R song titles containing girls' names; besides Sally, he scored with LUCILLE (Collins/ Penniman)** (Specialty: 1957), JENNY, JENNY (Johnson/ Penniman)**(1957), MISS ANN (Johnson/ Penniman) (1957) and GOOD GOLLY MISS MOLLY (Marascalco/ Blackwell)** (1958).

   Performed by Little Richard in "Don't Knock The Rock" (Columbia: 1956).

LONG TALL SALLY
Little Richard, during one of his UK visits in the 1960s, standing on the steps of EMI Records' headquarters in Manchester Square, London. This is the cover of an Edsel album containing tracks recorded by Richard for Epic's R&B subsidiary, Okeh, which included ROSEMARY, a song written by Fats Domino for his wife Rosemary, though when the Fat Man originally recorded it for Imperial in 1953, it was spelt out ROSE MARY.

US HITS: Little Richard (Specialty: 1956) Black & Pop
Pat Boone (Dot: 1956) Pop

UK HITS: Pat Boone (London: 1956)
Little Richard (London: 1957)

Other recordings: The Beatles (Parlophone); Eddie Cochran (Liberty); The Swinging Blue Jeans (HMV); Amos Milburn Jr (LeCam); The Kinks (Pye); Jerry Lee Lewis (Mercury); The Merseybeats (Fontana).

The colourfully titled girl songs had a heavy New Orleans connection. The great forerunner of them all was LAWDY MISS CLAWDY** by Lloyd Price. Little Richard recorded all of his 'girl' songs in New Orleans with the studio band. Price's cousin, Larry Williams, took off on Richard's LONG TALL SALLY with SHORT FAT FANNIE. He also recorded LAWDY MISS CLAWDY**, BONY MORONIE and DIZZY MISS LIZZY**.

LOUIE, LOUIE
(Richard Berry)
Much recorded and widely revered rock song, originally cut by R&B singer Richard Berry himself with his Californian band, The Pharoahs (Flip: 1957). Four years later, it was semi-adopted as a local anthem by Rockin' Robin Roberts and The Wailers, out of the Pacific North-west. Then came The Kingsmen who took LOUIE, LOUIE into the national American charts for the first time, in fact right up to the Number Two slot. The folkish Sandpipers were next in line, releasing it as their follow-up to GUANTANAMERA. It became an official frat-party song after being featured in the comedy movie, "National Lampoon's Animal House" (1978).

    Fuelled along the way by unfounded rumours that the title had dubious connotations, LOUIE, LOUIE has gone from strength to strength in popularity with radio stations even mounting special programmes just to play as many of the over one-hundred recorded versions of the song as possible...and Rhino Records even released an entire album of different cuts of the song!

US HITS: The Kingsmen (Wand: 1963 & 66) Pop
The Sandpipers (A&M: 1966) Pop
John Belushi (MCA: 1978) Pop

UK HITS: The Kingsmen (Pye International: 1964)
Motorhead (Bronze: 1978)

Other recordings: The Beach Boys (Capitol); Paul Revere and The Raiders (Columbia); Sir Arthur aka Ian Whitcomb (Tower); Travis Wammack (Atlantic); The Kinks (Pye); Otis Redding (Volt); The Troggs (Fontana); The Ventures (Dolton); The Beau Brummels (Autumn); Jan and Dean (Liberty); Sandy Nelson (Imperial); Wilbert Harrison; Toots and The Maytals (Trojan).

LOVE HURTS
(Boudleaux Bryant)
Heartbreaking love song written for and originally recorded by The Everly Brothers on their *A Date With The Everly Brothers* album (Warner Bros: 1960), but which finally charted for former Traffic drummer Jim Capaldi in Britain and Scottish band Nazareth in the States.

US HIT: Nazareth (A&M: 1976) Pop
UK HIT: Jim Capaldi (Island: 1975)

Other recordings: Roy Orbison (Monument); Suzi Quatro (RSO); Gram Parsons (Reprise); Jennifer Warnes (Arista).

See: BYE BYE LOVE for Boudleaux and Felice Bryant songs.

LOVE IS STRANGE
(Mickey Baker/Ethel Smith/Sylvia Robinson)
Mickey 'Guitar' Baker joined with Sylvia Vanderpool (aka Robinson) and as 'Mickey and Sylvia' they cut this duet in 1956 which has since become an R&B classic; featured on the soundtrack of the movie "Dirty Dancing" (Vestron:1987), to which stars Patrick Swayze and Jennifer Grey lip synch the words. The track became the B-side of that movie's initial hit record and subsequently one of the first 'oldies' to be released on cassette single. The song was written by Bo Diddley under the name of his wife, Ethel Smith, who is the sole writer credited on the original single.

US HITS: Mickey and Sylvia
           (Groove:1957)
           Pop & Black
           Peaches and Herb
           (Date:1967)
           Pop & Black
UK HIT: The Everly Brothers
           (Warner Bros: 1965)

Other recordings: Sylvia (Vibration); Donnie Elbert (All Platinum); Dale and Grace (Montel); Wings (Capitol); Betty Everett and Jerry Butler (Vee-Jay); Buddy Holly (Decca); Caesar and Cleo (aka Sonny and Cher) (Reprise); Bo Diddley (Checker).

See: BO DIDDLEY for other Bo Diddley songs.

Mickey and Sylvia left their mark on another R&B classic. IT'S GONNA WORK OUT FINE (McKinney/McCoy) was one of Ike and Tina Turner's early R&B charters; co-written by Sylvia, the 1961 single was on the Sue label. Mickey is the voice you hear answering Tina's calls, and Sylvia was also on the session playing guitar.

LOVE ME TENDER
(Vera Matson/Elvis Presley)
Title song from Elvis' first movie, written by its musical director, Ken Darby, using his wife's maiden name as a pseudonym. Melody was taken from the civil war song, AURA LEE.

Though no one has ever come near to matching Elvis' original chart-topping performance, some remakes made impressions on the bestseller lists, including one from actor Richard Chamberlain; in the wake of the heady success that the young actor was having on MGM Television's "Dr Kildare" series, he was being groomed as a popular vocalist recording a song based on the show's signature theme, followed by some re-makes including LOVE ME TENDER, ALL I HAVE TO DO IS DREAM** and one of Metro's musical movie hits, HI-LILI, HI-LO (Deutsch/Kaper).

Song performed by Willie Nelson on the soundtrack of "Porky's Revenge" (20th Century Fox: 1985).

US HITS: Elvis Presley (RCA: 1956)
           Black & Pop
           Richard Chamberlain
           (MGM: 1962) Pop
           Percy Sledge (Atlantic:
           1967) Black & Pop
UK HITS: Elvis Presley (HMV: 1956)
           Richard Chamberlain
           (MGM: 1962)
           Roland Rat Superstar
           (Rodent: 1984)

Other recordings: Linda Ronstadt (Asylum); Merle Haggard (MCA); Engelbert Humperdinck (Epic); Ace Cannon (Hi); B.B. King (MCA); Henri Rene (RCA); Frank Sinatra (Reprise); Ray Price; Albert King (Stax).

LOVE POTION NUMBER NINE
(Jerry Leiber/Mike Stoller)
When The Clovers came to United Artists, Leiber and Stoller blessed them with the same kind of magic that had been rubbing off on The Coasters. LOVE POTION NUMBER NINE is part novelty, particularly because of its fortune-telling angle about the gypsy 'with the gold-

capped tooth' and as such, annually makes its way onto halloween playlists! Song was a much bigger pop hit when it was revived by Britain's The Searchers, though it never meant anything in their homeland. By the way, the lyrics just before the fade-out on The Clovers' record differ between the original mono single and the stereo version released on their subsequent album.

US HITS: The Clovers (UA: 1959)
Black & Pop
The Searchers (Kapp: 1965) Pop
UK HIT: Tygers Of Pan Tang (MCA: 1982)

Other recordings: Sam The Sham and The Pharoahs (MGM); Jewel Akens (Era); The Coasters (King); The Surfaris (Decca); The Ventures (Liberty); Elkie Brooks (A&M); Gary Lewis (Liberty); Wayne Fontana and The Mindbenders (Fontana).

See: JAILHOUSE ROCK for other Jerry Leiber and Mike Stoller songs.

LOVE'S MADE A FOOL OF YOU

(Buddy Holly/Bob Montgomery)
A Buddy Holly song with which his former group, The Crickets (Jerry Allison, Sonny Curtis, Glen D. Hardin) scored overseas after Buddy's death in 1959. Holly's own version was released as a UK single three years later and it too made the charts.

The song was later a hit for The Bobby Fuller Four, whose biggest single I FOUGHT THE LAW, was written by Cricket Sonny Curtis.

US HITS: The Bobby Fuller Four (Mustang: 1966) Pop
UK HITS: The Crickets (Coral: 1959)
Buddy Holly (Coral: 1964)
Matchbox (Magnet: 1981)

Other recordings: Tom Rush (Elektra); Cochise (Liberty); Bobby Vee (Liberty); Greg Kihn

(Beserkley); Susie Allanson (Elektra); Ruby Starr (Capitol).

Covers of Buddy Holly hits
Among the Buddy Holly hits which were cut by other artists:

EVERYDAY (Hardin/Petty)** by Don McLean (UA: 1973)
HEARTBEAT (Petty/Montgomery) by Showaddywaddy (Bell: 1975)
I'M GONNA LOVE YOU TOO (Mauldin/Sullivan/Petty) by The Hullaballoos (Roulette: 1964) by Blondie (Chrysalis)
IT DOESN'T MATTER ANYMORE (Anka)** by Linda Ronstadt (Asylum: 1975)
IT'S SO EASY (Holly/Petty)** by Linda Ronstadt (Asylum: 1977)
NOT FADE AWAY (Hardin/Petty)**by The Rolling Stones (UK Decca: 1964)
OH BOY (Petty/West/Tilghman)** by Mud (RAK: 1975)
PEGGY SUE (Allison/Holly/Petty)** by The Beach Boys (Brother: 1978)
RAINING IN MY HEART (Bryant)** by Leo Sayer (Chrysalis: 1978)
THAT'LL BE THE DAY (Allison/Holly/Petty)** by The Everly Brothers (Warner Bros: 1965)
TRUE LOVE WAYS (Holly/Petty) by Peter and Gordon (Capitol: 1965)
WELL ALL RIGHT (Allison/Holly/Petty/Mauldin) by Blind Faith (Atco: 1969) by Santana (Columbia: 1978)
WORDS OF LOVE (Holly) by The Diamonds (Mercury: 1957) by The Beatles (Parlophone: 1964)

Long-time British Buddy Holly admirer Mike Berry – he'd recorded a fine tribute single after Holly's death – recorded STAY CLOSE TO ME, a Buddy Holly song never previously available.

NB: Where more than one hit cover version exists on a song which is individually covered elsewhere in this book, only the first revival is quoted above.

LUCILLE

(Albert Collins/Richard Penniman)
Another of Richard's string of
successful girl songs (see also LONG
TALL SALLY).

Performed by Little Richard in the
movies "Mister Rock And Roll"
(Paramount: 1957), "Sweet Toronto"
(Pennebaker: 1971), "Let The Good
Times Roll" (Columbia: 1973) and
"The London Rock 'N' Roll Show"
(Clifton Films: 1974). The original
Little Richard record was heard on
the soundtrack of "Porky's Revenge"
(20th Century Fox: 1985).

US HITS: Little Richard (Specialty:
           1957) Black & Pop
           The Everly Brothers
           (Warner Bros: 1960)
           Pop
UK HITS: Little Richard (London:
           1957)
           The Everly Brothers
           (Warner Bros: 1960)

Other recordings: Waylon Jennings
(RCA); The Osmonds (MGM); Jerry
Lee Lewis (Mercury); Otis Redding
(Atlantic); John Mayall (UK Decca);
The Hollies (Parlophone); Bobby
Vee and The Crickets (Liberty); Bill
Haley and His Comets; Jimmy
Gilmer and The Fireballs (Dot); John
Entwhistle (MCA); Jimi Hendrix;
Deep Purple; Brian Protheroe
(Chrysalis).

MAKE IT EASY ON YOURSELF

(Burt Bacharach/Hal David)
Burt Bacharach and Hal David were
staff writers with Scepter Records;
one day, they cut a demo of MAKE
IT EASY ON YOURSELF and played
it to Florence Greenberg, Scepter's
president. After it finished, they
asked Florence if she liked MAKE
IT EASY, to which her response was
'To hell with the song, who's the
singer?' That was actually a
milestone moment in the history of
the Scepter label because the girl
singer was Dionne Warwick, who
went on to become the company's
biggest-selling artist and her
collaboration with Bacharach and
David is unsurpassed in the number
of hit singles they had together. The
irony was that Burt and Hal thought
that Florence Greenberg had
preferred the singer to the song and
so they gave MAKE IT EASY ON
YOURSELF initially to Jerry Butler.

Dionne did however cut the song
herself and it also provided The
Walker Brothers with a hit, in fact
their first UK Number One.

The Walker Brothers made Number One in Britain
with their cover of Jerry Butler's hit.

US HITS: Jerry Butler (Vee-Jay:
              1962) Black & Pop
           The Walker Brothers
              (Smash: 1965) Pop
           Dionne Warwick
              (Scepter: 1970) Black &
              Pop
           Ron Banks (CBS
              Associated: 1984) Black
UK HIT: The Walker Brothers
              (Philips: 1965)

Other recordings: Cissy Houston
(Private Stock); Burt Bacharach
(A&M); Earl 'Fatha' Hines and Marva
Josie (Vee-Jay); Michael Henderson
(Buddah); The Four Seasons
(Philips); Little Anthony and The
Imperials (DCP); Cilla Black
(Parlophone); Long John Baldry
(UA); Jordan Christopher (UA).

Bacharach and David songs
Among the hit records of other Burt
Bacharach and Hal David songs:

ALFIE by Cilla Black (Parlophone:
   1966)
   by Cher (Imperial: 1966)
   by Dionne Warwick (Scepter:
   1967)
(THERE'S) ALWAYS SOMETHING
   THERE TO REMIND ME by Lou
   Johnson (Big Top: 1964)
   by Sandie Shaw (Pye: 1964)
   by R. B. Greaves (Atco: 1970)
   by Naked Eyes (RCA: 1983)
ANYONE WHO HAD A HEART by
   Dionne Warwick (Scepter: 1964)
   by Cilla Black (Parlophone: 1964)
(THEY LONG TO BE) CLOSE TO
   YOU by The Carpenters (A&M:
   1970)
DO YOU KNOW THE WAY TO SAN
   JOSÉ by Dionne Warwick
   (Scepter: 1968)
DON'T MAKE ME OVER by Dionne
   Warwick (Scepter: 1963)
   by Sybil (Champion: 1989)
I JUST DON'T KNOW WHAT TO DO
   WITH MYSELF by Dusty
   Springfield (Philips: 1964)
I SAY A LITTLE PRAYER** by
   Dionne Warwick (Scepter: 1967)

ANYONE WHO HAD A HEART
Dionne Warwick's long list of Burt Bacharach/Hal
David songs marks the longest hit collaboration
between a singer and songwriters. Their 1967
charter, I SAY A LITTLE PRAYER was revived in
1988 by Britain's Bomb The Bass.

by Aretha Franklin (Atlantic: 1968)
I'LL NEVER FALL IN LOVE AGAIN
by Dionne Warwick (Scepter:
1970)
THE LOOK OF LOVE by Dusty
Springfield (Philips: 1967)
THE MAN WHO SHOT LIBERTY
VALANCE by Gene Pitney
(Musicor: 1962)
A MESSAGE TO MICHAEL by
Dionne Warwick (Scepter: 1966)
ONE LESS BELL TO ANSWER by
The 5th Dimension (Bell: 1970)
ONLY LOVE CAN BREAK A HEART
by Gene Pitney (Musicor: 1962)
RAINDROPS KEEP FALLIN' ON MY
HEAD by B. J. Thomas (Scepter:
1970)
TWENTY-FOUR HOURS FROM
TULSA by Gene Pitney (Musicor:
1963)
WALK ON BY by Dionne Warwick
(Scepter: 1964)
WHAT THE WORLD NEEDS NOW
IS LOVE** by Jackie DeShannon
(Imperial: 1965)
WISHIN' AND HOPIN' by Dusty
Springfield (Philips: 1964)
by The Merseybeats (Fontana:
1964)

The above list is restricted to hit
recordings, but among the other
versions of Bacharach and David
songs you might not instantly
remember is Elvis Costello singing I
JUST DON'T KNOW WHAT TO DO
WITH MYSELF on the *Stiff's Live
Stiff's* album (Stiff: 1978).

MANNISH BOY
(Ellas McDaniel/Melvin London/
McKinley Morganfield)
Adapted from Bo (aka Ellas
McDaniel) Diddley's I'M A MAN, this
was a Top 5 R&B record for blues
legend Muddy Waters. Twenty-
three years later, Muddy performed
MANNISH BOY in the Martin
Scorsese movie of "The Last Waltz"
(UA: 1978).

US HIT: Muddy Waters (Chess:
1955) Black

Other recording: The Rolling Stones
(Rolling Stones).

See also: I'M A MAN.

Muddy Waters songs
Known as the Father of the Electric
Blues, Muddy Waters has given
inspiration to a myriad of
contemporary bands from The
Rolling Stones, who were named
after his ROLLIN' STONE, through to
ZZ Top. Muddy is associated with
songs which he didn't always write
but to which he made a significant
contribution. It was his
interpretations of I'M YOUR
HOOCHIE COOCHIE MAN** and
BABY PLEASE DON'T GO** which
inspired many of the later versions
we know and our entry on GOT MY
MOJO WORKING** explains how
such adaptations have come about.
   In addition to the tunes mentioned
above, the following are also key
covers of songs either written or
arranged by Muddy Waters:

BOTTOM OF THE SEA
(Morganfield) by George
Thorogood and The Destroyers
(EMI America: 1986)
I CAN'T BE SATISFIED (Waters) by
The Rolling Stones (UK Decca:
1965)
LOOK WHAT YOU'VE DONE
(Morganfield) by The Rolling
Stones (UK Decca: 1971)
ROLLIN' AND TUMBLIN' (Waters)
by Canned Heat (Liberty: 1967)
by Cream (Reaction: 1966)
ROLLIN' STONE (Waters) by
Humble Pie (A&M: 1971)

MANY RIVERS TO CROSS
(Jimmy Cliff)
One of the highlights of Jimmy Cliff's
song score for the Jamaican movie,
"The Harder They Come" (1972).
   Original studio recording on

Island with a 'live' version on Cliff's *In Person* album (Reprise).

UK HIT: UB40 (Dep International: 1983)

Other recordings: Linda Ronstadt (Asylum); Stanley Turrentine (Fantasy); The Animals (UA); Nilsson (RCA); Joe Cocker.

MAYBE
(George Goldner)
This song provided the first female R&B vocal group hit, by the east coast quintet (later a quartet), The Chantels. Lead singer was Arlene Smith whose majestic voice gave out a memorable, mournful cry on this song which was later performed by The Delights on the soundtrack of "American Hot Wax" (Paramount: 1978).

US HITS: The Chantels (End: 1958) Black & Pop
The Three Degrees (Roulette: 1970) Black & Pop

MAYBE
The wonderful Chantels, whose second best single was the hypnotizing LOOK IN MY EYES (Barrett) which was also revived years later by The Three Degrees.

Other recordings: Peabo Bryson and Roberta Flack (Capitol); The Shangri-Las (Red Bird); The Spaniels (Buddah).

MAYBELLENE
(Chuck Berry)
Originally titled IDA MAY, Chuck Berry drew his inspiration from an old hillbilly tune called IDA RED. MAYBELLENE was in fact, not only Chuck Berry's first chart record, but also his first-ever release!

One of his great 'motorvatin' car songs, of which NO PARTICULAR PLACE TO GO was another prime example. He performed MAYBELLENE in both "Go, Johnny, Go" (Hal Roach: 1959) and "Hail! Hail! Rock 'N' Roll" (Universal: 1987), while his original Chess recording was utilized to great effect in Ralph Bakshi's animated feature "Heavy Traffic" (AIP: 1973).

US HITS: Chuck Berry (Chess: 1955) Black & Pop
Johnny Rivers (Imperial: 1964) Pop

Other recordings: Bob Luman (Epic); Conway Twitty (MCA); Jerry Lee Lewis (Mercury); Hoyt Axton (A&M); Carl Perkins (Jet); Gerry and The Pacemakers (UK Columbia); Amboy Dukes (Discreet); Tommy Sands (Capitol); George Jones and Johnny Paycheck (Epic); The Everly Brothers (Warner Bros).

See: MEMPHIS for other Chuck Berry songs.

Car songs
Among other R&B/R&R car songs are:

BEEP BEEP (Claps/Cicchetti) by The Playmates (Roulette: 1958)
BRAND NEW CADILLAC (Taylor) by The Clash (CBS: 1979)
BUICK 59 (Green) by The Medallions (Dootone: 1954).

MEMPHIS
The Thornton Wilder of rock 'n' roll! Chuck Berry's
songs tell in-depth stories and give detailed
descriptions of American culture and lifestyles.

CAR WASH (Whitfield) by Rose
Royce (MCA: 1976)

CARS (E.REG. MODEL) (Numan) by
Gary Numan (Beggars Banquet:
1979)

CRUISIN' (Robinson/Tarplin) by
Smokey Robinson (Tamla: 1979)

DEAD MAN'S CURVE (Berry/
Christian/Kornfeld/Wilson) by Jan
and Dean (Liberty: 1964)

DRIVIN' (Davies) by The Kinks (Pye:
1969)

DRIVE MY CAR (Lennon/
McCartney) by The Beatles
(Parlophone: 1965)

DRIVING IN MY CAR (Barson) by
Madness (Stiff: 1982)

FAST CAR (Chapman) by Tracy
Chapman (Elektra: 1988)

FREEWAY OF LOVE (Walden/
Cohen) by Aretha Franklin
(Arista: 1985)

G.T.O. (Wilkin) by Ronny and The
Daytonas (Mala: 1964)

HOT ROD LINCOLN (Ryan/
Stevenson)** by Johnny Bond
(Republic: 1960)
by Commander Cody and His
Lost Planet Airmen
(Paramount:1972) of the original
version by Charlie Ryan (Four
Star: 1960)

I GET AROUND (Wilson) by The
Beach Boys (Capitol: 1964)

LITTLE RED CORVETTE (Nelson)
by Prince (Warner Bros: 1983)

MUSTANG SALLY (Rice) by Wilson
Pickett (Atlantic: 1966)

NO MONEY DOWN (Berry) by
Chuck Berry (Chess: 1955)

NO PARTICULAR PLACE TO GO
(Berry) by Chuck Berry (Chess:
1964)

PINK CADILLAC (Springsteen)** by
Natalie Cole (Manhattan: 1988)

ROCKET 88 (Brenston) by Jackie
Brenston and His Delta Kings
(Chess:1951)

RED CADILLAC AND A BLACK
MOUSTACHE (Thompson/Lillie)
by Bob Luman (Imperial: 1957)

TELL LAURA I LOVE HER (Barry/
Raleigh)** by Ray Peterson (RCA:
1960)

MEMPHIS

(Chuck Berry)
Also known as MEMPHIS
TENNESSEE, this contains rock 'n'
roll's finest lyric reference to the
telephone system ('Long distance,
information'). It is one of Chuck
Berry's pivotal compositions though
he never charted with it in the
States. His original recording was
made in 1958 but it was not until the
British Pye label coupled his LET IT
ROCK with MEMPHIS on a 1963
reissue in their 'R&B Series' that the
song achieved chart status...it was a
double A-sided release.

Around this same time (1963),

Johnny Rivers, who not only cut a string of hit
revivals of classic rock 'n' roll songs, but also
owned the record label Soul City, for whom The
5th Dimension recorded most of their huge sellers,
including the Laura Nyro songs STONED SOUL
PICNIC and WEDDING BELL BLUES. His live
album, *The Last Boogie in Paris*, was a topically
titled release that included concert performances
of his *Blue Suede Shoes* studio LP.

guitarist Lonnie Mack cut a tightly rhythmic instrumental version, and it charted high on the US lists; that same track was reissued some fifteen years later and made a brief appearance in the British Top 50.

US HITS: Lonnie Mack (Fraternity: 1963) Black & Pop
Johnny Rivers (Imperial: 1964) Pop
UK HITS: Chuck Berry (Pye: 1963)
Dave Berry (UK Decca: 1963)
Lonnie Mack (Lightning: 1979)

Other recordings: Wilson Pickett (RCA); Bill Black's Combo (Hi); Elvis Presley (RCA); Conway Twitty (MCA); The Challengers (Crescendo); Harry Belafonte (RCA); The Hollies (Parlophone); The Ventures (Liberty); Jerry Lee Lewis (Mercury); Bo Diddley (Checker); Jan and Dean (Liberty); Buck Owens (Capitol); The Animals (MGM); Wayne Fontana and The Mindbenders (Fontana).

Sequel record: LITTLE MARIE (Berry) by Chuck Berry (Chess:1964).

See: CHANTILLY LACE for other telephone songs.

Chuck Berry Songs
Berry's own self-written hit records include: MAYBELLENE** (1955), SCHOOL DAY** and ROCK AND ROLL MUSIC** (both 1957), SWEET LITTLE SIXTEEN**, JOHNNY B.GOODE**, and RUN, RUDOLPH, RUN (co-written by Johnny Marks)**(all 1958), NADINE and NO PARTICULAR PLACE TO GO (both 1964), and MY DING-A-LING**(1972).

Among the *hit* records by other artists of Chuck Berry songs:

BACK IN THE USA** by Linda Ronstadt (Asylum: 1978)
BROWN-EYED HANDSOME MAN**
by Buddy Holly (Coral: 1963)
CAROL by Tommy Roe (ABC/Paramount: 1964)
FORTY DAYS by Ronnie Hawkins (Roulette: 1959) (Actually this was Chuck Berry's 1955 song THIRTY DAYS!)
MAYBELLENE** by Johnny Rivers (Imperial: 1964)
PROMISED LAND by Elvis Presley (RCA: 1974)
REELIN' AND ROCKIN'** by The Dave Clark Five (UK Columbia: 1965)
ROCK AND ROLL MUSIC** by The Beach Boys (Capitol: 1976)
ROLL OVER BEETHOVEN** by The Velaires (Jamie: 1961)
by The Beatles (Capitol: 1964)
by Electric Light Orchestra (UA: 1973)

Though never a hit, Johnnie Allan's cajun version of PROMISED LAND (Oval: 1974) is also considered a classic version.

Chuck Berry songs recorded by The Rolling Stones include: AROUND AND AROUND, BYE BYE JOHNNY, CAROL, COME ON, I'M TALKING ABOUT YOU (aka TALKIN' ABOUT YOU), YOU CAN'T CATCH ME. Of course, many other artists cut Chuck Berry songs, but his compositions played a particularly important role in the Stones' early work.

MERRY CHRISTMAS BABY
(Lou Baxter/Johnny Moore)
The all-time greatest R&B Christmas song, first recorded by Charles Brown with Johnny Moore's Three Blazers for Exclusive in 1947. Re-cut in 1956 by Charles Brown for Aladdin.

US HITS: Johnny Moore's Three Blazers (Exclusive: 1948) (plus successful reissues in later years) Black

Other recordings: Chuck Berry (Chess); Bruce Springsteen (A&M); Elvis Presley (RCA); Otis Redding (Atlantic); James Brown (King); Don Julian (Classic Artists); Lou Rawls (Capitol); Booker T. and The M.G.'s (Atlantic); Ike and Tina Turner (Warner Bros).

Christmas has been particularly good for Charles Brown who went on to record PLEASE COME HOME FOR CHRISTMAS (Brown/Redd) (King: 1960), while his wife Mabel Scott charted with BOOGIE WOOGIE SANTA CLAUS (Exclusive: 1949).

Christmas songs

Other key R&B/R&R Christmas songs and records:

BLUE CHRISTMAS (Hayes/Johnson) by Elvis Presley (RCA: 1964)
CHRISTMAS (BABY, PLEASE COME HOME) (Spector/Barry/Greenwich) by Darlene Love (Philles: 1961)
CHRISTMAS BLUES (Cook/Taylor/Vestine/Wilson/Taylor/Hite Jr) by Canned Heat (Liberty: 1968)
CHRISTMAS IN THE CONGO (Botkin/Masten) by The Marquees (Warner Bros: 1959)
EMPTY STOCKING BLUES (Moore/Huntley) by Floyd Dixon (Aladdin: 1950)
GEE WHIZ IT'S CHRISTMAS (Thomas/Cropper/Trouth) by Carla Thomas (Atlantic: 1963)
JINGLE BELL ROCK (Beal/Boothe) by Bobby Helms (Decca: 1957)
LITTLE SAINT NICK (Wilson) by The Beach Boys (Capitol: 1963)
(IT'S GONNA BE A) LONELY CHRISTMAS (Sprung/Rose) by The Orioles (Jubilee: 1948)
LONESOME CHRISTMAS (Glenn) by Lowell Fulson (Swingtime: 1950)
MONSTERS' HOLIDAY (Underwood) by Bobby (Boris) Pickett and The Crypt-Kickers (Garpax: 1962)

Petite Brenda Lee cut her perennial stocking stuffer, ROCKIN' AROUND THE CHRISTMAS TREE, in amongst her long list of tear-jerking ballads from I'M SORRY (Self/Allbritten) (Decca: 1960) to ALL ALONE AM I (Decca: 1962). With an English lyric by Arthur Altman, ALL ALONE was composed by Manos Hadjidakis of NEVER ON SUNDAY fame.

ROCKIN' AROUND THE CHRISTMAS TREE (Marks) by Brenda Lee (Decca: 1960) by Mel and Kim aka Mel Smith and Kim Wilde, recorded as a 'Comic Relief' charity single (Ten: 1987).
RUN RUDOLPH RUN (Brodie/Marks) by Chuck Berry (Chess: 1958)
SANTA CLAUS IS COMING (Ballard) by Hank Ballard and The Midnighters (King: 1963)
SANTA CLAUS IS COMIN' TO TOWN (Gillespie/Coots) by The Four Seasons (Vee-Jay: 1962)
WHITE CHRISTMAS (Berlin) by The Drifters featuring Clyde McPhatter and Bill Pinkney (Atlantic: 1954)

THE MIGHTY QUINN
(Bob Dylan)
Sub-titled QUINN THE ESKIMO, it
was one of three Dylan songs to
become hits for British group
Manfred Mann, along with IF YOU
GOTTA GO, GO NOW (HMV: 1965)
and JUST LIKE A WOMAN (Fontana:
1966).

In 1989, it became the title song of
the Denzel Washington/Robert
Townsend movie, "The Mighty
Quinn" (MGM: 1988) and is heard
three times in the film; performed
most memorably by Sheryl Lee
Ralph.

US HIT: Manfred Mann
                 (Mercury: 1968) Pop
UK HIT: Manfred Mann
                 (Fontana: 1968)

Other recordings: The Hollies
(Parlophone); Ian and Sylvia
(Vanguard); Brothers and Sisters
with Merry Clayton (Ode); Bob
Dylan (Columbia); Gary Puckett and
The Union Gap (Columbia).

See: BLOWIN' IN THE WIND for
other Bob Dylan songs.

MR TAMBOURINE MAN
(Bob Dylan)
One of folk-rock's greatest hits, this
was the song which launched The
Byrds' career. Dylan himself had
recorded it on his fifth album,
Bringing It All Back Home
(Columbia: 1965).

In a recent interview with Robert
Hilburn (of the "Los Angeles Times"),
David Crosby admitted that he hated
the song when he first heard it!

US HIT: The Byrds (Columbia:
                 1965) Pop
UK HIT: The Byrds (CBS: 1965)

Other recordings: Bob Dylan
(Columbia); Judy Collins (Elektra);
John Denver and The Chad Mitchell
Trio (Mercury); Melanie (Buddah);
The Barbarians (Laurie); Marmalade
(CBS); Johnny Rivers (Imperial);

Johnny Cash and Tammy Wynette
(Columbia); The Buckinghams
(U.S.A.); Lester Flatt and Earl
Scruggs (Columbia); Jonathan King;
Odetta (RCA); Glen Campbell
(Capitol); The Brothers Four
(Columbia).

MR. TAMBOURINE MAN was one of
thirteen Dylan compositions
recorded by The Byrds; the other
songs were:

ALL I REALLY WANT TO DO**
CHIMES OF FREEDOM
IT'S ALL OVER NOW, BABY BLUE
LAY DOWN YOUR WEARY TUNE
LAY, LADY, LAY
MY BACK PAGES
NOTHING WAS DELIVERED
POSITIVELY 4TH STREET
SPANISH HARLEM INCIDENT
THIS WHEEL'S ON FIRE**
THE TIMES THEY ARE
    A-CHANGIN'** and
YOU AIN'T GOING NOWHERE.

See: BLOWIN' IN THE WIND for
other Bob Dylan songs.

MOCKINGBIRD
(Inez Foxx/Charlie Foxx)
Sue Records' owner–producer Juggy
Murray tells of leaving Dempsey's
Restaurant in New York one morning
in 1963, when Inez Foxx and her
brother Charlie stopped him and
asked that he hear a song. Juggy fell
in love with MOCKINGBIRD and
called up arranger Bert Keyes to do
the session, but insisted that Bert
'write it the way they play it'. Inez got
solo artist credit, but it was Charlie
who sang those chanting answers.
Song became an R&B standard and,
eleven years later, James Taylor
adapted it for him and his wife, Carly
Simon; they later performed it in the
concert movie, "No Nukes" (Warner
Bros: 1980). MOCKINGBIRD was also
featured in "Eddie And The
Cruisers" (Embassy: 1983).

US HITS: Inez Foxx (*Symbol: 1963)
                 Pop & Black

MOCKINGBIRD
Charlie Foxx, his sister Inez, and the producer of
their million-selling MOCKINGBIRD, Juggy
Murray. Inez and Charlie cut a number of follow-
up singles for Symbol, a label within the Sue
Records group of which Juggy was and is still
president. Charlie Foxx recorded a solo single,
HERE WE GO ROUND THE MULBERRY BUSH
(Foxx) which was released under the name Chuck
Johnson (Symbol: 1963).

	Carly Simon and James Taylor (Elektra: 1974) Pop
UK HITS:	Inez and Charlie Foxx (Re-release of the Inez Foxx original) (UA: 1969) Carly Simon and James Taylor (Elektra: 1974)

Other recordings: Aretha Franklin
(Columbia); Inez and Charlie Foxx
(Re-recording: Dynamo); The
Banshees (EMI); Dusty Springfield
(UK Philips).

* On the Symbol label, a Sue subsidiary.

MONEY (THAT'S WHAT I WANT)
(Janie Bradford/Berry Gordy Jr)
A monster hit from the early days of
Motown. Originally recorded in 1960
by Barrett Strong, it became lodged
in many of our consciences, not just
because of Barrett's own version, but
also due to the ongoing number of
covers over the years. The Beatles
did it on their second album in 1963,
the LOUIE, LOUIE-famed Kingsmen
brought it back a year later, followed
by Motown's own in-house sax giant
Jr Walker, not forgetting The Rolling
Stones.
  The late John Belushi performed
MONEY in the 1978 movie "National
Lampoon's Animal House", and
Barrett Strong's hit version was
heard on the soundtrack of 1984's
"The Flamingo Kid" (20th Century
Fox).

US HITS:	Barrett Strong (Anna: 1960) Black & Pop

The Kingsmen (Wand:
1964) Pop
Jr Walker and The All
Stars (Soul: 1966) Black
& Pop
The Flying Lizards
(Virgin: 1979) Pop
The Contours (Motown:
1988) Pop

UK HITS: Bern Elliott and The
Fenmen (Decca: 1963)
The Flying Lizards
(Virgin: 1979)

Other recordings: The Supremes
(Motown); Jerry Lee Lewis (Sun);
The Miracles (Tamla); The Beatles
(Parlophone); Buddy Guy
(Vanguard); The Shakers (Polydor);
The Undertakers (Pye); The Rolling
Stones (UK Decca); Little Richard
(Okeh); The Plastic Ono Band
(Apple); Kingsize Taylor and The
Dominoes (Polydor); The Everly
Brothers (Warner Bros); Freddie and
The Dreamers (UK Columbia);
Waylon Jennings (Coral).

See: DEVIL WITH A BLUE DRESS
ON for other Motown hits.

MONEY HONEY
(Jesse Stone)
The very first Drifters' record was
MONEY HONEY, written by one of
the key black writers in early R&B
music; using either 'Jesse Stone' or
his real name 'Charles Calhoun', he
created or co-created these other
milestone songs: SHAKE, RATTLE
AND ROLL**, FLIP, FLOP AND FLY
(Joe Turner on Atlantic: 1955), YOUR
CASH AIN'T NOTHIN' BUT TRASH
(by The Clovers on Atlantic: 1954),
RAZZLE DAZZLE (by Bill Haley and
His Comets on Decca: 1955), and
COLE SLAW, a 1949 double-header
for both Frank Culley (Atlantic) and
Louis Jordan (Decca).

US HITS: Clyde McPhatter and The
Drifters (Atlantic: 1953)
Black
Elvis Presley (RCA: 1956)
Pop

UK HIT: The Bay City Rollers
(Bell: 1975)

Other recordings: Little Richard
(Vee-Jay); Ella Mae Morse (Capitol);
Tom Rush (Elektra); The Flying
Burrito Bros (A&M); Gary Glitter
(Bell); Ry Cooder (Reprise); 38
Special (A&M); Alvin Lee.

MONSTER MASH
(Bobby Pickett/Lenny Capizzi)
Actor Bobby Pickett took on the
guise of Boris Karloff and came up
with this all-time Halloween
favourite. Released originally by
Gary Paxton on his Garpax label
(see also under ALLEY OOP).

US HIT: Bobby 'Boris' Pickett and
The Crypt-Kickers
(Garpax: 1962) Pop
UK HIT: Bobby 'Boris' Pickett and
The Crypt-Kickers
(London: 1962)

Other recordings: The Beach Boys
(Capitol); The Bonzo Dog Doo Dah
Band (UA).

Bobby Pickett attempted to follow up

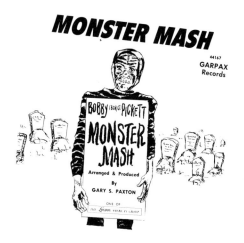

MONSTER MASH
The original single from 1962.

this with other Monster-related singles, including:

MONSTERS' HOLIDAY (Underwood) (Garpax: 1962)
THE MONSTER SWIM (Denos/ Paxton) c/w THE WEREWOLF WATUSI (Pickett/Paxton) (RCA: 1964)
ME AND MY MUMMY (Metromedia: 1968).

Monster records
Other key R&B/R&R Monster records are:

APE CALL (Drake) by Nervous Norvus (Dot: 1956)
THE CREATURE (FROM A SCIENCE FICTION MOVIE) by Buchanan and Ancell (Flying Saucer: 1957)
DINNER WITH DRAC Parts 1 and 2 (Sheldon/Land) by John Zacherle 'The Cool Ghoul' (Cameo: 1958)
FRANKENSTEIN OF '59 (Goodman/ Goodman) by Buchanan and Goodman with Count Dracula (Novelty: 1959)
FRANKENSTEIN'S DEN (Johnson/ Murry) by The Hollywood Flames (Ebb: 1958)
HAUNTED HOUSE (Geddins) by Jumpin' Gene Simmons (Hi: 1964) original version by Johnny Fuller (Specialty: 1959) also recorded by Roy Buchanan (Polydor: 1972)
I PUT A SPELL ON YOU (Hawkins)** by Screamin' Jay Hawkins (Okeh: 1956)
THE IDOL WITH THE GOLDEN HEAD (Leiber/Stoller) by The Coasters (Atlantic: 1957)
MIDNIGHT STROLL (Jackson/ Coman/Guerra) by The Revels (Norgolde: 1959)
MORGUS THE MAGNIFICENT (Clesi/Bayhi) by Morgus and The Ghouls (Vin: 1959)*
THE PURPLE PEOPLE EATER (Wooley) by Sheb Wooley (MGM: 1958)
SCREAMIN' BALL AT DRACULA HALL (Brandon/Williams) by The

Duponts (Roulette: 1958)
THE SHADOW KNOWS (Leiber/ Stoller) by The Coasters (Atlantic: 1958)
THE SPIDER AND THE FLY (Strong/ Stevens) by Bobby Christian With The Allen Sisters (Mercury: 1963)
WELCOME TO MY NIGHTMARE (Cooper/Wagner) by Alice Cooper (Atlantic: 1975)
WEREWOLF (Wadsworth/Hodge) by The Frantics (Dolton: 1960)

*'Morgus The Magnificent' was a local TV personality who introduced horror movies on a New Orleans station in the 1950s. Frankie Ford, Dr John and Jerry Byrne got together with The Clowns (Huey Smith's band) and recorded this one-off novelty for Ace's subsidiary label, Vin.

MONY, MONY
(Tommy James/Bobby Bloom/Ritchie Cordell/Bo Gentry)
Tommy James tells of looking out a window and seeing the Mutual of New York insurance company sign, the initials of which gave him the title for this song. Co-written with MONTEGO BAY hitmaker Bobby Bloom. Billy Idol's remake came around the same time that Tiffany was charting with another of Tommy James' hits, I THINK WE'RE ALONE NOW**.

US HITS: Tommy James and The Shondells (Roulette: 1968) Pop
Billy Idol (Chrysalis: 1987) Pop
UK HITS: Tommy James and The Shondells (Major Minor: 1968)

Other recording: Celia and The Mutations (UA).

MOTHER-IN-LAW
(Allen Toussaint)
Among the most successful New Orleans crossover hit songs, full of tongue-in-cheek humour and Allen Toussaint's jaunty rhythms. The bass voice on the original was provided

by Benny Spellman who drove around New Orleans telling everybody 'that's me on the record'! Toussaint remembers feeling that they should give Benny his own song; in fact, he gave him two: LIPSTICK TRACES and FORTUNE TELLER, both of which became classics in their own right.

US HITS: Ernie K-Doe (Minit: 1961)
           Black & Pop
           Clarence Carter (Fame:
           1973) Black
UK HIT: Ernie K-Doe (London:
           1961)

Other recordings: The Kingsmen (Wand); Herman's Hermits (UK Columbia); Gary Paxton (Capitol); The Newbeats (Hickory); The Laddins (Relic).

Answer records: GET OUT OF MY HOUSE by Ernie K-Doe (Minit: 1962) MY MOTHER-IN-LAW (IS IN MY HAIR AGAIN) by Ernie K-Doe (Duke: 1964) BROTHER-IN-LAW (HE'S A MOOCHER) by Paul Peek (Fairlane: 1961) SON-IN-LAW by The Blossoms (Challenge: 1961) by Louise Brown (Witch: 1961).

Allen Toussaint songs

Formidable force in contemporary New Orleans music, singer–songwriter–producer Toussaint was particularly associated with the local Minit label output from late 1959 through early 1963 and thereafter with the late Lee Dorsey.

Among the hit records of other Allen Toussaint songs:

ALL THESE THINGS by The Uniques featuring Joe Stampley (Paula: 1966)
A CERTAIN GIRL by Warren Zevon (Asylum: 1980)
GET OUT OF MY LIFE, WOMAN by Lee Dorsey (Amy: 1966)
HOLY COW by Lee Dorsey (Amy: 1966)
I CRIED MY LAST TEAR by Ernie K-Doe (Minit: 1961)
IT'S RAININ' by Shakin' Stevens (Epic: 1981)
JAVA (with Alvin Tyler and Freddy Friday) by Al Hirt (RCA: 1964)
LIPSTICK TRACES by Benny Spellman (Minit: 1962) by The O'Jays (Imperial: 1965)
PAIN IN MY HEART by Otis Redding (Volt: 1963)
PLAY SOMETHING SWEET (BRICKYARD BLUES) by Three Dog Night (Dunhill: 1974)
RIDE YOUR PONY by Lee Dorsey (Amy: 1965)
SHOORAH SHOORAH by Betty Wright (Alston: 1974)
SNEAKIN' SALLY THROUGH THE ALLEY by Robert Palmer (Island: 1974)
SOUTHERN NIGHTS by Glen Campbell (Capitol: 1977)
WHIPPED CREAM by Herb Alpert and The Tijuana Brass (A&M: 1965)
WORKING IN THE COAL MINE** by Lee Dorsey (Amy: 1966)
YES WE CAN CAN by The Pointer Sisters (Blue Thumb: 1973)

Singer–songwriter–producer Allen Toussaint, whose string of influential hits helped to solidify New Orleans' place on the musical map and whose efforts continue to this day.

MY BABE

(Willie Dixon/Charles Stone)
Little Walter (Muddy Waters'
harmonica player) originally refused
to sing this because it was based on
the gospel song, THIS TRAIN
(DON'T CARRY NO GAMBLERS),
but it ultimately became a Number
One hit for him. The Righteous
Brothers' version made it just into the
Top 75 in America in 1963.

US HIT: Little Walter (Checker:
            1955) Black

Other recordings: The Righteous
Brothers (Moonglow); Lightnin'
Hopkins (Excello); Jimmy
Witherspoon (Prestige); Long John
Baldry (UA); The Everly Brothers
(Warner Bros); Elvis Presley (RCA);
Albert King (Tomato); Gerry and
The Pacemakers (UK Columbia);
Mickey Gilley (Playboy); Frances
Faye (Crescendo); Willie Dixon;
Ricky Nelson (Imperial); Lightnin'
Slim (Excello); John Hammond
(Vanguard); Roy Head (Back Beat);
Cliff Richard (UK Columbia); Gene
Ammons (Prestige); The Spencer
Davis Group (Fontana); The
Romaines (Epic).

See: I'M YOUR HOOCHIE
COOCHIE MAN for other Willie
Dixon songs.

MY BOY LOLLIPOP

(Robert Spencer/Johnny Roberts/
Morris Levy)
The first blue-beat hit which was an
Island Records production. Written
by the same Bobby Spencer (a
member of The Cadillacs) who
wrote I'M NOT A JUVENILE
DELINQUENT. Millie's original
record featured Rod Stewart playing
harmonica.
    Performed by Millie in "Go-Go Big
Beat", a 1965 British concoction.

UK HITS: Millie (Fontana: 1964)
          Bad Manners (recorded
          as MY GIRL

LOLLIPOP) (Magnet:
1982)

US HIT: Millie Small (Smash: 1964)
            Pop

MY BOYFRIEND'S BACK

(Robert Feldman/Gerald Goldstein/
Richard Gottehrer)
One of the great girl-group anthems,
written and originally produced by
Feldman, Goldstein and Gottehrer,
who also wrote other 1960s hits like I
WANT CANDY (they actually *were*
The Strangeloves!). The Angels
(three white girls) were heard
singing MY BOYFRIEND'S BACK on
the soundtrack of Kenneth Anger's
short film, "Scorpio Rising", in 1963.
Performed by Sandy Duncan, Jill
Eikenberry and Judith Light in the
TV movie, "My Boyfriend's Back"
(NBC: 1989), in which Mary Wells,
Gary Puckett, Peggy March, Gary
Lewis and the then-current line-up of
The Penguins also appeared.

US HIT: The Angels (Smash: 1963)
            Pop

Other recordings: The Chiffons
(Laurie); Sarah Brightman (Whisper);
Melissa Manchester (Arista); Martha
and The Vandellas (Gordy); Kristy
and Jimmy McNichol (RCA).

Answer record: YOUR
BOYFRIEND'S BACK by Bobby
Comstock (Lawn: 1963)

Sequel record: THE GUY WITH THE
BLACK EYE (Feldman/Goldstein/
Gottehrer/Kalina) by The Angels
(Smash: 1963).

Messrs Feldman/Goldstein/Gottehrer
also wrote SORROW, the single hit
by British group The Merseys
(Fontana: 1966).

Answer records

Answer records usually make direct
reference to the lyric of the former
song and are obvious from their
titles. The 'answer song' craze was

particularly rife in the 1950s and 1960s and there was often more than one answer to a given hit; for instance, as the entry on WILL YOU LOVE ME TOMORROW indicates, there were at least three reply songs. Throughout this book, references are made to answer songs where relevant but here is a selective list of songs which answered hits that are not individually covered in this volume.

BALLAD OF THE YELLOW BERET by The Beach Bums (actually Bob Seger) (Are You Kidding Me?: 1966) answering BALLAD OF THE GREEN BERETS (Sadler/Moore) by Sgt Barry Sadler (RCA: 1966)

(HEY THERE) BIG BAD WOLF (Blackwell/Kapuzyski) by The Sham-ettes (MGM: 1966) answering LIL' RED RIDING HOOD (Blackwell) by Sam The Sham and The Pharoahs (MGM: 1966)

BILLY, I'VE GOT TO GET TO TOWN (Tillis/Dana) by Geraldine (aka Dodie) Stevens (World Pacific: 1969) answering RUBY, DON'T TAKE YOUR LOVE TO TOWN (Tillis) by Kenny Rogers and The First Edition (Reprise: 1969)

BY THE TIME YOU GET TO PHOENIX by Wanda Jackson (Capitol: 1968) answering BY THE TIME I GET TO PHOENIX (Webb) by Glen Campbell (Capitol: 1967)

FOUR SHY GIRLS (IN THEIR ITSY BITSY TEENIE WEENIE YELLOW POLKA DOT BIKINIS (Vance/Pockriss) by The Girlfriends (Pioneer: 1960) answering ITSY BITSY TEENIE WEENIE YELLOW POLKA DOT BIKINI (Vance/Pockriss) by Brian Hyland (Leader: 1960)

GO AWAY LITTLE BOY (Goffin/ King) by Marlena Shaw (Cadet: 1967) answering GO AWAY LITTLE GIRL (Goffin/King) by Steve Lawrence (Columbia: 1962)

HIPPIE FROM OLEMA (Levinger) by The Youngbloods (Raccoon: 1970) answering OKIE FROM MUSKOGEE (Haggard/Burris) by Merle Haggard (Capitol: 1969)

I PUT THE BOMP (Mann/Goffin) by Frankie Lymon (Roulette: 1961) and WE'RE THE GUYS by Morecambe & Wise (Pye 1961), both answering WHO PUT THE BOMP (IN THE BOMP BA BOMP BA BOMP) (Mann/Goffin) by Barry Mann (ABC/Paramount: 1961)

I'M JUST A DOWN HOME GIRL (Taylor) by The Ad Libs (Blue Cat: 1965) answering DOWN HOME GIRL (Leiber/Butler) by Alvin Robinson (Blue Cat/ 1965)

I'M THE GIRL ON WOLVERTON MOUNTAIN by Jo Ann Campbell (Cameo: 1962) answering WOLVERTON MOUNTAIN (Kilgore/King) by Claude King (Columbia: 1962)

I'M YOUR WILD THANG (Mamado) by Mamado and She (Attitude: 1989) answering WILD THING (Young/Smith/Dike/Ross) by Tone Loc (Delicious Vinyl: 1988)

NOW I'VE GOT A WITNESS (Phelge) by The Rolling Stones (UK Decca: 1964) answering CAN I GET A WITNESS (Holland/ Dozier/Holland) by Marvin Gaye (Tamla: 1963)

QUEEN OF THE HOUSE (Miller/ Taylor) by Jody Miller (Capitol: 1965) answering KING OF THE ROAD (Miller) by Roger Miller (Smash: 1965)

THE SOUND OF MY MAN (Cooke) by Theola Kilgore (Candix: 1960)

answering CHAIN GANG (Cooke) by Sam Cooke (RCA: 1960)

WE TOLD YOU NOT TO MARRY by Titus Turner (Glover: 1959) answering I'M GONNA GET MARRIED (Logan/Price) by Lloyd Price (ABC/Paramount: 1959)

WHY DON'T I RUN AWAY FROM YOU? (Berns) by Kiki Dee (Fontana: 1971) answering I'M GONNA RUN AWAY FROM YOU (Berns) by Tami Lynn (Atlantic: 1966; released by Mojo: 1971)

YES, I AM EXPERIENCED by Eric Burdon and The Animals (MGM: 1967) answering ARE YOU EXPERIENCED? (Hendrix) by The Jimi Hendrix Experience (Reprise: 1967)

YOU THREW A LUCKY PUNCH (Robinson/White/Covay) by Gene Chandler (Vee-Jay: 1962) answering YOU BEAT ME TO THE PUNCH (Robinson/White) by Mary Wells (Motown: 1962)

Occasionally, answer songs have been more personal, as in the case of Carole King writing and recording OH, NEIL (Alpine: 1960), directly responding to Neil Sedaka's OH! CAROL smash (RCA: 1959), which was written specifically for her. Which also brings to mind another song which is not an answer in any way, but Connie Francis asked Neil Sedaka and his then writing partner, Howard Greenfield, to write a song for teen idol, Frankie Avalon. They wrote it, Connie recorded it and it became a Top 10 song in the States; complete with a brief, spoken introduction, it was called FRANKIE (MGM: 1959).

For answer records to songs detailed elsewhere in this book, see individual entries on the following:

ARE YOU LONESOME TONIGHT?
BILLIE JEAN
BRING IT ON HOME TO ME
CAN I GET A WITNESS
CHANTILLY LACE
DADDY'S HOME

DONNA
DUKE OF EARL
EVE OF DESTRUCTION
GET A JOB
HE'LL HAVE TO GO
HIGH HEEL SNEAKERS
HIT THE ROAD JACK
HOUND DOG
I GOT A WOMAN
I'M GONNA BE A WHEEL SOMEDAY
I LIKE IT LIKE THAT
I'M A WOMAN
IF I WERE A CARPENTER
IN THE MIDNIGHT HOUR
IT'S A MAN'S MAN'S MAN'S WORLD
IT'S YOUR THING
LITTLE SISTER
MOTHER-IN-LAW
MY BOYFRIEND'S BACK
SAVE THE LAST DANCE FOR ME
SHERRY
SHOP AROUND
SIXTEEN CANDLES
SOLDIER BOY
TAKE GOOD CARE OF MY BABY
TELL LAURA I LOVE HER
THIS DIAMOND RING
UNIVERSAL SOLDIER
WILL YOU LOVE ME TOMORROW.

You will also find reference throughout this book to 'female versions' of key songs. These are usually the lyrics of the original song with simply the relevant genders altered; for example, SHE CRIED became HE CRIED, and TELL HIM became TELL HER. Another example is Otis Redding's MR PITIFUL (Redding/Cropper) (Volt: 1965) which was followed by MISS PITIFUL by Etta James (Cadet: 1969).

MY DING-A-LING

(Dave Bartholomew/Chuck Berry) Here's a song full of double-meanings, in whichever version you may hear! Dave Bartholomew is the New Orleans trumpeter–bandleader who co-wrote most of

Fats Domino's million-selling hits. He wrote this novelty song first as MY DING-A-LING (referring specifically to the male sexual organ) and recorded it himself on King Records in 1951. He re-cut it in 1952 on Imperial under the revised title LITTLE GIRL SING DING-A-LING and then two years later, he produced another variation called TOY BELL sung by a group called The Bees.

Also in 1954, Dave Bartholomew took the premise a step further with his song THE REAL THING (recorded by The Spiders on Imperial), the lyric of which states: 'It was the real thing that made my ding-a-ling ring!' Some years later, Chuck Berry adapted the same song and began singing it as MY TAMBOURINE, which he later recorded as MY DING-A-LING on a live album in 1972. Eventually it was released as a single which topped the charts in both Britain and the USA.

US HIT: Chuck Berry (Chess: 1972) Black & Pop
UK HIT: Chuck Berry (Chess: 1972)

See: I HEAR YOU KNOCKING for other Dave Bartholomew songs.

See: MEMPHIS for other Chuck Berry songs.

MY GENERATION

(Pete Townshend)
Townshend wrote this as a send-up of blues songs which went 'talkin' about' something or other, little knowing that he was indeed writing an anthem for his generation, or as he says, 'the hymn. The patriotic song they sing at Who football matches'. The one line 'Hope I die before I get old' perhaps sums up the essence of rock 'n' roll better than any other. For the record, the group added Roger Daltrey's memorable stutter and John Entwhistle's remarkable bass solo to produce one of the all-time classics. In 1978, Billy Idol had his first hit with his group Generation X with the punk rock answer to MY GENERATION – YOUR GENERATION.

The Who's memorable instrument-smashing performance at the 1967 Monterey Pop Festival was immortalized in the "Monterey Pop" film (Pennebaker: 1968). Song also is a highlight of "The Kids Are Alright" (New World: 1979), the retrospective of The Who's career.

UK HIT: The Who (Brunswick: 1965)
US HIT: The Who (Decca: 1966) Pop

Other recordings: Patti Smith (Arista); Count Five (Double Shot).

Answer record: YOUR GENERATION by Generation X (with Billy Idol) (Chrysalis: 1977)

MY GIRL

(William Robinson/Ronald White)
Not the first Temptations hit, but the song which really launched the group into superstar status. Their record showed off David (brother of Jimmy) Ruffin as one of the great Motown group singers. The song, co-written by Smokey Robinson, is a kind of sequel to the previous year's Mary Wells success, MY GUY (Robinson), without being strictly an answer song.

MY GIRL has been used in a number of medley singles including the two listed below, plus one by Amii Stewart and Johnny Bristol (Handshake: 1980) which actually blended MY GUY with MY GIRL together on the same record; Amii Stewart later re-cut virtually the same medley, this time with Deon Estus on Sedition in 1986.

In England, EMI were only semi-successful in getting The Temps' original record off the ground in early 1965, but the Otis Redding version was a much bigger hit later the same year.

US HITS: The Temptations (Gordy: 1965) Black & Pop
Bobby Vee: Medley with HEY GIRL (Goffin/King) (Liberty: 1968) Pop
Eddie Floyd (Stax: 1970) Black
Daryl Hall, John Oates, David Ruffin and Eddie Kendrick: Medley with THE WAY YOU DO THE THINGS YOU DO (Robinson/Rogers) (RCA: 1985) Black & Pop
Suave (Capitol: 1988) Black & Pop
UK HITS: The Temptations (Stateside: 1965)
Otis Redding (Atlantic: 1965)
Amii Stewart and Johnny Bristol: Medley with MY GUY (Robinson) (Hansa: 1980)

Other recordings: The Rolling Stones (UK Decca); Jackie Wilson and Count Basie (Brunswick); Al Green (Hi); The Whispers (Solar); Glen Campbell (Capitol); Georgie Fame and The Blue Flames (UK Columbia); Stevie Wonder (Tamla); Country Joe and The Fish (Vanguard); David Ruffin (Motown); Willie Mitchell (Hi); Earl Van Dyke and The Soul Brothers (Soul); The Mamas and The Papas (Dunhill); The American Breed (Acta); Helen Shapiro (UK Columbia); The Outsiders (Capitol); Carl Wayne and The Vikings (ABC).

See: DEVIL WITH A BLUE DRESS ON for other Motown hits.

See: SHOP AROUND for other songs by Smokey Robinson.

MY GUY
(William Robinson)
The song which took Motown to the top of the American charts for the very first time. Written and produced by Smokey Robinson, this was Mary Wells' shining hour after a series of memorable singles which included two R&B Number Ones, YOU BEAT ME TO THE PUNCH (Robinson/White) (Motown: 1962) plus TWO LOVERS (Robinson), released by Motown in late 1962 and which peaked early the following year. Mary Wells was one of Motown's first major stars and she was the key supporting act on The Beatles' UK tour of 1964.

The Amii Stewart/Johnny Bristol medley which included MY GUY was a minor US hit in 1980, the year it made it into the British Top 40.

US HITS: Mary Wells (Motown: 1964) Black & Pop

MY GUY
Mary Wells was one of the Motown family's first superstars, racking up a series of R&B sellers between 1960 and 1964. Her other most popular titles were YOU BEAT ME TO THE PUNCH (Robinson/White) and TWO LOVERS (Robinson) (both Motown: 1962). Mary later married Cecil Womack.

Sister Sledge (Cotillion: 1982) Black & Pop

UK HITS: Mary Wells (Stateside: 1964)

Mary Wells (Tamla Motown: 1972 Re-release)

Amii Stewart and Johnny Bristol: Medley with MY GIRL (Robinson/White) (Hansa: 1980)

Other recordings: Margo Smith (Warner Bros); Dara Sedaka (RSO); Petula Clark (MGM).

See: DEVIL WITH A BLUE DRESS ON for other Motown hits.

See: SHOP AROUND for other Smokey Robinson songs.

MY LITTLE RED BOOK

(Burt Bacharach/Hal David)
Sub-titled ALL I DO IS TALK ABOUT YOU. Written for and first performed by Manfred Mann on the soundtrack of "What's New Pussycat" (United Artists: 1965), the Woody Allen-scripted comedy, directed by Clive Donner and starring Peter Sellers, Peter O'Toole, Romy Schneider, Capucine and Woody himself in a supporting role. Manfred's lead singer at that time was Paul Jones, who embarked on a solo career in 1966.
   RED BOOK was never a hit for the Manfreds and it took American group, Love (led by guitarist-singer Arthur Lee), to give the song chart status.

US HIT: Love (Elektra: 1966) Pop

Other recordings: Greg Kihn (EMI America); The Wild Ones (UA); Burt Bacharach with Tony Middleton (Kapp); The Rockin' Berries (Piccadilly); Toni Basil (Chrysalis); Ted Nugent (Epic); Wild Thing (Warner Bros).

See: MAKE IT EASY ON YOURSELF for other Burt Bacharach and Hal David songs.

MY TOOT-TOOT

(Simien)
Cajun novelty song, originally recorded by Rockin' Sidney.

US HITS: Rockin' Sidney (Epic: 1985) Country

Jean Knight (Mirage: 1985) Pop

Other recordings: Fats Domino and Doug Kershaw (Toot Toot); Denise La Salle (Malaco) (credited as: MY TU-TU); John Fogerty (Warner Bros); Jimmy C. Newman (RCA).

The Fats Domino/Doug Kershaw version was released on a single which was a promotional release produced for a New Orleans-based fast food chain, Popeye's Famous Fried Chicken And Biscuits, Inc., and a Crescent City radio station, WTIX 690AM. B-side of the record was the same melody to which Fats sang a lyric re-written as a commercial for the chain: DON'T MESS WITH MY POPEYE!.

MYSTERY TRAIN

(Sam Phillips/Herman Parker)
Rockabilly song originally styled as a straight blues. Written by Sam Phillips (founder of Sun Records, the first label to which Elvis was signed) and (Little) Junior Parker, a blues singer/harmonica player who cut the original of MYSTERY TRAIN with his group, Little Junior and The Blue Flames on Sun in 1953. The first Presley version was the singer's final single on Sun in 1955. Elvis later re-cut the song on 'live' albums for RCA. As legendary as this song became, it has never figured on any of the major American charts. Performed by Paul Butterfield and Levon Helm in the concert movie, "The Last Waltz" (United Artists: 1978).

US HIT: Elvis Presley (RCA: 1956) Country

UK HIT: Elvis Presley (HMV: 1957)

Other recordings: Paul Butterfield Blues Band (Elektra); The Band (Capitol); The Staples (Warner Bros); James Burton (A&M); The Amazing Rhythm Aces (ABC); John Hammond (Atlantic); Jerry Reed and Chet Atkins (RCA); Junior Wells (Vanguard); Bob Luman; Phil Sweet (Charly).

See: SUSPICIOUS MIND for other Elvis Presley hits.

NA NA HEY HEY KISS HIM GOODBYE
(Gary DeCarlo/Dale Frashuer/Paul Leka)
British girl group Bananarama started their own trend of covering earlier American hits, beginning with HE WAS REALLY SAYING SOMETHING (Whitfield/Stevenson/Holland) (Deram: 1962) which had originally charted for The Velvelettes on Motown's V.I.P. label in 1965; they revived NA NA HEY HEY in 1983, and not long afterwards, brought Shocking Blue's VENUS back to the charts. More recently the girls worked on another Motown song, NATHAN JONES (Wakefield/Caston) with which The Supremes first scored on Motown in 1971.

US HITS: Steam (Fontana: 1969)
           Black & Pop
           The Nylons (Open Air: 1987) Pop
UK HITS: Steam (Fontana: 1970)
           Bananarama (London: 1983)

Other recordings: J. J. Mack (Salsoul); Manchester United Supporters Club (Jet).

The Nylons are a Canadian group who specialize in singing a capella versions of golden oldies, including NA NA re-titled simply KISS HIM GOODBYE, as well as the Turtles' classic, HAPPY TOGETHER (Bonner/Gordon); they also sing (with Diana Canova) the title song to the American television series, "Throb" (Cooper).

NATHAN JONES
(Kathy Wakefield/Leonard Caston)
Bananarama's re-working of this Supremes oldie was produced by the powerhouse British team of Stock, Aitken and Waterman who have, coincidentally, been compared in the trade press as following in the footsteps of Motown's original in-house trio: Holland, Dozier and Holland.
    The Bananarama record was used on the soundtrack of the Dustin Hoffman/Tom Cruise oscar winning movie, "Rain Man" (UA: 1988).

US HIT: The Supremes (Motown: 1971) Black & Pop
UK HITS: The Supremes (Tamla Motown: 1971)
           Bananarama (London: 1988)

This was, by comparison, a much more successful revival of a Motown girl-group oldie than Sheena Easton's 1986 cover of JIMMY MACK (Holland/Dozier/Holland), the Martha and The Vandellas classic from 1967.

See: DEVIL WITH A BLUE DRESS ON for other Motown hits.

NEEDLES AND PINS
(Jack Nitzsche/Salvatore Bono)
Key love song of the 1960s written by Jack Nitzsche, arranger of many Phil Spector productions, and Sonny Bono, whose own studio work attempted to emulate Spector's 'wall of sound' trademark. Bono's wife and singing partner, Cher, cut the song

on an album, but its initial popularity was the result of a single by Jackie DeShannon (herself a songwriter), though her version was outstripped by British group, The Searchers, who took it to Number One at the height of the 'Mersey Beat' era.

US HITS: Jackie DeShannon
(Liberty: 1963) Pop
The Searchers
(Kapp:1964) Pop
Smokie (RSO: 1977) Pop
Tom Petty and The
Heartbreakers with
Stevie Nicks (MCA:
1986) Pop
UK HITS: The Searchers (Pye: 1963)
Smokie (RSO: 1977)

Other recordings: Cher (Imperial); The Ramones (Sire); Del Shannon (Amy); Gary Lewis and The Playboys (Liberty); Crack The Sky (Lifesong); Bobby Vee (Liberty); Love And Tears.

Among the other American songs 'covered' by The Searchers were: WHEN YOU WALK IN THE ROOM**, LOVE POTION NUMBER NINE** and DON'T THROW YOUR LOVE AWAY (Wisner/Jackson) which was originally released by The Orlons (Cameo: 1963) but which became a Number One in the UK for The Searchers (Pye: 1964) and a subsequent Top 10 single in the US (Kapp: 1964). The Searchers' first British chart-topper was SWEETS FOR MY SWEET (Pomus/ Shuman) which had initially been a big song for The Drifters on Atlantic in 1961.

See: WHEN YOU WALK IN THE ROOM for songs by Jackie DeShannon.

NEVER BEEN TO SPAIN
(Hoyt Axton)
Most popular of all the songs written by actor-singer Hoyt Axton. His mother was the composer of HEARTBREAK HOTEL** and Hoyt's highest charted song to date was

JOY TO THE WORLD, an American Number One for Three Dog Night (Dunhill: 1971). The same group had the original hit with NEVER BEEN TO SPAIN which was heard in the documentary, "Elvis On Tour" (MGM: 1972).

US HIT: Three Dog Night (Dunhill: 1972) Pop

Other recordings: Morning (Fantasy); Waylon Jennings (RCA); Three Dog Night (Dunhill); Elvis Presley (RCA); Ike and Tina Turner (UA).

Hoyt Axton's other compositions include NO NO SONG, a US Top 5 song for Ringo Starr (Apple: 1975), and THE PUSHER which Steppenwolf performed on the soundtrack of Peter Fonda and Dennis Hopper's movie, "Easy Rider" (Columbia: 1969).

NEVER CAN SAY GOODBYE
(Clifton Davis)
Written for The Jackson 5 by Clifton Davis (composer of another Jacksons' hit LOOKIN' THROUGH THE WINDOWS in 1972), NEVER CAN SAY GOODBYE was first revived four years later. The song was arranged to a crackling disco dance beat, launching former Soul Satisfier Gloria Gaynor's solo career, which later peaked with I WILL SURVIVE (Fekaris/Perren).

Writer Clifton Davis is currently the star of the American television sitcom, "Amen".

Jimmy Somerville and Richard Coles aka the two Communards had previously covered another old hit, DON'T LEAVE ME THIS WAY**.

US HITS: The Jackson 5 (Motown:
1971) Black & Pop
Isaac Hayes (Enterprise:
1971) Black & Pop
Gloria Gaynor (MGM:
1975) Black & Pop
UK HITS: The Jackson 5 (Tamla
Motown: 1971)

Gloria Gaynor (MGM: 1974)

Other recordings: The Osmonds
(MGM); The Sandpipers (A&M); Cal
Tjader (Fantasy); Little Beaver (Cat).

See: DEVIL WITH A BLUE DRESS
ON for other Motown hits.

NEW ORLEANS
(Frank Guida/Joseph Royster)
Unlike WALKING TO NEW
ORLEANS, which Fats Domino
recorded in that very city, US Bonds'
original version of NEW ORLEANS
came booming out of Norfolk,
Virginia! Legrand Records president
Frank Guida rightly claims that this
was the first record to use the
double bass beat. It also began the
hit-making career of Gary Bonds,
whose 1981 comeback records were
produced by Bruce Springsteen and
Miami ('Little Steven') Steve van
Zandt.

US HITS: US Bonds (Legrand: 1960)
        Pop & Black
        Eddie Hodges
          (Aurora: 1965) Pop
        Neil Diamond
          (Bang: 1968) Pop
UK HITS: US Bonds
          (Top Rank: 1961)
        Bern Elliott and The

NEW ORLEANS
Gary Bonds' follow-up hit to NEW ORLEANS was
QUARTER TO THREE (Barge/Guida/Royster/
Anderson), a song based on an earlier record
called A NIGHT WITH DADDY G. Daddy G was
saxman Gene Barge who was heard on all the
early Gary Bonds classics.

Fenmen
(UK Decca: 1964)
Harley Quinne (Bell: 1972)
Gillan (Virgin: 1981)

Other recordings: The Dirt Band
(UA); Don Lang and His Twisters
(UK Decca); Cash McCall
(Plantation); The Ventures (Liberty);
Tommy Jennings (Monument); Bill
Haley and His Comets (Sonet); Big
Boy Myles (Ace); Hank Williams Jr
(Warner/Curb).

NIGHT TRAIN
(Jimmy Forrest/Oscar Washington/
Lewis C. Simpkins)
Tenor saxman Jimmy Forrest spent
time in the Duke Ellington Orchestra
and was inspired to write NIGHT
TRAIN after one of the Duke's
compositions, HAPPY GO LUCKY
LOCAL.
   James Brown's version heard on
the soundtrack of "Quadrophenia"
(Who Films: 1979).

US HITS: Jimmy Forrest (United:
          1952) Black
        Buddy Morrow (RCA:
          1952) Pop
        James Brown (King: 1962)
        Black & Pop

Other recordings: The Dirty Dozen
Brass Band (Rounder); The Viscounts
(Madison); Maynard Ferguson
(Mainstream); Richard Hayman
(Mercury); Oscar Peterson (Verve);
Louis Prima (Capitol); Georgie Fame
and The Blue Flames (UK Columbia);
Lionel Hampton (Audio Fidelity);
King Curtis.

NOT FADE AWAY
(Norman Petty/Charles Hardin)
Buddy Holly's song, co-written under
his pseudonym of Charles Hardin in
the style of Bo Diddley, became a
raw, R&B classic as styled by The
Stones, and released on their fourth
UK single.
   There have been two mini-hit
revivals in the States, by Tanya

Tucker (MCA: 1979) and Eric Hine (Montage: 1981).

The original Crickets' record (Brunswick: 1957) was heard on the soundtrack of John Carpenter's movie, "Christine" (Columbia: 1983).

UK HIT: The Rolling Stones
            (Decca: 1964)
US HIT: The Rolling Stones
            (London: 1964)
            Pop

Other recordings: Buddy Holly (Coral); Stephen Stills (Columbia); The Dave Clark Five (UK Columbia); The Everly Brothers (RCA); Dick and Dee Dee (Warner Bros); Bo Diddley (RCA); Black Oak Arkansas (Capricorn); Dave Berry (UK Decca).

See: LOVE'S MADE A FOOL OF YOU for other Buddy Holly songs.

OH! CAROL
(Neil Sedaka/Howard Greenfield)
Neil Sedaka's first US Top 10 hit was this song, dedicated to fellow songwriter, Carole King, whose name was professionally spelt 'Carol' in those days. Her reply version was not widely released but obviously is a valuable collector's item because of Carole King's later success as both writer and performer.

US HIT: Neil Sedaka (RCA: 1959)
            Pop
UK HIT: Neil Sedaka (RCA: 1959)
            Neil Sedaka (RCA: 1972
            Re-release)

Other recordings: Smokie (RSO); Fumble (Capitol).

Answer record: OH, NEIL (Sedaka/ Greenfield/Goffin) by Carole King (Alpine: 1960)

OH PRETTY WOMAN
(Roy Orbison/Bill Dees)
One of the great Roy Orbison classics and not a heartbroken tearjerker which so many of his other hits were. Sung over a dominant marching beat, it includes Roy's famous growl, 'Mercy!', which was used in a number of American TV commercials, one of which he even briefly appeared in himself.

US HITS: Roy Orbison (Monument:
            1964) Pop
            Van Halen: Billed as (OH)
            PRETTY WOMAN
            (Warner Bros: 1982)
            Pop
UK HIT: Roy Orbison (London:
            1964)

Other recordings: Del Shannon (Liberty); Al Green (Hi); The Ventures (Liberty); Leroy Van Dyke (Plantation).

Roy Orbison songs
Roy Orbison was the supreme master of the teary-eyed ballad with such bittersweet classics as ONLY THE LONELY (KNOW THE WAY I FEEL) (Orbison/Melson) and IT'S OVER (Orbison/Dees), just two of his own million-sellers on the Monument label in 1960 and 1964 respectively. IN DREAMS (Orbison) with which he scored in 1963 was chosen by film director David Lynch for a sequence in his movie, "Blue Velvet" (De Laurentis: 1986) and for which Orbison re-recorded the song.

Two of Roy's songs which have also been successfully revived by other artists were BLUE BAYOU (Orbison/Melson), originally an Orbison Top 10 single (Monument: 1960) and a huge Pop & Country record for Linda Ronstadt (Asylum: 1977), plus CRYING (Orbison/ Melson) which, after being a Top 5 song for Roy in 1961 (on Monument), was first returned to the best sellers five years later by Jay and The Americans (UA: 1966) and then revived once more in 1981 by Don McLean (Millennium).

Roy re-recorded CRYING himself as a duet with k.d. Lang for the soundtrack of Bob Giraldi's teen comedy movie "Hiding Out" (De Laurentis: 1987), and their single (Virgin: 1987) became a US Country hit.

ON BROADWAY
(Jerry Leiber/Mike Stoller/Barry Mann/Cynthia Weil)
Barry Mann and Cynthia Weil originally wrote this for The Cookies, the girl group who scored with Goffin/King's CHAINS**. But when Leiber and Stoller picked the song out to record with The Drifters, some re-structuring was required and so Jerry and Mike re-wrote the song from the male point of view. On the actual Drifters' record, Phil Spector, who was a staff writer in the early days with Leiber and Stoller, played the guitar solo.

Song was memorably revived by George Benson on the soundtrack of Bob Fosse's fantasy film, "All That Jazz" (20th Century Fox: 1979), in which a sequence showing auditioning and rehearsing members of a chorus line is edited to the beat of the Benson record.

US HITS: The Drifters (Atlantic: 1963) Black & Pop
George Benson (Warner Bros: 1978) Black & Pop

Other recordings: King Curtis (Atco); Eric Carmen (Arista); Bobby Darin (Capitol); Nancy Sinatra (RCA); The Coasters (King); The Jazz Crusaders (MCA); Barry Mann (New Design); Illinois Jacquet (Cadence); Lou Rawls (Capitol); The Dave Clark Five (UK Columbia); Long John Baldry; Livingston Taylor (Capricorn); Clyde McPhatter.

See: JAILHOUSE ROCK for other Jerry Leiber and Mike Stoller songs.

See: YOU'VE LOST THAT LOVIN' FEELIN' for other Barry Mann and Cynthia Weil songs.

ONE FINE DAY
(Gerry Goffin/Carole King)
First recorded with Little Eva, the same track was supposedly used for what we now know as The Chiffons' version.

A rare example of a song which became a Top 20 hit the second time around for one of its writers. Rita Coolidge's version made it only to the charts' lower region. The Chiffons' original hit was heard on the soundtrack of "The Hollywood Knights" (Columbia: 1980).

US HITS: The Chiffons (Laurie: 1963) Pop & Black
Rita Coolidge (A&M: 1979) Pop
Carole King (Capitol: 1980) Pop
UK HIT: The Chiffons (Stateside: 1963)

Other recordings: The Carpenters (A&M); Susie Allanson (Elektra); Johnny Adams (Ariola).

See: SEE YOU LATER ALLIGATOR for other hits that got away.

See: UP ON THE ROOF for other Gerry Goffin and Carole King songs.

ONE MINT JULEP
(Rudolph Toombs)
Classic R&B story song about the effects of whisky... 'One Mint Julep was the start of it all'! Originally by The Clovers on Atlantic, it became one of the first songs recorded by Ray Charles after he switched from Atlantic to ABC/ Paramount and, very briefly, ABC's jazz label called Impulse.

US HITS: The Clovers (Atlantic: 1952) Black
Ray Charles (Impulse: 1961) Black & Pop

Other recordings: Louis Prima (Capitol); Count Basie (Capitol); Buddy Morrow (Mercury and RCA); Earl Palmer (Liberty); Chet Atkins (RCA); Sounds Incorporated (UK Columbia); Eric Delaney Band (Pye); Jack Sheldon (Reprise); Bob James (CTI); The Ventures (Liberty); Xavier Cugat (Mercury).

ONE NIGHT
(Dave Bartholomew/Pearl King)
The original opening line was 'One night of sin', recorded by Smiley Lewis with Dave Bartholomew producing at Cosimo's Studio in New Orleans in October, 1955. Lewis, who was also a guitarist, had a rich, demanding voice which, at full throttle, grabbed your attention from the beginning of a song to the end. Imperial released his single of ONE NIGHT in January 1956 but a jinx, which haunted Smiley throughout his career, prevented the record from ever taking off. Dave Bartholomew sums it up as being a case of continued bad luck...Smiley Lewis got the songs but just couldn't break through.

Elvis had heard ONE NIGHT and even took a swing at the original lyric, but prior to an early 1957 recording session, the opening phrase was amended to 'One night with you' and it became a bona fide Presley smash.

The most recent (and welcome) revival was by Joe Cocker (Capitol: 1989) who sang the original Dave Bartholomew lyric; the track and the album were titled ONE NIGHT OF SIN and capping it all off, the subsequent Joe Cocker concerts were billed as the 'One Night Of Sin' tour!

The song has been heard in various movies, including "Elvis – That's The Way It Is" (MGM: 1970), "Heartbreak Hotel" (Touchstone: 1988) and "Everybody's All-American" (Warner Bros: 1988).

US HIT: Elvis Presley (RCA: 1958)
Pop & Black & Country
UK HIT: Elvis Presley (RCA: 1959)

Other recordings: Fats Domino (Imperial); Roy Head (MCA); Jeannie C. Riley (MGM); Arlo Guthrie (Warner Bros); Pat Boone (Dot); Terry Tigre (Starday); Albert King (Stax); Fancy (Big Tree).

See: I HEAR YOU KNOCKING for other Dave Bartholomew songs.

ONLY SIXTEEN
(Sam Cooke)
Along with ANOTHER SATURDAY NIGHT, CHAIN GANG, A CHANGE IS GONNA COME, TWISTIN' THE NIGHT AWAY** and YOU SEND ME**, one of the finest of Sam Cooke's own hits. The message, with its 'too young to fall in love' lines, was typical of the moral thinking of the 1950s, but far outmoded by today's standards.

Besides Sam Cooke, Gene McDaniels (*below*) also had songs 'covered' by Craig Douglas. Gene notched up a series of his own hit records including TOWER OF STRENGTH (Bacharach/Hilliard), but later wrote hits for other artists including FEEL LIKE MAKIN' LOVE, a million seller by Roberta Flack (Atlantic: 1974).

US HITS: Sam Cooke (Keen: 1959)
          Black & Pop
          Dr Hook (Capitol: 1976)
          Pop & Country
UK HITS: Sam Cooke (HMV: 1959)
          Craig Douglas (Top Rank:
          1959)
          Al Saxon (Fontana: 1959)

Other recordings: The Supremes
(Motown); West Virginia Slim (Kent).

In Britain, ONLY SIXTEEN provided
local artist Craig Douglas with his
only Number One; many of his other
records were covers of American
hits including Frankie Lymon's A
TEENAGER IN LOVE** (1959),
Steve Lawrence's PRETTY BLUE
EYES (Randazzo/Weinstein) (1960),
Gene McDaniels' A HUNDRED
POUNDS OF CLAY (Elgin/Roger/
Dixon) (1961), The Drifters' WHEN
MY LITTLE GIRL IS SMILING**
(1962) and Gary Criss' OUR
FAVOURITE MELODIES (Farrell/
Elgin) in 1962, all on Top Rank
except for OUR FAVOURITE
MELODIES on UK Columbia.

Sam Cooke songs

Singer–songwriter Sam Cooke
emerged from a gospel background
(he was one of the legendary Soul
Stirrers) to become one of the first
black superstars of pop music. His
records were also fine examples of
the in-roads that soul music was
making in the early sixties, prior to
Cooke's tragic death in Los Angeles
in 1964. Sam's influence is easily
measured by the ongoing popularity
of his songs and is also evident in
recordings of Otis Redding and Rod
Stewart among others.
    Among the hit records by other
artists of Sam Cooke songs:

ANOTHER SATURDAY NIGHT by
    Cat Stevens (Island: 1974)
BRING IT ON HOME TO ME** by
    The Animals (UK Columbia: 1965)
    by Rod Stewart (Mercury: 1974)
CHAIN GANG (medley) by Jim
    Croce (Lifesong: 1976)

CUPID** by Johnny Nash (JAD: 1969)
    by The Spinners (Atlantic: 1980)
    by Ray Tierney (Fontana: 1959)
HAVING A PARTY** by The
    Osmonds (MGM: 1975)
SHAKE** by Otis Redding (Volt:
    1967)
SWEET SOUL MUSIC** by Arthur
    Conley (Atco: 1967)
TWISTIN' THE NIGHT AWAY** by
    Rod Stewart (Mercury: 1973)

A fine rap version of CHAIN GANG
is included on Shinehead's album,
Unity (African Love/Elektra: 1988).

OOH POO PAH DOO

(Jessie Hill)
The wild call-and-response chant by
New Orleans artist Jessie Hill; in
origin, it's similar to the chants heard
by blacks who dress up as 'Mardi
Gras Indians' at carnival time in the
Crescent City. Arranged and
produced by Allen Toussaint, it
became one of the first true 'funk'
records.
    Jessie Hill was originally a
drummer with Professor Longhair
and has, in recent years, often been
the opening act for Fats Domino. A
listener to Steve Propes' "Rock 'N'
Roll and Rhythm and Blues" show on
KLON radio out of Long Beach,
California, once claimed that Jessie
Hill had vouched that the song was
about his (Hill's) obsession with
singer Barbara George (of I
KNOW** fame), hence the line 'I
won't stop trying till I create a
disturbance in your mind'.
(Copyright EMI Unart).
    The original Jessie Hill record was
heard on the soundtrack of the
Jessica Lange/Dennis Quaid movie,
"Everybody's All-American" (Warner
Bros: 1988).

US HITS: Jessie Hill (Minit: 1960)
          Black & Pop
          Ike and Tina Turner (UA:
          1971) Black & Pop

Other recordings: Wilson Pickett (Atlantic); Paul Revere and The Raiders (Columbia); The Standells (Liberty); Mitch Ryder and The Detroit Wheels (New Voice); Rufus Thomas (Stax); The Escalators (Atlantic); The Righteous Brothers (Verve); Freddy Fender (Intermedia); Chubby Checker (Parkway); Sandy Nelson (Imperial); The Kingsmen (Wand); Teddy Randazzo (ABC/Paramount); Trini Lopez; The Shirelles.

Sequel record: CAN'T GET ENOUGH (OF THAT OOH POO PAH DOO) (Neville aka Allen Toussaint) by Jessie Hill (Minit: 1962).

(Chubby Checker even recorded something called OOH POO PAH DOO SHIMMY!)

OUT OF TIME
(Mick Jagger/Keith Richards)
Originally released by Chris Farlowe on Andrew Oldham's Immediate label in 1966. Produced by Mick Jagger, it was also recorded by The Stones in March that year at a session in Hollywood. When released in the States, the Stones' version was only a minor hit.
Song featured on the soundtrack of Hal Ashby's post-Vietnam drama, "Coming Home" (UA: 1978).

UK HITS: Chris Farlowe and The
          Thunderbirds
          (Immediate: 1966)
          Dan McCafferty
          (Mountain: 1975)
          The Rolling Stones (UK
          Decca: 1975)
          Chris Farlowe and The
          Thunderbirds
          (Immediate: 1975 Re-
          release)

Other recordings: P. J. Proby (Liberty); Carillo (Atlantic); Kris Ife (MGM).

The original release of Chris

Farlowe's OUT OF TIME single gave Immediate its only Number One record; the label was the brainchild of the Stones' manager, Andrew Loog Oldham, and its other local acts included The Small Faces, The Nice and P. P. Arnold. Farlowe's first chart single was another Jagger/Richards song, THINK.

See: PAINT IT BLACK for other Mick Jagger and Keith Richards songs.

OVER AND OVER
(Robert Byrd)
Bobby Day's second hit after LITTLE BITTY PRETTY ONE** was ROCKIN' ROBIN**, the B-side of which was this which, like LITTLE BITTY, was covered by Thurston Harris, though his record hardly made a dent on the Top 100. Britain's Dave Clark Five not only revived the song seven years later, but took it all the way to Number One in the States, though their version hardly cracked the Top 50 at home.

US HITS: Bobby Day (Class: 1958)
          Black & Pop
          The Dave Clark Five
          (Epic: 1965) Pop
UK HIT: The Dave Clark Five (UK
          Columbia: 1965)

Other recordings: Jewel Akens (Era); The Righteous Brothers (Philles); Bobby Shafto (Parlophone).

Another of Bobby Day's revived songs was BUZZ-BUZZ-BUZZ which Bobby and his group The Satellites recorded as The Hollywood Flames (Ebb: 1957) and on which Earl Nelson was lead singer; together, Bob(by) and Earl did the original HARLEM SHUFFLE**. BUZZ-BUZZ-BUZZ was covered by, amongst others, Huey Lewis and The News on their *Picture This* album (Chrysalis: 1982).

JAGGER AND RICHARD SONGS
THINK was Chris Farowe's second single on Andrew Oldham's Immediate label and marked his UK chart debut; his follow-up OUT OF TIME was produced by Mick Jagger and gave Farlowe his only Number One.

PAINT IT BLACK
(Mick Jagger/Keith Richard)
The song which gave The Rolling Stones their sixth British Number One and their third American chart-topper. Their original record is used as the signature song for the Vietnam-based US television series, "Tour Of Duty" which debuted on CBS in 1988. It was also featured on the soundtrack of Stanley Kubrick's war movie, "Full Metal Jacket" (Warner Bros: 1987). The song's foreboding tone turned it into one of the darkest records of the Stones' early days and Eric Burdon's voice also lent credence to it when Eric Burdon and The Animals cut it on their *Winds Of Change* album (MGM: 1967). The 1980 revival by British girl group, The Modettes, was a minor Top 50 seller.

UK HITS: The Rolling Stones
                  (UK Decca: 1966)
              The Modettes
                  (Deram: 1980)
US HIT: The Rolling Stones
                  (London: 1966) Pop

Other recordings: The Flamin' Groovies (Sire); The London Symphony Orchestra and The Royal Choral Society (on the first *Classic Rock* album in 1977) (K-Tel); Gabor Szabo (Impulse); Chris Farlowe (Immediate); Echo and The Bunnymen (Sire).

Covers of Jagger and Richard songs
Among the Mick Jagger and Keith Richards songs which were hits by artists other than The Rolling Stones:

AS TEARS GO BY** by Marianne
   Faithfull (UK Decca: 1964)
BLUE TURNS TO GREY by Cliff
   Richard (UK Columbia: 1966)
(I CAN'T GET NO) SATISFACTION
   by Otis Redding (Volt: 1966)
JUMPIN' JACK FLASH** by Aretha
   Franklin (Arista: 1986)
LADY JANE by David Garrick
   (Piccadilly: 1966)
THE LAST TIME/UNDER MY
   THUMB by The Who (Track: 1967)

OUT OF TIME by Chris Farlowe
(Immediate: 1966)
RUBY TUESDAY by Melanie
(Buddah: 1971)
UNDER MY THUMB by Wayne
Gibson (Pye: 1974 re-release)

PAPA-OOM-MOW-MOW
(Al Frazier/Carl White/Turner
Wilson Jr/John Harris)
Great nonsense chorus from the Los
Angeles-based Rivingtons
punctuates this celebration of a
dance called THE BIRD, hence
follow-ups such as MAMA-OOOM-
MOW-MOW (Liberty: 1963) and
THE BIRD'S THE WORD

PAPA-OOM-MOW-MOW
The sound of The Rivingtons, which in turn gave
birth to THE BIRD'S THE WORD and the dance
they're demonstrating here.

(Liberty:1963), THE SHAKY BIRD
PTS. 1 AND 2, on Liberty in 1963 and
all written by the same guys, namely
the group themselves.

The Rivingtons later went to court
successfully claiming that a surf
group called The Trashmen had
plagiarized their song, combining it
with THE BIRD'S THE WORD as
SURFIN' BIRD, a major US hit in 1963
on the Garrett label.

The Rivingtons' original record
was heard on the soundtrack of
Steven Spielberg's fantasy movie,
"E.T. The Extra-Terrestrial"
(Universal: 1982) as a request on the
radio. Song was performed by Pee
Wee Herman in the Frankie
Avalon/Annette Funicello movie,
"Back To The Beach" (Paramount:
1987).

US HIT: The Rivingtons (Liberty:
1962) Black & Pop

UK HITS: Gary Glitter (Bell: 1975)
           The Sharonettes (Black
           Magic: 1975)

Other recordings: The Beach Boys
(Capitol), The California Raisins
(Atlantic); The Rivingtons (re-
recording: Wand).

PAPA-OOM-MOW-MOW was a UK
hit for Gary Glitter, whose other
'revival' records included AND
THEN SHE KISSED ME, a gender-
altered version of THEN HE KISSED
ME (Greenwich/Barry/Spector),
originally by The Crystals (Philles:
1963). Long before his rock 'n' roll
medley (Bell: 1972) launched the
string of 'Glitter' hits, Gary recorded
under other names; as Paul Raven,
for instance, he covered TOWER OF
STRENGTH (Bacharach/David) for
Parlophone in 1961, the year of the
original version by Gene McDaniels
on Liberty.

PAPA'S GOT A BRAND NEW BAG
(James Brown)
Brown's first major cross-over pop
hit, it was a two-parter single.

US HITS: James Brown and The
           Famous Flames (King:
           1965) Black & Pop
           Otis Redding (Atco: 1969)
           Black
UK HIT: James Brown and The
           Famous Flames
           (London: 1965)

Other recordings: The McCoys
(Bang); Georgie Fame and The Blue
Flames (UK Columbia).

James Brown's most unexpected UK
success came in 1988 when Polydor
took his 1974 R&B hit, THE
PAYBACK (Brown/various) and
re-structured it for the house music
audience.

See: PLEASE, PLEASE, PLEASE for
other James Brown songs.

PARTY DOLL
(Jimmy Bowen/Buddy Knox)
Featured on the soundtrack of
George Lucas' movie, "American
Graffiti" (Universal: 1973).

US HITS: Buddy Knox (Roulette:
           1957) Pop & Black
           Steve Lawrence (Coral:
           1957) Pop
           Wingy Manone (Decca:
           1957) Pop
           Roy Brown (Imperial:
           1957) Black
UK HIT: Buddy Knox (UK
           Columbia: 1957)

Other recordings: Leroy van Dyke
(Mercury); Rodney Lay (Sun).

PEGGY SUE
(Buddy Holly/Jerry Allison/Norman
Petty)
Originally written by Buddy Holly as
CINDY LOU, it was changed in
honour of his drummer Jerry Allison's
fiancée, Peggy Sue Gerow. Allison's
drumming was unique in its use of
light drum rolls. The song became
highly influential to hits like SUSIE
DARLIN' (Luke) by Robin Luke (Dot:
1958), SHEILA (Roe) by Tommy Roe
(ABC/ Paramount: 1962) and was
later revived by Tommy Roe (ABC/
Paramount: 1962).

US HITS: Buddy Holly (Coral: 1957)
           Black & Pop
           The Beach Boys (Brother:
           1978) Pop
UK HIT: Buddy Holly (Coral: 1957)

Other recordings: Billy 'Crash'
Craddock (ABC); John Lennon
(Apple); Mike Berry (Polydor); The
Tremeloes (CBS); Sandy Nelson
(Imperial); Hank C. Burnette (Sun);
Bobby Vinton (Epic).

Recorded by Waylon Jennings and
The Crickets in a Buddy Holly
medley produced by Duane Eddy
for Waylon's *I've Always Been Crazy*
album (RCA: 1978); other songs in
the medley: WELL ALL RIGHT

(Holly/Allison/Mauldin/Petty), IT'S SO
EASY (Holly/ Petty) and MAYBE
BABY (Holly/Petty).

Sequel record: PEGGY SUE GOT
MARRIED by Buddy Holly which
was a UK hit (Coral: 1959) and gave
its title to the Kathleen Turner/
Nicholas Cage movie, "Peggy Sue
Got Married" (Tri-Star: 1986); the
movie's plotline was unrelated to the
song, but the Buddy Holly record
was featured on the film's
soundtrack.

See: LOVE'S MADE A FOOL OF
YOU for other Buddy Holly songs.

PEOPLE GET READY

(Curtis Mayfield)
Socially conscious Curtis Mayfield
song which was originally recorded,
as so many of his songs were, by the
R&B trio he led until going solo in
1970.

US HITS: The Impressions
(ABC/Paramount: 1965)
Pop & Black
Jeff Beck and Rod Stewart
(Epic: 1985) Pop

UK HIT: Bob Marley and The
Wailers (Island: 1984)

Other recordings: Sonny Terry and
Brownie McGhee (A&M); Aretha
Franklin (Atlantic); The Chambers
Brothers (Fantasy); Vanilla Fudge
(Atco); Jeff Beck and Karen
Lawrence (Epic); The Everly
Brothers (Warner Bros); The Staple
Singers; The Walker Brothers
(Philips).

Curtis Mayfield songs

Significant R&B composer, Mayfield
spent twelve years as the hub of The
Impressions, writing and producing
most of their hits as well as being the
group's key voice. The following is a
list of his major hit songs, both with
and without The Impressions:

AMEN by The Impressions
(ABC/Paramount: 1965)
CHOICE OF COLORS by The
Impressions (Curtom: 1969)
FIND ANOTHER GIRL by Jerry
Butler (Vee-Jay: 1961)
FOOL FOR YOU by The
Impressions (Curtom: 1968)
FREDDIE'S DEAD by Curtis
Mayfield (Curtom: 1972)
GYPSY WOMAN by The
Impressions (ABC/Paramount:
1961) by Brian Hyland (Uni: 1970)
HE DON'T LOVE YOU (LIKE I LOVE
YOU) by Dawn (Elektra: 1975)
as HE WILL BREAK YOUR
HEART by Jerry Butler (Vee-Jay:
1960)
HEY LITTLE GIRL by Major Lance
(Okeh: 1963)
I'M SO PROUD by The Impressions
(ABC/Paramount: 1964)
by The Main Ingredient (RCA:
1971)
IT'S ALL RIGHT by The Impressions
(ABC/Paramount: 1963)
JUMP by Aretha Franklin (Atlantic:
1976)
KEEP ON PUSHING by The
Impressions (ABC/Paramount:
1964)
LET'S DO IT AGAIN by The Staple
Singers (Curtom: 1975)
LOOK INTO YOUR HEART by
Aretha Franklin (Atlantic: 1977)
MONKEY TIME by Major Lance
(Okeh: 1963)
NOTHING CAN STOP ME by Gene
Chandler (Constellation: 1965)
ON AND ON by Gladys Knight and
The Pips (Buddah: 1974)
SOMETHING HE CAN FEEL by
Aretha Franklin (Atlantic: 1976)
SUPERFLY by Curtis Mayfield
(Curtom: 1972)
UM, UM, UM, UM, UM, UM** by
Major Lance (Okeh: 1964)
by Wayne Fontana (Fontana: 1964)
WOMAN'S GOT SOUL by The
Impressions (ABC/Paramount:
1965)

PIECE OF MY HEART

(Jerry Ragovoy/Bert Berns)
'Take another piece of my heart
now, baby...'

A classic from the San Francisco
days of the late 1960s immortalized
when the raw, emotive vocals of
Janis Joplin soared above Big
Brother and The Holding Company
who had started out as house band at
the city's famed Avalon Ballroom.
Featured in the 1975 documentary
film, "Janis".

US HITS: Erma Franklin (Shout:
     1967) Pop
     Big Brother and The
     Holding Company
     (Columbia: 1968) Pop
     Sammy Hagar (Geffen:
     1982) Pop
UK HIT: Sammy Hagar (Geffen:
     1982)

Other recordings: Etta James
(Warner Bros); Bryan Ferry (Island);
Bonnie Tyler (Chrysalis); Delaney
and Bonnie (Atco); Marmalade
(CBS); The Ikettes (Liberty); Sandy
Kroft (Capitol); Jimmy Barnes
(Geffen); Rough Cut (Warner Bros).

See: CRY BABY for other Jerry
Ragovoy songs.

See: TWIST AND SHOUT for other
Bert Berns songs.

PINBALL WIZARD

(Pete Townshend)
Pete Townshend wrote this tribute to
the 'Bally table king' to interest
writer and pinball fanatic Nik Cohn
in his plans for the rock opera,
"Tommy". The song became the
opera's centrepiece, a celebration of
trivia in the great rock 'n' roll
tradition, surrounded by Freudian
suggestions.

Performed by Elton John in the
movie of The Who's rock opera,
"Tommy" (Columbia: 1975).

UK HITS: The Who (Track: 1969)
     The New Seekers:

medley with SEE ME,
FEEL ME (Townshend)
(Polydor: 1973)
Elton John (DJM: 1976)
US HITS: The Who (Decca: 1969)
     Pop
     The New Seekers:
     Medley with SEE ME,
     FEEL ME (Verve: 1973)
     Pop

Other recording: Rod Stewart
(Mercury).

PINK CADILLAC

(Bruce Springsteen)
PINK CADILLAC, which Bruce
Springsteen cut in 1984, spawned
Natalie Cole's spectacular comeback
hit, returning her to the glory days of
the previous decade; it was then that
she clocked up three US Top 10 pop
singles with THIS WILL BE (Capitol:
1975), I'VE GOT LOVE ON MY
MIND (Capitol: 1977) and OUR
LOVE (Capitol: 1978), all written by
Chuck Jackson and Marvin Yancy.

US HIT: Natalie Cole (Manhattan:
     1988) Black & Pop
UK HIT: Natalie Cole (Manhattan:
     1988)

Other recording: Southern Pacific
(Warner Bros).

Bruce Springsteen songs

Rock superstar Bruce Springsteen,
whose anthems BORN TO RUN and
BORN IN THE USA confirmed his
status as 'The Boss' with his millions
of fans, wrote some songs which
have scored for other artists. They
include:

BECAUSE THE NIGHT, written by
Patti Smith and Bruce Springsteen,
was a US Top 20 hit for the Patti
Smith Group (Arista: 1978).
BLINDED BY THE LIGHT...a smash
on both sides of the Atlantic for
Manfred Mann's Earth Band. It
initially scored in Britain in 1976
on Bronze and a few months later

in the States where Manfred also charted with a cover of Bruce's SPIRIT IN THE NIGHT (Warner Bros: 1977).

DANCING IN THE DARK by American group Big Daddy was a Top 30 UK hit (Making Waves: 1985).

FIRE, on which Robert Gordon cut the original version (Private Stock) and with which The Pointer Sisters had a Top 5 single in early 1979 (Planet). Robert Gordon later cut a second version with guitarist Link Wray (RCA).

NB: Bruce Springsteen has done his own share of covers, see for instance, the entry on DEVIL WITH A BLUE DRESS ON.

PLEASE MR POSTMAN
(Georgia Dobbins/William Garrett/ Brian Holland/Robert Bateman/ Freddie Gorman)
PLEASE MR POSTMAN heavily

PLEASE MR. POSTMAN
The Marvelettes, whose very first hit went all the way to Number One! Their other winners included PLAYBOY(Holland/Horton/Bateman/Stevenson) (Tamla: 1963).

influenced MASHED POTATO TIME (Sheldon/Land) by Dee Dee Sharp (Cameo: 1962).

US HITS: The Marvelettes (Tamla: 1961) Black & Pop
The Carpenters (A&M: 1975) Pop

UK HIT: The Carpenters (A&M: 1975)

Other recordings: The Beatles (Parlophone); Bern Elliott and The Fenman (UK Decca); Diana Ross (Motown).

Sequel record: TWISTIN' POSTMAN (Bateman/Holland/Stevenson) by The Marvelettes (Tamla: 1962)

See: DEVIL WITH A BLUE DRESS ON for other Motown hits.

See: HOW SWEET IT IS for Holland/ Dozier/Holland songs.

Few artists make their initial entry onto the pop charts on two different but simultaneous hits. The very week that Dee Dee's MASHED POTATO TIME entered the official best seller list, Chubby Checker's record of SLOW TWISTIN' (Sheldon) also popped on for the first time. Chubby's name was on the label, but the other voice on the record was that of Dee Dee. Chubby had been scoring with dance-oriented songs since Hank Ballard's THE TWIST** took him to Number One in the fall of 1960. The twist craze had exploded and Checker was drafted into low-budget teen-music movies to capitalize on the public's fascination with the new dance sensation. Dee Dee appeared performing SLOW TWISTIN' with Chubby in the movie, "Twist Around The Clock" (Columbia: 1961). Meanwhile, her own dance records were taking off... MASHED POTATO TIME was followed by (GRAVY) FOR MY MASHED POTATOES (Mann/ Appell), RIDE! (Sheldon/Leon) and a variation on the steps created by PAPA-OOM-MOW-MOW** under the title, DO THE BIRD (Mann/ Appell).

PLEASE, PLEASE, PLEASE

The Godfather of Soul himself, James Brown, with The Famous Flames and The James Brown Orchestra. Hearing James Brown on record is an experience, but seeing him live is a revelation. His concerts have been captured on film, video and on record; in fact, his *Live At The Apollo* album (King: 1962) is a milestone in capturing a R&B revue in orgasmic action! His first ever UK appearance was on the stage of the Granada Cinema, Walthamstow, East London.

PLEASE, PLEASE, PLEASE

(James Brown/Johnny Terry)
Though never a major hit (the original record barely scraped into the Hot 100 when it was first released by King in 1964), it remains among the most influential songs of James Brown's career. It's also the number which he performed in "The TAMI Show/Gather No Moss" (1964), an appearance which is virtually impossible to ignore or forget; it's the classic stage routine when his pleading vocals become so intense that his whole body quivers and he collapses onto the floor several times, requiring members of The Famous Flames to come forward, place a cape over his shoulders and, making various false exits, attempt to escort him off-stage! James Brown is

rightly named the 'Godfather of Soul' not just in recognition of his powerhouse vocals but also his unique stature as the ultimate rhythm and blues showman.

Other recordings: Stevie Wonder (Tamla); The Who (Brunswick); Ike and Tina Turner (Kent); Mitch Ryder and The Detroit Wheels (New Voice); Little Milton (Checker); Soul Survivors (Crimson); The Isley Brothers (UA); Syl Johnson (Federal); Alexis Korner's Blues Incorporated (Parlophone).

James Brown songs

The 'Godfather of Soul' (or even 'Mr Please Please Please' which he used in the wake of this hit) has logged countless inspired moments on record. Many were with his own songs, but not always, as in the case of the wild rebirth he gave to THINK (Pauling), the old Five Royales song from 1957 which gave him a Top 10 R&B smash in 1960 on Federal. But then there are the songs he wrote himself, including SAY IT LOUD, I'M BLACK AND I'M PROUD (King: 1968) and PAPA'S GOT A BRAND

NEW BAG (King: 1965).
Following are a few of the cover versions of James' songs:

I DON'T MIND by The Who (Brunswick: 1965)
I'LL GO CRAZY by The Moody Blues (Deram: 1965)
MOTHER POPCORN (with Alfred Ellis) by Aerosmith (Columbia: 1979)
PAPA'S GOT A BRAND NEW BAG** by Otis Redding (Atco: 1968)
SEX MACHINE (with Bobby Byrd/ Ronald Lenhoff) by The Clash (CBS)
TELL ME WHAT YOU'RE GONNA DO/I DO JUST WHAT I WANT by Bo Street Runners (UK Columbia: 1964)
THERE WAS A TIME (with Buddy Hobgood) by Gene Chandler (Brunswick: 1968)

PLEASE SEND ME SOMEONE TO LOVE
(Percy Mayfield)
Milestone ballad which was a Number One R&B tune for its writer, Percy Mayfield, who also wrote one of Ray Charles' biggest hits, HIT THE ROAD JACK (ABC Paramount: 1961).

US HITS: Percy Mayfield (Specialty: 1950) Black
            The Moonglows (Chess: 1957) Black & Pop

Other recordings: Lou Rawls (Capitol); Garnet Mimms (UA); Irma Thomas (Imperial); Solomon Burke (Atlantic); B. B. King (MCA); Paul Butterfield (Bearsville); Nancy Wilson (Capitol); Jimmy Witherspoon (JZM); The Animals (UA); Ramsey Lewis (Columbia); Count Basie and Joe Williams (Verve); Toots Thielemans (Grand Award); Brook Benton (Atlantic); Philip Upchurch (Blue Thumb); James Brooker (Rounder); Damita Jo (Mercury); Plas

Johnson (Concord); Peggy Lee (Capitol); Mickey Newbury (Elektra); Lloyd Price (ABC/Paramount); Etta James and Eddie 'Cleanhead' Vinson (Fantasy).

PLEDGING MY LOVE
(Don Robey/Ferdinand Washington)
Significant posthumous Number One R&B hit for the legendary Memphis-born baritone Johnny Ace, who accidently took his own life while playing Russian roulette in 1954. Co-credited to Don Robey, founder of Duke Records.
Performed by Elvis Presley in "Elvis On Tour" (MGM: 1979). The original Johnny Ace record was used in Martin Scorsese's "Mean Streets" (Warner Bros: 1973).

US HITS: Johnny Ace (Duke: 1955) Pop & Black
            Teresa Brewer (Coral: 1955) Pop
            Roy Hamilton (Epic: 1958) Pop
            Johnny Tillotson (Cadence: 1960) Pop
            Laura and Johnny (Silver Fox: 1969) Black
            Kitty Wells (Decca: 1971) Country
            Emmylou Harris (Warner Bros: 1984) Country

Other recordings: Delbert McClinton (ABC); O. V. Wright (MCA); LaVern Baker (Brunswick); Laura Green and Johnny McKinnis (SSS); Diana Ross and Marvin Gaye (Motown); The Platters (Musicor); Jackie Wilson (Brunswick); Elvis Presley (RCA); Charles Brown (Mainstream); Aaron Neville (Passport); Jerry Lee Lewis (Mercury); Country Joe McDonald (Rag Baby); The Four Coins (MGM); Kitty Wells (Decca); Chubby Checker and Dee Dee Sharp (Cameo).

Johnny Tillotson also covered another of Johnny Ace's hits, NEVER LET ME GO (Scott) (Duke: 1954).

PRETTY LITTLE ANGEL EYES
(Tommy Boyce/Curtis Lee)
After racking up their biggest hit
with Curtis Lee's 1961 success,
UNDER THE MOON OF LOVE,
British revival group
Showaddywaddy cut ANGEL EYES,
Curtis Lee's initial American hit,
which like his MOON OF LOVE
record, was produced by Phil
Spector.

US HIT: Curtis Lee (Dunes: 1961)
           Pop
UK HITS: Curtis Lee (London: 1961)
           Showaddywaddy (Arista:
           1978)

See: DA DOO RON RON for other
Phil Spector classics.

PROUD MARY
(John Fogerty)
Among the most enduring of
Creedence Clearwater songs, it was
originally part of their *Bayou Country*
album (Fantasy: 1969). The single
was a two-sided smash coupling
PROUD MARY with BORN ON THE
BAYOU. Creedence's first two chart
singles had been revivals, firstly of
Dale Hawkins' SUZIE Q and then
Screamin' Jay (no relation) Hawkins'
classic, I PUT A SPELL ON YOU,
both Fantasy singles in 1968. But
PROUD MARY literally pushed the
boat out, with John Fogerty's urgent
vocals leading a pack of solid gold
singles for the next two and a half
years.
    Covered at the same time as
Creedence's own hit by Solomon
Burke, as well as (less successfully)
by the Checkmates Ltd, PROUD
MARY had a tremendous
resurgence two years later when Ike
and Tina Turner took it on; as the
soul duo's single opened, Tina
declared 'We never do nothin' nice
and easy...we always do it nice and
rough!' after which the Turners'
duetted on a slow-tempoed version
of the tune and then slammed into a
powerhouse race to the finish, with

Tina backed up by the chanting
Ikettes.

US HITS: Creedence Clearwater
           Revival (Fantasy: 1969)
           Pop
           Solomon Burke (Bell:
           1969) Black & Pop
           Ike and Tina Turner
           (Liberty: 1971) Black &
           Pop
UK HITS: Creedence Clearwater
           Revival (Liberty: 1969)
           The Checkmates Ltd
           (A&M: 1969)

Other recordings: Elvis Presley
(RCA); Woody Herman (Fantasy);
George Jones and Johnny Paycheck
(Epic); Ace Cannon (Hi); Tom Jones
(UK Decca); Tina Turner (Capitol).

Creedence in the movies
Creedence Clearwater have been
heard on a number of movie soundtracks in addition to "Who'll Stop the
Rain" (UA: 1978) which, incidentally,
also used HEY TONIGHT (Fogerty)
plus, of course, his title song which
was adopted by the film's producers
in America after they decided
against using the picture's working
title and the name of the book on
which it's based, "The Dog
Soldiers";when UA finally released
the film in Europe, they reverted to
using the original title. Though the
strategy didn't pay off in box-office
receipts, the idea of using "Who'll
Stop the Rain" was sound, as it had
been the co-hit of a Top 5
Creedence single in the States in
1970 and as such, the song was much
better known there than in Britain
where only the A-side, TRAVELIN'
BAND (Fogerty) had left an
impression on the charts.
Creedence's (or rather John
Fogerty's) adaptation of the old
Huddie Ledbetter folk song,
MIDNIGHT SPECIAL, from their
Willy And The Poor Boys album
(Fantasy: 1969) was audible in
"Twilight Zone – The Movie"

Tina Turner (*right*) has always kept good
company! Here she is in 1975, guesting on Cher's
Sunday night TV variety series on CBS.

(Warner Bros: 1983), and BAD
MOON RISING (Fogerty), the
Creedence follow-up to PROUD
MARY, was heard in both "An
American Werewolf In London"
(Universal: 1981) and the film which
almost single-handedly gave birth to
the baby-boomer era, "The Big Chill"
(Columbia: 1983).

Finally, you may have heard KEEP
ON CHOOGLIN' (Fogerty) along
with Creedence's version of I
HEARD IT THROUGH THE
GRAPEVINE (Whitfield/Strong)** in
"Where The Buffalo Roam"
(Universal: 1980) and FORTUNATE
SON (Fogerty) was featured on the
track of Jonathan Demme's escapade
comedy "Melvin And Howard"
(Universal: 1980).

PURPLE HAZE
(Jimi Hendrix)
Hendrix supposedly wrote this about
the effects of a drug popularly
known as PURPLE HAZE. In any
event, the song has become a great
psychedelic rock anthem,
punctuated by Jimi's memorable
request: 'Scuse me, while I kiss the
sky!'

The original Hendrix record was
heard on the soundtrack of the Bill
Murray comedy, "Where The Buffalo
Roam" (Universal: 1980). Performed
by Jimi in the rock movies,
"Experience" (1969), "Jimi Plays
Berkeley" (1971), and "Jimi Hendrix"
(1973).

US HIT: Jimi Hendrix
          (Reprise: 1967) Pop
          Dion (Laurie: 1969) Pop

Other recordings: Joe Smooth
(Westside); Frank Marino and
Mahogany Rush (Columbia); Jose
Feliciano (RCA); Winger (Atlantic).

Parody record: GREEN HAZE (Pts. 1
& 2) (the theme song from TV's
"Green Acres" series sung to the
tune of PURPLE HAZE) by Elvis
Hitler (Restless: 1988)

Devo (Warner Bros) covered
another of the Hendrix classics, ARE
YOU EXPERIENCED and the same
tune was more recently revived by
Caresse And Sickmob (Temple).

PUT A LITTLE LOVE IN YOUR HEART
(Jackie DeShannon/Randy Myers/
Jimmy Holiday)
This spiritually uplifting ballad is the
most enduring of the songs on which
pop singer–songwriter Jackie
DeShannon collaborated with R&B
singer and Ray Charles' protégé, the
late Jimmy Holiday. Jackie's original
record of the song was used on the
soundtrack of the Karel Reisz movie,
"Who'll Stop The Rain" (UK Title:
"The Dog Soldiers") (UA: 1978). Ten
years later, Dave Stewart produced
fellow-Eurythmic Annie Lennox
duetting a remake version with the
soul of gospel music, Al Green, on
the soundtrack of the Bill Murray
farce, "Scrooged" (Paramount: 1988).

US HITS: Jackie DeShannon
          (Imperial: 1969) Pop
          Susan Raye (Capitol:
          1970) Country
          Annie Lennox and Al
          Green (A&M: 1988)
          Pop
UK HITS: The Dave Clark Five (UK
          Columbia: 1969)
          Annie Lennox and Al
          Green (A&M: 1988)

Other recordings: Martha and The
Vandellas (Gordy); Cilla Black
(Parlophone); Ella Fitzgerald (Pablo);
Ray Sanders (UA); David Ruffin
(Motown); The Trinidad Tripoli Steel
Band (AVI); Eddy Arnold (RCA);
The Four Freshmen (Liberty); Sandy
Nelson (Liberty).

See: WHEN YOU WALK IN THE
ROOM for other Jackie DeShannon
songs.

QUEEN OF HEARTS

(Hank DeVito)
One of two Hank DeVito songs
which Dave Edmunds included on
his *Repeat When Necessary* album
(Swan Song: 1979).

US HIT: Juice Newton (Capitol:
                1981) Pop & Country
UK HIT: Dave Edmunds (Swan
                Song: 1979)

Other recording: Rodney Crowell
(Warner Bros: 1980).

RAVE ON

(Sonny West/Bill Tighman/Norman
Petty)
Buddy Holly classic and originally
recorded by Sonny West for Atlantic
in 1958.
    Buddy Holly's version was heard
on the soundtrack of "American Hot
Wax" (Paramount: 1978), but it was
Gary Busey himself singing the song
when he starred in "The Buddy Holly
Story" (Columbia: 1978).
    Revived by John Cougar
Mellencamp for the soundtrack of
the Tom Cruise movie "Cocktail",
released on Elektra.

US HIT: Buddy Holly (Coral: 1958)
                Pop
UK HITS: Buddy Holly (Coral: 1958)
                Buddy Holly (MCA: 1968
                Re-release)

Other recordings: Waylon Jennings
(A&M); The Nitty Gritty Dirt Band

(UA); The Hullaballos (Roulette);
Jackson Highway (Capitol); Steeleye
Span (Chrysalis); Jesse Colin Young
(Elektra); Commander Cody and
The Lost Planet Airmen (Paramount);
The Buddy Holly Story soundtrack
(Epic).

See: LOVE'S MADE A FOOL OF
YOU for other Buddy Holly songs.

REACH OUT I'LL BE THERE

(Brian Holland/Lamont Dozier/Eddie
Holland)
Pinnacle of the Four Tops' Motown
output, and one of Holland/Dozier/
Holland's finest songs and
productions.
    The Tops' original record turned
REACH OUT into a rhythmically
driven love song, fully orchestrated
by Levi Stubbs' extraordinary,
desperate vocal, with the other
voices swelling out the unforgettable
chorus.
    Several attempts at re-kindling the
chart potential of this song have
been mounted over the years by
such as Merrilee Rush, Gloria
Gaynor and even Motown's own
Diana Ross, but the original
performance has never been
surpassed.

US HITS: The Four Tops (Motown:
                1966) Black & Pop
                Diana Ross (Motown:
                1971) Black & Pop
                Gloria Gaynor (MGM:
                1975) Pop
UK HITS: The Four Tops (Tamla
                Motown: 1966)
                Gloria Gaynor (MGM:
                1975)

Other recordings: David Johansen
(Blue Sky); P. J. Proby (Liberty);
Chris Farlowe (Immediate); Count
Basie (Brunswick); Thelma Houston
(Motown); Narada Michael Walden
(Atlantic); Petula Clark (Warner
Bros).

In 1989, the re-formed Doobie
Brothers (on their Capitol album,

Cycles) revived ONE CHAIN DON'T MAKE NO PRISON which had been a Four Tops hit on Dunhill in 1974. Song was written by the songwriting team of Britisher Dennis Lambert and New Yorker Brian Potter. Incidentally, Lambert co-wrote (with Bernie Taupin, Peter Wolf and Martin Page) Starship's international smash, WE BUILT THIS CITY (Grunt: 1985).

See: DEVIL WITH A BLUE DRESS ON for other Motown hits.

See: HOW SWEET IT IS for other Holland/Dozier/Holland songs.

READY TEDDY

(John Marascalco/Robert Blackwell) One of the many Little Richard hits co-written by Robert 'Bumps' Blackwell, his producer. Performed by Richard in the rock movie "The Girl Can't Help It" (20th Century Fox: 1956). Song featured by a Little Richard impersonator in the classic Federico Fellini movie, "La Dolce Vita" (1961) and by Elvis Presley in "Elvis On Tour" (MGM: 1972).

Recorded in a medley with RIP IT UP** by John Lennon on his *Rock 'N' Roll* album (Apple: 1975).

US HIT: Little Richard (Specialty: 1956) Black & Pop

Other recordings: Buddy Holly (Coral); Elvis Presley (RCA); Gene Vincent and His Blue Caps (Capitol); Big Wheelie and The Hubcaps (Scepter).

See: RIP IT UP for other John Marascalco songs.

See: TUTTI FRUTTI for other Little Richard songs.

RED, RED WINE

(Neil Diamond) British reggae band UB40 teamed up for a second time with the Pretenders lead singer Chrissie Hynde for a revival of RED, RED

WINE. The single was a smash on both sides of the Atlantic, and in America, A&M (their US label) took an advertisement in Billboard magazine trumpeting the record's success by claiming that it was the first Number One reggae single in history ; this was not entirely true, because Johnny Nash's I CAN SEE CLEARLY NOW, which was recorded in Jamaica with members of Bob Marley's group, had topped the Stateside charts almost sixteen years earlier.

But the story doesn't end there, because UB40's RED, RED WINE single was originally released in 1984 when it made it into the Top 50. Then in the early summer of 1988 a radio station in Phoenix, Arizona started playing it again, and the record's popularity spread like wildfire!

RED, RED WINE
Neil Diamond's original version of RED, RED WINE was released just prior to his switching labels to MCA's Uni from Bang, the label so-named after the initials of its partner-owners: Bert Berns, Ahmet Ertegun, Nesuhi Ertegun and Gerald Wexler. Neil's records on Bang, including his own CHERRY CHERRY and SOLITARY MAN, plus the covers listed on this album jacket, were produced by Jeff Barry and Ellie Greenwich.

US HITS: Neil Diamond (Bang:
             1968) Pop
           Vic Dana (Liberty: 1970)
             Pop
           UB40 (A&M: 1984) Pop
           UB40 (A&M: 1988 Re-
             release) Pop
UK HITS: Jimmy James and The
             Vagabonds (Pye: 1968)
           Toni Tribe (Downtown:
             1969)
           UB40 (Dep International:
             1983)
           . UB40 (Dep International :
             1988 Re-release)

Other recordings: Johnny Duncan
(Columbia); David Frizzell (MCA);
Ace Cannon (Hi).

See: I'M A BELIEVER for other Neil
Diamond songs.

REET PETITE

(Berry Gordy Jr/Tyran Carlo)
Sub-titled THE FINEST GIRL YOU
EVER WANT TO MEET, this was
Jackie Wilson's debut hit in 1957.
Twenty-nine years later, it was used
on the soundtrack of a British TV
commercial and made the Christmas
Number One spot.

US HIT: Jackie Wilson (Brunswick:
             1957) Pop
UK HITS: Jackie Wilson (Coral:
             1957)
           Jackie Wilson (SMP: 1986
             Re-release)

(Original records are not always
used in television ads; for instance,
the soundbed of the 501 Jeans
commercial which utilized I HEARD
IT THROUGH THE GRAPEVINE
featured a duplicate of the original
arrangement, along with singer Tony
Jackson re-creating Marvin Gaye's
vocal part; the session was produced
by ex-Soft Machine members Mike
Ratledge and Karl Jenkins.)

RESPECT

(Otis Redding)
Original version recorded by its
composer for his *Otis Blue* album
(Volt: 1965). Aretha Franklin's
subsequent cover was her first
British hit, and to date, her only
Number One pop hit in the States.
Song was revived with a rap version
by The Real Roxanne in 1988 and
another charter by Adeva early the
following year.

Aretha's version was heard on the
soundtrack of the movie, "Mystic
Pizza" (Samuel Goldwyn: 1988) and
"Back To School" (Orion: 1986).

US HITS: Otis Redding (Volt: 1965)
             Black & Pop
           Aretha Franklin (Atlantic:
             1967) Black & Pop
UK HITS: Aretha Franklin (Atlantic:
             1967)
           Adeva (Cooltempo: 1989)

Other recordings: The Staple
Singers (Stax); The Vagrants (Atco);
Ike and Tina Turner (Liberty); Jackie
Wilson and Count Basie (Brunswick);
Stevie Wonder (Tamla); Sam and
Dave (Stax); Nicci (Sedition); Reba
McEntire (MCA); Chris Hunter
(Atlantic); Diana Ross and The
Supremes and The Temptations
(Motown); St Louis Union (UK
Decca); Geno Washington and the
Ram Jam Band (Piccadilly).

RESPECT YOURSELF

(Luther Ingram/Mack Rice)
To the amazement of many, TV actor
(and now movie star) Bruce Willis
cut a remake of this Staple Singers
hit and soared up the American
charts with it.

Performed by The Kane Gang on
the soundtrack of "Bad Guys"
(InterPictures: 1986)

US HITS: The Staple Singers (Stax:
             1971) Pop
           Bruce Willis (Motown:
             1987) Pop & Black

UK HIT: Bruce Willis (Motown:
                1987)

Other recordings: Blue Mitchell
(Mainstream); Stevie Wonder
(Tamla).

'Sir' Mack Rice also wrote and
originally recorded MUSTANG
SALLY (on Blue Rock), the song with
which Wilson Pickett scored on
Atlantic in 1967. Singer–songwriter
Luther Ingram's biggest hit of his
own was (IF LOVING YOU IS
WRONG) I DON'T WANT TO BE
RIGHT (Koko: 1972).

RIOT IN CELL BLOCK NUMBER 9

(Jerry Leiber/Mike Stoller)
Never a chart record, but a key
West-Coast R&B milestone. First
recorded by Bobby Nunn and The
Robins (Spark: 1954) with Richard
Berry setting the scene via the
words 'On July 2nd, 1953...', the
chorus chanting 'There's a riot going
on', punctuated this memorable
narrative song. Also recorded by
such as Wanda Jackson (Capitol);
Commander Cody (Paramount); The
Beach Boys (Reprise); Johnny Winter
(Columbia) and British group, Dr
Feelgood (UA). Also recorded by
Darts in a medley with Willie
Mabon's I'M MAD, FRAMED
(Leiber/Stoller) and TROUBLE
(Leiber/Stoller/Pomus) (Magnet).

See: JAILHOUSE ROCK for other
Jerry Leiber and Mike Stoller songs.

RIP IT UP

(John Marascalco/Robert Blackwell)
Another Little Richard classic which
he performed in various concert
movies including "Sweet Toronto"
(Pennebaker: 1971), "Let The Good
Times Roll" (Columbia: 1973) and
"The London Rock 'N' Roll Show"
(1974).
    But his classic movie version of the
song was in "Don't Knock The Rock"
(Columbia: 1956) and his original

record is heard on a number of
contemporary soundtracks.
    By the last count, RIP IT UP has
been recorded by more rock 'n' roll
legends than any other song.

US HITS: Little Richard (Specialty:
                1956) Pop & Black
                Bill Haley and His Comets
                (Decca: 1956) Pop
UK HITS: Bill Haley and His Comets
                (Brunswick: 1956)
                Little Richard (London:
                1956)
                Elvis Presley (HMV: 1957)

Other recordings: Buddy Holly
(Coral); John Lennon (Capitol);
Chuck Berry (Chess); The Everly
Brothers (Cadence); Wanda Jackson
(Capitol); Commander Cody and
The Lost Planet Airmen (MCA);
Chubby Checker (Parkway); Gene
Vincent (Capitol); Gerry and The
Pacemakers (UK Columbia); Carl
Perkins (Columbia).

John Marascalco songs
John Marascalco is rarely written
about or spoken of, but he is
credited as co-writer on the
following other rock 'n' roll classics:
BE MY GUEST, recorded by Fats
Domino (Imperial: 1958), GOOD
GOLLY MISS MOLLY** for Little
Richard (Specialty: 1957),
GOODNIGHT MY LOVE** by Jesse
Belvin (Modern: 1956), HEEBIE
JEEBIES by Little Richard (Specialty:
1956), SEND ME SOME LOVIN' by
Little Richard (Specialty: 1957),
SHE'S GOT IT again for Little
Richard (Specialty: 1956) and
READY TEDDY** for the same Little
Richard (Specialty: 1956).

RIVER DEEP, MOUNTAIN HIGH

(Phil Spector/Jeff Barry/Ellie
Greenwich)
This powerful song came from the
album concept which combined for
the first time Ike and Tina Turner
with producer Phil Spector.

RIVER DEEP—MOUNTAIN HIGH
(Spector, Barry, Greenwich)
IKE & TINA TURNER

Spector's identity had been built on dynamically opulent productions built around a succession of girl groups and marrying his technique with the voice of Tina Turner seemed a natural. The result was nothing short of magnificent, with Tina's pleading vocals spectacularly bathed in a cavernous hallway of sound. What has never been entirely explained is why the record was a smash hit in Britain and only a minor chart success in the States, despite critical praise. Ike and Tina's record (Philles: 1986) didn't even make it into the US Top 75 and the Deep Purple cover three years later just missed breaking into the Top 50. The song had to wait until the Supremes/Four Tops combination which finally took it into the American Top 20.

Song featured in the Broadway musical, "Leader Of The Pack".

US HITS: Deep Purple
          (Tetragrammaton:
          1969) Pop
          The Supremes and The
          Four Tops (Motown:
          1971) Black & Pop

UK HITS: Ike and Tina Turner
          (London: 1966)
          Ike and Tina Turner
          (London: 1969 Re-
          release)
          The Supremes and The
          Four Tops (Tamla
          Motown: 1971)

Other recordings: Bob Seger (Capitol); Darlene Love (Elektra); Leslie Uggams (Atlantic); Eric Burdon and The Animals (MGM); Ellie Greenwich (Verve); Dobie Gray (Capitol); The Easybeats (UA); Nilsson (RCA); Long John Baldry (Pye); Erasure (Sire).

See: DA DOO RON RON for other Phil Spector classics.

Barry and Greenwich songs
Jeff Barry and his wife Ellie Greenwich were performers as well as one of the foremost songwriting teams of the 1960s. They sang as part of a trio called The Raindrops, charting with their own THE KIND OF BOY YOU CAN'T FORGET (Jubilee: 1963) and they also recorded simply as Jeff and Ellie, cutting another of their collaborations, I KNOW IT'S ALRIGHT (Red Bird). Yet their mainstay was writing for other acts in general, and girl-groups in particular.

Among the hit records of other Barry and Greenwich songs were:

BABY I LOVE YOU** (with Phil
    Spector) by The Ronettes (Philles:
    1964)
BE MY BABY** (with Phil Spector)
    by The Ronettes (Philles: 1963)
CHAPEL OF LOVE** (with Phil
    Spector) by The Dixie Cups (Red
    Bird: 1964)
DA DOO RON RON** (with Phil
    Spector) by The Crystals (Philles:
    1963)
DO WAH DIDDY DIDDY** by The
    Exciters (UA: 1964)
    by Manfred Mann (HMV: 1964)
GIVE US YOUR BLESSING by The

Shangri-Las (Red Bird: 1965)
HANKY PANKY by Tommy James
and The Shondells (Roulette: 1966)
I CAN HEAR MUSIC (with Phil
Spector) by The Ronettes (Philles:
1966)
by The Beach Boys (Capitol: 1969)
I WANNA LOVE HIM SO BAD by
The Jelly Beans (Red Bird: 1964)
THE KIND OF BOY YOU CAN'T
FORGET by The Raindrops
(Jubilee: 1963)
LEADER OF THE PACK** (with
George Morton) by The Shangri-
Las (Red Bird: 1964)
LOOK OF LOVE by Lesley Gore
(Mercury: 1965)
MAYBE I KNOW by Lesley Gore
(Mercury: 1964)
NOT TOO YOUNG TO GET
MARRIED (with Phil Spector) by
Bob B. Soxx and The Blue Jeans
(Philles: 1963)
PEOPLE SAY by The Dixie Cups
(Red Bird: 1964)
THEN HE KISSED ME** (with Phil
Spector) by The Crystals (Philles:
1963)
WAIT TILL MY BOBBY GETS
HOME (with Phil Spector) by
Darlene Love (Philles: 1963)

ROCK AND ROLL MUSIC
(Chuck Berry)
Rock's eternal anthem. One of two
Chuck Berry tunes recorded by The
Beatles, this one on their *Beatles For
Sale* album (Parlophone: 1964).
Performed by Etta James in the
Chuck Berry movie "Hail! Hail! Rock
'N' Roll" (Universal: 1987).

US HITS: Chuck Berry (Chess:
1957) Black & Pop
The Beach Boys (Brother:
1976) Pop
UK HIT: The Beach Boys (Reprise:
1976)

Other recordings: REO Speedwagon
(Epic); Billy 'Crash' Craddock (ABC);
Bill Haley and His Comets (Sonet);

The Everly Brothers (Warner Bros).

See: MEMPHIS for other Chuck
Berry songs.

ROCK AROUND THE CLOCK
(Max Freedman/Jimmy DeKnight)
'(WE'RE GONNA) ROCK AROUND
THE CLOCK' was, for many, a first in
rock 'n' roll history. It marked the
official entrance of rock 'n' roll into
the world of pop music and it also
became the title of Hollywood's first
rock movie, but let's step back and
examine some other facts. First of all,
Bill Haley's was not the original
version of the song. Co-written by
Jimmy DeKnight, which was actually
a pseudonym for music publisher
Jimmy Myers, the song was first
recorded by Sonny Dae and The
Knights on the Arcade label.
   Bill Haley switched from a smaller
label to American Decca and ROCK
AROUND THE CLOCK was one of
the tunes on his first session there.
MGM were finishing "Blackboard
Jungle" (1955), a picture about a
teacher (Glenn Ford) confronting
tough teenage pupils at a New York
School. They leased some jazz
records by Stan Kenton and Bix
Biederbecke for the soundtrack, in
addition to Haley's ROCK AROUND
THE CLOCK which was used under
the opening and closing titles. The
picture exploded and the Bill Haley
record took off.
   The song was heard again on the
screen, this time in "Rock Around
The Clock" (Columbia: 1956), the
movie which showcased Haley and
The Comets along with d-j Alan
Freed and other musical acts. The
original Decca recording was also
heard years later on the sound-track
of George Lucas' "American Graffiti"
(Universal: 1973) and it was also
performed by Paul Rodgers on the
track of "The Karate Kid Part II"
(Columbia: 1986).
   ROCK AROUND THE CLOCK by
Bill Haley was also used as the

(WE'RE GONNA)
ROCK AROUND THE CLOCK
Words and Music by MAX C. FREEDMAN and JIMMY DE KNIGHT A.S.C.A.P.

5 0 ¢

DECCA RECORDS

MYERS MUSIC

BILL HALEY and his COMETS

ROCK AROUND THE CLOCK
The song that ignited a storm! Bill Haley (in the dark suit) and His Comets topped hit-parade charts around the globe with this song, first heard on the soundtrack of the Glenn Ford movie, "Blackboard Jungle".

theme song on the early episodes of the "Happy Days" television show

(ABC Televsion: 1974), hence the return to the American charts of the record that year.

US HITS: Bill Haley and His Comets
(Decca: 1955) Black &
Pop
Bill Haley and His Comets

(MCA: 1974 Re-
release) Pop
UK HITS: Bill Haley and His Comets
(Brunswick: 1955, 1956
and 1957)
Bill Haley and His Comets
(MCA: 1968 Re-
release)
Bill Haley and His Comets
(MCA: 1974 Re-
release)
The Sex Pistols (Virgin:
1979)
Telex (Sire: 1979)

Other recordings: Nilsson (RCA);
The Mark Four (Mercury); Rodney
Lay and The Wild West (Sun);
Buddy Knox; Joey Welz (formerly of
'The Comets') (Fraternity); The Isley
Brothers (RCA); Freddy Cannon;
Mae West; Carl Perkins (Jet).

The 1959 hit record, CHARLIE
BROWN (Leiber/Stoller) by The
Coasters (Atco), contains the line
'Who calls the English teacher
Daddy-O?' which supposedly refers
to the "Blackboard Jungle" film in
which Glenn Ford's character is
referred to as 'Daddy-O'.

SWING THE MOOD:
Probably the oddest revival record
in recent times was the Number One
UK hit, SWING THE MOOD by Jive
Bunny and The Mastermixers (Music
Factory Dance: 1989). A mixture of
sampling and straightforward
medley, it began and ended with the
1938 Glenn Miller tune IN THE
MOOD (Garland/Razaf); interspersed
were portions of the original Bill
Haley recordings of ROCK AROUND
THE CLOCK and another of his 1955
hits, ROCK-A-BEATIN' BOOGIE
(Haley), The Everly Brothers doing
WAKE UP LITTLE SUSIE
(Bryant/Bryant)** plus extracts from
HOUND DOG (Leiber/Stoller)**,
ALL SHOOK UP (Blackwell/
Presley)** and JAILHOUSE ROCK
(Leiber/Stoller)**, all sung by an
Elvis soundalike. Also integrated at
various points were the chorus from

SHAKE, RATTLE AND ROLL
(Calhoun)**, some vocal phrases
from AT THE HOP (Madara/
Singer/White)**, Little Richard's
famed opening vocal line (albeit
rhythmically restructured) from
TUTTI FRUTTI (Penniman/
LaBostrie/Lubin)** plus Eddie
Cochran's strident guitar intro from
C'MON EVERYBODY
(Cochran/Capehart).
   The follow-up single, THAT'S
WHAT I LIKE (Music Factory Dance:
1989) used the TV theme HAWAII
FIVE-O (Stevens) as the musical
base, along with the OH BABY,
THAT'S WHAT I LIKE tagline from
the close of the Big Bopper's
CHANTILLY LACE** hit; the
interpolated songs in this Jive Bunny
medley included Chubby Checker's
remakes of both LET'S TWIST
AGAIN (Mann/Appell) and THE
TWIST (Ballard)**, Jerry Lee's
GREAT BALLS OF FIRE
(Blackwell/Hammer)**, Little
Richard's GOOD GOLLY MISS
MOLLY (Blackwell/Marascalco)**
and Dion's RUNAROUND SUE
(DiMucci/Maresca)**. In 1989 this
single reached Number One on the
British charts and there will
undoubtedly be more sequels and
further variations on this formula.

ROCKIN' AT MIDNIGHT
See: GOOD ROCKIN' TONIGHT.

**ROCKIN' PNEUMONIA AND THE
BOOGIE WOOGIE FLU**
(Huey Smith/Johnny Vincent)
Huey 'Piano' Smith earned his
nickname as a regular session player
in his native New Orleans. He
played on the dates of key R&B
figures including Little Richard,
Lloyd Price and Guitar Slim and he
claims that the piano intro on Smiley
Lewis' original version of Dave
Bartholomew's I HEAR YOU
KNOCKING** is his.
   What we can be sure of is that it's

Huey's pounding keyboard on his original record of this song, for which Ace Records owner Johnny Vincent is credited as co-writer. Huey himself recalls getting the inspiration for the title from Chuck Berry who referred to 'rockin' pneumonia' in his ROLL OVER BEETHOVEN** lyric.

Performed by Aerosmith on the soundtrack of "Less Than Zero" (20th Century Fox: 1987).

US HITS: Huey 'Piano' Smith and
           The Clowns (Ace:
           1957) Black & Pop
           Johnny Rivers (UA: 1972)
           Pop

Other recordings: Patti LaBelle (Philadelphia International); The Flamin' Groovies (Epic); Chris Farlowe (Immediate); Bobby Marchan (Cameo); Professor Longhair; Jerry Lee Lewis (Smash); Georgie Fame (UK Columbia); P. J. Proby (Liberty).

ROCKIN' ROBIN
(Jimmie Thomas)
Originally spelled out 'Rock-in Robin', this was Bobby Day's biggest hit, written by Leon Rene under the name Jimmie Thomas (see also GLORIA). Day's backing group singing the 'Tweet, tweet, tweedly-dee' phrases were credited as The Satellites but were actually The Hollywood Flames, a recording group in their own right.

US HITS: Bobby Day (Class: 1958)
           Black & Pop
           Michael Jackson
           (Motown: 1972) Black &
           Pop
UK HITS: Bobby Day (London:
           1958)
           Michael Jackson (Tamla
           Motown: 1972)

Other recordings: Clyde McPhatter (Mercury); The Hollies (Parlophone); Cliff Bennett and The Rebel Rousers (Parlophone); The Rivieras (Riviera);

Ernie Fields Orchestra (Rendezvous); Freddy Cannon (Buddah).

Bobby Day's other two major hits were LITTLE BITTY PRETTY ONE** and OVER AND OVER**.

ROLL OVER BEETHOVEN
(Chuck Berry)
Seminal statement in rock 'n' roll's language book of rebellion. Covered memorably by The Beatles on their *With The Beatles* LP (Parlophone: 1963), it was also the second chart record for ELO. In the States, the Beatles track became a semi-hit.

Early footage of The Beatles performing the song in concert was included in the TV special, "The Beatles Come To Town" (1963), while it is understandably one of the key numbers performed by the master himself in "Chuck Berry: Hail! Hail! Rock 'N' Roll" (Universal: 1987).

US HITS: Chuck Berry (Chess:
           1956) Black & Pop
           The Velaires (Jamie:
           1961) Pop
           The Beatles (Capitol:
           1964) Pop
           Electric Light Orchestra
           (UA: 1973) Pop
UK HIT: Electric Light Orchestra
           (Harvest: 1973)

Other recordings: Jerry Lee Lewis (Smash); Pat Wayne and The Beachcombers (UK Columbia); Mountain (Columbia); The Powder Blues (Flying Fish); Gerry and The Pacemakers (UK Columbia); Bill Black's Combo (Hi); Johnny Rivers (Imperial); The Royal Waterford Showband (HMV); The Astronauts (RCA); Carl Perkins (Sun).

See: MEMPHIS for other Chuck Berry songs.

See: DIZZY MISS LIZZY for other Beatles' re-makes.

ROLL WITH ME HENRY
See: WORK WITH ME ANNIE.

RUBY BABY

(Jerry Leiber/Mike Stoller)
An early Leiber and Stoller hit cut
first by The Drifters and later
covered by Dion, formerly of Dion
and The Belmonts. Dion's revival was
so successful that he re-worked
another of the old Drifters' tunes,
namely Leiber and Stoller's DRIP
DROP. RUBY BABY by The Drifters
was featured on the soundtrack of
the Matt Dillon movie, "The Big
Town" (Columbia: 1987).

US HITS: The Drifters (Atlantic:
           1956) Black
           Dion (Columbia: 1963)
           Pop & Black
           Billy 'Crash' Craddock
           (ABC: 1975) Pop &
           Country

Other recordings: Tony Sheridan
and The Beatles (Polydor); Donald
Fagen (Warner Bros); Ronnie
Hawkins (Roulette); Dion and The
Belmonts (Warner Bros).

See: JAILHOUSE ROCK for other
Jerry Leiber and Mike Stoller songs.

RUNAROUND SUE

(Dion DiMucci/Ernie Maresca)
The song which provided Dion with
his first major hit after splitting from
The Belmonts. Written with Ernie
Maresca, an artist in his own right
who cut SHOUT, SHOUT (KNOCK
YOURSELF OUT) on Seville in 1962.
The Dion original was heard on the
soundtrack of "The Flamingo Kid"
(20th Century Fox: 1984), while John
Cafferty and The Beaver Brown
Band performed the song for the
"Eddie and The Cruisers" movie
(Embassy: 1983).

RUNAROUND SUE
Dion as he appeared in one of the tinted, musical
numbers inserted into the tepid "Teenage
Millionaire" movie (UA: 1961) which starred Jimmy
Clanton.

US HITS: Dion (Laurie: 1961) Black
           & Pop
           Leif Garrett (Atlantic:
           1977) Pop
UK HITS: Dion (Top Rank: 1961)
           Doug Sheldon (UK Decca:
           1961)
           Racey (RAK: 1980)

Other recordings: Del Shannon (Big
Top); The Four Preps (Capitol);
Leroy van Dyke (Plantation); *Eddie
And The Cruisers* soundtrack (Scotti
Bros).

RUNAWAY
(Del Shannon/Max Crook)
One day, Guinness will probably
inform us that RUNAWAY has
achieved at least one astounding feat
in pop history, if not more. It seems
as though this archetypal rocker
from 1960 has been included on
more TV-advertised oldies packages
than any other. Del's original hit

RUNAWAY
Two rock 'n' roll legends who wrote most of their
own million selling songs! Del Shannon (left)
started with RUNAWAY while Paul Anka debuted
with DIANA and both their records went to
Number One in the States. (See also DIANA.)

single has also appeared on various movie soundtracks ranging from "American Graffiti" and "That'll Be The Day" (both 1973) to "Dusty And Sweets McGee", released two years earlier. Bonnie Raitt performed RUNAWAY in the concert movie "No Nukes" (Warner Bros: 1980) and, six years later, Del himself recorded a new version (with slightly altered lyric) for the main title soundtrack of the Michael Mann NBC Television series, "Crime Story".

US HITS: Del Shannon (Big Top: 1961) Pop & Black
          Lawrence Welk and His Orchestra (Dot: 1962) Pop
          Charlie Kulis (Playboy:1975) Pop
          Bonnie Raitt (Warner Bros: 1977) Pop
          Narvel Felts (ABC: 1978) Country
UK HIT: Del Shannon (London: 1961)

Other recordings: Elvis Presley (RCA); Sha Na Na (Kama Sutra); Bonnie Leigh (RCP); The Shirelles (Scepter); The McCoys (Bang); Dawn featuring Tony Orlando (in a medley with HAPPY TOGETHER) (Bell); Luis Cardenas (Allied Artists); Small Faces (UK Decca); The Ventures (Dolton); The Hunters (Fontana).

Other artists recorded Del Shannon songs, most notably British duo Peter and Gordon, whose version of I GO TO PIECES (Capitol: 1965) was a Top 10 record in the States; Rachel Sweet did a fine revival on Stiff in 1979.

SATISFACTION.
See: (I CAN'T GET NO) SATISFACTION.

SAVE THE LAST DANCE FOR ME
(Doc Pomus/Mort Shuman)
A number one R&B and number one Pop ballad, sung memorably by the legendary Drifters in 1960 with Ben E. King supplying the lead vocal. It was the group's biggest single seller and was produced by Jerry Leiber and Mike Stoller.

US HITS: The Drifters (Atlantic: 1960) Pop & Black
          Buck Owens (Capitol:1962) Country
          The De Franco Family (20th Century Fox: 1974) Pop
          Dolly Parton (RCA: 1983) Pop & Country
UK HITS: The Drifters (London: 1960)
          The Drifters (Lightning: 1979 Re-release)
          Ben E. King (EMI Manhattan: 1987)

Other recordings: Dion (Laurie); The Swinging Blue Jeans (HMV); Jerry Lee Lewis (Sun); Nilsson (RCA); Emmylou Harris (Warner Bros); Buck Owens (Capitol); Ben E. King (EMI-Manhattan); Cliff Richard (UK Columbia); Ike and Tina Turner (A&M); Jay and The Americans (UA); Patti LaBelle.

Answer records: I'LL SAVE THE LAST DANCE FOR YOU by Damita Jo (Mercury: 1960) YOU'RE HAVING THE LAST DANCE WITH ME by Billy Fury (UK Decca: 1961).

See: A TEENAGER IN LOVE for other Doc Pomus and Mort Shuman songs.

Harry Nilsson's version was on his celebrated *Pussy Cats* album (RCA: 1974) which John Lennon produced and on which such fellow luminaries as Ringo Starr and Keith Moon sit in as Nilsson also covered ROCK AROUND THE CLOCK**, Johnny Thunder's hit LOOP DE LOOP (Vann) and Dylan's quintessential SUBTERRANEAN HOMESICK BLUES. Aside from his own significant body of compositions which include COCONUT, JUMP INTO THE FIRE and ME AND MY ARROW (all Nilsson hits on RCA), he is best remembered for his American and British Number One, WITHOUT YOU (RCA: 1972), written by Peter Ham and Tom Evans of Badfinger.

SAY A LITTLE PRAYER
See: I SAY A LITTLE PRAYER.

SCHOOL DAY
(Chuck Berry)
Among Chuck Berry's most descriptive songs, telling of the classroom, lunchbreak and the afternoon class until three o'clock, and the welcome dash to the 'juke joint'! Performed by him in the Alan Freed movie, "Go Johnny Go" (Hal Roach: 1959), it is also the song from which the line, 'Hail! Hail! Rock 'N' Roll' comes, and that became the title of the 1987 Chuck Berry concert movie.

The original Chuck Berry record was featured on the soundtrack of The Ramones' high school-blasting flick, "Rock 'N' Roll High School" (New World: 1979).

US HIT: Chuck Berry (Chess: 1957) Black & Pop
UK HITS: Chuck Berry (UK Columbia: 1957)
Don Lang and His Frantic Five (HMV: 1957)

Other recordings: New Riders Of The Purple Sage (Columbia); The Beach Boys (Caribou).

See: MEMPHIS for other Chuck Berry songs.

Juke boxes in rock 'n' roll
Other songs which refer to jukeboxes include:

MUSIC, MUSIC, MUSIC (PUT ANOTHER NICKEL IN) (Weiss/Baum) by Teresa Brewer (Coral: 1950)
IF I DIDN'T HAVE A DIME (TO PLAY THE JUKE BOX) (Russell/Medley) by Gene Pitney (Musicor: 1962)
JUKE BOX MUSIC (Davies) by The Kinks (Arista: 1976)
A PRAYER AND A JUKE BOX (Shelton) by Little Anthony and The Imperials (End: 1959)
LET THE JUKE BOX KEEP ON PLAYING (Perkins) by Carl Perkins (Sun: 1955)
SOMEBODY PUT A JUKE BOX IN THE STUDY HALL (Hayes/Bartholomew) by Shirley and Lee (Imperial: 1963)

SEA CRUISE
(Huey P. Smith)
Originally recorded at an Ace Records session with Huey 'Piano' Smith, but his vocals were replaced by those of Frankie Ford; Huey therefore lost the chance at having the original SEA CRUISE hit even though his group, The Clowns, are the backing musicians. The Johnny Rivers revival was a semi-hit, making it into the bottom half of the Top 100.

The original Frankie Ford record was heard on the soundtrack of "American Hot Wax" (Paramount: 1978).

US HITS: Frankie Ford (Ace: 1959) Black & Pop
Johnny Rivers (UA: 1971) Pop

Other recordings: Robert Gordon and Link Wray (Private Stock); Jose Feliciano (RCA); Jerry Lee Lewis

(Mercury); Billy 'Crash' Craddock (Capitol); John Fogerty (Asylum); Herman's Hermits (UK Columbia).

Sound effects in rock 'n' roll

The Frankie Ford record of SEA CRUISE opened with the clanging of a ship's bell, rippling water and the blast of a ship's horn. Many R&B/R&R records utilized sound effects which were relevant to the song lyrics and other nautical sounds were heard on YELLOW SUBMARINE (Lennon/McCartney) by The Beatles (Parlophone: 1966) and CAPTAIN OF YOUR SHIP (Young/Yardley), a big UK hit for American girl group, Reparata and The Delrons (Mala: 1968).

Inclement weather is particularly common on pop singles with some of the best thunderclaps and/or rainstorms occurring on the following records:

FLOWERS IN THE RAIN (Wood) by The Move (Regal Zonophone: 1967)
IN THE RAIN (Hester) by The Dramatics (Volt: 1972)
RAINDROPS (Clark) by Dee Clark (Vee-Jay: 1961)
RHYTHM OF THE RAIN (Gummoe) by The Cascades (Valiant: 1963)
WALKIN' IN THE RAIN WITH THE ONE I LOVE (White) by Love Unlimited (Uni: 1972)

(This last entry also contains the sound of a telephone call, together with Barry White answering the 'phone and talking; as such, the record would also qualify as a telephone song, a category which is briefly explored under CHANTILLY LACE.)

Obviously, monster records benefit from creaks and screams and all manner of noises-off (Bobby Pickett's MONSTER MASH being a prime example), so refer to the Monster Records list under MONSTER MASH for other Halloween-type concoctions.

Following is a checklist of some other R&B/R&R singles and their sound effect ingredients:

BEEP BEEP (Cicchetti/Claps) by The Playmates (Roulette: 1958) – motor horn
FIRE BRIGADE (Wood) by The Move (Regal Zonophone: 1968) – fire truck siren and bell
GROOVIN' (Cavaliere/Brigati)** by The Young Rascals (Atlantic: 1967) – bird calls
LEADER OF THE PACK (Morton/Barry/Greenwich)** by The Shangri-Las (Red Bird: 1964) – motorcycle engine, car motors, brakes screeching and crash
(REMEMBER) WALKIN' IN THE SAND (Morton) by The Shangri-Las (Red Bird: 1964) – seagulls crying and waves on the shore
SHOTGUN WEDDING (Hammond) by Roy C (Island: 1966) - gun shots
SO MUCH IN LOVE (Straigis/Jackson/Williams) by The Tymes (Parkway: 1963) - seagulls and waves on the shore
STICK SHIFT (Bellinger) by The Duals (Sue: 1961) – car starting, fast take-off, screeching wheels
WESTERN MOVIES (Goldsmith/Smith) by The Olympics (Demon: 1958) – gun shots

SEA OF LOVE

(George Khoury/Philip Baptiste)
Lazy swamp-rock from the depths of Louisiana, recorded originally by the rich-textured tone of Phil Phillips, aided by doo-wop background vocals from The Twilights.

The most recent revival was by supergroup The Honeydrippers, including Jeff Beck, Jimmy Page and Nile Rodgers, with lead vocal by Robert Plant.

The recent Al Pacino movie, "Sea Of Love" (Universal: 1989), uses the song extensively; the original Phil Phillips record plays a prominent role in the picture's key murder sequence, actor John Goodman spoofs a few lines himself and the movie's end-title sequence features a reprise of the song newly recorded by Tom Waits.

US HITS: Phil Phillips with The
            Twilights (Mercury:
            1959) Black & Pop
            Del Shannon (Network:
            1982) Pop
            The Honeydrippers
            (Es Paranza: 1985) Pop
UK HITS: Marty Wilde (Philips:
            1959)
            The Honeydrippers
            (Es Paranza: 1985)

SEALED WITH A KISS

(Peter Udell/Gary Geld)
Classic American high-school teen love song; it was Brian Hyland's biggest record after his ITSY BITY TEENIE WEENIE YELLOW POLKADOT BIKINI (Vance/ Pockriss) smash on Leader in 1960. Song immediately followed the release of Brian's other romantic teen single, GINNY COME LATELY, again by Peter Udell and Gary Geld who also wrote SAVE YOUR HEART FOR ME for Gary Lewis and The Playboys (Liberty: 1965) and HURTING EACH OTHER, which eventually became a huge stateside hit for The Carpenters (A&M: 1972).

Brian Hyland's original hit was heard on the soundtrack of "That'll Be The Day" (EMI: 1973).

US HITS: Brian Hyland
            (ABC/Paramount: 1962)
            Pop
            Gary Lewis and The
            Playboys (Liberty:
            1968) Pop
            Bobby Vinton (Epic: 1972)
            Pop
UK HITS: Brian Hyland (HMV: 1962)
            Brian Hyland (ABC: 1975
            Re-release)
            Jason Donovan (PWL:
            1989)

Other recordings: The Happenings (B. T. Puppy); The Lettermen (Capitol); Nelson Riddle and His Orchestra (UA); The Flying Pickets (10); Gary Solomon (Pyramid).

Brian Hyland's official follow-up to SEALED WITH A KISS was another Udell/Geld song, WARMED OVER KISSES (LEFT OVER LOVE) (ABC/Paramount: 1962) and it was revived in 1982 by Dave Edmunds.

SEARCHIN'

(Jerry Leiber/Mike Stoller)
The only song in rock 'n' roll history that mentions six fictional detectives: Boston Blackie, Bulldog Drummond, Charlie Chan, Sam Spade, Sherlock Holmes and Sgt Joe Friday. It became the very first R&B Number One and the first Pop Top 5 record for The Coasters.

Recorded in a medley with Sam Cooke's hit CHAIN GANG (Quasha/ Yakus/Scott) and Jerry Butler's immortal HE DON'T LOVE YOU (LIKE I LOVE YOU) (Mayfield/ Carter) by the late Jim Croce (Lifesong: 1976) which made a brief appearance at the bottom of the American charts.

US HIT: The Coasters (Atco: 1957)
            Black & Pop
UK HITS: The Coasters (London:
            1957)
            The Hollies (Parlophone:
            1963)

Other recordings: Frankie Lymon and The Teenagers (Gee); Wanda Jackson (Capitol); The Lovin' Spoonful (Elektra); The Spencer Davis Group (Fontana); Buzzy Linhart (Kama Sutra); Alvin Robinson (Tiger); McCoy Tyner (Impulse); The Crew Cuts (Warwick); Ace Cannon (Hi); Johnny Rivers (UA); Otis Blackwell (Inner City); The Mugwumps (Warner Bros).

See: JAILHOUSE ROCK for other Jerry Leiber and Mike Stoller songs.

SEE SEE RIDER/C.C. RIDER
(Ma Rainey) (Chuck Willis)
'See See Rider...See what you have done'. Traditional blues song, re-worked as SEE SEE RIDER by Ma Rainey in 1925 and successfully revived by Bea Booze on Decca in 1942. However, the majority of versions in the rock era are indebted to R&B singer Chuck Willis' inspired update; it was far less frantic than certain other interpretations, and its walking-pace rhythm prompted a dance craze called 'The Stroll' to be built around it. Ironically, Chuck Willis' name became linked with the huge success of the dance, though he had nothing to do with it!

Performed by Janis Joplin in the film "Janis" (Universal: 1975).

US HITS: Chuck Willis (as
           C.C.RIDER) (Atlantic:
           1957) Black & Pop
           LaVern Baker (as
           C.C.RIDER) (Atlantic:
           1963) Black & Pop
           Bobby Powell (as
           C.C.RIDER) (Whit:
           1966) Black & Pop
           The Animals (as SEE SEE
           RIDER) (MGM: 1966)
           Pop

Other recordings: The Animals (UK Decca); The Strollers (with Earl Palmer) (Aladdin); Charlie Rich (Sun); Jimmy Witherspoon (Fantasy); Ian and Sylvia (Vanguard); Elvis Presley (RCA); The Youngbloods (RCA); Roy Buchanan (Polydor); Chuck Berry (Chess); Jerry Lee Lewis (Sun); Jimmy Rushing (Vanguard); Bill Haley and His Comets (Sonet); Esther Phillips (Atlantic); Alexis Korner's Blues Incorporated (Fontana); Dave Berry and The Cruisers (UK Decca).

Songwriter–producer (and occasional artist) Bob Crewe constructed a medley incorporating JENNY, JENNY ** (Johnson/ Penniman), a Little Richard hit (Specialty: 1957), and SEE SEE RIDER ; the result was JENNY TAKE A RIDE ** (Johnson/Penniman/ Crewe) with which Mitch Ryder and The Detroit Wheels charted in the US on New Voice in 1966, and in Britain on Stateside the same year. JENNY TAKE A RIDE was revived by Bruce Springsteen and The E Street Band in the concert movie, "No Nukes" (Warner Bros: 1980).

SEE YOU LATER ALLIGATOR
(Robert Guidry)
Originally written and first recorded by its composer Robert Guidry aka Bobby Charles under the title: 'LATER ALLIGATOR (Chess: 1955). Bill Haley covered it a few months later, making not only the song a world-wide hit, but turning the extended title into a piece of slang that everybody was using as a parting gesture!

Performed by Bill Haley and His Comets in the musical, "Rock Around The Clock" (Columbia: 1956).

US HITS: Bobby Charles (Billed as
           'LATER ALLIGATOR)
           (Chess: 1956) Black
           Bill Haley and His Comets
           (Decca: 1956) Black &
           Pop
UK HIT: Bill Haley and His Comets
           (Brunswick: 1956)

Other recordings: Winifred Atwell (UK Decca); Freddie and The Dreamers (UK Columbia).

Robert Guidry's name was also found on the credits of Fats Domino's 1960 classic, WALKING TO NEW ORLEANS (Guidry/Domino/ Bartholomew) and Clarence 'Frogman' Henry's hit, BUT I DO (Guidry/Gayten)**.

The hits that got away
Bill Haley was not the first artist to have the chance of recording SEE YOU LATER ALLIGATOR. It was originally offered to Fats Domino

back in 1954 but, as with more rock
classics than you might expect, the
song was either discarded or turned
down or simply passed over in
favour of other material.

The following is a checklist of
some of the R&R/R&B classics which
were originally written for or initially
offered to artists other than those
who ended up recording the now-
classic versions.

DANCING IN THE STREET (Gaye/
   Stevenson)**
   Intended for Kim Weston
   Actually a hit for Martha and The
   Vandellas (Gordy: 1964)
DO YOU LOVE ME (Gordy Jr.)**
   Written for The Temptations
   Actually a hit for The Contours
   (Gordy: 1962)
DON'T BE CRUEL (Blackwell/
   Presley)**
   Offered to The Four Lovers,
   Frankie Valli's first group before
   The Four Seasons
   Actually a hit for Elvis Presley
   (RCA: 1956)
EVE OF DESTRUCTION (Sloan/
   Barri)**
   Turned down by The Turtles as a
   follow-up to IT AIN'T ME BABE
   (Dylan), their debut hit (White
   Whale: 1965), though they did
   record it on their first album
   (White Whale: 1965)
   Actually a hit for Barry McGuire
   (Dunhill: 1965)
HE'S A REBEL (Pitney)**
   Turned down by The Shirelles
   Actually a hit for The Crystals
   (Philles: 1962)
IT MIGHT AS WELL RAIN UNTIL
   SEPTEMBER (Goffin/King)
   Intended for Bobby Vee (who did
   record it)
   Actually a hit for Carole King
   (Dimension: 1962)
LAY LADY LAY (Dylan)
   Offered to The Everly Brothers
   Actually a hit for Bob Dylan
   (Columbia: 1969)
MY GIRL (Robinson/White)
   Written for The Miracles

Actually a hit for The Temptations
   (Gordy: 1965)
ON BROADWAY (Mann/Weil/
   Leiber/Stoller)**
   Written for The Cookies
   Actually a hit for The Drifters
   (Atlantic: 1963)
ONE FINE DAY (Goffin/King)
   Written for Little Eva
   Actually a hit for The Chiffons
   (Laurie: 1963)
ONLY IN AMERICA (Mann/Weil/
   Leiber/Stoller)
   First recorded by The Drifters in
   the days before integration and
   subsequently released by white
   group Jay and The Americans
   whose voices replaced those of
   The Drifters on the master track
   produced by Leiber and Stoller.
   A hit for Jay and The Americans
   (UA: 1963)
ONLY THE LONELY (Orbison/
   Melson)
   Offered to The Everly Brothers
   Actually a hit for Roy Orbison
   (Monument: 1960)
RUBBER BALL (Schroeder/Orlowski)
   Turned down by Jimmy Jones
   Actually a hit for Bobby Vee
   (Liberty: 1961)
RUN TO HIM (Goffin/Keller)
   Written for The Everly Brothers
   Actually a hit for Bobby Vee
   (Liberty: 1961)
SAVE THE LAST DANCE FOR ME
   (Pomus/Shuman)**
   Offered to Jimmy Clanton
   Actually a hit for The Drifters
   (Atlantic: 1960)
SHOP AROUND (Robinson/Gordy
   Jr.)**
   Intended for Barrett Strong
   Actually a hit for The Miracles
   (Tamla: 1961)
STUPID CUPID (Sedaka/Greenfield)
   Turned down by The Shepherd
   Sisters (who sang ALONE in 1957)
   Actually a hit for Connie Francis
   (MGM: 1958)
TEENAGE IDOL (Lewis)
   Offered to Bobby Vee
   Actually a hit for Ricky Nelson
   (Imperial: 1962)

THIS DIAMOND RING (Kooper/
Brass/Levine)★★
Intended for The Drifters
Actually a hit for Gary Lewis and
The Playboys (Liberty: 1965)
WE GOTTA GET OUT OF THIS
PLACE (Mann/Weil)
Intended for The Righteous
Brothers
Actually a hit for The Animals (UK
Columbia: 1965)
WHERE DID OUR LOVE GO
(Holland/Dozier/Holland)
Intended for Mary Wells
Actually a hit for The Supremes
(Motown: 1964)
WILL YOU LOVE ME TOMORROW
(Goffin/King)★★
Written for Johnny Mathis
Actually a hit for The Shirelles
(Scepter: 1961)

SEND ME SOME LOVIN'

(Leo Price/John Marascalco)
Written by Leo Price, Lloyd Price's
brother, with lyrics addded by John
Marascalco, this rock 'n' roll standard
was first recorded by Little Richard.

Recorded in a medley with BRING
IT ON HOME TO ME (Cooke)★★ by
John Lennon on his *Rock 'N' Roll*
album (Apple: 1975) which was later
re-released by Capitol.

US HITS: Little Richard (Specialty:
            1957) Black & Pop
            Sam Cooke (RCA: 1963)
            Black & Pop

Other recordings: Buddy Holly and
The Crickets (Brunswick); Thurston
Harris (Aladdin); Sleepy Labeef
(Sun); King Curtis (Capitol); Dean
Martin (Reprise); Solomon Burke
(Atlantic); Brenda Lee (Decca);
Stevie Wonder (Tamla); Hank
Williams Jr (MGM); Neil Sedaka
(MCA); Lloyd Price

SEVENTH SON

(Willie Dixon)
Originally recorded by Chess

bluesman Willie Mabon, of I DON'T
KNOW fame.

Johnny Rivers was no stranger to
cover versions of other people's
songs (see under MEMPHIS) and
took SEVENTH SON into the Top 10
of 1965, while four years later,
Georgie Fame successfully revived
it again, this time in Britain.

With his group The Blue Flames,
organist–singer Georgie Fame was a
fixture at London's Flamingo club in
the early 1960s and his first records
were covers of American songs like
SHOP AROUND (Gordy Jr/Robinson)
originally by The Miracles (Tamla:
1960) and the instrumental GREEN
ONIONS (Cropper/Jones/Jackson
Jr/Steinberg), the 1962 smash for
Booker T. and The M.G.'s on Stax.
Another of Georgie's hits, produced
independently for EMI's Columbia
label, was SUNNY, released in
direct competition with the original
version, sung by its composer,
Bobby Hebb (Philips: 1966).

US HIT: Johnny Rivers (Imperial:
           1965) Pop
UK HIT: Georgie Fame (CBS:
           1969)

Other recordings: Mose Allison
(Atlantic); Willie Dixon (Columbia);
The Climax Chicago Blues Band
(Sire); John Hammond (Vanguard);
The Mindbenders (Fontana).

See: I'M YOUR HOOCHIE
COOCHIE MAN for other Willie
Dixon songs.

SHAKE

(Sam Cooke)
Graphically instructional ('Move
Your Body Like A Whip') dance
song from the same singer–
songwriter who had earlier twisted
'the night away'! Sam Cooke's last
major hit, it entered the American
charts the month after he was
gunned down in Los Angeles.

US HIT: Sam Cooke (RCA: 1965)
           Black & Pop

Otis Redding (Volt: 1965)
Black & Pop
The Gap Band (Mercury:
1979) Black
UK HIT: Otis Redding (Stax: 1967)

Other recordings: Rod Stewart (UK
Columbia); The Supremes (Motown);
Tom Jones (UK Decca); The
Shadows Of Knight (Team); GQ
(Arista); The Small Faces (UK
Decca); Oscar Brown Jr.

See: DO YOU WANT TO DANCE for
other dance songs.

See: ONLY SIXTEEN for other Sam
Cooke songs.

SHAKE, RATTLE AND ROLL
(Charles Calhoun)
Another of the earliest rock'n' roll
anthems which we all seemed to be
singing at the time...but which
version were we listening to? Yes,
this was another rhythm and blues
lyric which had been whitewashed
on its way to rock 'n' roll's marketing
machine. Teddy boys were being
spurred to rioting by Bill Haley, and
his rock 'n' roll shows...cinema seats
were slashed during showings of
those early rock movies...just think
what might have happened if they'd
have been listening to the real thing!
 Song was written by Jesse Stone
(aka Charles Calhoun)...the same
Jesse Stone whose MONEY
HONEY** was a huge Clyde
McPhatter record. SHAKE was sung
in its original form by blues shouter
Joe Turner, whose 78 began: 'Get out
of that bed and wash your face and
hands'; the lyric went on to refer to a
couple living together and this had
to be watered down for the mass
audience; by contrast, Bill Haley's
million-selling version opens with:
'Get out of that kitchen and rattle
those pots and pans', immediately
deleting the reference to sleeping
facilities! Yes, that *was* rock 'n' roll
and we've luckily come a long way
from that.

Whereas Joe Turner's previous
release, HONEY HUSH**, was cut in
New Orleans with Edgar Blanchard's
band, SHAKE, RATTLE AND ROLL
was recorded with New York
musicians. The original record was
heard on the soundtrack of the Matt
Dillon/Diane Lane movie, "The Big
Town" (Columbia: 1987), while The
Beatles performed their own version
in "Let It Be" (Apple: 1970).

US HITS: Joe Turner (Atlantic: 1954)
Black & Pop
Bill Haley and His Comets
(Decca: 1954) Pop
Arthur Conley (Atco:
1967) Black & Pop
UK HIT: Bill Haley and His Comets
(Brunswick: 1954)

Other recordings: Elvis Presley
(RCA); The Swinging Blue Jeans
(HMV); Billy Swan (Monument);
NRBQ (Mercury); Chubby Checker
(Parkway); Vern Gosdin (Elektra);
Fats Domino (Silver Eagle); Jerry
Lee Lewis (Mercury); The Deep
River Boys (EMI); Canned Heat
(Liberty).

Another Joe Turner original which
was successfully covered by Bill
Haley was FLIP, FLOP AND FLY
(Calhoun/Turner).

See: ROCK AROUND THE CLOCK
for the SWING THE MOOD record.

SHAKIN' ALL OVER
(Freddie Heath)
Arguably the best British rock 'n' roll
song from the pre-Beatle days.
Written and recorded by Freddie
Heath aka Johnny Kidd and revived
in the States by The Guess Who.
Kidd's group, The Pirates, were only
a three-piece, but guitarist Mick
Green really shone on their hit.

UK HIT: Johnny Kidd and The
Pirates (HMV: 1960)
US HIT: The Guess Who (Scepter:
1965) Pop

Other recordings: The Who (Track);

The Searchers (UK Philips); Suzi Quatro (Bell); Billy Idol (Chrysalis); The Pirates (Warner Bros).

Additional note: In the 1950s and 1960s, many artists who were attempting to regain chart status recorded new versions of their earlier hits; they identified these by adding the year of the new release... for instance, instrumental group The Ventures had launched their career in 1960 with WALK, DON'T RUN (Smith) on Dolton; for the same label four years later, they cut a new version of the same tune, titled: WALK DON'T RUN '64. Johnny Kidd tried the same approach with his biggest hit which became SHAKIN' ALL OVER '65 (HMV).

SHARE YOUR LOVE WITH ME
(Al Braggs/Deadric Malone) Crossover song which was first a success for blues giant Bobby 'Blue' Bland and then Aretha Franklin. The Band included it in their memorable *Moondog Matinee* set (Capitol: 1973).

US HITS: Bobby Bland (Duke: 1964) Black & Pop
Aretha Franklin (Atlantic: 1969) Black & Pop
Kenny Rogers (Liberty: 1981) Pop & Country

Other recordings: Charlie Rich (RCA); Jacky Ward (Mercury); Lanier and Company (Larc); Jerry Jaye (Mega).

SH-BOOM (LIFE COULD BE A DREAM)
(James Keyes/Claude Feaster/Carl Feaster/Floyd McRae/ James Edwards)
Written by The Chords themselves, a New York doo-wop group who also recorded an R&B cover version of Patti Page's pop success, CROSS OVER THE BRIDGE (Benjamin/ Weiss).

The original British release of the Chords' record was credited on the label to 'The Chordcats', one of the group's several aliases.

US HITS: The Chords (Cat: 1954) Pop & Black
The Crew-Cuts (Mercury: 1954) Pop
Stan Freberg (Capitol: 1954) Pop
Billy Williams Quartet (Coral: 1954) Pop
UK HITS: The Crew-Cuts (Mercury: 1954)
Stan Freberg (Capitol: 1954)
Darts (Magnet: 1980)

Other recordings: The Marvels (UA); Big Wheelie and The Hubcaps (MCA).

Parody record: SH-BOOM by Stan Freberg (Capitol: 1954).

SHE CRIED
(Ted Daryll/Greg Richards) Heartbroken ballad which became the debut hit for the original Jay and The Americans (lead singer Jay Traynor left soon afterwards and was replaced for the balance of their recording career by Jay Black). Ted Daryll recorded the original version himself and later wrote COUNTRY GIRL–CITY MAN with Chip Taylor for Billy Vera and Judy Clay (Atlantic: 1968).

Jay and The Americans' record was produced, as a number of their early singles were, by Jerry Leiber and Mike Stoller. The Shangri-Las' version in 1966 and the Lettermen's revival four years after that made minimal impact on the US charts.

US HIT: Jay and The Americans (UA: 1962) Pop

Other recordings: The Lettermen (Capitol); Roy Clark (Dot); Billy Fury (UK Decca); Del Shannon (Amy).

Female version: HE CRIED by The Shangri-Las (Red Bird: 1966).

...visual sound STEREO

JAN & DEAN take LINDA SURFIN'

LINDA ● MR. BASS MAN ● SURFIN' SAFARI ● RHYTHM OF THE RAIN ● WALK LIKE A MAN
● THE BEST FRIEND I EVER HAD ● MY FOOLISH HEART ● SURFIN' ● THE GYPSY CRIED ●
● ● WALK RIGHT IN ● ● ● LET'S TURKEY TROT ● ● ● WHEN I LEARN HOW TO CRY ● ●

LIBERTY

From the days when rock and pop stars filled out
their albums with covers of other artists' hits; *Jan
And Dean Take Linda Surfin'* (Liberty: 1963)
offered The Four Seaons' WALK LIKE A MAN
(Crewe/Gaudio), The Rooftop Singers' WALK
RIGHT IN (Woods/Cannon), Little Eva's LET'S
TURKEY TROT (Goffin/Keller) plus Johnny
Cymbal's own MR. BASS MAN.

SHERRY

(Bob Gaudio)

The Four Seasons' first Number One
song in the States was written by
member Bob Gaudio who co-wrote
with producer Bob Crewe the
following other major hits for the
group: BIG GIRLS DON'T CRY (Vee-
Jay: 1962), WALK LIKE A MAN
(Vee-Jay: 1963) and RAG DOLL
(Philips: 1964), plus DAWN (GO

AWAY) (Philips: 1964) which he
wrote with Sandy Linzer and LET'S
HANG ON! (Philips: 1965) which he
and Sandy composed with Denny
Randell.

US HIT: The Four Seasons (Vee-
Jay: 1962) Black & Pop
UK HITS: The Four Seasons
(Stateside: 1962)
Adrian Baker (Magnet:
1975)

Answer record: JERRY, (I'M YOUR
SHERRY) by Tracey Dey (Vee-Jay:
1962)

SHE'S NOT THERE

(Rod Argent)
British group The Zombies, with
singer Colin Blunstone, recorded
existing songs such as the blues
standard GOT MY MOJO
WORKING** and Little Anthony's
hit, GOIN' OUT OF MY HEAD**, but
the song which established them
was written by their keyboard
player Rod Argent, who went on to
form his own group, Argent,
following the break-up of The
Zombies in 1967.

US HITS: The Zombies (Parrot:
         1964) Pop
         Santana (Columbia: 1977)
         Pop
UK HITS: The Zombies (Decca:
         1964)
         Santana (CBS: 1977)
         UK Subs (Gem: 1979)

Other recordings: Vanilla Fudge (Atco).

Colin Blunstone later embarked on a
solo career, even re-recording
SHE'S NOT THERE under the
pseudonym Neil McArthur.
However, he switched back to Colin
Blunstone for some successful
singles on Epic in the 1970s, and on
PRT in 1982 when he charted briefly
with a remake of The Miracles'
TRACKS OF MY TEARS**. See also
the entry on WHAT BECOMES OF
THE BROKENHEARTED.

THE SHOOP SHOOP SONG (IT'S IN HIS KISS)

(Rudy Clark)
Originally recorded by Merry
Clayton (Capitol: 1963) as IT'S IN HIS
KISS. Betty Everett had the hit
version using the title THE SHOOP
SHOOP SONG, so named because of
the 'shoops' in the background
vocals.

    The Betty Everett version is the
one most often revived and it was
used under the main titles of
Madonna's first movie, "Desperately
Seeking Susan" (Orion: 1985).

THE SHOOP SHOOP SONG

Merry Clayton, whose singing in The Rolling
Stones' "Gimme Shelter" performance film (1970) is
now part of rock 'n' roll history, actually recorded
the *first* version of THE SHOOP SHOOP SONG,
even though Betty Everett is pictured on the sheet
music.

    Former member of backup group
The Blossoms, Merry Clayton is
particularly remembered for her
spine-tingling performance of
GIMME SHELTER (Jagger/Richard)
which she duetted with Mick Jagger
in the concert movie of the same
name (Maysles/Fox: 1970). She finally
got to sing IT'S IN HIS KISS on-
screen in the 1987 Ally Sheedy
movie, "Maid To Order" (New
Century).

US HITS: Betty Everett (Vee-Jay:
         1964) Black & Pop
         Kate Taylor (Columbia:
         1977) Pop
UK HITS: Betty Everett (Fontana:
         1965)
         Linda Lewis (Arista: 1975)

Other recordings: The Searchers
(Pye); Linda Ronstadt (Asylum).

THE SHOOP SHOOP SONG
Beautiful Betty Everett sang the original of IT'S IN
HIS KISS, composed by Rudy Clark, who also
co-wrote the Young Rascals' hit, GOOD LOVIN'.

For their version, The Searchers
changed genders in the song's title
to make it read IT'S IN HER KISS.
Similar switches have often occurred
throughout rock history; another
example is that after Bobby Vee
charted with Gerry Goffin & Jack
Keller's RUN TO HIM (Liberty:1961),
it was recorded several times as
RUN TO HER, most notably by Little
Eva (Dimension: 1964).

SHOP AROUND
(William Robinson/Berry Gordy Jr)
The record on which Berry Gordy
played piano has more than just his
stamp as co-writer on it, for a first
version of the Miracles' record was
already pressed and on the streets
when the Motown boss woke
Smokey Robinson out of a deep
sleep and a head cold imploring him
to gather the group together and
immediately rush over to the studio

where Berry wanted to re-cut the
song! Smokey followed through and
in the early hours of a cold, Detroit
morning, SHOP AROUND was re-
recorded and it became the classic
version of the song.

US HITS: The Miracles (Tamla:
          1961) Black & Pop
          The Captain and Tennille
          (A&M: 1976) Pop

Other recordings: Johnny Kidd and
The Pirates (HMV); Mary Wells
(Motown); Helen Shapiro (UK
Columbia); Georgie Fame and The
Blue Flames (UK Columbia); Lloyd
Price (ABC Paramount); Bobby Vee
(Liberty); Bern Elliott and The
Fenmen (UK Decca); The Spinners
(Motown).

Answer records: DON'CHA SHOP
AROUND (Barrett/Clowney) by
Laurie Davis (Guaranteed: 1961)
DON'T LET HIM SHOP AROUND by
Debbie Dean (Motown: 1961)

See: DEVIL WITH A BLUE DRESS
ON for other Motown songs.

Smokey Robinson songs
Without William 'Smokey' Robinson,
there probably wouldn't have been a
Motown Records. As a teenager in
1958 Robinson showed over 100
songs to Berry Gordy, who picked
out a likely commercial candidate,
GOT A JOB, an answer record to
GET A JOB, and leased it to End. It
was on the next Miracles release,
BAD GIRL that Smokey first
revealed his breathtaking alto.
Gordy leased it to Chess, but not
before releasing it locally in Detroit
under the designation it was worthy
of – 'Motown 1'.
  The Miracles' WAY OVER
THERE in 1960 was Gordy's first
nationally distributed record. SHOP
AROUND, which was originally
offered to Barrett Strong, was
Smokey's first million seller.
  Of course, Smokey is not only a
great writer, the Shakespeare of the

Motor City, he has also one of the greatest voices on the planet. Bob Dylan once called him 'the world's greatest living poet'. The Beatles listed him as one of their favourite artists (George Harrison recorded two Robinson tributes – OOH BABY and PURE SMOKEY). ABC had the hit WHEN SMOKEY SINGS in 1987 – yet another tribute.

Here's a sampling of hits written by Smokey, several in collaboration with the other members of The Miracles.

AIN'T THAT PECULIAR (with Warren Moore, Marvin Tarplin and Robert Rogers) by Marvin Gaye (Tamla: 1965)
BEING WITH YOU by Smokey Robinson (Tamla: 1981)
CRUISIN' by Smokey Robinson (Tamla: 1980)
GET READY** by The Temptations (Gordy: 1966)
by Rare Earth (Rare Earth: 1970)
GOING TO A GO-GO (with Warren Moore, Marvin Tarplin and Robert Rogers) by The Miracles (Tamla: 1966)
by The Rolling Stones (Rolling Stones: 1982)
I SECOND THAT EMOTION (with Al Cleveland) by The Miracles (Tamla: 1967)
I'LL BE DOGGONE (with Warren Moore and Marvin Tarplin) by Marvin Gaye (Tamla: 1965)
I'LL TRY SOMETHING NEW by The Miracles (Tamla: 1962)
by The Supremes and The Temptations (Motown: 1969)
by A Taste of Honey (Capitol: 1982)
MORE LOVE by Smokey Robinson and The Miracles (Tamla: 1967)
by Kim Carnes (EMI America: 1980)
MY GIRL ** (with Ronald White) by The Temptations (Gordy: 1966)
MY GUY ** by Mary Wells (Motown: 1964)
THE ONE WHO REALLY LOVES YOU by Mary Wells (Motown: 1962)

OOH BABY BABY (with Warren Moore) by The Miracles (Tamla:1965)
by Linda Ronstadt (Asylum:1979)
SINCE I LOST MY BABY (with Warren Moore) by The Temptations (Gordy: 1965)
by Luther Vandross (Epic: 1983)
STILL WATER (LOVE) by The Four Tops (Motown: 1970)
TEARS OF A CLOWN (with Henry Cosby and Stevie Wonder) by Smokey Robinson and The Miracles (Tamla:1970)
TWO LOVERS by Mary Wells (Motown: 1963)
THE WAY YOU DO THE THINGS YOU DO ** (with Warren Moore, Marvin Tarplin and Robert Rogers) by The Temptations (Gordy: 1964)
by Rita Coolidge (A&M: 1978)
by Hall and Oates with David Ruffin and Eddie Kendrick (medley) (RCA: 1985)
YOU BEAT ME TO THE PUNCH (with Ronald White) by Mary Wells (Motown: 1962)

A SHOT OF RHYTHM AND BLUES
(Terry Thompson)
This became a regular number with many of the British groups during the 1960s beat boom and The Beatles sang it in live performances.

Song performed by The Stray Cats, produced by Dave Edmunds for the soundtrack of the David Essex/Adam Faith movie, "Stardust" (1974).

Soulman Arthur Alexander also wrote and recorded the original version of ANNA (GO TO HIM) which The Beatles covered, EVERY DAY I HAVE TO CRY SOME (Buddah: 1975) which was cut by Steve Alaimo (Checker: 1963) and also by The Gentrys (Phoenix) and by The Bee Gees (Polydor).

Arthur's original of SHOT OF RHYTHM AND BLUES was actually the flipside of YOU BETTER MOVE ON (Dot: 1961).

UK HIT: Johnny Kidd and The Pirates (HMV: 1963)

Other recordings: The Swinging Blue Jeans (HMV); Jimmy Hughes (Fame); Gerry and The Pacemakers (UK Columbia).

Johnny Kidd's earlier cover singles included the Marv Johnson hit YOU GOT WHAT IT TAKES ** and Ray Sharpe's own song LINDA LU (Jamie: 1959).

SHOUT
(O'Kelly Isley/Ronald Isley/Rudolph Isley)
Written by the three original brothers, this was the great Isley Brothers mover which launched their long hit-making career.
    Covered first by Joey Dee and, although it wasn't the actual follow-up, SHOUT was Dee's only other record to come near to the success of PEPPERMINT TWIST (Dee/Glover) (Roulette: 1961). Two years later, a fifteen year old Scottish lass with a powerhouse voice zoomed up the British charts, taking the Isleys' song with her!
    Song performed by Otis Day and The Knights in "National Lampoon's Animal House" (Universal: 1978).

US HITS: The Isley Brothers (RCA: 1959) Black & Pop
Joey Dee and The Starliters (Roulette: 1962) Pop
UK HITS: Lulu and The Luvvers (Decca: 1964)
Lulu (Jive: 1986 Re-recording) (Decca: 1986 Re-release)

Other recordings: Dion (Laurie); Tommy James (Roulette); The Chambers Brothers (Vault); The Shangri-Las (Red Bird); The Mighty Clouds Of Joy (MCA).

Sequel records: TWIST AND SHOUT (Russell/Medley)** by The Isley Brothers (Wand: 1962)

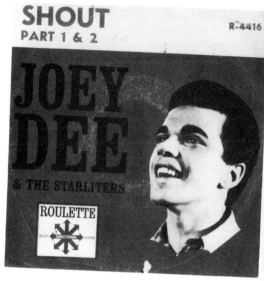

SHOUT
Joey Dee's biggest selling single after his PEPPERMINT TWIST (Dee/Glover) hit was a remake of The Isley Brothers' classic, SHOUT. As with PEPPERMINT TWIST and his later HOT PASTRAMI WITH MASHED POTATOES, Joey's version of SHOUT was spread over two sides of the single, with Part 1 being designated the 'A' side.

SURF AND SHOUT (Russell/Bachelor) by The Isley Brothers (UA: 1963)

Lulu also cut the original of HERE COMES THE NIGHT (Berns) which was later a hit for Van Morrison's group, Them (UK Decca: 1965).

SILHOUETTES
(Frank Slay/Bob Crewe)
Doo-wop ballad which became a major R&B crossover for the four-man vocal group, The Rays. Messrs. Slay and Crewe wrote and produced other hits including TALLAHASSIE LASSIE for Freddy Cannon, before splitting up. Crewe went on to produce The Four Seasons and Mitch Ryder, and some years later, Slay re-emerged as producer of Sugarloaf. Mickie Most produced the

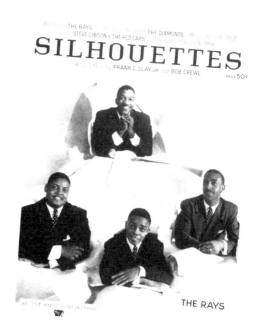

THE RAYS

SILHOUETTES
Two songsheets from different eras: the original 1957 issue showing The Rays who recorded the original version, alongside the 1965 sheet released to coincide with British group Herman's Hermits' revival. That's Peter Noone (aka Herman) in the centre of the shot.

major revival of SILHOUETTES by Herman's Hermits in 1965.

US HITS: The Rays (Cameo: 1957)
                 Pop & Black
                 The Diamonds (Mercury:
                     1957) Pop
                 Steve Gibson and The
                     Red Caps (ABC/
                     Paramount: 1957) Pop
                 Herman's Hermits (MGM:
                     1965) Pop
UK HIT: Herman's Hermits (UK
                 Columbia: 1965)

Other recordings: The Four Seasons (Vee-Jay); Sha Na Na (Buddah); Frankie Lymon (Gee); The Ronettes (May).

Parody record: SILHOUETTES by Andy Griffith (Capitol: 1958).

SINCERELY
(Harvey Fuqua/Alan Freed)
Classic sentimental ballad, first cut by The Moonglows, of which Harvey Fuqua was one of their two lead singers. Covered by The McGuire Sisters, whose version was featured prominently on the soundtrack of Robert Altman's movie "Come Back To The Five And Dime Jimmy Dean, Jimmy Dean" (Cinecom: 1982). The Moonglows' original was heard in the Alan Freed biopic, "American Hot Wax" (Paramount: 1978). A 1988 remake by The Forester Sisters was a hit on the American country charts (Warner Bros).

US HITS: The Moonglows (Chess:
                     1954) Black & Pop
                 The McGuire Sisters
                     (Coral: 1955) Pop
                 The Four Seasons (Vee-
                     Jay: 1964) Pop
                 The Forester Sisters
                     (Warner Bros: 1989)
                     Country
UK HIT: The McGuire Sisters
                 (Vogue Coral: 1955)

Other recordings: Paul Anka (RCA);
The Mills Brothers (Dot); Bobby Vee
(Liberty); The Four Amigos
(Capitol); Bobby Vinton (Epic).

SINGING THE BLUES
(Melvin Endsley)
This became a key song in the
development of the British rock 'n'
roll scene. First recorded by country
singer Marty Robbins, it was
covered for the US pop market by
Guy Mitchell, even though both
artists were on the same label. Guy's
record was a huge world-wide
smash, and in England it was his
third Number One single; but he had
huge competition from the hottest
young local star yet...Tommy Steele.
Decca rushed it out as the follow-up
to Steele's debut hit, ROCK WITH
THE CAVEMAN (Bart/Steele/Pratt)
(1956).

US HITS: Marty Robbins
           (Columbia: 1956) Pop &
           Country
           Guy Mitchell (Columbia:
           1956) Pop & Black
UK HITS: Guy Mitchell (Philips:
           1956)
           Tommy Steele (UK
           Decca: 1956)

Other recordings: Hank Locklin
(RCA); The Knightsbridge Strings
(Top Rank); Eddy Arnold (RCA);
Winifred Atwell (Decca); Connie
Francis (MGM); Jerry Lee Lewis
(Sun); Black Oak Arkansas (Atco);
Dave Edmunds (Swan Song); Jason
Eddie (Parlophone).

(SITTIN' ON) THE DOCK OF THE BAY
(Otis Redding/Steve Cropper)
The record with which Otis Redding
had the most success was, ironically,
not even a finished master when he
was killed in a 'plane wreck in
December 1967. During his career,
he'd picked out songs from a
number of different sources; PAIN

IN MY HEART (Neville) (Volt: 1963)
was a re-working of the Irma
Thomas record, RULER OF MY
HEART... SHAKE (Volt: 1967)** was
the Sam Cooke song... (I CAN'T GET
NO) SATISFACTION (Volt: 1966)
was of course the Rolling Stones'
classic, and he even dug way back
to the 1930s for TRY A LITTLE
TENDERNESS (Woods/Campbell/
Connelly)** (Volt: 1967). But Otis'
own songs were standouts also,
including three he co-wrote with
Stax's own house guitarist (and
member of Booker T. and The
M.G.'s), Steve Cropper: MR.
PITIFUL, FA-FA-FA-FA-FA (SAD
SONG) and (SITTIN' ON) THE
DOCK OF THE BAY. As it turned
out, DOCK OF THE BAY was one of
the last songs Otis recorded;
production was completed shortly
after his death and it became a
posthumous Number One pop
record in the States and a Top 5
single in Britain.

There have been a number of
remakes of this song over the years,
most notably by The Dells, The
Reddings (a group formed by Otis'
sons) and Michael Bolton. The Dells
made it inside the Top 50 pop chart,
The Reddings lodged just outside
and the Michael Bolton record
almost made the Top 10 in the
Spring of 1988.

As a tribute to Otis, Paul Rodgers
of Bad Company performed the song
at the Atlantic Records' 40th
Anniversary Concert in New York in
May 1988.

US HITS: Otis Redding (Volt: 1968)
           Black & Pop
           The Dells (Cadet: 1969)
           Black & Pop
           The Reddings (Believe:
           1982) Black & Pop
           Michael Bolton
           (Columbia: 1988) Black
           & Pop
UK HIT: Otis Redding (Stax: 1968)

Other recordings: T. Graham Brown
(Capitol); Waylon Jennings and

Willie Nelson (RCA); Billy Burnette (Polydor); King Curtis (Atco); Al Jarreau (Warner Bros); Eric Andersen (Vanguard); Joe Simon (Sound Stage 7); Tom Jones (UK Decca); Glen Campbell (Capitol); Waldo De Los Rios (A&M); Cher (Kapp); John Rowles (MCA); Don Partridge (UK Columbia); The Staple Singers (Stax).

With Mark Mangold, Michael Bolton wrote the song I FOUND SOMEONE; he produced Cher's version (Geffen: 1987) which was a significant UK hit in 1988, following Laura Branigan's unsuccessful version of the same song (Atlantic: 1986).

SIXTY MINUTE MAN
(William Ward/Rose Marks)
The Dominoes, Billy Ward's group with bassist Bill Brown singing lead, were the originators of SIXTY MINUTE MAN which, years later, became one of the stalwart 'beach music' favourites.

The record was one of the earliest R&B crossovers to pop, a fact which is particularly surprising considering the song's risqué lyric.

The original Dominoes recording was used to memorable effect during a candlelit bathroom sequence in the Kevin Costner/Susan Sarandon movie, "Bull Durham" (Orion: 1988) although amazingly, Capitol Records failed to include the track on the soundtrack album!

US HITS: The Dominoes (Federal: 1951) Black & Pop
           Clarence Carter (Fame: 1973) Black & Pop
UK HIT: Trammps (Buddah: 1975)

Other recordings: Jerry Lee Lewis (Mercury); Rufus Thomas (Stax); The Persuasions (Elektra); Hardrock Gunter and Roberta Lee (Decca).

Answer record: CAN'T DO SIXTY NO MORE by The Du Droppers and The Dominoes (Federal: 1951)

SLIPPIN' AND SLIDIN'
(Albert Collins/Edwin J. Bocage/James Smith/Richard Penniman)
Based on a song called I'M WISE written and recorded by Eddie Bocage on Apollo, which in turn was derived from I GOT THE BLUES FOR YOU by Albert Collins on Ace. Little Richard's record featured on the soundtrack of Peter Bogdanovich's movie, "Mask" (Universal: 1985).

US HITS: Little Richard (Specialty: 1956) Black & Pop
           Billy 'Crash' Craddock (ABC: 1973) Country

Other recordings: The Everly Brothers (Warner Bros); Jim and Monica (Betty); Otis Redding (Atlantic); Ronnie Milsap (RCA); Buddy Knox (Liberty); Billy Preston (Vee-Jay); Buddy Holly (Coral); Johnny and Edgar Winter (Columbia); Mickey Gilley; Willie (Bill Wyman) and The Poor Boys (Passport); Sandy Nelson (Imperial); James Cotton (Vanguard); Willie Mitchell (Hi); John Lennon (Apple); Billy Farrell (Imperial).

SLOW DOWN
(Larry Williams)
Great teen rocker, driven along on the original version by a wild piano intro. Amazingly though, it was first released on the B-side of Larry Williams' DIZZY MISS LIZZY** single (Specialty: 1958). It was later 'discovered' by John Lennon who sang it on a Beatles EP in the UK in 1964.

Track subsequently made it on to the Beatles' *Something New* album in America (Capitol: 1964) after which it was released as a US single.

Song was heard in both "That'll Be The Day" (Mayfair: 1973) and "Where The Boys Are '84" (Tri-Star: 1984), but its third movie use was its most memorable...as sung by Billy Vera and The Beaters on the soundtrack of Blake Edwards'

SLIPPIN' AND SLIDIN'
1956 was a banner year for Little Richard, seen
here as he appears in the all-star rock musical,
"The Girl Can't Help It" (20th Century Fox); he
sang three songs in the picture, READY TEDDY
(Blackwell/Marascalco) and SHE'S GOT IT
(Penniman/Marascalco), plus the movie's title song.

comedy, "A Fine Mess" (Columbia:
1986).

US HIT: The Beatles (Capitol:
1964) Pop

Other recordings: Mickey Gilley
(Epic); The Jam (Polydor); The
Young Rascals (Atlantic).

See: DIZZY MISS LIZZY for other
Beatle remakes.

SMOKESTACK LIGHTNING

(Chester Burnett)
Best-known of the repertoire of
Howlin' Wolf, the Mississippi-born
blues singer–songwriter whose
instruments were harmonica and
guitar. He was a key influence on the
British R&B and blues resurgence of
the 1960s, and even cut an album in
London for the Rolling Stones' label.

US HIT: Howlin' Wolf (Chess:
1956) Black
UK HIT: Howlin' Wolf (Pye
International: 1964)

Other recordings: Manfred Mann (HMV); The Yardbirds (UK Columbia); The Grateful Dead (Warner Bros); The V.I.P.'s (Island); George Thorogood (EMI America); Quicksilver Messenger Service (Psycho).

SO YOU WANT TO BE A ROCK 'N' ROLL STAR

(Roger McGuinn/Chris Hillman) Roger McGuinn and Chris Hillman were inspired to write this devastating satire of the rock 'n' roll star-maker machinery by looking at teeny-bop magazines that had new fave raves coming and going non-stop. They added a recording of screaming girls from one of their concerts in England and pretty well summed up rock 'n' roll in the 1960s.

US HIT: The Byrds (Columbia: 1967) Pop

Other recordings: The Move (Regal Zonophone); Patti Smith Group (Arista); Black Oak Arkansas (Atco); The Royal Guardsmen (Laurie); Tom Petty and The Heartbreakers (MCA); Nazareth (A&M).

SOLDIER BOY

(Luther Dixon/Florence Greenberg) The four-girl group, The Shirelles, had enjoyed huge success during 1961 in which they'd racked up their first American Number One with WILL YOU LOVE ME TOMORROW **. This, their second chart-topping song, began in the mind of Florence Greenberg, who was president of their label, Scepter Records.

Florence had seen a TV ad one morning and dreamt up a marching chorus which she called I'LL BE TRUE TO YOU. At the office that day, she laughingly told Luther Dixon, who produced The Shirelles' records, that she'd written a song. A couple of days later, Luther reported to Florence that he was about to go into the studio with The Shirelles and

that he was going to record *her* song! Dixon had extended Greenberg's original chorus and added the winning line, 'Soldier boy, oh my little soldier boy'.

US HIT: The Shirelles (Scepter: 1962) Black & Pop
UK HITS: The Shirelles (HMV: 1962) The Cheetahs (Philips: 1965)

Answer records: HURRY HOME TO ME (SOLDIER BOY) (Dixon/Green/Rogers/Elgin) by Valli (Scepter: 1962)
I'M YOUR SOLDIER BOY by The Soldier Boys (Scepter: 1962)

Of these, HURRY HOME TO ME was the cheapest attempt to capitalize on the success of The Shirelles' hit; it began with Valli bleating out that she is sending her guy this record now that he is 'oh so far away' and then they simply play the original SOLDIER BOY track, over which Valli sings alternative responses to the original lyrics. And if that wasn't enough, Valli also speaks over the guitar and organ instrumental break!

SOME GUYS HAVE ALL THE LUCK/ SOME GIRLS HAVE ALL THE LUCK

(Jeff Fortgang) Melodic ballad built around a confirmed loser's philosophy! Nine years after the initial version, Robert Palmer revived the song, and two years later Rod Stewart provided a further first-class example of a white singer's re-working of a black group's original. Then Barbara Mandrell's sister Louise took the song the country route, cutting it as SOME GIRLS HAVE ALL THE LUCK.

US HITS: The Persuaders (Atco: 1973) Pop & Black
Rod Stewart (Warner Bros: 1984) Pop
Louise Mandrell (RCA:1986) Country

UK HITS: Robert Palmer (Island:
1982)
Rod Stewart (Warner
Bros: 1984)

SOME OTHER GUY
(Richard Barrett/Elmo Glick/Mike
Stoller)
Originally recorded by Ritchie
Barrett (Atlantic: 1962), it was one of
the most performed songs in British
clubs in the early 1960s. The earliest
sound film of The Beatles features
them singing SOME OTHER GUY at
the Cavern in Liverpool in 1962.
Performed by The Stray Cats for the
David Essex/Adam Faith movie
"Stardust" (Goodtimes: 1974).

UK HIT: The Big Three (UK
Decca: 1963)

Other recordings: The Searchers
(Pye); Wayne Fontana and The
Mindbenders (Fontana); Freddie
and The Dreamers (UK Columbia).

Richard (aka Ritchie) Barrett was
involved with a number of major
R&B acts including The Chantels,
The Isley Brothers and Frankie
Lymon and The Teenagers, whose
WHY DO FOOLS FALL IN LOVE
(Levy/Lymon) (Gee: 1956) Barrett
produced. He also worked with
Little Anthony and The Imperials
and, in the erstwhile British
magazine, "Black Music" (April 1974),
Tony Cummings related the story of
when Barrett gave TEARS ON MY
PILLOW (Bradford/Lewis) to Little
Anthony and The Imperials. Because
Anthony had a lisp, Barrett had him
break the song up into syllables:
'You/don't/re/mem/ber/ me, but/I/re/
mem/ber/you', thereby creating the
phrasing which virtually sold the
song and guaranteed the hit (End:
1958).

SOMEBODY TO LOVE
(Darby Slick)
Written by Grace Slick's husband

and originally recorded by their San
Francisco underground band, The
Great Society.
   The Jefferson Airplane hit, also
featuring Grace Slick, was used in
the Ralph Bakshi animated feature
"American Pop" (Columbia: 1981).

US HIT: Jefferson Airplane (RCA:
1967) Pop

Another song originally recorded by
The Great Society was Grace's own
WHITE RABBIT which also later
became a Jefferson Airplane success
(RCA: 1967).
   During 1989, the year that
witnessed the twentieth anniversary
of the Woodstock festival as well as
what seemed to be reunion tours of
more '60s bands than ever before,
Jefferson Airplane flew again. Grace
Slick, Marty Balin, Jorma Kaukonen,
Jack Casady and Paul Kantner
gathered together to make a new
album as well as to play concerts in
13 US cities. The classic songs are
still there and, as evidence of the
passage of time, China Kantner
(daughter of Paul Kantner and Grace
Slick) is an occasional vee-jay on
MTV.

SOMETHIN' ELSE
(Bob Cochran/Sharon Sheeley)
Like SUMMERTIME BLUES, another
great teenage rocker from the late
Eddie Cochran, written by his
brother and his fiancée.

US HIT: Eddie Cochran (Liberty:
1959) Pop
UK HIT: Eddie Cochran (London:
1959)

Other recordings: The Move (Regal
Zonophone); Kathi McDonald
(Capitol); The Sex Pistols (Virgin).

Sharon (Shari) Sheeley was one of
the first girls to write a Number One
rock 'n' roll classic, namely POOR
LITTLE FOOL, for Ricky Nelson
(Imperial: 1958); she also wrote with
Jackie DeShannon (*see under*
BREAK-A-WAY).

SOMETHING YOU GOT
(Chris Kenner)
The year before New Orleans singer–songwriter Chris Kenner laid down the original version of LAND OF 1000 DANCES (Kenner/Domino)**, he turned in this song which became a big local hit (Instant: 1961) and set off the Popeye dance craze. Fats Domino, Kenner's co-writer on LAND OF 1000 DANCES, re-cut SOMETHING YOU GOT three years later and within the next few months, three different versions made inroads on to the American R&B Charts; those by Al(vin) Robinson and Ramsey Lewis were minor hits, but the Chuck Jackson/Maxine Brown duet made it to the Top 10 R&B listings.

US HITS: Alvin Robinson (Tiger: 1964) Black & Pop
The Ramsey Lewis Trio (Argo: 1964) Black & Pop
Chuck Jackson and Maxine Brown (Wand: 1965) Black & Pop

Other recordings: Fats Domino (ABC/Paramount); The Moody Blues (UK Decca); Johnny Rivers (UA); The Searchers (Pye); Wilson Pickett (Atlantic); Peaches and Herb (Date); Eddie Floyd (Stax); The Righteous Brothers (Verve); Bobby Womack (UA); Them featuring Van Morrison (UK Decca); The American Breed (Acta); Barbara George; Dr John; The James Cotton Blues Band; Johnny Copeland

SOMETHING'S GOTTEN HOLD OF MY HEART
(Roger Cook/Roger Greenaway)

UK HITS: Gene Pitney (Stateside: 1967)
Mark Almond featuring Gene Pitney (Parlophone: 1989)

Other recording: Cilla Black (Parlophone).

Songwriters Roger Cook and Roger Greenaway also recorded together under the name David and Jonathan; their biggest seller was their own LOVERS OF THE WORLD UNITE (UK Columbia: 1966). Their other chart single was a version of MICHELLE (Lennon/McCartney) (UK Columbia: 1966)**.

Other Cook and Greenaway hits include:

YOU'VE GOT YOUR TROUBLES by The Fortunes (UK Decca: 1965)
GREEN GRASS by Gary Lewis and The Playboys (Liberty: 1966)

SON OF A PREACHER MAN
(John Hurley/Ronnie Wilkins)
Dusty Springfield's hit from her triumphant album *Dusty In Memphis*, produced by Jerry Wexler, Tom Dowd and Arif Mardin, and which featured background vocals by The Sweet Inspirations.

US HIT: Dusty Springfield (Atlantic: 1969) Pop
UK HIT: Dusty Springfield (Philips: 1969)

Other recordings: Mavis Staples (Stax); Tanya Tucker (MCA); Aretha Franklin (Atlantic); Gene Ammons (Prestige); Honey Cone (Hot Wax); Bobbie Gentry (Capitol); Erma Franklin (Brunswick).

Dusty Springfield hits
Britain's premier female pop/R&B singer of the 1960s, Dusty's single hits came from a wide range of composers; SOME OF YOUR LOVIN' and GOING BACK, both in 1966, were Gerry Goffin and Carole King songs; I ONLY WANT TO BE WITH YOU (1963)** and STAY AWHILE (1964) were by Britons Mike Hawker and Ivor Raymonde; I JUST DON'T KNOW WHAT TO DO WITH MYSELF (1964), WISHIN' AND HOPIN' (1964) and THE LOOK OF LOVE (1967) were all by Burt Bacharach And Hal David; LOSING

YOU (1964) was co-written by Dusty's brother Tom with another British writer, Clive Westlake, who singly gave Dusty I CLOSE MY EYES AND COUNT TO TEN four years later and co-wrote ALL I SEE IS YOU (1966) with American Ben Weisman who penned many of Elvis Presley's movie songs.

IN THE MIDDLE OF NOWHERE (1965) came from American writers Bea Verdi and Buddy Kaye, the same Buddy Kaye who co-wrote 'A' YOU'RE ADORABLE in 1949 for Perry Como and The Fontane Sisters as well as SPEEDY GONZALES which was first recorded in France but made famous the world round by bubbling Pat Boone (Dot: 1961)!

In 1970, Dusty charted in the UK with a cover of HOW CAN I BE SURE, the Young Rascals hit of 1967, written by members Felix Cavaliere and Eddie Brigati, which went on to be covered a second time by David Cassidy (Bell: 1972). Around the same time, Dusty also borrowed from AM I THE SAME GIRL (Record/Sanders) from Barbara Acklin.

The other great source of Dusty hit material was the continent, where Peter Callendar found the song for which he wrote English lyrics before it became GIVE ME TIME (1967); a year earlier, Dusty hit Number One in her homeland with the glorious ballad, YOU DON'T HAVE TO SAY YOU LOVE ME, further details of which are listed under this title's own entry.

SOUL MAN
(Isaac Hayes/David Porter)
Emphatic statement ('I'm a Soul Man') from the jubilant voices of Sam and Dave, a duo silenced by the death of Dave Prater, but immortally vivid in the Stax Records' Hall of Fame. Isaac Hayes and David Porter wrote this and other hits for the team, including HOLD ON, I'M

COMIN' ** and SOUL SISTER, BROWN SUGAR (Atlantic: 1968), an anthem celebrating black womanhood.

Sam and Dave performed SOUL MAN years later on TV's "Saturday Night Live" at the invitation of John Belushi and Dan Aykroyd, alias The Blues Brothers, who recorded the song on their *Briefcase Full Of Blues* album. Sam and Dave also performed it in the Paul Simon movie, "One-Trick Pony" (Warner Bros: 1980).

Song also became the title tune of a comedy film starring C. Thomas Howell and Rae Dawn Chong; released by New World Pictures in 1986, the A&M *Soul Man* soundtrack album included a re-make of the title song featuring Sam Moore with Lou Reed.

US HITS: Sam and Dave (Stax: 1967) Black & Pop
The Blues Brothers (Atlantic: 1978) Pop
UK HIT: Sam and Dave (Stax: 1967)

Other recordings: Philly Cream (WMOT); Johnny Winter and Edgar Winter (Blue Sky); Ramsey Lewis (Cadet).

SPANISH HARLEM
(Jerry Leiber/Phil Spector)
Ben E. King's first solo hit after leaving The Drifters was this love song set in the section of New York's Harlem populated by Puerto-Ricans and Latin-Americans.

The original Ben E. King record was featured on the soundtrack of the musical movie, "Salsa" (Cannon: 1988).

US HITS: Ben E. King (Atco: 1961) Black & Pop
Aretha Franklin (Atlantic: 1971) Black & Pop
UK HITS: Jimmy Justice (Pye: 1962)
Sounds Incorporated (Columbia: 1964)

Aretha Franklin (Atlantic: 1971)

Other recordings: Lloyd Price (ABC/Paramount); King Curtis (Atco); Tom Jones (UK Decca); Arthur Alexander (Monument); Leon Russell (Monument); Tony Orlando and Dawn (Elektra); Long John Baldry (Pye); Clyde McPhatter (Mercury); Cliff Richard (UK Columbia); Laura Nyro and Patti LaBelle (Columbia); Chet Atkins (RCA); Gene McDaniels (Liberty); John Barry (UK Columbia); The Crusaders (Motown); Sonny Charles and The Checkmates (A&M); Jay and The Americans (UA); Bobby Vee (Liberty); The Mamas and The Papas (Dunhill); Santo and Johnny (Canadian-American); Sam Butera and The Witnesses (Dot).

See: JAILHOUSE ROCK for other Jerry Leiber and Mike Stoller songs.

SPIRIT IN THE SKY
(Norman Greenbaum)
Folksinger and founder of Dr West's Medicine Show and Junk Band (their one claim to fame was THE EGGPLANT THAT ATE CHICAGO on Go-Go in 1966), Norman Greenbaum wrote and recorded an international hit called SPIRIT IN THE SKY on his debut solo album.

British group Doctor and The Medics scored again with the song in 1986 when it became a number one single in England and a lesser chart success in the US.

US HITS: Norman Greenbaum
          (Reprise: 1970) Pop
          Doctor and The Medics
          (IRS: 1986) Pop
UK HITS: Norman Greenbaum
          (Reprise: 1970)
          Doctor and The Medics
          (IRS: 1986)

Other recordings: Morgan Superstars and Blue Mink (Philips); Dorothy Morrison (Buddah); The Stovall Sisters (Reprise).

Doctor and The Medics later teamed up with Roy Wood (formerly of The Move, ELO and Wizzard) to successfully revive the Abba song WATERLOO (IRS: 1986).

SPLISH SPLASH
(Bobby Darin/Jean Murray)
The rock 'n' roll song with that watered-down feeling with which a diminutive British comedian outsold the late, great Bobby Darin on the UK charts! (Incidentally, the B-side of Charlie Drake's record was a song written around his catch-phrase Hello, my darlings!) Bobby Darin's original record was heard on the soundtrack of the Floyd Mutrux movie, "American Hot Wax" (Paramount: 1978).

US HIT: Bobby Darin (Atco: 1958)
          Black & Pop
UK HITS: Bobby Darin (London:
          1958)
          Charlie Drake
          (Parlophone: 1958)

Other recordings: Barbra Streisand (Columbia); Marc Benno (A&M); Dee Dee Sharp (Cameo); Conway Twitty (MGM); Frankie Avalon (Delite); Sandy Nelson (Imperial);

Freddy Cannon (Swan); Kenny Lynch (HMV); Leroy Kirkland (Imperial); Tommy Sands (Capitol).

SPLISH SPLASH
The late Bobby Darin's star rose swiftly on the Atlantic Records' horizon. SPLISH SPLASH was followed by QUEEN OF THE HOP and another self-penned hit, DREAM LOVER. Later, he would cover the influential Tim Hardin song, IF I WERE A CARPENTER, but he also sang adaptations of a French song which became BEYOND THE SEA (Trenet/Lawrence) and a finger-clicking MACK THE KNIFE (Weill/Blitzstein) based on a song from "The Threepenny Opera".

STAGGER LEE

(Lloyd Price/Harold Logan)
Old American folk legend about a shoot-out between two gamblers which has been written and copyrighted as several different songs.

Archibald (aka Leon T. Gross) wrote and recorded it as STACK-A-LEE (Imperial: 1950), Fats Domino sang STACK AND BILLY (Domino/Bartholomew) for the same label in

1957, and Ike and Tina Turner recorded Ike's version called STAGGER LEE AND BILLY (Sue: 1965).

You are probably most familiar with the Lloyd Price interpretation known as STAGGER LEE, although the Wilson Pickett record credited Messrs Price and Logan as writers, but initially gave the title as STAG-O-LEE, though later pressings were changed to the more familiar title.

When some American radio stations refused to play his record, Lloyd Price re-cut STAGGER LEE with a lyric which was less graphic about the actual shooting. The revised version was played on the air, though the record which was sold in stores was not altered and it became a Number One.

The Fabulous Thunderbirds performed STAGGER LEE on the soundtrack of the teen comedy, "Porky's Revenge" (20th Century Fox: 1985).

US HITS: Lloyd Price (ABC: 1958)
           Black & Pop
           Wilson Pickett (Atlantic:
           1967) Black & Pop
           Tommy Roe (ABC: 1971)
           Pop
UK HIT: Lloyd Price (HMV: 1959)

Other recordings: Shirley Ellis (Congress); James Brown and The Famous Flames (King); Bill Haley (Warner Bros); Mary Wells (20th Century Fox); Dion and The Belmonts (Laurie); P. J. Proby (Liberty); Taj Mahal (Columbia); Johnny Rivers (Imperial); The Righteous Brothers; Neil Diamond (Columbia); Professor Longhair (Dancing Cat).

Sequel record: THE RETURN OF STAGOLEE by Titus Turner (King: 1959)

STAIRWAY TO HEAVEN

(Robert Plant/Jimmy Page)
From the fourth Led Zeppelin album (Atlantic: 1971), *Stairway To Heaven*

was a crowning moment in the band's long career, although the song was never released as a single.

Featured in Zeppelin's 1976 movie, "The Song Remains The Same", it epitomizes American FM radio output in the seventies. During the 1988 Atlantic Records Anniversary concert at New York's Madison Square Gardens, STAIRWAY TO HEAVEN was performed by the re-formed Led Zeppelin which included John Bonham's son, Jason, filling in for his late father on drums.

Other recordings: The Wonder Band (Atco); Far Corporation (Atco).

Parody record: STAIRWAY TO GILLIGAN'S ISLAND by Little Roger and The Goose Bumps. This was an unofficial record of the "Gilligan's Island" TV theme song to the tune of STAIRWAY TO HEAVEN. It was popularized on Barret Hansen's "Dr Demento" syndicated radio show in America, but was suppressed by Led Zeppelin.

As with STAIRWAY TO HEAVEN, Deep Purple's SMOKE ON THE WATER (Blackmore/Gillan/Glover/Lord/Paice) occupies a similar place in the annals of British rock milestones. Originally a hit for Deep in 1977 on their own Purple label, the song was revived in 1989 for a Life-Aid Armenia charity by an assembled group of luminaries including Deep's own Ian Gillan, Jon Lord and Ritchie Blackmore, Black Sabbath's Tony Iommi, Queen's Roger Taylor and Brian May, Bad Company's one-time member Paul Rodgers, plus Chris Squire from Yes and Dave Gilmour of Pink Floyd.

STAND BY ME
(Ben E. King/Jerry Leiber/Mike Stoller)
Gospel-tinged ballad from Ben E.King (former lead singer with The Drifters), the title of which became a hit movie in 1986 with King's original

1961 record featured on the soundtrack of Rob Reiner's movie of the same name (Columbia: 1986).

Coincidentally, the single was re-released and returned to the charts providing a welcome shot-in-the-arm to Ben's career, not the least effect of which was his getting a new record deal. In Britain, the record also had a huge resurgence of popularity but this reissue was prompted by the song being prominently heard in a TV jeans commercial.

Mickey Gilley recorded a version which was featured in the 1980 movie "Urban Cowboy" (Paramount: 1980), the country and western version of "Saturday Night Fever" (both movies starred John Travolta) and among the other songs on its soundtrack was LYIN' EYES (Henley/Frey) by The Eagles (Asylum: 1975).

US HITS: Ben E. King (Atco: 1961) Pop & Black
Little Junior Parker (Duke: 1961) Black
Mickey Gilley (Full Moon: 1980) County & Pop
Earl Grant (Decca: 1965) Pop
Spyder Turner (MGM: 1967) Black & Pop
David and Jimmy Ruffin (Soul: 1970) Black & Pop
John Lennon (Apple: 1975) Pop
Maurice White (Columbia: 1985) Black & Pop
Ben E. King (Atlantic: 1986 Re-issue) Pop
UK HITS: Ben E. King (London: 1961)
Kenny Lynch (HMV: 1964)
John Lennon (Apple: 1975)
Ben E. King (Atlantic: 1987 Re-issue)

Other recordings: Muhammed Ali (aka Cassius Clay) (Columbia); Ry Cooder (Reprise); Earl Van Dyke

STAND BY ME
Former lead singer with The Drifters, Ben E. King
co-wrote his biggest solo hit, STAND BY ME,
which came back as strong as ever 25 years after
it was first released.

(Motown); Barbara Lewis (Atlantic);
The Kingsmen (Wand); Wilbert
Harrison (Sue); The Searchers (Pye);
The Walker Brothers (Philips); Ike
and Tina Turner (UA); Jimmy Ruffin
(Motown); Gene Chandler (Vee-Jay);

Little Eva ; Julian Lennon.

Answer record: I'LL BE THERE by
Damita Jo (Mercury: 1961)

See: JAILHOUSE ROCK for other
Jerry Leiber and Mike Stoller songs.

STAY

(Maurice Williams)
Maurice Williams had lost out to a cover version by The Diamonds on his earlier song, LITTLE DARLIN'**, but with STAY, he had the intial hit himself. It has become an almost timeless rock 'n' roll song, being covered in other decades and by a wide range of performers. The Maurice Williams record was heard on the soundtrack of "American Graffiti" (Universal: 1973).

Performed by Bruce Springsteen in the "No Nukes" concert movie (Warner Bros: 1980).

US HITS: Maurice Williams and The Zodiacs (Herald: 1960) Black & Pop
The Four Seasons (Vee-Jay: 1964) Pop
Jackson Browne (Asylum: 1978) Pop

UK HITS: Maurice Williams and The Zodiacs (Top Rank: 1961)
The Hollies (Parlophone: 1963)
Jackson Browne (Asylum: 1978)

Other recording: Andrew Gold (Asylum).

STAY WITH ME

(Jerry Ragovoy/George Weiss)
This song was immortalized via one of the finest female R&B performances in years...by Lorraine Ellison. The song's title in Britain was changed to STAY WITH ME BABY. STAY WITH ME was revived by Bette Midler in her first movie, "The Rose" (20th Century Fox: 1979).

US HIT: Lorraine Ellison (Warner Bros: 1966) Pop

UK HITS: The Walker Brothers (Philips: 1967)
David Essex (CBS: 1978)

See: CRY BABY for other Jerry Ragovoy songs.

SUCH A NIGHT

(Lincoln Chase)
Clyde McPhatter and The Drifters cut the first hit version of SUCH A NIGHT, the song into which white heartthrob Johnnie Ray injected sexual shrieks, causing his single to be banned in the States where it made inroads into the Top 20.

In England, where the original was virtually unknown, the Johnnie Ray record topped the hit parade, becoming the first of three such UK achievements for the 'prince of wails'.

A decade later, Elvis Presley introduced the song to a new generation.

US HITS: The Drifters Featuring Clyde McPhatter (Atlantic: 1954) Black
Johnnie Ray (Columbia: 1954) Pop
Elvis Presley (RCA: 1964) Pop

UK HITS: Johnnie Ray (Philips: 1954)
Elvis Presley (RCA: 1964)

Other recordings: Dinah Washington (Mercury); David Bromberg Band (Fantasy); Emile Ford (Transdisc); The Cadets (Modern); Conway Twitty.

Composer Lincoln Chase was the husband of Shirley Ellis, for whom he wrote the novelty hits, THE NAME GAME (Congress: 1965) and THE CLAPPING SONG (Congress: 1965).

SUGAR, SUGAR

(Jeff Barry/Andy Kim)
Novelty song written for a Saturday morning cartoon show, "The Archie Show" based on the American 'Archie' comic. The series began on CBS Television in September 1968 and out of it came the 'group' known as The Archies. Singing voices were supplied by Ron Dante and Toni Wine. Ron Dante was later the singer on The Cuff Links' record of

TRACY (Vance/Pockriss) (Decca:
1969), while Toni Wine was the
co-writer of, amongst other songs, A
GROOVY KIND OF LOVE**.

SUGAR, SUGAR was included in
the Number One STARS ON 45
medley single (Radio: 1981).

US HITS: The Archies (Calendar:
           1969) Pop
           Wilson Pickett (Atlantic:
           1970) Black & Pop
UK HITS: The Archies (RCA: 1969)
           Sakkarin (alias Jonathan
           King) (RCA: 1971)

Other recordings: Ron Dante (RCA);
Screaming Mothers and Ernie
Wilkins (Mainstream); Shirley
(Whiz); Tommy Roe (Accord); Jimmy
McGriff (Capitol); El Chicano (Kapp);
Jimmy Smith (Polydor); Helmut
Zacharias (EMI).

SUGAR, SUGAR was the third of six
singles by 'The Archies' to figure on
the American charts and was their
only Number One record; second
bestseller of the batch was JINGLE,
JANGLE, the official follow-up to
SUGAR, SUGAR which was released
in late 1969 on the Kirshner label,
owned by Don Kirshner who had
created the studio group concept.

Jeff Barry and singer Bobby Bloom
had written Bobby's 1970 hit,
MONTEGO BAY (L&R) after which
Jeff Barry and Andy Kim came up
with HEAVY MAKES YOU HAPPY
(SHA-NA-BOOM-BOOM), which was
initially recorded by Bloom but then
became a hit for The Staple Singers
(Stax: 1971). Jeff and Andy went on to
compose Andy's own series of hits
on Jeff's Steed label: HOW'D WE
EVER GET THIS WAY (1968),
SHOOT 'EM UP BABY (1968) and SO
GOOD TOGETHER (1969). Andy
subsequently wrote his own Number
One single, ROCK ME GENTLY
(Capitol: 1974).

See: RIVER DEEP, MOUNTAIN
HIGH for songs by Jeff Barry and
Ellie Greenwich.

SUMMER IN THE CITY

(John Sebastian/Steve Boone/Mark
Sebastian)
Highest-charted song from The
Lovin' Spoonful, the New York-based
group formed by singer–songwriter
John Sebastian.

Their other key hits were DO
YOU BELIEVE IN MAGIC
(Sebastian), DAYDREAM
(Sebastian), DID YOU EVER HAVE
TO MAKE UP YOUR MIND
(Sebastian), and YOU DIDN'T HAVE
TO BE SO NICE (Sebastian/Boone),
all in 1965 or 1966.

These were, of course, the heady
days of Beatlemania, and the fab
four's pressman supreme, Derek
Taylor, was one of the first to wire

SUMMER IN THE CITY
From Greenwich village came the good-time
sounds of The Lovin' Spoonful, led by John
Sebastian (*far left*). When folk rock–singer–
songwriter Paul Simon made his first feature film
"One Trick Pony" (Warner Bros: 1980) he enlisted
the aid of several music performers, among them
The Lovin' Spoonful, who sang the first of their
seven Top 10 songs, DO YOU BELIEVE IN MAGIC
(Sebastian).

back to England with the news of the
Spoonful's formula: 'The music they
play represents America's vast
cross-section – a combination of jug
band, light blues, swing tunes and
heavy, bloodbucket rock 'n' roll!'

Song performed by Celebration
featuring Mike Love on the
soundtrack of "Almost Summer"
(Universal: 1978).

US HIT: The Lovin' Spoonful
            (Kama Sutra: 1966) Pop
UK HIT: The Lovin' Spoonful
            (Kama Sutra: 1966)

Other recordings: Quincy Jones
(A&M); Del Shannon (Liberty);
Barbara Mason (Arctic); The Flying
Pickets (10); B. B. King (ABC
Probe/Dunhill); Eat (Fiction).

SUMMERTIME BLUES
(Eddie Cochran/Jerry Capehart)
Timeless teenage anthem and a
standout performance from the late
rock 'n' roll idol, Eddie Cochran. His
single was first released in July 1958
and it has been reissued countless
times since Cochran's untimely
death two years later.

Song performed by Brian Setzer
(as Eddie Cochran) in the movie, "La
Bamba" (Columbia: 1987), and by
The Who in their movie "The Kids
Are Alright" (New World: 1979).

US HITS: Eddie Cochran (Liberty:
            1958) Pop
            Blue Cheer (Philips: 1968)
            Pop
            The Who (Decca: 1970)
            Pop
UK HITS: Eddie Cochran (London:
            1958)
            The Who (Track: 1970)
            Eddie Cochran (Liberty :
            1968 Re-release)

Other recordings: Robert Gordon
and Link Wray (Private Stock); The
Beach Boys (Capitol); Dick Dale and
The Del Tones; The Swinging Blue
Jeans (HMV); The Nite People
(Fontana); The Legends (Capitol);

Olivia Newton-John (MCA); Heinz
(UK Decca); The Flying Lizards
(Virgin).

THE SUN AIN'T GONNA SHINE ANYMORE
(Bob Gaudio/Bob Crewe)
Written for and originally recorded
by Frankie Valli (of The Four
Seasons) on Smash in 1965, THE SUN
AIN'T GONNA SHINE turned out to
be the second Number One in the
UK for three Californians known as
The Walker Brothers, actually Scott
Engel, John Maus and Gary Leeds.

UK HIT: The Walker Brothers
            (Philips: 1966)
US HITS: The Walker Brothers
            (Smash: 1966) Pop
            Nielsen/Pearson (Capitol:
            1981) Pop

Other recordings: Neil Diamond
(Columbia); Jay and The Americans
(UA).

The Walkers' other hits included
covers of MAKE IT EASY ON
YOURSELF**, originally by Jerry
Butler (Vee-Jay: 1962), and
ANOTHER TEAR FALLS
(Bacharach/David) which Gene
McDaniels had recorded (Liberty:
1961) and sung on-screen in the 1962
British pop movie, "It's Trad, Dad!"
which was released in the US as
"Ring-A-Ding Rhythm".

The Tremeloes had a huge hit
with the cover of a Four Seasons'
original, SILENCE IS GOLDEN
(Gaudio/Crewe), the song which was
the original B-side of RAG DOLL
(Philips: 1964). The Trems' version
was a Number One single in Britain
(CBS: 1967) and the record was
subsequently a big record in the
States as well.

SURF CITY
(Jan Berry/Brian Wilson)
Jan and Dean's Two Girls For Every
Boy anthem was their only Number
One record on the American charts.

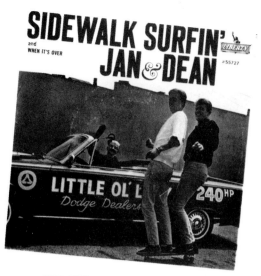

SURF CITY
Jan Berry (*right*) and Dean Torrence on a skateboard, along with the lady who posed as THE LITTLE OLD LADY FROM PASADENA for Liberty's promotional shots in the heady days of 1964!

Co-written by surf's mentor and leader of The Beach Boys, Brian Wilson, it ushered in a group of big selling Jan and Dean singles on Liberty. The guys did everything...when they weren't riding the wild surf, they were drag racing or sidewalk surfin'! DRAG CITY, their Top 10 single of early 1964, was again co-written by Brian Wilson and also with Roger Christian, a Hollywood disc-jockey with KFWB.

Jan and Dean's 1964 hit, DEAD MAN'S CURVE (Christian/Kornfeld/Berry/Wilson), proved more than a little prophetic, for Jan's Corvette slammed into a truck in the spring of 1966; when he came out of his coma months later, he had suffered brain damage and it is one of the great miracles that he and Dean are back performing today.

US HIT: Jan and Dean (Liberty: 1963) Pop
UK HIT: Jan and Dean (Liberty: 1963)

Not all Jan and Dean hits were original songs. In 1963, they had US chart success with a song that dated back to the 1940s and its origin is particularly interesting today.

Attorney and music publisher Lee Eastman had a song dedicated to his wife, but nothing for his daughter, Linda. So in 1946 he commissioned Jack Lawrence (who would later write the English lyric to Charles Trenet's French hit LA MER which Bobby Darin recorded as BEYOND THE SEA for Atco in 1960) to write LINDA...the song became a Number One US Pop song in 1947 by Ray Noble and His Orchestra with singer Buddy Clark; Eastman's daughter grew up and married Paul McCartney and, incidentally, McCartney's MPL Communications now owns the publishing rights to this song.

It was a pop hit years later for Jan and Dean who had already clocked up success with other 'standard' revivals such as CLEMENTINE (Dore: 1960), HEART AND SOUL (Challenge: 1961) and A SUNDAY KIND OF LOVE** (Liberty: 1962).

SURFIN' U.S.A.
(Brian Wilson/Chuck Berry)
This was the Beach Boys' first Top 10 hit and showed how much of Chuck Berry's motorvatin' rhythms influenced their own car and surfing songs.

Brian Wilson adapted SURFIN' U.S.A. from Chuck Berry's SWEET LITTLE SIXTEEN and the Beach Boys performed it in the legendary concert movie, "The TAMI Show" (aka "Teenage Command Performance" and "Gather No Moss") in which, incidentally, Mr Berry also sang the original !

US HITS: The Beach Boys (Capitol: 1963) Pop
            Leif Garrett (Atlantic: 1977) Pop
UK HIT: The Beach Boys (Capitol: 1963)

Other recordings: Wayne Warner
(Surf).

See: GOOD VIBRATIONS for other
Beach Boys hits.

SUSIE Q
(Dale Hawkins/Stanley Lewis)
Dale Hawkins of Bossier City,
Louisiana, came up with the ultimate
swampy guitar sound in a club and
with his band, including studio
legends James Burton and bassist
Joe Osborne, built the song SUZIE Q
around it. Dale's record is also
notable for the most prominent use
of a cow bell in rock 'n' roll history –
downhome music, indeed! Eleven
years later, swamp music revivalists
Creedence Clearwater Revival had
an even bigger hit than Dale's
original.

US HITS: Dale Hawkins (Checker:
            1957) Black & Pop
            Creedence Clearwater
            Revival (Fantasy: 1968)
            Pop

Other recordings: Lonnie Mack
(Fraternity); Bobby McFerrin (EMI);
Jose Feliciano (RCA); The
Barbarians (Laurie); The Everly
Brothers (Warner Bros); James
Burton (A&M); Sonny Boy
Williamson.

SUSPICIOUS MINDS
(Mark James)
Songwriter Mark James (see also
under ALWAYS ON MY MIND) cut
the original version of this song
himself on Scepter in 1968. Elvis
Presley recorded the song the
following year.

Waylon Jennings and his wife Jessi
Colter recorded it for RCA in 1970
and their version was a moderately
sized country hit that year, but
achieved much greater acclaim
when re-released in early 1976.

SUSPICIOUS MINDS was heard on
the soundtrack of the American

remake of the French classic,
"Breathless" (Orion: 1983).

US HIT: Elvis Presley (RCA: 1969)
            Pop
UK HITS: Elvis Presley (RCA: 1969)
            Candi Staton (Sugar Hill:
            1982)
            Fine Young Cannibals
            (London: 1986)

Other recordings: Thelma Houston
(RCA); Judy Cheeks (Salsoul); Dee
Dee Warwick (Atco).

Covers of Elvis Presley hits
One of the most recent revivals of an
Elvis hit was The Pet Shop Boys'
version of ALWAYS ON MY MIND
(Thompson/James/Christopher)**
which the duo had initially
performed on a British TV show
celebrating the King's music.

A song from much earlier in Elvis'
career was PARTY (Robinson) which
was written for him to sing in the

WOODEN HEART
Though hard to believe, Joe Dowell was an
unknown artist who went to Number One in the
States with a cover version of an Elvis Presley
tune, sung partly in German!

movie, "Loving You" (Paramount: 1957). Three years later, rockabilly singer Wanda Jackson charted with her version of the song, re-titled LET'S HAVE A PARTY (Capitol: 1960).

YOU DON'T KNOW WHAT YOU'VE GOT
The late Ral Donner not only sounded like Elvis, he had a hit with a Presley song when he covered THE GIRL OF MY BEST FRIEND (Ross/Bobrick).

Elvis Presley remakes
Not all Elvis Presley hits were songs written specifically for him and the following list details the original versions of some of what we regard as 'Presley classics':

AN AMERICAN TRILOGY (Newbury) by Mickey Newbury (Elektra: 1971)
BABY LET'S PLAY HOUSE (Gunter)** by Arthur Gunter (Excello: 1954)
BIG BOSS MAN (Smith/Dixon)** by Jimmy Reed (Vee-Jay: 1961)
BLUE MOON OF KENTUCKY (Monroe) by Bill Monroe

(Columbia: 1947)
BLUE SUEDE SHOES (Perkins)** by Carl Perkins (Sun: 1956)
BOSSA NOVA BABY (Leiber/Stoller) by Tippie and The Clovers (Tiger: 1962)
CRYING IN THE CHAPEL (Glenn)** by Darrell Glenn (Valley: 1953)
A FOOL SUCH AS I (Trader)** by Hank Snow (RCA: 1952)
HOUND DOG (Leiber/Stoller)** by Willie Mae Thornton (Peacock: 1953)
LAWDY MISS CLAWDY (Price)** by Lloyd Price (Specialty: 1952)
MONEY HONEY (Stone)** by The Drifters (Atlantic: 1953)
MYSTERY TRAIN (Phillips/Parker)** by Little Junior and The Blue Flames (Sun: 1953)
OLD SHEP (Foley) by Red Foley (Decca: 1940)
ONE NIGHT (Bartholomew/King)** by Smiley Lewis (Imperial: 1955)
SUCH A NIGHT (Chase)** by The Drifters (Atlantic: 1954)
THAT'S ALL RIGHT (Crudup)** by Arthur Crudup (RCA: 1946)
WITCHCRAFT (Bartholomew/King)** by The Spiders (Imperial: 1955)
THE WONDER OF YOU (Knight) by Ray Peterson (RCA: 1959)
YOU DON'T HAVE TO SAY YOU LOVE ME** (Donaggio/Pallavicini/Wickham/Napier-Bell) by Dusty Springfield (Philips: 1966) (English version)

Certain other Presley hit songs dated back way before the rock era. For instance, LOVE LETTERS was the Victor Young theme from a 1945 Joseph Cotten/Jennifer Jones movie of the same name; after the picture's completion, Edward Heyman wrote a lyric and the song was popular for a number of years before sultry Ketty Lester cut it on Era in 1962 which became a huge international hit. Elvis revived it four years later and again, the song soared up the charts. The most recent revival was by Alison Moyet (CBS: 1987) which was a Top 5 hit in the UK and the arrangement was a virtual copy of the Ketty Lester record.

Finally, there were also R&B songs which Elvis revived and which were in turn, subsequently re-cut by other artists. One case in point was MY BABY LEFT ME, another of Arthur Crudup's original tunes which he himself recorded for RCA in 1950; Elvis' version was a hit on RCA six years later and British singer Dave Berry successfully revived it on UK Decca in early 1964.

SWEET LITTLE SIXTEEN
(Chuck Berry)
One of Chuck Berry's greatest songs, and among his own highest-charted singles. In fact, it topped the R&B chart in early 1958, the year in which Chuck sang it at the Newport Jazz Festival; this performance was captured in the "Jazz On A Summer's Day" documentary and a later performance is available in the 1970 release, "Sweet Toronto".

Brian Wilson used SWEET LITTLE SIXTEEN as the musical base for SURFIN' USA**.

US HIT: Chuck Berry (Chess: 1958) Pop & Black
UK HITS: Chuck Berry (London: 1958)
         Jerry Lee Lewis (London: 1962)

Other recordings: John Lennon (Capitol); Bill Black's Combo (Hi); Bobby Vee (Liberty); Jesse Colin Young (Warner Bros); The Beatles (Bellaphon); The Animals (MGM).

Also available on early 'live' recordings of The Beatles (Polydor), and on the United Artists release of a British TV soundtrack featuring Eddie Cochran.

See: MEMPHIS for other Chuck Berry songs.

SWEET SOUL MUSIC
(Otis Redding/Sam Cooke/Arthur Conley)
Based on a Sam Cooke song called YEAH MAN. This was one of the great name-dropping songs, where Conley mentions individual R&B legends, paying tribute to Lou Rawls, Wilson Pickett, Sam and Dave, Otis Redding and James Brown. The brass phrase which opened the Arthur Conley single consisted of eighteen notes from Elmer Bernstein's theme from "The Magnificent Seven" western (United Artists: 1960); at the time, this movie theme was being used in a Marlboro Cigarettes TV commercial and the ad directly influenced the arrangement of SWEET SOUL MUSIC.

US HITS: Arthur Conley (Atco: 1967) Black & Pop
         Otis Redding and Carla Thomas (Stax: 1967) Black & Pop
         Amii Stewart (Ariola: 1979) Black & Pop
UK HITS: Arthur Conley (Atlantic: 1967)
         Otis Redding and Carla Thomas (Stax: 1967)
         David Bowie (RCA: 1974)
         Amii Stewart (Hansa: 1979)
         Amii Stewart (Sedition: 1985 Re-release)

Other recording: Ike and Tina Turner (Liberty).

See: ONLY SIXTEEN for other Sam Cooke songs.

That same "Magnificent Seven" opening phrase was integrated into the instrumental track of the hit I BEG YOUR PARDON by Canadian group Kon Kan (Atlantic: 1989).

Name dropping songs
My favourite other name-dropping song was LET'S THINK ABOUT

The Edsels' biggest song was RAMA LAMA DING DONG and is referred to by Barry Mann in WHO PUT THE BOMP. Later Edsels' releases included Jeff Barry's tune, SHAKE SHAKE SHERRY (Capitol: 1962).

LIVING (Bryant) by rockabilly star Bob Luman (Warner Bros: 1960) in which he refers to song titles as well as artists themselves; the premise was that characters were being killed off in song lyrics and it mentioned, for instance, CATHY'S CLOWN and Don and Phil (The Everly Brothers).

Other R&B/R&R songs which refer to artists and song titles and which were not specifically tribute records, included:

BELIEVE IT OR NOT (Rudolph) – refers to dances and song titles in its lyric and is set up by the spoken introduction, 'Hey Peggy, there's the cat that made Chantilly Lace talking to all of the disc-jockeys' by Don Covay (Sue: 1958)

EVERYBODY'S GOT A DANCE BUT ME (Ervin/St.John/Goffin) – the backup chorus echoes phrases from then-current dance songs including C'MON BABY, DO THE LOCOMOTION (Goffin/King) and 'It's the latest, it's the greatest' from MASHED POTATO TIME** by Big Dee Irwin (Dimension: 1962)

DEDICATED TO THE SONGS I LOVE (Smith/Goldsmith) – using nonsense phrases (RAMA LAMA DING DONG) and working hit tune titles into the lyric, e.g: 'He Walked Right Back to a Spanish Harlem', etc. by The Three Friends (Imperial: 1961)

(HERE THEY COME) FROM ALL OVER THE WORLD (Sloan/Barri) – actually the Theme from the rock 'n' roll concert movie, "The TAMI Show" (1965), released in Britain as both "Gather No Moss" and "Teenage Command Performance". Jan and Dean opened the movie, riding skateboards and singing this song which names the artists about to

appear from Chuck Berry and Lesley Gore to the 'Baby Lovin' Supremes and Marvin Gaye, though the lyric wrongly indicates that the Stones came from Liverpool – by Jan And Dean (Liberty: 1965)
LITTLE EVA (Zober) – dedicated to you know who! – by The Locomotions (Gone: 1962)
OUR FAVORITE MELODIES (Farrell/Elgin) – referring to HIT THE ROAD JACK, TAKE GOOD CARE OF MY BABY, etc. by Gary Criss (Wand: 1962), very successfully covered in Britain by Craig Douglas (UK Columbia: 1962)
SHORT FAT FANNIE (Williams) – as Charlie Gillett memorably pointed out in his "Sound Of The City" book, SHORT FAT FANNIE interwove at least a dozen rock 'n' roll song titles and/or references including mentions of BLUE SUEDE SHOES, HEARTBREAK HOTEL, LONG TALL SALLY and JIM DANDY...to the rescue, of course! – by Larry Williams (Specialty: 1957)

T

TAINTED LOVE
(Ed Cobb)
It never made any chart when it first came out, but the initial version of TAINTED LOVE by west coast R&B artist, sometime session singer (and also later, Mark Bolan's lady) Gloria Jones, became a Northern club dance favourite.
Song was written by Ed Cobb, an original member of singing group The Four Preps and the composer of the early punk classic DIRTY

WATER by The Standells (Tower: 1966), also recorded in Britain by the Inmates (WB: 1979), and as FRUSTRATED WOMEN by Freedom (ABC Probe/Dunhill: 1970).
Gloria Jones' original version of TAINTED LOVE was released on Champion in 1964 and the contemporary remake was by Britain's techno-pop couple, Soft Cell.
Song performed by Rupert Everett in the movie "Hearts Of Fire" (Lorimar: 1987), in which he stars with Bob Dylan.

US HIT: Soft Cell (Sire: 1982) Pop
UK HIT: Soft Cell (Some Bizarre: 1981)

Aside from being an artist, Gloria Jones herself has had success as a composer, most notably with HAVEN'T STOPPED DANCING YET recorded by British group Gonzalez (Sidewalk: 1979), and as co-writer of IF I WERE YOUR WOMAN (Jones/Sawyer/McMurray), a hit for Gladys Knight and The Pips (Soul: 1970).

TAKE GOOD CARE OF MY BABY
(Gerry Goffin/Carole King)
Bobby Vee's biggest hit on both sides of the Atlantic, although THE NIGHT HAS A THOUSAND EYES (Weisman/Wayne/Garrett) attained equal chart status in England in 1963. Dion recorded the song first but his version was never released as a single.

US HIT: Bobby Vee (Liberty: 1961) Pop
          Bobby Vinton (Epic: 1968) Pop
UK HITs: Bobby Vee (London: 1961)
          Smokie (RAK: 1980)

Answer records: HE TAKES GOOD CARE OF YOUR BABY by Dora Dee & Lora Lee (Liberty: 1961)
I'LL TAKE GOOD CARE OF YOUR BABY by Ralph Emery (Liberty: 1961)
YOU SHOULD KNOW I'M STILL YOUR BABY by Sammi Lynn (Sue: 1961)

See: UP ON THE ROOF for other Gerry Goffin and Carole King songs.

it really was a different Bobby Vee, displaying rich, resonant-toned vocals and a group of self-written folk ballads, except for MY GOD AND I composed by John Buck Wilkin (Ronny of Ronny and The Daytonas who'd also struck out on a new course), and TAKE GOOD CARE OF MY BABY which Bobby sang against just acoustic guitars and a pedal steel.

TAKE GOOD CARE OF MY BABY
On one of his UK visits in the early 1960s, Bobby Vee meets ballad singer Matt Monro, plus teenage sensation Helen Shapiro. Produced by her recording manager Norrie Paramor, Helen's early hits were brand-new songs such as DON'T TREAT ME LIKE A CHILD, YOU DON'T KNOW and WALKIN' BACK TO HAPPINESS, all written by Mike Hawker and EMI staffer, John Schroeder. Later, Helen cut some 'covers', including a revival of the Little Willie John/Peggy Lee hit, FEVER (see separate entry).

Bobby Vee records
TAKE GOOD CARE OF MY BABY was one of a string of Goffin and King songs which Bobby Vee recorded in his early years. He also had hits with these titles: HOW MANY TEARS (Liberty: 1961) SHARING YOU (Liberty: 1962) WALKIN' WITH MY ANGEL (Liberty: 1961) and HEY GIRL which he recorded in a medley with the Motown song MY GIRL (Robinson/White)** for Liberty in 1968.

He also charted with two songs which Gerry Goffin wrote with Jack Keller, A FOREVER KIND OF LOVE (Liberty: 1962) and RUN TO HIM (Liberty: 1961).

In 1972, Bobby cut an album called *Nothin' Like A Sunny Day* (UA), using his real name, Robert Thomas Velline;

A TEENAGER IN LOVE
(Doc Pomus/Mort Shuman)
TEENAGER IN LOVE was the biggest of Marty Wilde's many cover records in the late 1950s and early 1960s. Father of contemporary hitmaker Kim Wilde, Marty successfully recorded British versions of the American hits: ENDLESS SLEEP**, A TEENAGER IN LOVE, SEA OF LOVE** and RUBBER BALL (Schroeder/Orlowski).

US HIT: Dion and The Belmonts
          (Laurie: 1959) Pop
UK HITS: Dion and The Belmonts
          (London: 1959)
          Marty Wilde (Philips: 1959)
          Craig Douglas (Top Rank: 1959)

Pomus and Shuman songs
Among the hit records of other Doc Pomus and Mort Shuman songs:

CAN'T GET USED TO LOSING YOU by Andy Williams (Columbia: 1963) by The Beat (Go Feet: 1983)
GO, JIMMY, GO by Jimmy Clanton (Ace: 1959)
(MARIE'S THE NAME) HIS LATEST FLAME by Elvis Presley (RCA: 1961)
HOUND DOG MAN by Fabian (Chancellor: 1959)
HUSHABYE by The Mystics (Laurie: 1959)
I COUNT THE TEARS by The Drifters (Atlantic: 1960)
LITTLE SISTER by Elvis Presley (RCA: 1961)

SAVE THE LAST DANCE FOR ME**
by The Drifters (Atlantic: 1960)
SURRENDER by Elvis Presley (RCA:
1961)
SUSPICION by Terry Stafford
(Crusader: 1964)
SWEETS FOR MY SWEET** by The
Drifters (Atlantic: 1961)
by The Searchers (Pye: 1963)
THIS MAGIC MOMENT** by The
Drifters (Atlantic: 1960)
by Jay and The Americans (UA:
1969)
TURN ME LOOSE by Fabian
(Chancellor: 1959)

TELL HIM

(Bert Russell)

'I know something about love' sang
Brenda Reid of The Exciters, a New
York three girls-one guy R&B group,
produced in their early days by Jerry
Leiber and Mike Stoller. Though the
era of the music video was still eons
away, The Exciters did shoot (miming
to playback) a 'scopatone', a short-
lived process whereby short films
showing singers performing current
hits (or would-be-hits) were made

specifically to be shown on jukebox
apparatus, similar to the video-jukes of
today. Luckily, the Exciters' clip still
exists, otherwise a colour record of
them 'doing' their biggest song would
not exist.

The original British cover version
was the only Top 10 single by Billie
Davis who was the girlfriend of
guitarist Jet Harris, an original
member of The Shadows and, at that
time, a Decca recording artist himself
with both solo singles to his credit
plus three huge hits with drummer
Tony Meehan (also of The Shadows),
including their Number One,
DIAMONDS, written by Jerry Lordon
of APACHE fame.

US HIT: The Exciters (UA: 1963)
            Black & Pop
UK HITS: The Exciters (UA: 1963)
            Billie Davis (Decca: 1963)
            Hello (Bell: 1974)

TELL HIM

More great exponents of the classic 'girl group
sound', The Exciters recorded the original
versions of both TELL HIM and DO WAH DIDDY
DIDDY (see separate entry). Their lead singer
was Brenda Reid, the centre girl in the photo, and
the group's male voice belonged to her husband,
Herb Rooney, who is standing centre.

Male versions: TELL HER by Dean Parrish (Boom: 1966)
TELL HER by Ed Townsend (Liberty: 1962)
TELL HER by Kenny Loggins (Columbia: 1989)

R&B singer-songwriter Ed Townsend struck gold in 1958 with FOR YOUR LOVE, a ballad he wrote and recorded for Capitol and which was successfully re-cut by soul duo Peaches and Herb on Date in 1967. Townsend later co-wrote LET'S GET IT ON with Marvin Gaye whose version was a Number One R&B single (Tamla: 1973) and he was the sole writer of THE LOVE OF MY MAN, Theola Kilgore's hit record on Serock a decade earlier.

TELL IT LIKE IT IS

(George Davis/Lee Diamond)
Written by two New Orleans musicians, one of whom performed professionally as Lee Diamond though his real name was Wilbert Smith and he was a member of Little Richard's band, The Upsetters, in the 1950s. TELL IT LIKE IT IS was made famous by the songbird of the bayou, Aaron Neville, who today sings with the famed masters of New Orleans funk, The Neville Brothers. In 1980 the song was revived for a major US hit by Ann Wilson, with her group Heart. There had earlier been an MOR version by Andy Williams (Columbia: 1976) that just scraped into the US Top 75.

Performed by Aaron Neville and The Neville Brothers on the soundtrack of "The Big Easy" (Columbia: 1987).

US HITS: Aaron Neville (Par-Lo: 1967) Black & Pop
           Heart (Epic: 1981) Pop

Other recordings: Freddy Fender (ABC); Otis Redding.

TELL LAURA I LOVE HER
Ray Peterson's first US hit was the original version of Baker Knight's THE WONDER OF YOU which eventually became a worldwide smash for Elvis Presley. TELL LAURA is one of the all-time classic death songs and was followed up by Ray with CORINNA, CORINNA.

TELL LAURA I LOVE HER

(Jeff Barry/Ben Raleigh)
One of the great 'death' songs, telling of Tommy's fatal stock-car accident; the title is actually his message from heaven to girlfriend Laura!

The original was by Ray Peterson (see also under: CORINNA, CORINNA) but the British cover version ran into censorship problems.

I remember the BBC even playing an extract on the nine o'clock television news to illustrate the uproar that was being caused by folks who thought it was anti-religious.

Nevertheless the cover became a hit and Valance went on to 'borrow' another American song, JIMMY'S GIRL (Vance/Pockriss), originally by Johnny Tillotson on Cadence.

US HIT: Ray Peterson (RCA: 1960)
           Pop
UK HIT: Ricky Valance (UK
           Columbia: 1960)

Other recording: John Leyton
(Triumph).

Answer records: TELL TOMMY I
MISS HIM by Marilyn Michaels (RCA:
1960)
by Laura Lee (Triumph: 1960)
by Skeeter Davis (RCA: 1961).

Death songs
Other memorable R&B/R&R death
songs:

DEAD MAN'S CURVE (Christian/
    Wilson/Berry/Kornfeld) by Jan and
    Dean (Liberty: 1964)
THE HOMECOMING QUEEN'S GOT
    A GUN (Brown/Coffey/McNally/
    Calcord) by Julie Brown (Rhino:
    1984)
EBONY EYES (Loudermilk) by The
    Everly Brothers (Warner Bros:
    1961)
ENDLESS SLEEP (Reynolds/Nance)**
    by Jody Reynolds (Demon: 1958)
JOHNNY REMEMBER ME
    (Goddard)** by John Leyton (Top
    Rank: 1961)
LAST KISS (Cochran) by J. Frank
    Wilson (Josie: 1964)
LAURIE (STRANGE THINGS
    HAPPEN) (Addington) by Dickey
    Lee (TCF Hall: 1965)
LEADER OF THE PACK (Morton/
    Barry/Greenwich)** by The
    Shangri-Las (Red Bird: 1964)
PATCHES (Mann/Kolber) by Dickey
    Lee (Smash: 1962)
TEEN ANGEL (Surrey/Surrey) by
    Mark Dinning (MGM: 1960)
TERRY (Twinkle) by Twinkle (UK
    Decca: 1964)

The answer song to all death songs
was LET'S THINK ABOUT LIVING
(Bryant) recorded by Bob Luman
(Warner Bros: 1960), while a sick
parody of them was I WANT MY
BABY BACK (by Jimmy Cross
(Tollie:1965) in which the singer's

girlfriend gets killed in a car crash on
the way home from a Beatles' concert;
the singer wants to have her back so
desperately that he breaks open her
coffin and joins her!

TEQUILA
(Chuck Rio)
OK, so this is really an instrumental,
but the shouted repetition of its title
just about qualifies it as a semi-vocal!
Chuck Rio cut the song for the west-

Don Wilson (*left*) and Bob Bogle were the
founders of instrumental group, The Ventures,
whose debut hit WALK DON'T RUN was covered
in Britain by The John Barry Seven on Columbia.

coast Challenge label which was owned by cowboy star, Gene Autry, and the name of 'The Champs' was derived from Autry's screen horse, Champion.

Years after the original hit, Pee Wee Herman moonwalked to TEQUILA in a memorable scene from his "Pee Wee's Big Adventure" movie (Warner Bros: 1985); jumping on the bandwagon, a dance hit called PEE-WEE'S DANCE by Joeksi Love (Vintertainment: 1986) used TEQUILA as its recurring theme.

US HITS: The Champs (Challenge: 1958) Pop
Eddie Platt (ABC/ Paramount: 1958) Pop
UK HITS: The Champs (London: 1958)
Ted Heath and His Music (UK Decca: 1958)
No Way Jose (4th and Broadway: 1985)

Other recordings: Bill Black's Combo (Hi); The Ventures (Liberty); Boots Randolph (Monument); The Challengers.

Instrumental hits
Following is a selective list of other R&B/R&R instrumental hits:

GREEN ONIONS (Cropper/Jones/ Steinberg/Jackson Jr.) by Booker T. and The M.G's (Stax: 1962)
THE HAPPY ORGAN (Cortez/Wood) by Dave 'Baby' Cortez (Clock: 1959)
HIDE AWAY (King) by Freddy King (Federal: 1961)
HONKY TONK PARTS 1 & 2 (Doggett/Scott/Butler/Sheppard) by Bill Doggett (King: 1956)
I'VE GOT A WOMAN PART 1 (Charles)** by Jimmy McGriff (Sue: 1962)
LET THERE BE DRUMS by Sandy Nelson (Original Sound: 1961)
MEMPHIS (Berry)** by Lonnie Mack (Fraternity: 1963)

NIGHT TRAIN (Forrest)** by James Brown and The Famous Flames (King: 1962)
PETER GUNN (Mancini) – the 1958 TV movie theme – by Duane Eddy (Jamie: 1960)
by Art Of Noise with Duane Eddy (China: 1986)
PIPELINE (Spickard/Carman) by The Chantay's (Dot: 1963)
RAUNCHY (Justis/Manker) by Bill Justis (Phillips International: 1957)
REBEL-ROUSER (Eddy/Hazlewood) by Duane Eddy (Jamie: 1958)
RED RIVER ROCK (King/Mack/ Mendelsohn) by Johnny and The Hurricanes (Warwick: 1959)
RED'S BOOGIE (Perryman) by Piano Red (RCA: 1950)
RUMBLE (Wray) by Link Wray (Cadence: 1958)
SLEEP WALK (Farina/Farina/Farina) by Santo and Johnny (Canadian American: 1959)
SO FAR AWAY (Jacobs) by Hank Jacobs (Sue: 1963)
SOULFUL STRUT (Record/Sanders) by Young-Holt Unlimited (Brunswick: 1968)
STICK SHIFT (Bellinger) by The Duals (Sue: 1961)
TALL COOL ONE (Dangel/Greek) by The Wailers (Golden Crest: 1959)
TEEN BEAT (Nelson/Egnoian) by Sandy Nelson (Original Sound: 1959)
TOPSY PART 2 (Battle/Durham) by Cozy Cole (Love: 1958)
WALK DON'T RUN (Smith) by The Ventures (Dolton: 1960)
WALKIN' WITH MR. LEE (Allen) by Lee Allen (Ember: 1958)
WIPE OUT (Berryhill/Wilson/Fuller/ Connolly)** by The Surfaris (Dot: 1963)
YOU CAN'T SIT DOWN PART 2 (Mann/Clark/Muldrow)** by The Philip Upchurch Combo (Boyd: 1961)

THAT'LL BE THE DAY

(Jerry Allison/Norman Petty/Buddy Holly)

One of *the* best Buddy Holly and The Crickets' records, its title came from a line spoken by John Wayne in the John Ford western, "The Searchers" (Warner Bros: 1956). First cut for Decca who failed to release it, the guys recorded it again under their new contract with Brunswick.

This was the first song that The Beatles ever recorded on a demo which they paid for in 1958. It was also the song which launched Buddy Holly and The Crickets on the American charts though they were only billed as The Crickets to distinguish them from their Decca releases.

US HITS: The Crickets (Brunswick: 1957) Black & Pop
           Linda Ronstadt (Asylum: 1976) Pop
UK HITS: The Crickets (Vogue Coral: 1957)
           The Everly Brothers (Warner Bros: 1965)

Other recordings: Link Wray (Swan); Pure Prairie League (RCA); Cliff Richard (UK Columbia); The Ravens (Argo); Foghat (Bearsville); Tommy Roe (ABC); The Hullaballoos (Roulette); J. Frank Wilson (Jubilee); Françoise Hardy (Reprise); Kenny Vernon (Capitol); Pat Boone (Dot); The Allisons (Fontana); The Crossfires (aka The Turtles) (Lucky Token); Bobby Vee (Liberty); Gary Busey; *That'll Be The Day* soundtrack (Epic).

See: LOVE'S MADE A FOOL OF YOU for other Buddy Holly songs.

THAT'S ALL RIGHT

(Arthur Crudup)

One of Elvis Presley's early influences was Arthur 'Big Boy' Crudup, the Mississippi bluesman who recorded the first version of THAT'S ALL RIGHT in 1946. Elvis cut the song, also known as THAT'S ALL RIGHT, MAMA, in 1954 on his first session at Sun Records in Memphis.

Performed by Elvis in the rockumentary, "Elvis On Tour" (MGM: 1972).

UK HIT: Slade: Medley with MY BABY LEFT ME (Crudup) (Barn: 1977)

Other recordings: Carl Perkins (Columbia); Hoyt Axton (A&M); Marty Robbins (Columbia); Rod Stewart (Mercury); Lightnin' Slim (Excello); Blind Snooks Eaglin (Fantasy); Merle Haggard (MCA); Mike Bloomfield and Al Kooper (Columbia); Earl Scruggs Revue (Columbia); Geoff Muldaur (Flying Fish); Mahalia Jackson (Columbia); Paul McCartney (EMI); Wet Willie (Capricorn); Rick Nelson (Epic); Albert King (Fantasy); Canned Heat (Liberty); Chas and Dave and Friends (BBC).

Another medley of THAT'S ALL RIGHT and MY BABY LEFT ME was recorded by Waylon Jennings on his *Ol' Waylon* album (RCA: 1977).

Elvis Presley also covered Crudup's MY BABY LEFT ME (RCA: 1956) and his version made both the American pop and country charts. MY BABY LEFT ME was originally a hit in the UK for British singer Dave Berry (UK Decca: 1964); though his later and best-remembered songs were dramatic ballads such as Geoff Stephens' THE CRYING GAME (UK Decca: 1964), his first two charters were fine examples of early '60s British R&B. Besides MY BABY LEFT ME, Dave Berry scored with a cover of Chuck Berry's MEMPHIS TENNESSEE** (UK Decca: 1963).

THEN HE KISSED ME/THEN I KISSED HER

(Phil Spector/Jeff Barry/Ellie Greenwich)

As with DA DOO RON RON**, of which this was the follow-up, THEN

HE KISSED ME was a teen-dream come true saga etched into history by the five Crystals on a record produced by Phil Spector.

US HIT: The Crystals (Philles: 1963) Black & Pop
UK HITS: The Crystals (London: 1963)
The Beach Boys: Recorded as THEN I KISSED HER (Capitol: 1967)

Other recordings: Kiss (Casablanca); Martha and The Vandellas (Gordy).

See: DA DOO RON RON for other Phil Spector classics.

See: RIVER DEEP, MOUNTAIN HIGH for other Jeff Barry and Ellie Greenwich songs.

THERE'S SOMETHING ON YOUR MIND
(Cecil James McNeely)
Originally written as THERE'S NOTHING ON MY MIND by Cecil James (aka Big Jay) McNeely, R&B's legendary tenor sax player who was a seminal figure on the Los Angeles music scene in the 1950s and is still working crazy schedules to this day!

This blues ballad was first recorded by McNeely himself in 1959 with his Band and vocalist 'Little Sonny' Warner. This was followed by Bobby Marchan's cover version that took the song to the top of the R&B listings. The Baby Ray version made it on to the lower rungs of the pop charts in 1966.

US HITS: Big Jay McNeely (Swingin': 1959) Pop
Bobby Marchan (Fire: 1960) Black & Pop

Other recordings: Baby Ray (Imperial); Little Johnny Taylor (Ronn); Grady Gaines and The Texas Upsetters (Black Top); King Curtis; Professor Longhair.

THE THINGS THAT I USED TO DO
(Eddie Jones)
An eloquent, impassioned, slow-paced blues written and originally recorded by the late Eddie 'Guitar Slim' Jones. That 1953 session was arranged by Ray Charles who played piano on the date. The song had more than a passing influence on Charles and his own gospel-based blues records. Not only was this New Orleans' song widely recorded, but Guitar Slim's electric guitar style was said to have inspired many musicians including Jimi Hendrix.

US HIT: Guitar Slim (Specialty: 1954) Black

Other recordings: Earl King (Imperial); Chuck Berry (Chess); Little Milton (Checker); Ike and Tina Turner (Blue Thumb); Stevie Ray Vaughan and Double Trouble (Epic); Joe Turner (Pablo); Bill Black's Combo (Hi); Elvin Bishop (Columbia); Ike Turner (Liberty); Pee Wee Crayton (Epic); Freddie King (Atlantic); Earl Gaines (Starday); Buddy Guy (Vanguard); James Brown (King); B. B. King (Modern).

THIS DIAMOND RING
(Al Kooper/Bob Brass/Irwin Levine)
Comedian Jerry Lewis' son, Gary, hit paydirt with his first million-selling single, produced by Tommy 'Snuff' Garrett, Liberty's crack A&R whiz whose roster at the label also included Bobby Vee, Gene McDaniels (who later wrote Roberta Flack's 1974 hit, FEEL LIKE MAKIN' LOVE) and Johnny Burnette.

THIS DIAMOND RING was co-written by Al Kooper who had started out as a member of The Royal Teens who charted with SHORT SHORTS (Austin/Gaudio) on ABC in 1958; he later played organ with Bob Dylan, formed the legendary Blues Project and then began Blood, Sweat and Tears!

Bonnie Bramlett and which was a big hit by The Carpenters (A&M: 1971) and was also recorded by Bette Midler (Atlantic), Luther Vandross (Epic), Spring (UA) and Joe Cocker (A&M), plus THIS MASQUERADE which launched George Benson's hit-making career (Warner Bros: 1976).

THIS DIAMOND RING
Caught listening to record producer Snuff Garrett (*far right*), are (*from the left*) arranger Leon Russell, Patti Lewis (mother of Gary), and Gary Lewis who led his Playboys through a succession of huge American single hits. Gary later turned to other people's classics and scored with revivals of both SEALED WITH A KISS (Udell/Geld) (Liberty: 1968) and RHYTHM OF THE RAIN (Gummoe) (Liberty: 1969).

Kooper revived DIAMOND RING himself on a solo album cut for UA in 1977. Gary's original version was arranged by Leon Russell.

US HIT: Gary Lewis and The
          Playboys (Liberty:
          1965) Pop

Other recordings: Leroy Van Dyke (Plantation); Billy Fury (UK Decca).

Answer record: (GARY, PLEASE DON'T SELL) MY DIAMOND RING by Wendy Hill (Liberty: 1965).

The same team of writers of THIS DIAMOND RING also wrote one of Gene Pitney's ballad hits, I MUST BE SEEING THINGS (Musicor: 1965).
     The arranger on THIS DIAMOND RING and most of Gary Lewis' other Liberty hits was pianist–composer–performer Leon Russell who went on to back Joe Cocker on the legendary Mad Dogs and Englishmen tour in 1970. Russell's songs include SUPERSTAR which he co-wrote with

THIS MAGIC MOMENT
(Doc Pomus/Mort Shuman)
One of two ballad hits written by Doc and Mort specially for The Drifters; their other collaboration was I COUNT THE TEARS in 1961.
     Jay and The Americans revived THIS MAGIC MOMENT as part of a 1968 album of classic R&B songs called *Sands Of Time.* In 1983, British group The Beat injected a reggae rhythm into another Pomus and Shuman classic, CAN'T GET USED TO LOSING YOU, which was originally a 1963 international smash for Andy Williams.

US HITS: The Drifters
(Atlantic:1960) Pop &
Black
Jay and The Americans
(UA: 1969) Pop

Other recordings: Richie Furay
(Asylum); Marvin Gaye (Tamla); Rita
Remington (Plantation).

See: A TEENAGER IN LOVE for
other Doc Pomus and Mort Shuman
songs.

THIS OLD HEART OF MINE (IS WEAK FOR YOU)

(Brian Holland/Lamont Dozier/Eddie
Holland/Sylvia Moy)
From the Isley Brothers' brief (by
comparison with other artists) stay
with the Motown family, this was
their most successful side, coming as
it did from the Holland/Dozier/
Holland team along with Sylvia Moy
during the same year in which she
co-wrote Stevie Wonder's smash,
UPTIGHT (EVERYTHING'S
ALRIGHT).

US HITS: The Isley Brothers
(Tamla: 1966) Black &
Pop
Tammi Terrell (Motown:
1969) Black & Pop
UK HITS: The Isley Brothers (Tamla
Motown: 1966)
Rod Stewart (Riva: 1975)

Rod Stewart re-cut the song 14 years
later as a duet with Ronald Isley.

Other recordings: The Supremes
(Motown); Wild Cherry (Epic);
Shalamar* (Solar); The Zombies (UK
Decca).

*   Vocal group Shalamar, one of whom was Jody
    Watley, cut a medley of Motown songs on Soul
    Train in 1977. The tunes they included were:
    GOING TO A GO-GO, I CAN'T HELP MYSELF,
    IT'S THE SAME OLD SONG, STOP! IN THE
    NAME OF LOVE and UPTIGHT
    (EVERYTHING'S ALRIGHT).

The Isleys also cut a Motown song
usually associated with The Elgins; in
fact, PUT YOURSELF IN MY PLACE
(Holland/Dozier/ Holland) was an
Elgins hit in the US in 1966 on
Motown's V.I.P. label, but in Britain,
the Isleys' version was the first hit of
the song (Tamla Motown: 1969) and
only when the Elgins' record was
re-released two years later (on
Tamla Motown) did it enter the UK
Top 30.

See: DEVIL WITH A BLUE DRESS
ON for other Motown hits.

See: HOW SWEET IT IS for other
Holland/Dozier/Holland songs.

THIS WHEEL'S ON FIRE

(Bob Dylan/Rick Danko)
Song originally on The Band's debut
album, *Music From Big Pink*
(Capitol: 1968) – Danko was the
group's bass player – and it was also
included in Bob Dylan's *Basement
Tapes* collection (Columbia: 1975).

UK HITS: Julie Driscoll, Brian Auger
and The Trinity
(Marmalade: 1968)
Siouxsie and The
Banshees
(Wonderland: 1987)

Other recordings: Ian and Sylvia
(Vanguard); The Byrds (Columbia).

See: BLOWIN' IN THE WIND for
other Bob Dylan songs.

THRILL ON THE HILL

See: LET'S GO, LET'S GO, LET'S
GO.

TIME IS ON MY SIDE

(Norman Meade/James Norman)
Co-written by Norman Meade (aka
Jerry Ragovoy) who also composed
such dramatic R&B ballads as CRY
BABY (Garnet Mimms' 1963 charter)
and STAY WITH ME, Lorraine
Ellison's milestone hit of 1966.

TIME IS ON MY SIDE was initially
cut by New Orleans' soul queen
Irma Thomas in a fine, uptown R&B

THE TIMES THEY ARE A CHANGIN'
(Bob Dylan)
Surprisingly never a chart hit in America, this is however a key song from the early output of Bob Dylan when the singer–songwriter was adopted as the forefather of the 1960s folk-rock movement. THE TIMES THEY ARE A-CHANGIN' is an archetypal political statement by the artist who, along with Joan Baez, symbolizes the mood and unrest of that era. Performed by James Taylor, Carly Simon and Graham Nash in the 1980 rockumentary "No Nukes".

UK HITS: Peter, Paul and Mary
              (Warner Bros: 1963)
              Bob Dylan (CBS: 1965)

TIME IS ON MY SIDE
The Soul Queen of New Orleans is what they call the great Irma Thomas. After her time with producer Allen Toussaint on the Minit label between 1961 and 1963, she switched to Imperial Records; there she cut the original of TIME IS ON MY SIDE as well as BREAK-A-WAY (DeShannon/Sheeley) which Tracey Ullman revived two decades later.

production by Eddie Ray. Song covered by The Rolling Stones on a single first released in the US in September, 1964 where it became the group's first American Top 10 hit. It was finally released as a Stones single in England eighteen years later!

US HIT: The Rolling Stones
            (London: 1964) Pop
UK HIT: The Rolling Stones
            (Rolling Stones: 1982)

Other recordings: Unit Four Plus One (Parlophone); The In Crowd (Parlophone); Brian Poole and The Tremeloes (UK Decca).

See: CRY BABY for other Jerry Ragovoy songs.

THE TIMES THEY ARE A-CHANGIN'
Bob Dylan's first hit single was the British release of THE TIMES THEY ARE A-CHANGIN', followed by his SUBTERRANEAN HOMESICK BLUES which charted on both sides of the Atlantic.

The Ian Campbell Folk
Group (Transatlantic:
1965)

Other recordings: The Beach Boys
(Capitol); Cher (Imperial); Simon and
Garfunkel (Columbia); Bob Lind
(Verve); Billy Joel (Columbia); The
Seekers (UK Columbia); The Hollies
(Parlophone); The Byrds (Columbia);
Joan Baez (Vanguard); Carly Simon
and Graham Nash; Burl Ives
(Columbia); The Brothers And
Sisters (A&M).

TO BE YOUNG, GIFTED AND BLACK
See: YOUNG, GIFTED AND BLACK.

TO KNOW HIM IS TO LOVE HIM
(Phil Spector)
Wistful pop ballad, written by Phil
Spector and recorded by the Los
Angeles group he formed under the
name The Teddy Bears. He and
Marshall Leib provided back-up
vocals behind Annette Kleinbard
who sang lead on what became a
chart-topping record; shortening her
name, Annette Bard went on to cut a
solo single for Imperial, the label for
which the three cut a Teddy Bears
album.

Annette later changed her name
to Carol Connors, under which she
not only recorded but also co-wrote
such songs as HEY LITTLE COBRA
(for The Rip Chords in 1963),
GONNA FLY NOW (Theme from the
1976 "Rocky" movie), and WITH YOU
I'M BORN AGAIN, the Billy Preston
and Syreeta hit from the movie
"Spring Break" in 1980.

Phil Spector became one of rock's
finest record producers whose
haunting 'wall of sound' trademark
delivered a series of spine-tingling,
emotion-packed singles by such
artists as The Crystals, The Ronettes,
Ike and Tina Turner and the
Righteous Brothers. TO KNOW HIM
IS TO LOVE HIM (also recorded by
male artists as TO KNOW HER IS TO

TO KNOW HIM IS TO LOVE HIM
An original sheet for Phil Spector's debut hit; the
trio (*left to right*) is Marshall Leib, Annette
Kleinbard (aka Carol Connors) and Phil Spector
himself.

LOVE HER) was a Number One
country single for Dolly Parton,
Emmylou Harris and Linda Ronstadt
from their award-winning *Trio*
album, and as a result, BMI (the
American music licensing society)
awarded it their Most Performed
Country Song Of 1987 accolade.

US HITS: The Teddy Bears (Dore:
          1958) Pop & Black
          Peter and Gordon
          (Capitol: 1965) Pop
          Bobby Vinton (Epic: 1969)
          Pop
          Dolly Parton, Linda
          Ronstadt, Emmylou
          Harris (Warner Bros:
          1987) Country

UK HITS: The Teddy Bears
          (London: 1958)
          Peter and Gordon (UK
          Columbia: 1965)
          The Teddy Bears

(Lightning: 1979 Re-release)

Other recordings: Steeleye Span (Chrysalis); Nancy Sinatra (Reprise); Mick Farren (Big Sound); David Bromberg (Fantasy); The Fleetwoods (Dolton); Cleo (UK Decca); Cilla Black (EMI); The Beatles (Bellaphon); The Shirelles (Scepter).

See: DA DOO RON RON for other Phil Spector productions.

TO LOVE SOMEBODY
(Barry Gibb/Maurice Gibb/Robin Gibb)
The Bee Gees' second (following NEW YORK MINING DISASTER 1941) hit record. Nina Simone's cover was a Top 5 hit, much bigger than the boys' original.

UK HITS:	The Bee Gees (Polydor: 1967)
	Nina Simone (RCA: 1969)
US HITS:	The Bee Gees (Atco: 1967) Pop
	The Sweet Inspirations (Atlantic: 1968) Black & Pop
	James Carr (Goldwax: 1969) Black

Other recordings: Eric Burdon and The Animals (MGM); Janis Joplin (Columbia); Hank Williams Jr (Elektra); Flying Burrito Bros (A&M); Jackie DeShannon (Amherst); Roberta Flack (Atlantic); Johnny Rodriguez (Mercury); Little Joe (Brunswick); The Marbles (Polydor); Moulin Rouge (MCA); Tom Jones (UK Decca); Lulu (UK Columbia); The Mirettes; P. P. Arnold (Immediate); Mike Berry; Gary Puckett (Columbia); The Robert Stigwood Orchestra (Polydor); The Chambers Brothers (Columbia).

Bee Gees songs
The three Gibb Brothers wrote and had hits with a slew of songs from 1967 through to the late 1970s, but their songs were also successful for other artists as well. Here are a few of them:

EMOTIONS (Barry Gibb and Robin Gibb were the writers) by Samantha Sang (Private Stock: 1978)
AN EVERLASTING LOVE (Barry Gibb was the solo writer) by Andy Gibb (RSO: 1978)
GREASE (Barry Gibb only) by Frankie Valli (RSO: 1978)
JIVE TALKIN' by Boogie Box High (Hardback: 1987)
MORE THAN A WOMAN by Tavares (Capitol: 1977)
NIGHT FEVER by Carol Douglas (Gull: 1978)
SHADOW DANCING by Andy Gibb (RSO: 1978)
STAYIN' ALIVE by Richard Ace (Blue Inc: 1978)
YOU STEPPED INTO MY LIFE by Melba Moore (Epic: 1979)
WARM RIDE by Rare Earth (Prodigal: 1978)
WORDS by Rita Coolidge (A&M: 1978)

TOBACCO ROAD
(John D. Loudermilk)
Country writer John D. Loudermilk was supposedly inspired by his North Carolina upbringing and the Erskine Caldwell drama "Tobacco Road" to write this song. In Britain, The Nashville Teens from Weybridge, Surrey, did an inspired, nasty version that brought the song its just fame.

US HIT:	The Nashville Teens (London: 1964) Pop
UK HIT:	The Nashville Teens (Decca: 1964)

Other recordings: Jefferson Airplane (RCA); Edgar Winter's White Trash (Epic); The Blues Magoos (Mercury); Spooky Tooth (A&M); Lou Rawls (Capitol); Rare Earth (Rare Earth); John D. Loudermilk (Warner Bros);

TOBACCO ROAD

John D. Loudermilk wrote and recorded hits himself, either under his real name, as with LANGUAGE OF LOVE (RCA: 1961), or under the name Johnny Dee, which was on the label of the original version of SITTIN' IN THE BALCONY (Colonial: 1957) before Eddie Cochran cut it and made it his own. His other song-writing successes include ANGELA JONES, which charted in 1960 for both America's Johnny Ferguson (MGM) and Britain's Michael Cox (Triumph).

Dan Seals (EMI America); David Lee Roth (Warner Bros); Junior Wells (Vanguard); Eric Burdon and The Animals.

TOBACCO ROAD was written by the same John D. Loudermilk who wrote THEN YOU CAN TELL ME GOODBYE, the 1967 hit by The Casinos (Fraternity). ANGELA JONES was also his song, recorded originally in the States by Johnny Ferguson (MGM: 1960) and covered in Britain by Michael Cox (Triumph: 1960).

TOMORROW NIGHT

(Sam Coslow/Will Grosz)
A song from the big band era of the late 1930s which was revived a decade later by R&B singer–guitarist Lonnie Johnson. His record made Number One on the rhythm and blues charts in 1948 on the King label. The song had been recorded by various jazz artists over the years, but Lonnie Johnson's version must have contributed greatly to its ongoing popularity. It was later recorded by Elvis Presley (RCA), Charlie Rich (RCA) and LaVern Baker (Atlantic).

US HITS: Horace Heidt & His
                 Orchestra (Columbia:
                 1939) Pop
                 Lonnie Johnson (King:
                 1948) Black & Pop

Vintage popular standards

Some of the 1930s standards which have been recorded by R&B and R&R acts started out as movie songs. BLUE MOON** is a perfect example, as is OVER THE RAINBOW (Arlen/Harburg), the perennial Judy Garland classic from "The Wizard Of Oz" (MGM: 1939) which was a Top 20 US hit in 1960 for The Demensions (Mohawk) and part of a Top 20 UK medley hit single in 1980 for Matchbox on Magnet. OVER THE RAINBOW was also a Top 10 country seller for Jerry Lee Lewis on Elektra in 1980.

Following is a random selection of other songs which obviously came with built-in longevity. The approximate year of when the song was first published is shown, along with recommended versions from the rock era:

AS TIME GOES BY (Hupfeld) (1931) by Nilsson (RCA: 1973)
AT LAST (Warren/Gordon) (1942) by Etta James (Argo: 1961)
BLUE MOON (Rodgers/ Hart)**(1934) by The Marcels (Colpix: 1961)
BLUEBERRY HILL (Lewis/Stock/

Rose)**(1940) by Fats Domino
(Imperial: 1956)
DEEP PURPLE (Parish/DeRose)
(1934) by Billy Ward and The
Dominoes (Liberty: 1957)
by Nino Tempo and April Stevens
(Atco: 1963)
DOWN THE ROAD APIECE (Ray)
(1941) by the Rolling Stones (UK
Decca: 1965)
GEORGIA ON MY MIND
(Carmichael/Gorrell) (1930) by
Ray Charles (ABC/Paramount:
1960)
THE GLORY OF LOVE (Hill) (1936)
by The Five Keys (Aladdin: 1951)

Billy Fury sang JEALOUSY in 1961. Here he is the
year before at a Decca Records reception in
London. *Left to right.* Eddie Cochran, DJ Paul
Hollingdale, Fury, Joe Brown and TV producer
Jack Good.

The Five Keys' string of standard revivals included
THE GLORY OF LOVE (Hill) (1951), RED SAILS IN
THE SUNSET (Williams/Kennedy) (1952) and I
CRIED FOR YOU (Arnheim/Lyman/Freed) (1952),
all for Aladdin.

HEART AND SOUL (Carmichael/
Loesser) (1938) by The Cleftones
(Gee: 1961)

I ONLY HAVE EYES FOR YOU
(Warren/Dubin) (1934) by Art
Garfunkel (Columbia: 1975)
JEALOUSY (Gade/Bloom) (1938) by
Billy Fury (UK Decca: 1961)
LET IT BE ME (Becaud/Curtis)
(1955) by The Everly Brothers
(Cadence: 1960)
by Betty Everett and Jerry Butler
(Vee-Jay: 1964)
MY PRAYER (Kennedy/Boulanger)
(1939) by The Platters (Mercury:
1956)
SMOKE GETS IN YOUR EYES
(Kern/Harbach) (1933) by The
Platters (Mercury: 1958)
STORMY WEATHER (Arlen/
Koehler) (1933) by The Five
Sharps (Jubilee: 1952)
by The Leaders (Glory: 1955)
SUMMERTIME (Gershwin/Heyward)
(1935) by Billy Stewart (Chess:
1966)
A SUNDAY KIND OF LOVE (Prima/
Belle/Leonard/Rhodes) (1946) by

Jan and Dean (Liberty: 1962)
by The Van Dykes (Mala: 1967)
(THERE'LL BE BLUEBIRDS OVER)
THE WHITE CLIFFS OF DOVER
(Burton/Kent) (1942) by The
Caravans (Vee-Jay: 1961)
by The Righteous Brothers
(Philles: 1965)
TRY A LITTLE TENDERNESS
(Woods/Campbell/
Connelly)**(1932) by Otis
Redding (Volt: 1966)
THE WAY YOU LOOK TONIGHT
(Kern/Fields) (1936) by The
Jaguars (R-Dell: 1956)
WHISPERING (Schonberger/
Coburn/Rose) (1920) by Nino
Tempo and April Stevens (Atco:
1964)
YOU'RE A SWEETHEART (McHugh/
Adamson) (1937) by Little Willie
John (King: 1958)

TOWN WITHOUT PITY
The young singer-songwriter Gene Pitney who
had a series of UK hit records between 1961 and
1974, yet never reached the coveted Number One
position until 1989, when he guested on Marc
Almond's revival of Gene's 1967 success,
SOMETHING'S GOTTEN HOLD OF MY HEART
(Greenaway/Cook).

TOWN WITHOUT PITY

(Dimitri Tiomkin/Ned Washington)
'When you're young and so in love as
we...'

Was this the age of innocence or
what?! Actually written for a Kirk
Douglas movie (the song was played
on a juke-box) called "Town Without
Pity" (UA: 1961), it was nominated for
that year's Best Song Oscar. A
perfect ballad for the powerful
larynx of Gene Pitney, whose
original record was picked out by
outrageous moviemaker John Waters
for the soundtrack of his "Hairspray"
(New Line: 1988).

US HIT: Gene Pitney (Musicor:
            1961) Pop
UK HIT: Gene Pitney (HMV: 1962)

Other recordings: The Nylons (Open
Air); Ronnie Montrose (Warner
Bros); Herb Alpert (A&M); Don
Costa Orchestra (DCP).

THE TRACKS OF MY TEARS

(William Robinson/Warren Moore/
Marvin Tarplin)
'People say I'm the life of the party'
opens up this faultless love song
co-written and originally sung by the
wistful Smokey Robinson whom Bob
Dylan once tagged 'America's
greatest living folk poet'. Song's
other composers were the bass
voice of The Miracles, Warren
Moore, and their guitarist, Marv
Tarplin.

US HITS: The Miracles (Tamla:
           1965) Black & Pop
           Johnny Rivers (Imperial:
           1967) Pop
           Aretha Franklin (Atlantic:
           1969) Black & Pop
           Linda Ronstadt (Asylum:
           1976) Pop
UK HITS: The Miracles (Tamla
           Motown: 1969)
           Linda Ronstadt (Asylum:
           1976)

Other recordings: Bryan Ferry
(Island); Gladys Knight and The Pips

(Soul); The Boys On The Block (Fantasy); Martha and The Vandellas (Gordy); The Roulettes (Parlophone); The Powers Of Blue (CBS); Colin Blunstone (PRT).

THE TRAIN KEPT A-ROLLIN'

(Myron Bradshaw/Howie Kay/ Sydney Nathan)
A song which has become a mini rock 'n' roll anthem, with recordings over the years ranging from rockabilly to heavy metal versions. The original version was by R&B singer Tiny Bradshaw (King: 1951). It was the rockabilly treatment of the song by The Johnny Burnette Trio (Coral: 1956) which not only transformed the song but also inspired later rock covers.

Other recordings: Aerosmith (Columbia); The Yardbirds (UK Columbia), who also used an instrumental version called STROLL ON in the guitar-crunching club sequence in the Antonioni 1960s classic 'Swinging London' movie "Blow Up".

TRIBUTE TO BUDDY HOLLY

(Geoffrey Goddard)
'The wind was blowin', the snow was snowin"...a graphic tribute to the Texas-born singer-songwriter who was killed in the 1959 'plane-crash that also took the lives of Ritchie Valens and The Big Bopper.
British pop singer–actor Mike Berry struck a major chord in 1961 with his TRIBUTE TO BUDDY HOLLY record. Although nowhere near the size of his two Top Ten singles, DON'T YOU THINK IT'S TIME (Goddard/Meek) (HMV: 1963) and a revival of the pre-war SUNSHINE OF YOUR SMILE (Ray/ Cooke) (Polydor: 1980), the TRIBUTE record is by far his best-remembered. Written by Geoff Goddard and produced by Joe Meek, it shared the same style of

rhythmic narrative as John Leyton's first smash, JOHNNY REMEMBER ME**.

UK HIT: Mike Berry with The
            Outlaws (HMV: 1961)

Goddard and Meek were the team behind a second successful tribute record, JUST LIKE EDDIE by Heinz (UK Decca: 1963); Heinz Burt was one of Meek's biggest-selling acts, The Tornadoes (their TELSTAR was a Number One instrumental record on both sides of the Atlantic in '62) and the 'Eddie' in question was Eddie Cochran; the American teen rocker was killed in Wiltshire at the close of his 1960 UK tour and British fans, who'd already put his records considerably higher in the charts than their American counterparts, had obsessively canonized him with an unofficial sainthood, the kind of which is reserved for personalities who die while at the peak of popularity.
When the post-Buddy Holly group of The Crickets came to tour Britain in 1961, Mike Berry was booked for in the same package! Many years later, he cut a Holly song STAY CLOSE TO ME that the writer had never released on record.

Tribute songs
Other R&B/R&R songs paying tribute to other musical styles and artists have included:

Musical styles:
BRING BACK THOSE DOO-WOPS (Rodgers) – tribute to R&B songs of the past; titles only are either sung or spoken, among them CHERRY PIE, OVER THE MOUNTAIN, ACROSS THE SEA, DEDICATED TO THE ONE I LOVE, ONE SUMMER NIGHT, YOU CHEATED, etc. – by The Bagdads (Double Shot: 1968)
LOOKING FOR AN ECHO (Reicheg) – about New York's would-be doo-wop singers of the 1950s who

would congregate in subway stations where the acoustics simulated an echo chamber in which they harmonized after the style of such groups as The Moonglows, The Harptones and The Dells – by Kenny Vance (Atlantic: 1975)

MEMORIES OF EL MONTE (Zappa) – Frank Zappa's paean to the 1950s when they danced to such groups as The Five Satins, The Shields, The Heartbeats, The Medallions plus Marvin and Johnny and Tony Allen...All these acts are mentioned in the lyric along with some of their song titles; The Penguins then lead into an extract of their own signature song, EARTH ANGEL – by the Penguins (Original Sound: 1963)

WHO PUT THE BOMP (IN THE BOMP BA BOMP BA BOMP) (Mann/Goffin) – was a celebration of doo-wop catch phrases such as 'Rama Lama Ding Dong', and 'Bop sh-bop, sh-bop' – by Barry Mann (ABC Paramount: 1961)

Tributes to artists:

AMERICAN PIE (McLean) – a tribute to Buddy Holly and 'the day the music died' – by Don McLean (United Artists: 1972)

DEDICATED TO DOMINO (Bartholomew/King) dedicated to Fats Domino by Al(vin) Robinson (Imperial: 1962)
(Dave Bartholomew, Fats Domino's long time collaborator, wrote and recorded DEDICATED TO FATS with Frankie Ford; though it remains unissued, it was recorded within a few days of the Al Robinson session on DEDICATED TO DOMINO and may be the same song).

GOODBYE JESSE (Woods/Pride/Hastings) – tribute to Jesse Belvin by Billy Davis and The Legends (Peacock: 1960)

JAMES BROWN (Kirk/Mallinder) by Cabaret Voltaire (Virgin: 1984)

JAMES BROWN (Duncan) by Darryl

Duncan (Motown: 1988)

JOHNNY ACE'S LAST LETTER (Fuller/Rosenbaum/Geddins) by Johnny Moore's Three Blazers (Hollywood: 1955)

KING'S CALL (Lynott) – a tribute to Elvis Presley by Philip Lynott (Vertigo 1980)

MISSING YOU (Richie) – dedicated to Marvin Gaye by Diana Ross (RCA: 1985); written and produced by Lionel Richie

NIGHTSHIFT (Orange/Lambert/Golde) – a tribute to Marvin Gaye and Jackie Wilson by The Commodores (Motown: 1985)

ROCK AND ROLL HEAVEN (Stevenson/O'Day) referring to deceased rock legends including Hendrix, Janis, Otis, Morrison, Croce, Darin; by The Righteous Brothers (Haven/Capitol: 1974)

ROCKIN' WITH THE KING (Taylor/Penniman) – a tribute to Little Richard ('he's the king of rock 'n' roll') played and sung by Canned Heat and (uncredited), Richard himself (UA: 1972)

SIR DUKE (Wonder) – a tribute to Duke Ellington by Stevie Wonder (Tamla: 1977)

THREE STARS (Dee) recalling three stars who died in the same 1959 plan crash: Ritchie Valens, Buddy Holly, The Big Bopper; with a repeating chorus line 'Gee, we're gonna miss you, everybody sends their love', the original was cut by Tommy Dee himself (Crest: 1959), but a cover version by Eddie Cochran became ironically morbid as it was released some time after his tragic death in 1960.

TRIBUTE (The Pasadenas/Wingfield) saluting rock legends alive and dead, including Little Richard, Elvis, Sam Cooke, Jackie Wilson, Otis, James Brown, Marvin, Stevie, Smokey, The Supremes, Ike and Tina, Aretha, Hendrix and The Jackson 5, by The Pasadenas (CBS: 1988).

A TRIBUTE TO A KING (Jones/Bell) – dedicated to Otis Redding by

William Bell (Stax: 1968)
TRIBUTE TO GENE VINCENT:
BLACK LEATHER REBEL
(Weiser/Carroll) by Johnny
Carroll (Rollin' Rock: 1976)
A TRIBUTE TO THE FOUR
SEASONS (Gaudio/Petrillo/Cifelli/
Crewe/ Linzer) including extracts
from 'Sherry, Rag Doll, Dawn', etc.
by Society's Children (Atco: 1968)
WHEN SMOKEY SINGS – a tribute
to Smokey Robinson by ABC
(Neutron: 1987)

TRUE LOVE WAYS

(Buddy Holly/Norman Petty)
One of three orchestra-accompanied
songs which Buddy Holly recorded
in New York following his split from
The Crickets. The other songs on the
session were RAINING IN MY
HEART (Bryant) and IT DOESN'T
MATTER ANYMORE (Anka)**.

Performed by Gary Busey in the
biopic, "The Buddy Holly Story"
(Columbia: 1978).

US HITS: Peter and Gordon
              (Capitol: 1965) Pop

Mickey Gilley (Epic:
   1980) Pop & Country
UK HITS: Buddy Holly (Coral: 1960)
   Peter and Gordon (UK
      Columbia: 1965)
   Cliff Richard (EMI: 1983)

Other recordings: Frank Ifield (UK
Columbia); Randy Gurley (MCA);
Bobby Vee (Liberty); Rick Nelson.

See: LOVE'S MADE A FOOL OF
YOU for other Buddy Holly songs.

TRY A LITTLE TENDERNESS

(Harry Woods/Jimmy Campbell/Reg
Connelly)
A 1932 ballad which Otis Redding
heard Sam Cooke sing on his live
Copa album. Otis recorded the song
and it became a major R&B record
as well as a crossover pop hit.

The Otis Redding version was
used to great effect in John Hughes'
movie, "Pretty In Pink" (Paramount:
1986), in which Jon Cryer mimes to
it.

Performed by Bennie Wallace and
Dr John on the soundtrack of "Bull
Durham" (Orion: 1988).

Song sung by Miki Howard on
Atlantic Records 40th Anniversary
Celebration Concert held in 1988 at
Madision Square Garden, New York
and shown as an HBO cable special.

As with TOMORROW NIGHT,**
TRY A LITTLE TENDERNESS is a
vintage standard which transcends
time and style.

US ROCK   Otis Redding (Volt: 1966)
ERA HITS: Black & Pop
              Three Dog Night
                 (Dunhill: 1969) Pop
UK ROCK   Otis Redding
ERA HITS: (Atlantic: 1967)

Other recordings: Rod Stewart
(Warner Bros); Sam Cooke (RCA);
Jimmy Dean (Columbia); Bing
Crosby (Brunswick); Charlie Rich
(Columbia); Mel Torme (Musicraft);
Aretha Franklin (Columbia); Jackie
Wilson (Brunswick); Frank Sinatra
(Columbia); Three Dog Night (Dunhill).

TURN ON YOUR LOVE LIGHT
(Deadric Malone/Joseph Scott)

US HITS: Bobby Bland (Duke: 1961)
Black & Pop
Oscar Toney Jr (Bell:
1967) Black & Pop

Other recordings: Them (UK Decca);
Bill Black's Combo (Hi); Jerry Lee
Lewis (Smash); Bobby Hart (DCP);
Herbie Goins and The Night Timers
(Parlophone); Bob Seger (Reprise);
Long John Baldry (UA); The Grateful
Dead (Warner Bros); Mitch Ryder
and The Detroit Wheels (Virgo);
Edgar Winter's White Trash (Epic);
Conway Twitty (MCA); Johnny
Rivers (UA); James Cotton (Verve).

TUTTI FRUTTI
(Richard Penniman/Dorothy
La Bostrie/Joe Lubin)
'A Wop Bop A Loo Bop A Lop Bam
Boom'...The opening phrase of Little
Richard's wildest rocker which he
performed in the movie, "Don't
Knock The Rock" (Columbia: 1956).
    Pat Boone covered the song, but it
will always be 100 per cent
Richard's. Later, Little Richard
performed TUTTI FRUTTI in the
movies "Sweet Toronto"
(Pennebaker: 1971) and "The London
Rock 'N' Roll Show" (1974), while his
record was heard on various movie
soundtracks, including "American
Hot Wax" (Paramount: 1978) and
"The Year Of Living Dangerously"
(MGM: 1983).
    The "Don't Knock The Rock"
sequence was used in the movie,
"Down And Out In Beverly Hills"
(Touchstone: 1985). Song was also
performed by Sting in "Party Party"
(1982) and by Val Kilmer in "Top
Secret" (Paramount: 1984).
Performed by T-Rex in "Born To
Boogie" (Apple: 1972). TUTTI
FRUTTI was also the title song of a
BBC Television series in 1987.

US HITS: Little Richard (Speciality:
1956) Black & Pop

TUTTI FRUTTI
Little Richard's record as it was originally released
in Britain in 45 rpm form, with the legendary
London logo and the infamous triangular centre!

Pat Boone (Dot: 1956)
Pop
UK HIT: Little Richard (London:
1957)

Other recordings: Jerry Lee Lewis
(Mercury); Johnny Winter and Edgar
Winter (Columbia); MC5 (Atlantic);
Elvis Presley (RCA); Delaney and
Bonnie and Friends and Eric Clapton
(Atlantic); The Swinging Blue Jeans
(HMV); Johnny Paycheck and
George Jones (Epic); Rufus Thomas
(Stax); Johnny Rivers (Imperial);
Sting (A&M); Commander Cody and
The Lost Planet Airmen (Warner
Bros); Jimi Hendrix and Little
Richard (ALA); Carl Perkins
(Columbia); Trio (Mercury).

See: ROCK AROUND THE CLOCK
for the SWING THE MOOD record

Little Richard songs
Innovator Little Richard has
influenced many fellow performers.

There have been some great medleys of his songs recorded by Jerry Lee Lewis and by Delaney and Bonnie.

His songs have also been interpreted in a wide range of styles; for instance, Billy 'Crash' Craddock had a major country record with his SLIPPIN' AND SLIDIN'** on ABC in 1973.

Richard's inspiration for The Beatles is well known, as witnessed particularly on their version of his HEY HEY HEY HEY on their *Beatles For Sale* album (Parlophone: 1964).

Little Richard (Penniman)'s name is on the writing credits of many of his big hits and the listing of songs by John Marascalco in our entry on RIP IT UP shows a number of these titles. But Richard also cut significant covers of other writers' songs; for instance, GET DOWN WITH IT by Bobby Marchan was picked up and recorded by Little Richard for Okeh at Abbey Road Studios, London in 1966. British group Slade subsequently re-cut the song under the revised title GET DOWN AND GET WITH IT (Polydor: 1971).

TWEEDLEE DEE
Originally billed as Little Miss Sharecropper, LaVern Baker cut some unforgettable sides for Atlantic, which also included BOP-TING-A-LING (Scott) (Atlantic: 1955) and JIM DANDY (Chase) (Atlantic: 1956).

TWEEDLEE DEE
(Winfield Scott)
Not content with covering Etta James, Georgia Gibbs ripped off the great LaVern Baker, not only on TWEEDLEE DEE, but also with TRA LA LA (Parker) which LaVern had performed before the cameras in "Rock, Rock, Rock" (Vanguard: 1957).

Miss Baker was one of the premier Atlantic artists during that label's early years, and re-surfaced in 1988 at the Atlantic Records 40th Anniversary Concert in New York.

British heart-throb Frankie Vaughan also had his fair share of recording other people's songs from across the Atlantic: besides TWEEDLEE DEE he covered SEVENTEEN (Young Jr/Gorman/ Bennett) originally by Boyd Bennett

and His Rockets (King: 1955), GREEN DOOR (Moore/Davie) by Jim Lowe (Dot: 1956), KOOKIE LITTLE PARADISE (Hilliard/Pockriss) by Jo Ann Campbell (ABC:1960), plus TOWER OF STRENGTH (Bacharach/ Hilliard) which was an American hit for Gene McDaniels on Liberty in 1961.

Incidentally, Little Jimmy Osmond's record of TWEEDLEE DEE charted briefly in the States, but was a much bigger single in England.

US HITS: LaVern Baker (Atlantic: 1955) Black & Pop
Georgia Gibbs (Mercury: 1955) Pop

TEARDROPS ON YOUR LETTER
(Glover).

The Chubby Checker single became the first (and to date, the only) rock-era chart success to ever hit the Number One slot on the American charts on two separate occasions over twelve months apart by the same artist.

Further evidence of the power of this Ballard composition is that a contemporary rap version by The Fat Boys featuring Chubby Checker returned the song to the bestseller charts in 1988, and in Britain, the single topped the independent radio chart.

US HITS: Hank Ballard and The
Midnighters (King:
1959) Black
Chubby Checker
(Parkway: 1960) Pop &
Black
Chubby Checker
(Parkway: 1961) Pop &
Black
The Fat Boys with
Chubby Checker (Tin
Pan Apple: 1988) Pop
UK HITS: Chubby Checker (UK
Columbia: 1960)
Chubby Checker (UK
Columbia: 1962)
The Fat Boys with
Chubby Checker (Tin
Pan Apple: 1988)

Other recordings: King Curtis (RCA); The Olympics (Arvee); Sam Cooke (RCA); Bobby Rydell (Cameo); Duane Eddy (RCA); Dion (Laurie); Ernie Freeman (Imperial); Smokey Robinson and The Miracles (Tamla).

THE TWIST not only became the most popular of modern dance crazes, but it gave birth to a whole series of major twist-inspired hit records. Among these were:

DEAR LADY TWIST (Guida) by
Gary US Bonds (Legrand: 1961)
LET'S TWIST AGAIN (Mann/Appell)
by Chubby Checker (Parkway:
1961)

UK HITS: Georgia Gibbs (Mercury:
1955)
Frankie Vaughan (Philips:
1955)
Little Jimmy Osmond
(MGM: 1973)

Other recordings: Pat Boone (Dot); Vicki Young (Capitol); The Mirettes (MCA); Pee Wee King (RCA); Wanda Jackson (Capitol); Bill Haley and His Comets (Sonet); Elvis Presley (Louisiana Hayride/The Music Works).

THE TWIST
(Henry Ballard)
One of the most popular dance songs of all time, originally written and recorded by Hank Ballard in 1958; its biggest influence came from WHAT'CHA GONNA DO (Nugetre) (Atlantic: 1955), the Drifters' seventh R&B hit single. Hank instinctively knew that THE TWIST was a hit, but King Records didn't agree and when they first released his version, it ended up as the B-side of

THE TWIST

Hank Ballard twisting then and now! Hank was the originator and is still twisting thirty years later! Top shows Hank Ballard (*far left*) and The Midnighters at the Royal Theatre, Baltimore in 1959 (courtesy of Theresa MacNeil). Below shows Hank (in shades) demonstrating The Twist in 1988 to The Fat Boys, while BMI executives Mark Fried and Rick Sanjek look on. (Courtesy: Gary Gershoff.)

THE TWIST
Chubby Checker, who took THE TWIST to
Number One, recorded a series of follow-up
dance songs. One of them was SLOW TWISTIN'
which he is demonstrating in this scene from the
movie, "Don't Knock The Twist" (Columbia: 1962);
his partner here is singer Dee Dee Sharp (see
under MASHED POTATO TIME) who duetted with
Checker on this 1962 hit.

PEPPERMINT TWIST (Dee/Glover)
by Joey Dee and The Starliters
(Roulette: 1962)
SLOW TWISTIN' (Sheldon) by
Chubby Checker with Dee Dee
Sharp (Parkway: 1962)
TWIST, TWIST SENORA (Guida/

Royster/Barge) by Gary US Bonds
(Legrand: 1962)
TWISTIN' MATILDA (Span) by
Jimmy Soul (SPQR: 1962)
TWISTIN' THE NIGHT AWAY
(Cooke) by Sam Cooke (RCA:
1962)

There was even a song called
THANK YOU MISTER BALLARD
FOR CREATING THE TWIST
(Ballard/Barry/Bridge/Redd) released
by The Escos on Federal (sister
label of King, the company to which
Hank was signed) in 1961.

Hank Ballard songs

In our section on Dance Records in the DO YOU WANT TO DANCE entry, I list a few of the other dances which Hank created and recorded. There are, however, a number of other Hank Ballard songs which have been performed by other artists including LOOK AT LITTLE SISTER by Stevie Ray Vaughan and Double Trouble (Epic: 1986) and versions of TORE UP OVER YOU by rockabilly singer Ray Campi on Rollin' Rock, by the late Roy Hamilton on RCA and the 1960s classic version by Harmonica Fats, originally on the Darcey label.

THE CONTINENTAL WALK was covered around the time of Hank and The Midnighters' original record by a Southern Californian group called The Rollers, of whom Al 'Show and Tell' Wilson was a member, (Liberty: 1960). Much more recently, guitarist Lonnie Mack did a medley of ANNIE HAD A BABY and SEXY WAYS on an Epic album. Hank has, by the way, recorded his share of other writers' tunes, of which two standouts are Elmore James' mournful THE SKY IS CRYING and Henry Glover's passionate TEARDROPS ON YOUR LETTER.

Finally though, a mention of two of my personal favourites among Hank's originals: FINGER POPPIN' TIME ('hey now, hey now') from 1960 and the following year's stop-and-starter, THE HOOCHIE COOCHIE COO.

TWIST AND SHOUT
The Isley Brothers, whose version of TWIST AND SHOUT is considered the yardstick by which other recordings are measured. Their self-written SHOUT has also been widely covered, including the UK hit record by Lulu (Decca: 1964) which the same artist re-recorded successfully 22 years later!

TWIST AND SHOUT

(Bert Russell/Phil Medley)
Though often credited as an Isley Brothers' original, the very first version of TWIST AND SHOUT was by a group called The Top Notes (Atlantic: 1961), produced by session veterans Jerry Wexler and Phil Spector, while the young author Bert Berns (aka Bert Russell) looked on.

Berns promptly took the song to The Isleys and produced a smash hit. Incidentally, one of the 'Top Notes' was Derek Martin, whose DADDY ROLLIN' STONE (Crackerjack: 1959) was a turntable hit when it was released in the UK on Island's Sue label in the early 60s and covered by The Who (Brunswick: 1965).

The Beatles featured TWIST AND SHOUT as their playout tune on the *Please Please Me* album, and, though it was never a single for them in England, the independent US label, Tollie, released it.

The 1986 Danish teen movie, "Twist and Shout", understandably featured the song prominently while two American motion pictures released the same year featured it: "Ferris Bueller's Day Off" using the Beatles' version, while "Back To School" had comedian Rodney Dangerfield take the vocals! Capitol re-released the Beatles' single and it charted all over again. Song was also featured by Dale Gonyea in "Tuff Turf" (New World: 1985).

TWIST AND SHOUT was performed by Bruce Springsteen with Peter Gabriel and Sting on the 1988 Amnesty concert tour.

US HITS: The Isley Brothers (Wand: 1962) Pop & Black
The Beatles (Tollie: 1964) Pop
The Beatles (Capitol:1986) Pop
UK HITS: The Isley Brothers (Stateside: 1963)
Brian Poole and The Tremeloes (Decca: 1963)
Salt 'N' Pepa (ffrr/London: 1988)

Other recordings: Del Shannon (Big Top); Tina Turner; The Shirelles; Bobby Vee (Liberty); Salt-'N'-Pepa (Next Plateau); Tom Jones (UK Decca): The Searchers (Pye); The Blackberries (A&M); The Dave Clark Five (UK Columbia): The Mamas and The Papas (Dunhill); Chubby Checker (Parkway); The Who (MCA).

Though The Isley Brothers did not cut the first version of TWIST AND SHOUT, they did record the original of I'M GONNA KNOCK ON YOUR DOOR (Schroeder/Wayne), the 1961 hit for teenager Eddie Hodges on Cadence.

The Isleys' other hits have been covered and revived from time to time, particularly by British artists such as Salt 'N' Pepa, who re-made IT'S YOUR THING** as SHAKE

YOUR THANG (ffrr: 1988) and The Housemartins with their faithful recreation of CARAVAN OF LOVE (Isley/Isley/Jasper) on Go! Discs in late 1986. While with Tamla, the brothers' most memorable song was THIS OLD HEART OF MINE (IS WEAK FOR YOU)** and it was later refuelled by Rod Stewart (Riva: 1975).

Bert Berns songs

In addition to being a formidable music publisher, record producer and label owner (he formed Bang Records in the mid-1960s, signing such artists as Neil Diamond and Van Morrison), Bert Berns (aka Bert Russell and Russell Byrd) was also a writer of certain milestone R&B/R&R songs.

Among the original hit records of other Bert Berns songs are:

CRY BABY (Russell/Meade)** by Garnet Mimms and The Enchanters (UA: 1963)
CRY TO ME (Russell)** by Solomon Burke (Atlantic: 1962)
DOWN IN THE VALLEY (Berns/ Burke/Martin/Chivian by Solomon Burke (Atlantic: 1962)
EVERYBODY NEEDS SOMEBODY TO LOVE (Berns/Burke/Wexler) by Solomon Burke (Atlantic: 1964) by Wilson Pickett (Atlantic: 1967)
HANG ON SLOOPY (Russell/ Farrell)** by The McCoys (Bang: 1965)
HERE COMES THE NIGHT by Them (UK Decca: 1965)
I WANT CANDY (Feldman/ Goldstein/Gottehrel/Berns)** by The Strangeloves (Bang: 1965)
I'LL TAKE GOOD CARE OF YOU (with Jerry Ragovoy) by Garnet Mimms (UA: 1966)
A LITTLE BIT OF SOAP (Russell) by The Jarmels (Laurie: 1961)
ONE GIRL (Jerry Ragovoy/Berns) by Garnet Mimms (UA: 1967)
PIECE OF MY HEART (Ragovoy/ Berns)** by Big Brother and The Holding Company (Columbia: 1968)

TELL HIM (Russell)** by The
Exciters (UA: 1963)

Fields and Billie Barnum) on a
remake of TWIST AND SHOUT
(Russell/Medley) (A&M: 1973).

See: PEOPLE GET READY for other
Curtis Mayfield songs.

U

UM, UM, UM, UM, UM, UM
(Curtis Mayfield)
Also known as: CURIOUS MIND
Unexplained nonsense phrase
continuously uttered by a guy on a
fence, according to the singer of this
fine mid-tempo R&B ballad.
Originally recorded by Major Lance,
it was produced by Carl Davis who
was the key architect of what was
then referred to as the 'Chicago
sound'. This and their previous
collaboration, the dance song called
MONKEY TIME (also by Curtis
Mayfield) (Okeh: 1963), became
'beach' classics in the US and
Northern Soul favourites in the UK.

US HITS: Major Lance (Okeh: 1964)
    Black & Pop
    Johnny Rivers (Big Tree:
    1978) Pop
UK HITS: Major Lance (UK
    Columbia: 1964)
    Wayne Fontana and The
    Mindbenders (Fontana:
    1964)

At the time of writing the most
recent revival is by former member
of both The Small Faces and Humble
Pie, Steve Marriott (Trax: 1989).
Marriott's taste for American soul
and R&B pre-dates this and his
current album; Humble Pie's A&M
repertoire included such tunes as
Willie Dixon's I'M READY, Tina
Turner's BLACK COFFEE and Ann
Peebles' I CAN'T STAND THE RAIN,
while Steve produced The
Blackberries (Clydie King, Venetta

Major Lance whose 1960s soul records resulted in
him being a key favourite with the Northern club
circuit. He re-cut his classic UM, UM, UM, UM,
UM, UM, for Playboy in 1974. His first major
crossover hit, THE MONKEY TIME (written by
Curtis Mayfield) was on Georgie Fame and The
Blue Flames' second album (UK Columbia: 1965).

UNCHAINED MELODY
(Alex North/Hy Zaret)
This song started out as the theme
from the prison drama, "Unchained"
(Warner Bros: 1955). Initially a hit for
orchestral conductor Les Baxter (on

Capitol) and black singers Al Hibbler and Roy Hamilton, as well as white songstress June Valli on RCA. New York doo-wop group, Vito and The Salutations had a minor hit with their revival, and then the song was a Top 5 US single for The Righteous Brothers, though it was virtually a solo effort by Bobby Hatfield.

In later years, femme groups The Sweet Inspirations and Heart had minor success with their individual versions. In Britain, singer–dj Jimmy Young had the original chart-topping record of the song (UK Decca: 1955), though his competition had also included a strong selling version by pianist Liberace (Philips: 1955). Leo Sayer's revival three decades later lodged just outside the British Top 50.

US HITS: Al Hibbler (Decca: 1955)
            Black & Pop
           Roy Hamilton (Epic: 1955)
            Black & Pop
           Les Baxter Orchestra &
            Chorus (Capitol: 1955)
            Pop
           June Valli (RCA: 1955)
            Pop
           The Righteous Brothers
            (Philles: 1965) Black &
            Pop
UK HITS: Al Hibbler (Brunswick:
            1955)
           Les Baxter Orchestra &
            Chorus (Capitol: 1955)
           Jimmy Young (Decca:
            1955)
           Leo Sayer (Chrysalis:
            1986)

Other recordings: The Sweet Inspirations (Atlantic); Heart (Epic); Elvis Presley (RCA); Charlie Rich (Sun); Willie Nelson (Columbia); George Benson (Warner Bros); Sonny And Cher (Atco); Blue Haze (A&M); Sam Cooke (RCA); Conway Twitty (MGM); Gene Vincent (Capitol); Duane Eddy (RCA); Cliff Richard (UK Columbia); Vito and The Salutations (Herald); U2 (Island).

Another 1955 song, again originally cut by Al Hibbler, was revived by The Righteous Brothers, namely HE (Richards/Mullen), and their version made the US Top 20 in 1966 on Verve.

UNDER MY THUMB
(Mick Jagger/Keith Richards)
Early Rolling Stones' song, originally on their *Aftermath* album (UK Decca: 1966). Never on a Stones single, it was covered in Britain by both Wayne Gibson and The Who.

Following on the heels of their own PICTURES OF LILY (Track: 1967), The Who's version was on a moderately successful single (it made it just inside the Top 50) of two Jagger/Richard songs back-to-back, the other being THE LAST TIME.

Gibson's version was released on EMI's Columbia label some months earlier in 1966, but it didn't find chart fame until reissued by Pye in its Disco Demand series following extensive plays in the northern clubs.

UNDER MY THUMB is among the songs performed by the Stones at the famous Altamont concert in 1969 which subsequently became the "Gimme Shelter" movie in 1971.

UK HITS: The Who (Track: 1967)
           Wayne Gibson (Pye:
            1974)
Other recordings: Del Shannon (Liberty); Beverly Johnson (Buddah); Sweetheart (Atlantic); Tina Turner (UA).

UNDER THE BOARDWALK
(Artie Resnik/Kenny Young)
Bruce Willis, star of the then-hip and hot TV series "Moonlighting", followed up his revivals of a Staple Singers hit RESPECT YOURSELF and a Coasters oldie YOUNG BLOOD with this classic from the Drifters' repertoire.

In the States, Willis fever had

UNDER THE BOARDWALK

The Drifters were *the* vocal group on Atlantic Records. Not forgetting the many different group members who've come and gone over the years, the first Drifters hit was MONEY HONEY (Stone) (Atlantic: 1953) and they were still recording hits in the mid-1970s.

peaked as far as his records were concerned, and his BOARDWALK single barely scraped inside the Top 75, but in the UK, it leapt up as far as Number Two.

One of the song's writers is Kenny Young, most recently one-third of the A&M band, Gentlemen Without Weapons. His other song-writing successes have included DON'T GO OUT INTO THE RAIN, a US only hit for Herman's Hermits (MGM: 1967), and JUST A LITTLE BIT BETTER which charted for Herman (UK Columbia: 1965) on both sides of the Atlantic.

Performed by Bette Midler in her movie "Beaches" (Touchstone: 1988).

The original Drifters' record was heard on the soundtrack of the movie "Under The Boardwalk" (New World: 1989).

US HITS: The Drifters (Atlantic: 1964) Black & Pop
            Bruce Willis (Motown: 1987) Black & Pop
UK HITS: The Drifters (Atlantic: 1964)
            Tom Tom Club (Island: 1982)
            Bruce Willis (Motown: 1987)

Other recordings: Sam and Dave (UA); Rickie Lee Jones (Warner Bros); John Cougar Mellencamp (Riva); Lynn Anderson (Mercury); The Rolling Stones (UK Decca); Los Lobos.

UNIVERSAL SOLDIER
(Buffy Sainte-Marie)
One of rock's purest protest songs from folk singer Buffy Sainte-Marie, whose other memorable compositions included UNTIL IT'S TIME FOR YOU TO GO which charted for both Neil Diamond (Uni: 1970) and Elvis Presley (RCA: 1972). Years later she collaborated with Jack Nitzsche and Will Jennings to write UP WHERE WE BELONG, the theme song from the Richard Gere/Debra Winger movie, "An Officer and A Gentleman" (Paramount: 1982), in which it was performed by Joe Cocker and Jennifer Warnes (Island: 1982).

Buffy's original version of UNIVERSAL SOLDIER was on her debut album, *It's My Way* (Vanguard: 1964). The two 'hit' versions listed below hovered only around the centre of the Top 100 chart, but the impact of the song was widely felt as the reality of the Vietnam war began to take hold in America.

US HITS: Glen Campbell (Capitol: 1965) Pop
            Donovan (Hickory: 1965) Pop

Other recording: Joan Baez.

Answer record: THE UNIVERSAL COWARD by Jan Berry (Liberty: 1965)

Vietnam songs
Other records related to the Vietnam war era:

BALLAD OF THE GREEN BERETS (Sadler/Moore) by Staff Sgt.Barry Sadler (RCA: 1966)*

BRING THE BOYS HOME (Johnson/ Perry/Bond) by Freda Payne (Invictus: 1971)

CHRISTMAS IN VIETNAM (Taylor) by Pte.Charles Bowens and The Gentlemen From Tigerland (Rojac: 1966)

HELLO VIETNAM (Hall) by Johnny Wright (Decca: 1965)

HYMN TO A RETURNING SOLDIER (King) by Ric King (Capitol: 1967)

THE I-FEEL-LIKE-I'M-FIXIN'-TO-DIE RAG (McDonald) by Country Joe and The Fish (Vanguard: 1967)

MARCHING OFF TO WAR (Floyd/ Cropper) by William Bell (Stax: 1966)*

AN OPEN LETTER TO MY TEENAGE SON (Thompson) by Victor Lundberg (Liberty: 1967)*

RICE PADDY DADDY (Martin) by Dick 'Deacon' Martin (Film City: 1962)

SKY PILOT (Burdon/Briggs/Jenkins/ Weider/McCulloch) by Eric Burdon and The Animals (MGM: 1968)*

TALKING VIETNAM POT LUCK BLUES (Paxton) by Tom Paxton (Elektra: 1971)*

plus Mel Tillis' song, RUBY, DON'T TAKE YOUR LOVE TO TOWN*, a huge hit for Kenny Rogers and The First Edition (Reprise: 1969); however, it was actually written to suggest a Korean war setting.

In 1988, Britain's "New Musical Express" released a compilation of original American 'Vietnam' tracks including those marked * above; titled *Feel Like I'm Fixin' To Die.*

Eric Burdon and The Animals', similarly war-themed single, SKY PILOT, came from their *Twain Shall Meet* album (MGM: 1968).

UP ON THE ROOF

(Gerry Goffin/Carole King)
The second of two Goffin/King songs
which became 1962 hits for The
Drifters, the other one being WHEN
MY LITTLE GIRL IS SMILING. Two
British cover versions achieved chart
status, of which the Kenny Lynch
record even made the Top 10.

US HITS: The Drifters (Atlantic:
           1962) Black & Pop
           James Taylor (Columbia:
           1979) Pop
UK HITS: Kenny Lynch (HMV: 1962)
           Julie Grant (Pye: 1963)

Other recordings: Laura Nyro
(Columbia); Carole King (Ode); The
Nylons (Open Air); Dawn (Bell); The
Cryan' Shames (Columbia); Ike and
Tina Turner (UA); Clyde McPhatter
(Mercury).

By the way, Kenny Lynch is the
second face from the left in the front
cover picture on Paul McCartney's
Band On The Run album (Apple:
1973).

As a solo writer, Carole King's
successes included I FEEL THE
EARTH MOVE which was originally
the B-side to IT'S TOO LATE (King)
(Ode: 1971), the first single from her
milestone album, *Tapestry* (Ode:
1971). In 1989, I FEEL THE EARTH
MOVE was successfully revived by
Martika (Columbia).

Carole King made her first mark as a singer when
Don Kirshner rushed out her version of IT MIGHT
AS WELL RAIN UNTIL SEPTEMBER, a Goffin/King
song that had been intended for Bobby Vee who
also recorded it for Liberty. In 1971 Carole
launched a whole new phase of her performing
career, with her legendary *Tapestry* album for Lou
Adler's Ode label, from which the Number One
song IT'S TOO LATE (King/Stern) was lifted.

Goffin and King songs

Carole King became a fully-fledged
recording artist in 1962. Prior to that,
she had been musical director on
various recording sessions and you
could pick out her voice singing
backup on singles like NOT JUST
TOMORROW BUT ALWAYS, one of
the answer records to WILL YOU
LOVE ME TOMORROW**. But her
greatest contribution was as the
song-writing partner with her
husband Gerry Goffin. Their list of
successes is staggering and among
the many hit records of their other
songs were:

CHAINS by The Cookies**
   (Dimension: 1962)
DON'T BRING ME DOWN by The
   Animals (UK Columbia: 1966)
DON'T SAY NOTHIN' BAD (ABOUT
   MY BABY) by The Cookies
   (Dimension: 1963)
EVERY BREATH I TAKE by Gene
   Pitney (Musicor: 1961)
GO AWAY LITTLE GIRL by Steve
   Lawrence (Columbia: 1962)
   by Donny Osmond (MGM: 1971)
   (a double achievement this, as
   both versions went to Number
   One in the US)
HALFWAY TO PARADISE** by

Tony Orlando (Epic: 1961)
by Billy Fury (UK Decca: 1961)
HE'S IN TOWN by The Tokens
(B.T. Puppy: 1964)
HER ROYAL MAJESTY by James
Darren (Colpix: 1962)
HEY GIRL** by Freddie Scott
(Colpix: 1963)
HI-DE-HO (That Old Sweet Roll) by
Blood, Sweat and Tears
(Columbia: 1970)
I CAN'T HEAR YOU NO MORE by
Helen Reddy (Capitol: 1976)
I CAN'T STAY MAD AT YOU by
Skeeter Davis (RCA: 1963)
I'M INTO SOMETHING GOOD** by
Earl-Jean (Colpix: 1964)
by Herman's Hermits (UK
Columbia: 1964)
IT MIGHT AS WELL RAIN UNTIL
SEPTEMBER by Carole King
(Dimension: 1962)
JUST ONCE IN MY LIFE (written
with Phil Spector) by The
Righteous Brothers (Philles: 1965)
THE LOCO-MOTION** by Little Eva
(Dimension: 1962)
OH NO NOT MY BABY by Maxine
Brown (Wand: 1964)
ONE FINE DAY** by The Chiffons
(Laurie: 1963)
PLEASANT VALLEY SUNDAY by
The Monkees (Colgems: 1967)
SHARING YOU by Bobby Vee
(Liberty: 1962)
SOME KIND OF WONDERFUL by
The Drifters (Atlantic: 1961)
TAKE GOOD CARE OF MY BABY**
by Bobby Vee (Liberty: 1961)
WHEN MY LITTLE GIRL IS
SMILING by The Drifters
(Atlantic: 1962)
by Craig Douglas (Top Rank:
1962)
by Jimmy Justice (Pye: 1962)
WILL YOU LOVE ME
TOMORROW** by The Shirelles
(Scepter: 1961)
YOU MAKE ME FEEL LIKE (A
NATURAL WOMAN) (with Jerry
Wexler) by Aretha Franklin
(Atlantic: 1967)

NB: Where more than one hit
version exists on a song which is
individually covered elsewhere in
this book, only the first hit record is
quoted above.

V

VENUS
(Robbie van Leeuwen)
Rarely do two separate versions of
the same song both reach the
coveted Number One slot on the
American charts, but that's what
Shocking Blue's original and
Bananarama's cover records
achieved! Shocking Blue was not the

The other **VENUS**
Eleven years before the Shocking Blue song was
another VENUS, recorded by teenage heart-throb
Frankie Avalon whose hit was originally covered
in Britain by band vocalist Dickie Valentine on Pye
Nixa.

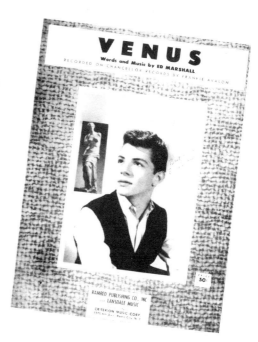

only Dutch group to break international borders down in 1970 when the George Baker Selection had their first American hits, though their most memorable seller, UNA PALOMA BLANCA (Bouwens) didn't come along until 1975 (Warner Bros).

UK HITS: Shocking Blue (Penny Farthing: 1970)
Bananarama (London: 1986)

US HITS: Shocking Blue (Colossus: 1970) Pop
Bananarama (London: 1986) Pop

Other recording: Nervus Rex (Dreamland).

Not to be confused with the earlier song VENUS (Marshall), a teen love ballad of the 1950s, originally recorded by Frankie Avalon (Chancellor: 1959); Avalon's own 1976 disco re-recording of VENUS charted in the States.

WAKE UP LITTLE SUSIE
(Boudleaux Bryant/Felice Bryant)
The Nashville-based husband and wife team of Boudleaux and Felice Bryant wrote a string of Everly Brothers hits including BYE BYE LOVE**, ALL I HAVE TO DO IS DREAM**, BIRD DOG and PROBLEMS as well as Buddy Holly's posthumous seller, RAINING IN MY HEART. WAKE UP LITTLE SUSIE was their most rousing composition and is still a highlight of the Everly's stage act, opening with those familiar eight guitar notes.

WAKE UP, LITTLE SUSIE
By Boudleaux Bryant and Felice Bryant
RECORDED BY THE EVERLY BROTHERS FOR CADENCE RECORDS

WAKE UP LITTLE SUSIE
The Everlys were what The Righteous Brothers were not – real brothers! Don (*right*) and Phil sang about girls and school and, in this case, falling asleep in front of a movie!

US HITS: The Everly Brothers (Cadence: 1957)
Country & Pop
Simon and Garfunkel (Warner Bros: 1982) Pop

UK HITS: The Everly Brothers (London: 1957)
The King Brothers (Parlophone: 1957)

Other recordings: The Flying Burrito Brothers (A&M); Frankie Lymon (Gee); Billy 'Crash' Craddock (MCA); Loggins and Messina (Columbia); The Grateful Dead (Warner Bros).

See: BYE BYE LOVE for other Boudleaux and Felice Bryant songs.

See: ROCK AROUND THE CLOCK for the SWING THE MOOD record.

WALK AWAY RENEE
(Mike Brown/Tony Sansone/Bob Calilli)
Soft-rock ballad co-written by The Left Banke's keyboard player, Mike Brown.

US HITS: The Left Banke (Smash: 1966) Pop
               The Four Tops (Motown: 1968) Black & Pop
UK HIT: The Four Tops (Tamla Motown: 1967)

Other recordings: Pink Lady (Elektra); Southside Johnny and The Jukes (Atlantic); Wishful Thinking (UK Decca).

WALK LIKE A MAN
(Bob Crewe/Bob Gaudio)
One of five Number One hits in America for The Four Seasons featuring the falsetto vocals of Frankie Valli.
    Written by the group's producer Bob Crewe and one of their members, keyboard player Bob Gaudio.
    The original Four Seasons record of the song was heard on the soundtrack of Phil Kaufman's gang drama, "The Wanderers" (Orion:1979), while the Mary Jane Girls' version was featured in Blake Edwards' comedy "A Fine Mess" (Columbia: 1986). It also became the title song of the Howie Mandel comedy "Walk Like A Man" (MGM/UA:1987).

US HITS: The Four Seasons (Vee-Jay: 1963) Pop & Black
               Mary Jane Girls (Motown: 1986) Pop
UK HITS: The Four Seasons (Stateside: 1963)
               Divine (Proto Bellaphon: 1985)

WALK ON THE WILD SIDE
(Lou Reed)
Leader of the legendary Velvet Underground, Lou Reed went on to a solo career which peaked with his *Transformer* album (RCA: 1972) from which WALK ON THE WILD SIDE originally came. Co-produced by David Bowie and Mick Ronson, it was successfully released as a single on both sides of the Atlantic, despite its sexually ambiguous references.

US HIT: Lou Reed (RCA: 1973) Pop
UK HIT: Lou Reed (RCA: 1973)

Another Lou Reed song, SWEET JANE which dates back to his Velvet Underground days and was covered by Mott The Hoople on their *All The Young Dudes* set (CBS: 1972), turned up again recently on the debut album by American group, Cowboy Junkies (RCA: 1988); Reed is quoted as saying that their remake is 'the best and most authentic version that I have ever heard'.

WALK THIS WAY
(Steve Tyler/Joe Perry)
New Hampshire five-man group Aerosmith released single covers of The Beatles' COME TOGETHER and The Shangri-Las' REMEMBER (WALKIN' IN THE SAND). Their first hit, DREAM ON (Tyler) charted higher when it reissued in 1976 than when they initially released it towards the end of 1973.
    WALK THIS WAY was written by their lead singer Steve Tyler and guitarist Joe Perry, both of whom performed with rap group Run-D.M.C. on their revival a decade later.

US HITS: Aerosmith (Columbia: 1976) Pop
               Run-D.M.C. (Profile: 1986) Pop & Black
UK HIT: Run-D.M.C. (London: 1986)

WALKING THE DOG
(Rufus Thomas)

Rufus Thomas Jr knew a good step when he saw one and, having cut the official answer song to Willie Mae Thornton's HOUND DOG, he almost built an entire career around his own 'Dog' dances! THE DOG (Thomas) (Stax: 1963) was first; then came WALKING THE DOG followed by CAN YOUR MONKEY DO THE DOG? (Thomas/Cropper) and then, SOMEBODY STOLE MY DOG (Thomas/Cropper).

US HIT: Rufus Thomas (Stax: 1963)
            Black & Pop

Other recordings: Roger Daltrey (MCA); The Rolling Stones (UK Decca); Aerosmith (Columbia); The Everly Bros (Warner Bros); Zoot Money's Big Roll Band (UK Decca); Georgie Fame (UK Columbia).

Rufus re-cut some of his classic dance songs with his beautiful daughter, Carla Thomas, whose own classic song, GEE WHIZ (LOOK IN HIS EYES), charted for her on Atlantic in 1961, and was successfully revived by actress–singer Bernadette Peters (MCA: 1980). See also under: KNOCK ON WOOD.

Rufus cut a slew of other dance songs including DO THE FUNKY CHICKEN (Thomas) (Stax: 1970), (DO THE) PUSH AND PULL (Nixon/Bell) (Stax: 1970), THE BREAKDOWN (Thomas/Rice/Floyd) (Stax: 1971) and even DO THE FUNKY PENGUIN (Thomas/Rice/Bridges/Nixon) (Stax: 1971).

THE WANDERER
(Ernie Maresca)

How did Dion follow his first solo Number One single?

With this first-rate rocker in which composer Ernie Maresca virtually turns the tables on RUNAROUND SUE by describing the subject of the song as 'the kind of guy who hates to settle down'. As with the 'Sue' song,

Leif Garrett tried to re-cut THE WANDERER but with less success, in fact his single barely scraped the Top 50.

US HITS: Dion (Laurie: 1961) Pop
            Leif Garrett (Atlantic: 1978) Pop
UK HITS: Dion (HMV: 1962)
            Status Quo (Vertigo: 1984)

Other recordings: Arthur Alexander (Dot); Adam Faith (Parlophone); Dave Edmunds (Swan Song); The Beach Boys (Capitol).

WATERLOO
(Benny Andersson/Stig Anderson/Bjorn Ulvaeus)

Abba is reportedly the best-selling pop group ever and this song typifies both their sound and their songwriting, a task they – Benny and Bjorn (the two guys in the group) – share with Abba's manager, Stig Anderson. Their first hit in both the US and the UK, WATERLOO, represented Sweden (which with Norway shares credit as the group's real homeland) and, more importantly, won the 1974 Eurovision Song Contest.

The revival by Doctor and The Medics featured Roy Wood, formerly of The Move, ELO and Wizzard.

UK HITS: Abba (Epic: 1974)
            Doctor and The Medics (IRS: 1986)
US HIT: Abba (Atlantic: 1974) Pop

Abba's chart reign lasted through until 1981, after which their singles could no longer be guaranteed a Top 10 position in the UK charts.

THE WAY YOU DO THE THINGS YOU DO
(William Robinson/Bobby Rogers)

The song which really started the Temptations' ball rolling, with Eddie Kendricks singing lead on a song he was to return to two decades later on

VOCO-INSTRUMENTAL

THE WAY YOU DO THE THINGS YOU DO

by WILLIAM ROBINSON and BOBBY ROGERS

Recorded by TEMPTATIONS on Gordy Records

75¢

05537

JOBETE MUSIC COMPANY, INC.

THE WAY YOU DO THE THINGS YOU DO

The Temptations with their legendary tenor, Eddie Kendricks, were previously known as The Distants until Motown's founder Berry Gordy signed them in 1960 and changed their name.

a live album with fellow-Temp David Ruffin when the two guested on Hall and Oates' Apollo project.

Performed by Smokey Robinson and Pee Wee Herman on an edition of NBC Television's "Motown Revue" (1985). Performed by UB40 on the soundtrack of the Michael Douglas movie, "Black Rain" (Paramount: 1989).

US HITS: The Temptations (Gordy: 1964) Black & Pop
Rita Coolidge (A&M: 1978) Pop

Daryl Hall, John Oates,
David Ruffin and Eddie
Kendrick: Medley with
MY GIRL (Robinson/
White) (RCA: 1985)
Black & Pop

Other recordings: Little Richard
(Reprise); Dr John (UA); Jerry Butler
and Betty Everett (Vee-Jay); Diana
Ross and The Supremes and The
Temptations (Motown); The
Mindbenders (Fontana).

See: DEVIL WITH A BLUE DRESS
ON for other Motown hits.

See: SHOP AROUND for other
Smokey Robinson songs.

THE WEIGHT
(Jaime Robbie Robertson)
The Band's debut hit single, it was a
highlight of their critically acclaimed
Music From Big Pink album (Capitol:
1968).
   Song was initally covered by (and
charted higher for) Jackie
DeShannon. A decade later it was
reprised by The Band along with
The Staple Singers when Robertson
and his cohorts played one final,
spectacular concert which was
filmed by Martin Scorsese as "The
Last Waltz" (UA: 1978).
   THE WEIGHT was also featured in
the Peter Fonda/Dennis Hopper
movie, "Easy Rider" (Columbia:
1969), but, although The Band were
heard on the soundtrack, Dunhill
couldn't get rights to their recording
for the album of songs from the
movie, so they substitued a
recording by their own act, Smith.

US HITS: The Band (Capitol: 1968)
Pop
Jackie DeShannon
(Imperial: 1968) Pop
Aretha Franklin (Atlantic:
1969) Black & Pop
Diana Ross and The
Supremes and The
Temptations (Motown:
1969) Black & Pop

UK HIT: The Band (Capitol: 1968)

Other recordings: King Curtis (Atco);
Mike Bloomfield and Al Kooper
(Columbia).

Robbie Robertson was the guitarist–
singer–songwriter–front man of The
Band which had started out as The
Hawks with rockabilly star Ronnie
Hawkins; they later began working
with Bob Dylan and were the
musicians on his legendary
Basement Tapes. For The Band,
Robbie also wrote UP ON CRIPPLE
CREEK, their second hit single
(Capitol: 1969) as well as THE
NIGHT THEY DROVE OLD DIXIE
DOWN which became Joan Baez's
most successful record (Vanguard,
1971). His first solo album, *Robbie
Robertson* (Geffen: 1987) bore the
UK hit single, SOMEWHERE DOWN
THE CRAZY RIVER which harked
back to Robertson's teenage days in
the American south.

WHAT AM I LIVING FOR
(Art Harris/Fred Jay)
Chuck Willis' original was a Number
One R&B record.

US HITS: Chuck Willis (Atlantic:
1958) Black & Pop
Conway Twitty (MGM:
1960) Pop
Ray Charles (ABC/
Tangerine: 1972) Pop

Other recordings: Percy Sledge
(Atlantic); The Everly Brothers
(Warner Bros); Carl Perkins (Koala);
Sleepy Labeef (Sun); Z. Z. Hill (Kent);
Solomon Burke (Bell); Millie
(Fontana); Johnny Tillotson (Amos);
Wilbert Harrison.

WHAT BECOMES OF THE BROKENHEARTED
(Paul Riser/James Dean/William
Weatherspoon)
The song which established Jimmy
Ruffin on both sides of the Atlantic,
but particularly in England where

Jimmy has toured regularly over the years; in fact, when WHAT BECOMES was reissued in 1974, it reached a higher position in the UK Top 10 than it did on its original release. Jimmy's brother is David Ruffin of The Temptations, the group whom Jimmy had once been invited to join.

WHAT BECOMES OF THE BROKENHEARTED became Jimmy's signature song and he did re-cut it as a duet with his brother. Song's most recent chart revival came courtesy of Eurythmic Dave Stewart with vocal assistance from Zombie Colin Blunstone.

US HIT: Jimmy Ruffin (Soul: 1966) Black & Pop
UK HITS: Jimmy Ruffin (Tamla Motown: 1966)
Jimmy Ruffin (Tamla Motown: 1974 Re-release)
Dave Stewart (Stiff: 1981)

Other recordings: Ruby Turner (Jive); Chris Farlowe (Immediate); Tom Jones (MCA); Diana Ross and The Supremes (Motown).

See: DEVIL WITH A BLUE DRESS ON for other Motown hits.

WHAT'D I SAY
(Ray Charles)
Supreme gospel-based Ray Charles classic with the traditional call and response vocal patterns sung on the original by Ray and his hand-picked group of Raelettes.

Performed by Charles himself in a 1964 British movie, "Ballad In Blue" (US Title: "Blues For Lovers"), and in "The Big TNT Show" (American International: 1966); while Ray's 1959 record was heard on the soundtrack of "The Hollywood Knights" (Columbia: 1980).

Performed by Elvis Presley in his movie, "Viva Las Vegas" (MGM: 1964) (UK Title: "Love In Las Vegas") and on a later 'live' album, *Elvis In Concert* (RCA: 1977). Performed by Andy Garcia in the Michael Douglas police thriller, "Black Rain" (Paramount: 1989).

US HITS: Ray Charles (Atlantic: 1959) Black & Pop
Jerry Lee Lewis (Sun: 1961) Black & Pop
Bobby Darin (Atco: 1962) Pop
Elvis Presley (RCA: 1964) Pop
Rare Earth (Rare Earth: 1972) Pop
UK HIT: Jerry Lee Lewis (London: 1961)

Other recordings: John Mayall and Eric Clapton (UK Decca); Cliff Richard (UK Columbia); Jackie Wilson (Brunswick); Lightnin' Hopkins (Tomato); The Crickets (Liberty); The Ronettes (Autumn); The Big 3 (UK Decca); Gerry and The Pacemakers (UK Columbia); Bill Black's Combo (Hi); Teddy Randazzo (ABC); Bill Haley and His Comets (Sonet); Earl Thomas Conley (RCA); Dee Clark (Vee-Jay); Clyde McPhatter (Mercury); The Beach Boys (Capitol); The Olympics; Freddie And The Dreamers (UK Columbia); plus an all-star version on Atco's *Apollo Saturday Night* album (1964) featuring Otis Redding, Ben E. King, Doris Troy, The Coasters, Rufus Thomas plus Wilson Pickett and The Falcons.

WHAT'S GOING ON
(Marvin Gaye/Al Cleveland/Renaldo Benson)
Co-written by Renaldo Benson of The Four Tops, this spiritually uplifting song marked a new era of Marvin Gaye records. A thought provoking message, it was the title track of his 1971 Tamla album, which also included the equally stirring MERCY MERCY ME (THE ECOLOGY).

More than ever before in his music career, Marvin was in charge of his own recording destiny, for he was the artist, composer, producer and musician.

US HITS: Marvin Gaye (Tamla: 1971) Black & Pop
            Cyndi Lauper (Portrait: 1987) Pop
UK HIT: Cyndi Lauper (Portrait: 1987)

Other recordings: Donny Hathaway (Atco); Quincy Jones and Valerie Simpson (A&M); Tim Weisberg (MCA); Ella Fitzgerald and Count Basie (Pablo); Weather Report (Columbia).

See: DEVIL WITH A BLUE DRESS ON for other Motown hits.

WHEN A MAN LOVES A WOMAN

(Calvin Lewis/Arthur Wright)
The 1960s gave us some memorable hits which featured dominant organ passages, including A WHITER SHADE OF PALE (Brooker/ Reid)** by Procol Harum and the Alan Price Set version of I PUT A SPELL ON YOU (Hawkins)**. The original version of WHEN A MAN LOVES A WOMAN was another case in point, with co-writer Arthur Wright's keyboard somberly paving the way for Percy Sledge's passionate, soulful performance.

The song's most recent revival in Britain was sparked by its use on the soundtrack of a Levi's 501 Jeans TV commercial.

Song featured in Bette Midler's first motion picture, "The Rose" (20th Century Fox: 1979).

US HITS: Percy Sledge (Atlantic: 1966) Black & Pop
            Bette Midler (Atlantic: 1980) Pop
UK HITS: Percy Sledge (Atlantic: 1966)
            Percy Sledge (Atlantic: 1987)

Other recordings: Burton Cummings (Portrait); Z. Z. Hill (Kent); O. V.

Wright (Hi); Leon Russell (Paradise); Art Garfunkel (Columbia); Solomon Burke (Rounder); Lou Rawls (Allegiance); Jerry Lee Lewis (Mercury); Narvel Felts (Evergreen); Thee Midniters (Whittier).

Recorded as WHEN A WOMAN LOVES A MAN by: Esther Phillips (Atlantic); Nancy Wilson (Capitol); Ketty Lester (Tower).

WHEN DOVES CRY

(Prince)
Prince's stark and compelling song about a love in turmoil came from his album *Purple Rain* (Warner Bros: 1984), which contained the score from his first movie...the semi-autobiographical, "Purple Rain" (Warner Bros: 1984). WHEN DOVES CRY also marked Prince's first time at the top of the top of the American charts.

US HIT: Prince (Warner Bros: 1984) Pop & Black
UK HIT: Prince (Warner Bros: 1984)

Prince is a most ambitious artist in that his music is constantly evolving and virtually always surprising in the directions it takes. He has written under several pseudonyms and for various other performers including funk band The Time (who originally included Morris Day, Terry Lewis, Jimmy Jam and Jesse Johnson) whose early hits included 777-9311 (Day) (Warner Bros: 1982), and Vanity 6, whose biggest seller was NASTY GIRL (Starr) on Warner Bros in 1982. Both these bands became part of Prince's touring revue and The Time, minus Terry Lewis and Jimmy Jam who'd left to become mega-producers in their own right, were featured in the "Purple Rain" movie, from which their JUNGLE LOVE (Day/ Johnson) hit emerged (Warner Bros: 1984).

For Nona Hendryx, Prince wrote BABY GO GO (the credited writer is

'Joey Coco') (EMI America: 1987)
and Sheena Easton recorded his
SUGAR WALLS (by 'Alexander
Nevermind'), a Top 10 smash in 1985
(EMI America). Veteran rocker
Mitch Ryder cut Prince's WHEN
YOU WERE MINE (Riva: 1983)
which was produced by John Cougar
Mellencamp. More recently, Sinead
O'Connor covered his NOTHING
COMPARES 2 U (Ensign: 1990).

One of the more bizarre versions
of a Prince song was Tom Jones' hit
recording of KISS (China: 1988) on
which he was joined by techno-pop
musicians, Art of Noise.

Prince's LITTLE RED CORVETTE
(see also our section on car songs
under MAYBELLENE) was
performed by actress Rebecca De
Mornay in Neil Simon's movie, "The
Slugger's Wife" (Columbia: 1985).

WHEN WILL I BE LOVED
(Phil Everly)

US HITS: The Everly Brothers
(Cadence: 1960) Pop
Linda Ronstadt (Capitol:
1975) Pop
UK HIT: The Everly Brothers
(London: 1960)

Other recordings: Tanya Tucker
(MCA); Rockpile (Columbia); Rita
Remington (Plantation); The
Chambers Brothers (Fantasy);
Manfred Mann (HMV); Saskia and
Serge (MCA).

Don Everly wrote ('TIL) I KISSED
YOU, their Top 5 hit (Cadence: 1959)
which they always seemed to sing
as: ('TIL) I KISSED YA ! Together,
Don and Phil wrote CATHY'S
CLOWN (Warner Bros: 1960) and
GONE, GONE, GONE (Warner Bros:
1964) plus THE PRICE OF LOVE
which never charted in the States
but was a huge hit for them in the UK
(Warner Bros: 1965) and the song
was back on the charts in early 1989
via a remix of Bryan Ferry's version
(EG/Virgin).

WHEN YOU WALK IN THE ROOM
The multi-talented singer-songwriter Jackie
DeShannon who once wrote songs with British
guitarist Jimmy Page. She travelled America in
1964 with a certain British group, causing Liberty
to release an album titled *Breakin' It Up On The
Beatles Tour!* containing studio versions of some of
the songs she had been performing on-stage;
WHEN YOU WALK IN THE ROOM was among
them.

WHEN YOU WALK IN THE ROOM
(Jackie DeShannon)
Classic 1960s teen love ballad, first
recorded by its composer with a
memorable Jack Nitzsche
arrangement...the same ingredient
that added much to Jackie's earlier
single, NEEDLES AND PINS which
Nitzsche wrote with Sonny Bono.
Both songs were successfully
covered by The Searchers, but they
were only two of many highspots in
DeShannon's musical career. Among

her other milestone songs of which she cut the first versions were: PUT A LITTLE LOVE IN YOUR HEART (DeShannon/Holiday/Myers) (Imperial: 1969), latterly a hit duet for Annie Lennox and Al Green (A&M: 1988), and BETTE DAVIS EYES (DeShannon/Weiss) which Jackie cut herself on an album (Columbia: 1975) and which Kim Carnes turned into an international smash (EMI America: 1981).

WHEN YOU WALK IN THE ROOM is another archetypal song of the girl group era of the 1960s.

US HITS: The Searchers (Kapp: 1964) Pop
           Paul Carrack (Chrysalis: 1988) Pop
UK HITS: The Searchers (Pye: 1964)
           Child (Ariola Hansa: 1978)
           Paul Carrack (Chrysalis: 1987)

Other recordings: Del Shannon (Liberty); The Ventures (Dolton); Karla Bonoff (Columbia); Bobby Vee (Liberty); Lynn Terry (Rust); Steve Forbert (Nemperor); Billy J. Kramer and The Dakotas (Parlophone); Stephanie Winslow (Warner-Curb); Bobbie McGee (EMI); Michelle Fisher (Pye).

Jackie DeShannon songs
Jackie DeShannon also made some fine versions of other songs... Her WHAT THE WORLD NEEDS NOW IS LOVE (Bacharach/David) is *the* classic record of the song (Imperial: 1965) and its that track which plays under the closing titles of Paul Mazursky's "Bob And Carol And Ted And Alice" (Columbia: 1969). She also charted with a cover of The Band's first single, THE WEIGHT (Robertson)** and was among the first artists to cut songs by both Bob Dylan and Randy Newman (the latter was, like Jackie, a staff writer with Liberty's Metric Music publishing house) plus she was produced by Bobby Womack at Muscle Shoals in

1969 including her version of Bobby's R&B hit, WHAT IS THIS. You may also recall the Jackie DeShannon best-selling record of Chip Taylor's I CAN MAKE IT WITH YOU (Imperial: 1966), around the same time as the version by The Pozo-Seco Singers (Columbia: 1966), featuring Don Williams singing lead.

Other memorable records of DeShannon compositions include:

COME AND STAY WITH ME by Marianne Faithfull (UK Decca: 1965)
DON'T DOUBT YOURSELF, BABE by The Byrds (Columbia: 1965)
plus her collaborations with Sharon Sheeley (see: BREAK-A-WAY).

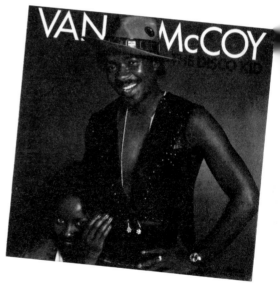

The late Van McCoy hit the top of the American charts with his dance tune, THE HUSTLE, in 1975 (Avco) backed by his Soul City symphony. Yet Van is particularly remembered as a key R&B songwriter and producer; aside from those hits listed on the opposite page, he wrote I GET THE SWEETEST FEELING recorded by Jackie Wilson (Brunswick: 1968), 5-10-15-20 (25-30 YEARS OF LOVE) by The Presidents (Sussex: 1970) and GIVING UP, first cut by Gladys Knight and The Pips (Maxx: 1964) and later by Donny Hathaway (Atco: 1972).

WHEN YOU'RE YOUNG AND IN LOVE

(Van McCoy)
The late Van McCoy wrote fine songs for girl singers...his BABY I'M YOURS became Barbara Lewis' seductive hit of 1965 (Atlantic) and Betty Everett's record of GETTIN' MIGHTY CROWDED (Vee-Jay) fairly leapt off the turntables in 1964, and that's not even counting his RIGHT ON THE TIP OF MY TONGUE scorcher by Brenda and The Tabulations (Top and Bottom: 1971). Both of the US hits on WHEN YOU'RE YOUNG are great girl-group versions and the song even comes off well by the British boy-group, The Flying Pickets!

WHEN YOU'RE YOUNG AND IN LOVE
Ruby and The Romantics rode the crest of the American pop charts in early 1963 with the classic OUR DAY WILL COME (Hilliard/Garson), which was also recorded by Cher and by Frankie Valli. WHEN YOU'RE YOUNG started out as Ruby's song but the later version by Tamla's Marvelettes eclipsed the original.

US HITS: Ruby and The Romantics (Kapp: 1964) Black & Pop
The Marvelettes (Tamla: 1967) Black & Pop
UK HITS: The Marvelettes (Tamla Motown: 1967)
The Flying Pickets (10: 1984)

Other recordings: Stacy Lattisaw (Cotillion); Ralph Carter (Mercury); Donny and Marie Osmond (MGM); Choice Four (RCA); Kathy Keegan (DCP); The Jets (MCA).

WHERE IS THE LOVE

(Ralph MacDonald/William Salter)

US HIT: Roberta Flack and Donny Hathaway (Atlantic: 1972) Black & Pop
UK HITS: Roberta Flack and Donny Hathaway (Atlantic: 1972)
Will Downing and Mica Paris (4th and Broadway: 1989)

Other recordings: Helen Reddy (Capitol); Ralph MacDonald (Marlin)

A WHITER SHADE OF PALE

(Gary Brooker/Keith Reid)
British group Procol Harum grew out of an earlier foursome known as The Paramounts who covered such R&B classics as LITTLE BITTY PRETTY ONE (Byrd)**, POISON IVY (Leiber/Stoller)** and A CERTAIN GIRL (Neville), all for Parlophone in the early 1960s. A WHITER SHADE launched Procol in a very different light with Matthew Fisher's organ intro leading into Gary Brooker's shadow-filled vocal and the spiritually symbolic lyric.

Though A WHITER SHADE draws musically from Bach, I had always imagined the song in Wagnerian terms, so for a hit (albeit outside the Top 30) revival to come from German group, Munich Machine, was more than a little appropriate! Curiously, the same Bach-based opening featured in BEWARE THE IDES OF MARCH by John Hiseman's Colosseum on their debut album

Those About To Die (Fontana: 1969).

UK HITS: Procol Harum (Deram: 1967)
          Munich Machine (Oasis: 1978)
US HIT: Procol Harum (Deram: 1967) Pop

Other recordings: Joe Cocker (Asylum); Herbie Mann (Atlantic); R. B. Greaves (Atco); Willie Nelson and Waylon Jennings (Epic); King Curtis (Atco); London Symphony Orchestra (K-Tel); Johnny Rivers (Imperial); The Everly Brothers (Warner Bros); Hugh Masekela (Uni); Bill Black's Combo (Hi); Jimmy Cliff (Island); The Box Tops (Mala).

WHO DO YOU LOVE

(Ellas McDaniel)
From Bo Diddley's first album came this self-written blues with its underlying syncopated rhythm. If for no other reason, the lyric will be remembered for describing Bo as having used 'a cobra snake for a necktie'! Song became a much-played favourite, particularly with British bands during the 1960s R&B boom. Recorded originally by Bo Diddley on Checker in 1956.

Performed by Ronnie Hawkins with Robbie Robertson in the concert movie, "The Last Waltz" (United Artists: 1978) – it had been a Canadian hit for The Hawks. Performed by Bo Diddley himself on the soundtrack of "La Bamba" (Columbia: 1987).

UK HIT: Juicy Lucy (Vertigo: 1970)

Other recordings: Quicksilver Messenger Service (Capitol); John Hammond (Vanguard); George Thorogood and The Destroyers (Rounder); The Woolies (Dunhill); Tom Rush (Elektra); Bob Seger (Reprise); Brownsville (Epic); Townes Van Zandt (Tomato); The Doors (Elektra); *The Last Waltz* soundtrack (Warner Bros); The Blues Project (Verve); Ronnie Hawkins

(Roulette and Atlantic); Jesus and Mary Chain (Warner Bros).

See: BO DIDDLEY for other Bo Diddley songs.

WHOLE LOTTA LOVE

(Robert Plant/Jimmy Page/John Paul Jones/John Bonham)
Key heavy-metal song from the *Led Zeppelin II* album in 1969. Featured in their movie, "The Song Remains The Same" (Columbia: 1976). Performed by Led Zeppelin, i.e: Robert Plant, Jimmy Page and John Paul Jones plus the late John Bonham's son Jason, on the Atlantic Records' 40th Anniversary Concert in New York in May 1988.

Most successful version of the song in England was by Alexis Korner's C.C.S. band.

UK HIT: C.C.S. (Rak: 1970)
US HITS: Led Zeppelin (Atlantic: 1970) Pop
          C.C.S. (Rak: 1971) Pop

Other recordings: King Curtis (Atco); The London Symphony Orchestra (RSO); The Wonder Band (Atco); Tina Turner (UA); Patti Smith Group.

Parody record: WHOLE LOTTA LUNCH by Weird Al Jankovic (Rock 'n' Roll)

WHOLE LOTTA SHAKIN' GOING ON

(Sunny David/Dave Williams)
First recorded by Big Maybelle (Okeh), followed by versions by Roy Hall (US Decca), Dolores Fredericks (US Decca), and The Commodores (Dot), all in 1955. Jerry Lee Lewis supposedly heard Roy Hall's version and cut his barnstorming classic two years later.

WHOLE LOTTA SHAKIN' was re-recorded by Jerry Lee for the soundtrack of his biopic, "Great Balls Of Fire" (Orion: 1989), for which he also re-cut GREAT BALLS itself, along with HIGH SCHOOL CONFIDENTIAL (Lewis/Hargrove), the title tune from MGM's 1958 teen drama in which Jerry Lee himself had appeared.

US HITS: Jerry Lee Lewis (Sun: 1957) Black & Pop
            Chubby Checker (Parkway: 1960) Pop
            Conway Twitty (MGM: 1960) Pop
UK HIT: Jerry Lee Lewis (London: 1957)

Other recordings: Carl Perkins (Columbia); Bill Haley and His Comets (Sonet); Little Richard (Vee-Jay); Cliff Richard (Columbia); Mae West (Tower); Mitch Ryder and The Detroit Wheels (New Voice); Valerie Wellington (*Great Balls Of Fire* soundtrack album on Polydor).

Jerry Lee recorded the original version of I WISH I WAS EIGHTEEN AGAIN (Throckmorton) (Elektra: 1979), the song which, just a few months later, became a big country-seller for 84-year-old comedian George Burns (Mercury: 1980).

WHY DO FOOLS FALL IN LOVE

(Morris Levy/Frankie Lymon)
The song that launched fourteen year-old Frankie Lymon and The Teenagers.

A year later, they sang the memorable I'M NOT A JUVENILE DELINQUENT (Levy) in the movie "Rock, Rock, Rock!" (Vanguard:1957).

The Teenagers Featuring Frankie Lymon (as they were originally billed) were forerunners of groups like The Jackson 5, though when Frankie went solo, his career plummeted and he eventually died of a drug overdose in 1968.

Co-writing credit originally went to George Goldner, owner of the Gee label which was named after the 1954 R&B hit GEE (Watkins/Norton/Davis) recorded by another of Goldner's acts, The Crows, on Rama.

Song was originally covered in England by Alma Cogan (known as 'the girl with the laugh in her voice') who had earlier covered hits by American girl singers, beginning

WHY DO FOOLS FALL IN LOVE
Frankie Lymon (*second from right*) and The Teenagers also made major inroads with songs such as I WANT YOU TO BE MY GIRL (Barrett/Goldner) (Gee: 1956) and THE ABC'S OF LOVE (Barrett/Levy).

with BELL BOTTOM BLUES (David/ Carr), a Teresa Brewer original on Coral in 1954.

The original Frankie Lymon and The Teenagers record was reissued in Britain by EMI in October 1989 following the song's use in a Persil TV advertisement. Appropriately, the single came out on the Roulette label, following EMI's buyout of the group of US labels owned by legendary industry figure, Morris Levy.

US HITS: The Teenagers Featuring Frankie Lymon (Gee: 1956) Black & Pop
Gale Storm (Dot: 1956) Pop
The Diamonds (Mercury: 1956) Pop
Diana Ross (RCA: 1981) Black & Pop

UK HITS: The Teenagers Featuring Frankie Lymon (UK Columbia: 1956)
Alma Cogan (HMV: 1956)
Diana Ross (Capitol: 1981)

Other recordings: The Beach Boys (Capitol); The Chiffons (Laurie); California Music (Equinox); The Happenings (B. T. Puppy); The Fourmost (Parlophone); The Four Seasons; Gloria Manne.

WILD THING

(Chip Taylor)
Here's a song that was so easy to parody that its composer did just that by producing 'Senator Bobby', featuring an imitation of Robert Kennedy performing the song as a political speech. The very first released version was by The Wild Ones (UA), a five-man American group who actually put out an album called *The Arthur Sound* named after a New York disco where they performed! One of the group's members was Jordan Christopher who also briefly tried a solo singing career and whose actress-wife Sybil had previously been married to

Richard Burton. Despite a publicity campaign, The Wild Ones weren't able to get much action and their single of WILD THING went largely unnoticed; luckily for the song, British producer Larry Page chose it for the second release by local group The Troggs, led by Reg Presley. Their version had strong punkish overtones and makes for interesting comparison with the one by X, Los Angeles' premier contemporary punk band. The song also became a highlight of Jimi Hendrix's appearance in the classic 1968 documentary of the "Monterey Pop" festival, and has been heard in various other movies including the Kevin Costner/Gene Hackman drama, "No Way Out" (Orion: 1987).

WILD THING became even more outrageous in 1988 when screaming, controversial American comic Sam Kinison used it to close his otherwise non-musical album on Warner Bros. Changing some of the lyrics to suit his style (though Chip Taylor's were always read as being more than a little suggestive!), Kinison appeared in the video of the track, writhing around with Jessica Hahn, a real(?)-life secretary whose reputation was derived from the US media's coverage of a sex scandal involving a television preacher. On-lookers in Kinison's WILD THING video included Billy Idol plus members of Ratt, Poison, Motley Crue and Bon Jovi.

US HITS: The Troggs (Fontana: 1966) Pop
Senator Bobby (Parkway: 1967) Pop
Fancy (Big Tree: 1974) Pop

UK HIT: The Troggs (Fontana: 1966)

Other recordings: The Ventures (Dolton); Manfred Mann (Fontana); Tommy Roe (ABC); The Kingsmen (Scepter); X (Slash); The Humans (IRS); Gary Lewis and The Playboys (Libery); Nancy Sinatra (Reprise);

The Jimi Hendrix Experience (Reprise).

Incidentally, composer Chip Taylor is the brother of actor Jon Voight and also wrote ANGEL OF THE MORNING and ANY WAY THAT YOU WANT ME. He tells an amusing story of his own version of ANGEL (and a lot about the US recording industry and race horses!) on his *Last Chance* album.

WILD WORLD
(Cat Stevens)
Song featured on Cat Stevens' *Tea For The Tillerman* album (Island: 1970). It was actually written about American actress Patti D'Arbanville, who inspired another Cat Stevens' song LADY D'ARBANVILLE on his *Mona Bone Jakon* set (Island: 1970).

US HIT: Cat Stevens (A&M: 1971)
           Pop
UK HITS: Jimmy Cliff (Island: 1970)
           Maxi Priest (Ten: 1988)

Other recordings: Jimmy Cliff ('live' reprise); The Gentrys (Sun); Jonathan King (Rhino); The Boys On The Block (Fantasy).

See: I SHOT THE SHERIFF for other reggae songs.

WILL YOU LOVE ME TOMORROW
(Gerry Goffin/Carole King)
All-time masterful pop song, often mistakenly titled 'Will You Still Love Me Tomorrow'.

Credit for the first Goffin and King Number One song in the US goes not only to the four Shirelles but also to their arranger and producer Luther Dixon. Song came to the group in the form of Carole King's own demo which was the way that Bobby Vee usually heard the Goffin and King hits which he cut; but this was before the world knew Carole as a recording artist in her own right, via IT MIGHT AS WELL RAIN UNTIL SEPTEMBER (Goffin/King) on

Dimension in 1962. However, when Carole released her legendary *Tapestry* album (Ode: 1971), she included a new version of WILL YOU LOVE ME TOMORROW on which, incidentally, James Taylor played acoustic guitar.

The original Shirelles record was featured on the soundtrack of "Dirty Dancing" (Vestron: 1987).

US HITS: The Shirelles (Scepter:
             1961) Black & Pop
           The Four Seasons
             (Philips: 1968) Pop
           Dave Mason (Columbia:
             1978) Pop

WILL YOU LOVE ME TOMORROW
One of the golden girls groups, The Shirelles, whose record of WILL YOU LOVE ME TOMORROW soared to the top of America's charts in early 1961, after which their earlier single DEDICATED TO THE ONE I LOVE was successfully re-released.

UK HITS: The Shirelles (Top Rank:
             1961)
           Melanie (Neighbourhood:
             1974)

Other recordings: Roberta Flack

(Atlantic); Linda Ronstadt (Capitol); The Chiffons (Laurie); Dionne Warwicke (Arista); Donnie Elbert (All Platinum: 1977); Dana Valery (Phantom): Michael Stanley Band (Elektra); Smokey Robinson (Motown); Shandi Sinnanon (Asylum); Mike Berry and The Outlaws (UK Decca); Laura Branigan (Atlantic); Bobby Vee (Liberty); Brenda Lee (Decca); Helen Shapiro (UK Columbia); Tony Orlando (Epic); Ben E. King (Atco); Lloyd Price (ABC/Paramount); Little Eva (Dimension); Joey Dee and The Starliters (Roulette); Cher (Imperial); The Righteous Brothers (Verve); Sandy Posey (MGM); The Raindrops (Jubilee); Peaches and Herb (Date); Cliff Richard (UK Columbia); The Bob Crewe Generation (Dynovoice); Françoise Hardy (UA); Cheryl Handy (Compleat); Millie Jackson (Jive).

Answer records: NOT JUST TOMORROW, BUT ALWAYS by Bertell Dache (aka Tony Orlando) (UA: 1961)
YES I WILL LOVE YOU TOMORROW by Jon E. Holiday (Atlantic: 1961)
YOU KNOW I'LL LOVE YOU TOMORROW by Ry-An Colly Williams.

WILLIE AND THE HAND JIVE
(Johnny Otis)
Song built around the hand-jive, a series of choreographed hand-movements (hitting your knees and elbows, then criss-crossing your hands without touching them, then drawing imaginary circles in the air, etc., etc.) all done to the beat of the music. This was simply a revival of an audience participation routine that dated back years, but it caught the imagination of the teenage audience on both sides of the Atlantic; it was introduced in Britain on the BBC's "Six-Five Special" Saturday night TV pop show and became an instant fad.

'The Johnny Otis Show' was a travelling rhythm-and-blues show led by composer–vibraphonist–showman extraordinaire, Johnny Otis. Johnny Otis' record was successfully covered by Eric Clapton in 1974, but George Thorogood's revival didn't make it into the Top 50.
Song performed by Johnny Otis in the rock 'n' roll B-feature movie, "Juke Box Rhythm" (Columbia: 1959), which starred Brian Donlevy, Jo Morrow and crooner Jack Jones.

US HITS: The Johnny Otis Show (Capitol: 1958) Black & Pop
Eric Clapton (RSO: 1974) Pop
George Thorogood and The Destroyers (EMI America: 1985) Pop

Other recordings: Cliff Richard (UK Columbia); Johnny Rivers (UA); Rinder and Lewis (AVI); Boots Randolph (Monument); The Crickets (Liberty); Dan Penn (MGM).

Sequel records: WILLIE DID THE CHA CHA (Otis) by The Johnny Otis Show (Capitol: 1958)
HAND JIVE ONE MORE TIME (Otis) by The Johnny Otis Show (King: 1961).

WITCH DOCTOR
(Ross Bagdasarian)
The novelty song with which Ross Bagdasarian (aka David Seville) experimented with speeded-up voices (for the 'oo-ee-oo-ah-ah, bing, bang, walla-walla-bing-bang' chorus) which he eventually used for his million(s)-selling THE CHIPMUNK SONG.
Bagdasarian was already a successful composer of, amongst other hits: COME ON-A MY HOUSE for Rosemary Clooney (Columbia: 1951), and went on to record a whole slew of both novelty and MOR singles for Liberty. Incidentally, the

Let's Have A Merry, Merry Christmas

BY ROSS BAGDASARIAN

40¢

FRANK MUSIC CORP.
Sole Selling Agents, FRANK DISTRIBUTING CORP.
119 WEST 57th STREET • NEW YORK 19, N Y

WITCH DOCTOR

Ross Bagdasarian took on the name of David
Seville and began making records in 1956 for the
new Los Angeles-based label, Liberty Records.
He'd been writing (and recording) MOR songs
such as this 1951 Christmas tune, but came up with
a novelty tune in 1958. This was WITCH DOCTOR,
performed by Don Lang on BBC TV's 'Six–Five
Special'! It was the first time that he used speeded-
up voices, which became his trademark and which
he used with the Chipmunks.

'names' of the Chipmunks came from
three executives of Liberty Records,
the Los Angeles-based label which
was virtually turned around by the
initial success of THE CHIPMUNK
SONG (CHRISTMAS DON'T BE
LATE) in 1958; the so-honoured
parties were: Alvin Bennett (the
label's then-president), Simon
Waronker (co-founder of Liberty and
the father of Warner Bros Records'
current president, Lenny Waronker),
and Theodore Keep, the chief
engineer at Liberty's studio.

US HIT: David Seville (Liberty:
            1958) Pop
UK HITS: David Seville (London:
            1958)

Don Lang and His Frantic
Five (HMV: 1958)

One of this author's favourite David
Seville comedy records is THE
TROUBLE WITH HARRY (Liberty:
1956).

Novelty songs:
Following is a selective list of other
novelty singles from the rock era:

AHAB THE ARAB (Stevens) by Ray
    Stevens (Mercury: 1962)
    by Jimmy Savile (UK Decca: 1967)
FLYING SAUCER (Axton) by
    Buchanan and Goodman
    (Luniverse: 1956)
THE OLD PAYOLA ROLL BLUES
    (Freberg) by Stan Freberg
    (Capitol: 1960)
THE PURPLE PEOPLE EATER
    (Wooley) by Sheb Wooley (MGM:
    1958)
TRANSFUSION (Drake) by Nervous
    Norvus (Dot: 1956)

FLYING SAUCER also qualifies as a
'Break-In' record, where brief clips
from other songs (usually from the
actual hit singles) are strung
together by a commentator or
narrator. Bill Buchanan and Dickie
Goodman started a mini-industry
with their 'Saucer' record, linking
one-liners and phrases from current
hits on a series of thematic singles to
which they would add, depending
usually on current events or seasonal
times of year. Among the other
Buchanan and Goodman singles:

BUCHANAN AND GOODMAN ON
    TRIAL (Luniverse: 1956)
FLYING SAUCER THE SECOND
    (Luniverse: 1957)
FLYING SAUCER GOES WEST
    (Luniverse: 1958)
FLYING SAUCER THE THIRD
    (Comic: 1959)
FRANKENSTEIN OF '59 (Novelty:
    1959)
SANTA AND THE SATELLITE
    (Luniverse: 1957)

Bill Buchanan made records both on his own and with Howard Greenfield and with Bob Ancell; the latter partnership produced THE CREATURE (FROM A SCIENCE FICTION MOVIE) (Flying Saucer: 1957), while Dickie Goodman cut a long line of solo singles, ranging from PRESIDENTIAL INTERVIEW: FLYING SAUCER '64 (Audio Spectrum: 1964), THE TOUCHABLES (Mark-X: 1961), BEN CRAZY (Diamond: 1962) and BATMAN AND HIS GRANDMOTHER (Red Bird: 1966) through to his biggest hit, MR JAWS (Cash: 1975).

In 1974, when a world shortage of vinyl threatened to restrict the numbers of records pressed, Neil Innes of The Bonzo Dog Doo-Dah Band, Monty Python's Flying Circus and Rutland Weekend Television (as well as the great Beatles' parody, "The Rutles"), took the cause to his heart and ran with it! He released a single called the RE-CYCLED VINYL BLUES on UA in which he adopted the premise that old songs had to be melted down to make way for new ones! He and an accompanying chorus sang extracts from such evergreens as TAKE GOOD CARE OF MY BABY (Goffin/King)**, WHITE CHRISTMAS (Berlin) and HALFWAY TO PARADISE (Goffin/King)** plus that Guy Mitchell chestnut, SHE WEARS RED FEATHERS (AND A HULA HULA SKIRT) (Merrill). All was not lost... Neil presented his case and the situation was averted!

WITH A LITTLE HELP FROM MY FRIENDS
(John Lennon/Paul McCartney)
Sung by Ringo Starr on the Beatles' album, *Sgt Pepper's Lonely Hearts Club Band* (Parlophone: 1967). Performed by Joe Cocker in the "Woodstock" movie (Warner Bros: 1970). Cocker's studio version featured on the soundtrack of Michael Apted's "Stardust" (EMI: 1974). Performed by Jeff Lynne, in a medley with NOWHERE MAN (Lennon/McCartney), on the soundtrack of "All This And World War II" (20th Century Fox: 1976). Performed by Peter Frampton and The Bee Gees in the movie version of "Sgt Pepper's Lonely Hearts Club Band" (Universal: 1978).

In the States, the Joe Cocker single made it briefly inside the Top 75 and an extract of the song appeared in the BEATLES MEDLEY single which Capitol released in 1978. Joe Cocker's version is heard each week under the opening of the American TV show, "The Wonder Years" (ABC).

UK HITS: Joe Brown (Pye: 1967)
          Joe Cocker (Regal Zonophone: 1968)
          The Young Idea (Columbia: 1967)
          Wet, Wet, Wet (Jewel: 1988)
US HIT: Joe Cocker (A&M: 1968)

WITH A LITTLE HELP by Wet, Wet, Wet, together with Billy Bragg singing SHE'S LEAVING HOME were two songs from the concept charity album, *Sgt Pepper Knew My Father,* created for and released though Britain's rock magazine, "New Musical Express" in 1988. The Billy Bragg side also figured prominently on the UK charts.

Other recordings: The Beach Boys (Capitol); Richie Havens (Verve); Barbra Streisand (Columbia); The Undisputed Truth (Gordy); Jeff Lynne: 'All This And World War II' soundtrack (20th Century); Betty Lavette (Karen).

Covers of Lennon and McCartney songs
Among the John Lennon and Paul McCartney songs which were hits by artists other than The Beatles:

BAD TO ME by Billy J. Kramer and The Dakotas (Parlophone: 1963)

COME TOGETHER** by Aerosmith (Columbia: 1978)
by Ike and Tina Turner (Minit: 1970)

DAY TRIPPER** by Otis Redding (Stax: 1967)

DO YOU WANT TO KNOW A SECRET by Billy J. Kramer and The Dakotas (Parlophone: 1963)

ELEANOR RIGBY by Ray Charles (Tangerine/ABC: 1968)
by Aretha Franklin (Atlantic: 1969)

THE FOOL ON THE HILL by Sergio Mendes and Brasil '66 (A&M: 1968)

GET BACK by Billy Preston (A&M: 1978)

GOODBYE by Mary Hopkin (Apple: 1969)

GOT TO GET YOU INTO MY LIFE by Cliff Bennett and The Rebel Rousers (Parlophone: 1966)
by Earth, Wind And Fire (Columbia: 1978)

HELLO LITTLE GIRL by The Fourmost (Parlophone: 1963)

HELP by Bananarama (London: 1989)

HERE, THERE AND EVERYWHERE by Emmylou Harris (Reprise: 1975)

HEY JUDE by Wilson Pickett (Atlantic: 1969)

I DON'T WANT TO SPOIL THE PARTY by Rosanne Cash (Columbia: 1989)

I SAW HER STANDING THERE ** by The Elton John Band featuring John Lennon (DJM: 1981)
by Little Richard (1969)

I SAW HIM STANDING THERE** by Tiffany (MCA: 1988)

I SHOULD HAVE KNOWN BETTER by The Naturals (Parlophone: 1964)

I WANT TO HOLD YOUR HAND by Dollar (Carrere: 1979)

I'LL KEEP YOU SATISFIED by Billy J. Kramer and The Dakotas (Parlophone: 1963)

IT'S FOR YOU by Cilla Black (Parlophone: 1964)

LET IT BE** by Joan Baez (Vanguard: 1971)
by Ferry Aid (The Sun/ Zeebrugge: 1987)

LUCY IN THE SKY WITH DIAMONDS by Elton John (DJM: 1974)

MICHELLE by David and Jonathan (UK Columbia: 1966)
by The Overlanders (Pye: 1966)

NOBODY I KNOW by Peter and Gordon (UK Columbia: 1964)

OB-LA-DI, OB-LA-DA by The Marmalade (CBS: 1968)

OH DARLING by Robin Gibb (RSO: 1978)

SHE CAME IN THROUGH THE BATHROOM WINDOW by Joe Cocker (A&M: 1970)

SHE'S LEAVING HOME by Billy Bragg (Jewel: 1988)

STEP INSIDE LOVE by Cilla Black (Parlophone: 1968)

WE CAN WORK IT OUT** by Stevie Wonder (Tamla: 1971)
by Chaka Khan (Warner Bros: 1981)

A WORLD WITHOUT LOVE by Peter and Gordon (UK Columbia: 1964)

YESTERDAY by Ray Charles (ABC: 1967)
by Marianne Faithfull (UK Decca: 1965)
by Matt Monro (Parlophone: 1965)

YOU WON'T SEE ME by Anne Murray (Capitol: 1974)

YOU'VE GOT TO HIDE YOUR LOVE AWAY by The Silkie (Fontana: 1965)

NB: The above does not include the STARS ON 45 single by Dutch group 'Stars On 45' (Radio: 1981) which reached Number One in the US with their medley which included Lennon and McCartney's DO YOU WANT TO KNOW A SECRET, DRIVE MY CAR, I SHOULD HAVE KNOWN BETTER, I'LL BE BACK, NO REPLY, NOWHERE MAN, WE CAN WORK IT OUT and YOU'RE GOING TO LOSE THAT GIRL.

WONDERFUL WORLD
(Barbara Campbell/Lou Adler/Herb Alpert)
Co-written by Sam Cooke using his wife's name, Barbara Campbell, as a pseudonym. His original record was heard (as was his TWISTIN' THE NIGHT AWAY) on the soundtrack of "National Lampoon's Animal House" (Universal: 1978).

US HITS: Sam Cooke (Keen: 1960)
                    Black & Pop
                Herman's Hermits (MGM:
                    1965) Pop
                Art Garfunkel With James
                    Taylor, Paul Simon
                    (Columbia: 1978) Pop
UK HITS: Sam Cooke (HMV: 1960)
                Herman's Hermits (UK
                    Columbia: 1965)
                Sam Cooke (RCA: 1986
                    Re-release)

Other recordings: Johnny Nash (Epic); Bryan Ferry (Island); The Tymes (Parkway); Roger Whittaker (RCA); Cliff Richard (UK Columbia).

See: ONLY SIXTEEN for other Sam Cooke songs.

WORDS
(Barry Gibb/Maurice Gibb/Robin Gibb)
One of the most recorded of all the Bee Gees songs. Performed by Elvis Presley in the rockumentary film, "Elvis – That's The Way It Is" (MGM: 1970).

UK HITS: The Bee Gees (Polydor:
                    1968)
                Rita Coolidge (A&M:
                    1978)
US HITS: The Bee Gees (Atco:
                    1968) Pop
                Susie Allanson (Elektra:
                    1979) Country

Other recordings: Cilla Black (Parlophone); Elvis Presley (RCA).

See: TO LOVE SOMEBODY for other Bee Gees' songs.

WORK WITH ME ANNIE
(Henry Ballard)
Hank Ballard created a storm of controversy back in 1954 when he wrote and, with his group The Midnighters, recorded WORK WITH ME ANNIE, an R&B song full of innuendo and explicit lyric lines like 'Annie please don't cheat, give me all your meat'.

    Not surprisingly, the record was banned, but that was just the beginning of a huge tidal wave. The Midnighters' record zoomed to the top of the race charts and Etta James cut an answer version, originally called ROLL WITH ME HENRY, but when that title seemed a little too spicy, it was released under the satirically expurgated title, THE WALLFLOWER (Ballard/Otis/James); the record opened with Richard 'Louie Louie' Berry asking 'Hey baby, what do I have to do to make you love me too?' to which Etta replied: 'You gotta roll with me Henry'.

    Etta James and The Peaches found themselves also storming up the charts while, over at Mercury, white singer Georgia Gibbs was in the studio recording an homogenized version called DANCE WITH ME HENRY. This latter song broke big with the mass hit parade audiences and the song became the title of an Abbott and Costello movie (UA: 1956).

    But the original lives on, and not just on revive-45's either; Hank is still on the road, introducing his first ANNIE song to today's audiences by saying: 'This is the reason your parents used to go around calling me a dirty old man!'

US HIT: The Midnighters
                    (Federal: 1954) Black

Annie and Henry songs
WORK WITH ME ANNIE and THE WALLFLOWER generated a whole series of sequel songs incorporating the Annie and Henry characters into a slew of different situations. Hank

Ballard himself took the lead with his own ANNIE HAD A BABY and ANNIE'S AUNT FANNIE (both Federal: 1954), followed by HENRY'S GOT FLAT FEET (Federal: 1955). Other artists climbed on the bandwagon and, among the results, were:

ANNIE DON'T LOVE ME NO MORE (Berry) by The Hollywood Flames (Symbol: 1965)
ANNIE KICKED THE BUCKET by The Nu-Tones (Hollywood Star: 1954)
ANNIE MET HENRY (Riley/Stone) by The Champions (Chart: 1954) by The Cadets (Modern: 1955)
ANNIE PULLED A HUMBUG by The Midnights (Music City: 1954)
ANNIE'S ANSWER (Smith/Price) by Al Smith Combo, Hazel McCollum and The El Dorados (Vee-Jay:1954)
ANNIE'S BACK (Anderson) by Little Richard (Specialty: 1964)
(ANNIE'S BEEN WORKING ON THE) MIDNIGHT SHIFT by Buddy Holly (Decca: 1958)
EAT YOUR HEART OUT ANNIE (Pingatore/Lytle) by The Jodimars*(Capitol: 1956)
HEY, HENRY! (Josea/Gallo) by Etta James (Modern: 1955)
I'M THE FATHER OF ANNIE'S BABY by Danny Taylor (Bruce)
MY NAME AIN'T ANNIE (Roberson/ Hayes) by Linda Hayes and The Platters (King)

* The Jodimars were actually three members of Bill Haley's Comets who constructed their group title from their respective names: JOey D'Ambrosia, DIck Richards and MARShall Lytle.

See: THE TWIST for other Hank Ballard songs.

WORKING IN THE COAL MINE
(Allen Toussaint)
Lee Dorsey's lazy, nasal twang was perfectly married to a slew of Allen Toussaint's jaunty songs, of which WORKING IN THE COAL MINE is perhaps the most durable.

Other key Toussaint/Dorsey collaborations were RIDE YOUR PONY (Amy: 1965); GET OUT OF MY LIFE, WOMAN (Amy: 1966), HOLY COW (Amy: 1966), plus YES WE CAN CAN of which Lee Dorsey's original went nowhere, but The Pointer Sisters' version rocketed up the bestsellers (Blue Thumb: 1973).

COAL MINE was performed by Devo on the soundtrack of the animated movie, "Heavy Metal" (Columbia: 1981).

US HITS: Lee Dorsey (Amy: 1966)
                   Black & Pop
                   Devo (Full Moon: 1981)
                   Pop
UK HIT: Lee Dorsey (Stateside: 1966)

Other recordings: Allen Toussaint (Scepter); Pure Prairie League (RCA); Levon Helm (MCA); The Meters ; The Judds (RCA).

See: MOTHER-IN-LAW for other Allan Toussaint songs.

YA YA
(Lee Dorsey/Clarence Lewis/ Morgan Robinson)
'Sittin' in my ya-ya, waitin' for my la-la' went this nursery-rhyme adaptation, which was the first single to chart for New Orleans singer, the late Lee Dorsey. It was also performed by The Beatles in their Hamburg appearances and was later re-cut by John Lennon.

Lee Dorsey's original record was heard on the soundtrack of "American Graffitti" (Universal: 1973).

The song had another life as well, when somebody adapted it to cash in on the dance craze of the day, and it became YA YA TWIST, sung in French by Petula Clark; the single made it into the British Top 20 in mid-1962 on the Pye label and 'Pet' dutifully performed it on TV's '"Thank Your Lucky Stars".

US HIT: Lee Dorsey (Fury: 1961)
            Black & Pop
UK HIT: Petula Clark : billed as
            YA YA TWIST (Pye:
            1962)

Other recordings: Georgie Fame (UK Columbia); Tony Orlando (Elektra); Steve Miller (Capitol); John Lennon (Capitol); Rufus Thomas (Stax); Joey Dee and The Starliters (Roulette); Tony Sheridan and The Beatles (Polydor).

YAKETY YAK

(Jerry Leiber/Mike Stoller)
'Yakety Yak, Don't Talk Back!' Leiber and Stoller injected slabs of great humour into a string of cartoon story songs for The Coasters, who grew out of the remains of west coast R&B group, The Robins.

Best remembered are YAKETY YAK, plus CHARLIE BROWN, ALONG CAME JONES and POISON IVY, all on Atco in 1959. YAKETY YAK was performed by 2 Live Crew on the soundtrack of the Arnold Schwarzenegger/Danny DeVito movie, "Twins" (Universal: 1988) and earlier, by Bad Manners for "Party Party" (A&M Sound Pictures: 1982).

The dominant sax on The Coasters' YAKETY YAK is the work of King Curtis, whose own hits include SOUL TWIST (Ousley) (Enjoy: 1962) and MEMPHIS SOUL STEW (Ousley) (Atco: 1967).

US HIT: The Coasters (Atco: 1958)
            Black & Pop
UK HIT: The Coasters (London:
            1958)

Other recordings: Wanda Jackson

(Capitol); Sam The Sham and The Pharoahs (MGM); Sha Na Na (Kama Sutra); Joe Turner (Polydor); Brian Poole and The Tremeloes (UK Decca); Ray Stevens (Barnaby); Boots Randolph (Monument); The Fourmost (Parlophone); Sandy Nelson (Imperial); Frankie Avalon; Eric Weisberg and Deliverance.

See: JAILHOUSE ROCK for other Jerry Leiber and Mike Stoller songs.

YOU ARE THE SUNSHINE OF MY LIFE

(Stevie Wonder)
Among the most recorded of Stevie Wonder's songs, it instantly became an easy listening/MOR ballad.

US HIT: Stevie Wonder (Tamla:
            1973) Black & Pop

US HIT: Stevie Wonder (Tamla
            Motown: 1973)

Other recordings: Mel Torme and Buddy Rich (Gryphon); Ella Fitzgerald (Pablo); Shirley Bassey (UA); Frank Sinatra (Reprise); Peter Nero (Columbia); Johnny Mathis (Columbia).

Stevie Wonder songs

Covers of Stevie Wonder songs include:

ALL IN LOVE IS FAIR by Barbra Streisand (Columbia: 1974).
HIGHER GROUND (Wonder) by The Red Hot Chili Peppers (EMI: 1989)
UNTIL YOU COME BACK TO ME (THAT'S WHAT I'M GONNA DO) (Wonder/Paul/Broadnax) by Aretha Franklin (Atlantic: 1973) by Luther Vandross (Epic: 1984)
UPTIGHT (EVERYTHING'S ALRIGHT)(Moy/Cosby/Wonder) by Jackie Wilson (Brunswick)

Luther Vandross' version was a medley incorporating UNTIL YOU COME BACK TO ME with SUPERSTAR by Leon Russell and Bonnie Bramlett. Luther has more recently covered another classic,

LOVE WON'T LET ME WAIT (Barrett/Eli) which was a Number One R&B single for Major Harris (Atlantic: 1975) who is still working as one of The Delfonics.

Dutch group Starsound followed on their STARS ON 45 tradition with a STARS ON STEVIE medley (CBS: 1982) which included the following songs: UPTIGHT (EVERYTHING'S ALRIGHT)(Moy/Cosby/Wonder), MY CHERIE AMOUR (Moy/Cosby/Wonder), YESTER-ME, YESTER-YOU, YESTERDAY (Miller/Wells) MASTER BLASTER (Wonder), YOU ARE THE SUNSHINE OF MY LIFE, ISN'T SHE LOVELY (Wonder), SIR DUKE (Wonder), I WISH (Wonder), I WAS MADE TO LOVE HER (Cosby/Hardaway/Wonder/Moy), FOR ONCE IN MY LIFE (Miller/Murden), SUPERSTITION (Wonder) and FINGERTIPS (Cosby/Paul).

YOU BETTER MOVE ON
(Arthur Alexander)
Southern soul singer Arthur Alexander wrote and recorded the original version of YOU BETTER MOVE ON which the Rolling Stones covered on a British EP (UK Decca: 1964) and on their American album *December's Children* (London: 1965).

US HIT:	Arthur Alexander (Dot: 1962) Black & Pop
UK HIT:	The Rolling Stones EP (Decca: 1964)

(According to author Roy Carr, The Rolling Stones EP made it on to the UK charts on the strength of YOU BETTER MOVE ON being one of the tracks.)

Other recordings: Johnny Rivers (Imperial); Johnny Paycheck and George Jones (Epic); Liza Minnelli (A&M); Billy 'Crash' Craddock; Tommy Roe (Warner Bros).

The Beatles covered three other Arthur Alexander records...for details of these, see the Beatle Remakes list following the entry on DIZZY MISS LIZZY .

Rolling Stones' remakes
Like The Beatles, the Stones recorded a number of American R&B songs on their early albums. Among them were these:

AIN'T THAT LOVIN' YOU BABY (Reed) by Jimmy Reed (Vee-Jay: 1956)
BRIGHT LIGHTS, BIG CITY (Reed) by Jimmy Reed (Vee-Jay: 1961)
CAN I GET A WITNESS (Holland/Dozier/Holland)** by Marvin Gaye (Tamla: 1963)
CONFESSIN' THE BLUES (Brown/McShann) by Jay McShann
CRY TO ME (Meade/Russell)** by Solomon Burke (Atlantic: 1962)
DOWN HOME GIRL (Leiber/Butler)
EVERYBODY NEEDS SOMEBODY TO LOVE (Russell/Burke/Wexler) by Solomon Burke (Atlantic: 1964)
FORTUNE TELLER (Neville) by Benny Spellman (Minit: 1962)
GOOD TIMES (Cooke) by Sam Cooke (RCA: 1964)
HI-HEEL SNEAKERS (Higginbotham)** by Tommy Tucker (Checker: 1964)
HITCH HIKE (Gaye/Paul/Stevenson) by Marvin Gaye (Tamla: 1963)
HONEST I DO (Reed) by Jimmy Reed (Vee-Jay: 1957)
I'M A KING BEE (Moore) by Slim Harpo (Excello: 1957)
I'VE BEEN LOVING YOU TOO LONG (Redding/Butler)** by Otis Redding (Volt: 1965)
IF YOU NEED ME (Pickett/Sanders/Batesman) by Wilson Pickett (Double-L: 1963) by Solomon Burke (Atlantic: 1963)
IT'S ALL OVER NOW (Womack/Womack)** by The Valentinos (Sar: 1964)
LET'S TALK IT OVER (Hooker) by John Lee Hooker

LOOK WHAT YOU'VE DONE
(Morganfield) by Muddy Waters
MERCY, MERCY (Covay/Miller) by
Don Covay (Rosemart: 1964)
MONEY (THAT'S WHAT I WANT)
(Gordy Jr/Bradford)** by Barrett
Strong (Tamla Anna: 1959)
MY GIRL (Robinson/White)** by
The Temptations (Gordy: 1965)
OH BABY, WE GOT A GOOD
THING GOIN' (Ozen) by Barbara
Lynn (Jamie: 1964)
PAIN IN MY HEART (Neville) by
Otis Redding (Volt: 1963) adapted
from RULER OF MY HEART
(Neville) by Irma Thomas (Minit:
1963)
POISON IVY (Leiber/Stoller) by The
Coasters (Atlantic: 1959)
SHE SAID YEAH (Christy/Jackson)
by Larry Williams (Specialty:
1959)
SUSIE Q (Hawkins/Lewis)** by Dale
Hawkins (Checker: 1957)
TIME IS ON MY SIDE (Meade/
Norman)** by Irma Thomas
(Imperial: 1964)
UNDER THE BOARDWALK (Resnik/
Young)** by The Drifters
(Atlantic: 1964)
WALKING THE DOG (Thomas)** by
Rufus Thomas (Stax: 1963)
YOU BETTER MOVE ON
(Alexander)** by Arthur
Alexander (Dot: 1962)

Plus various Chuck Berry, Bo
Diddley and Willie Dixon tunes; for
details of these see individual entries
on the songs MEMPHIS, BO
DIDDLEY and I'M YOUR HOOCHIE
COOCHIE MAN.

YOU CAN GET IT IF YOU REALLY WANT

(Jimmy Cliff)
Alongside MANY RIVERS TO
CROSS ** and the film's title song,
YOU CAN GET IT later became a
highlight of the soundtrack songs
written and performed by Jimmy
Cliff in the 1972 Jamaican production,

"The Harder They Come". The
original soundtrack film is on Island.

UK HIT: Desmond Dekker and
           The Aces (Trojan:
           1970)

YOU CAN'T HURRY LOVE

(Brian Holland/Lamont Dozier/Eddie
Holland)
This was the seventh of twelve
Number One hits that The Supremes
had between 1964 and 1969, the last
of which teamed them with The
Temptations. Their original record
was heard on the soundtrack of
Whoopi Goldberg's comedy movie,
"Jumpin' Jack Flash" (20th Century
Fox: 1986).

Phil Collins remake was a bigger
chart hit in Britain than the original
Supremes version had been and, in
an interesting side story, Collins has
recently been writing with Lamont
Dozier; together they won a Grammy
for their song TWO HEARTS, the
theme song from Phil Collins' first
motion picture, "Buster" (1988).

US HITS: The Supremes (Motown:
           1966) Black & Pop
           Phil Collins (Atlantic:
           1983) Pop
UK HITS: The Supremes (Tamla
           Motown: 1966)
           Phil Collins (Virgin: 1982)

Other recordings: The Four Tops
(Motown); Kate Taylor (Columbia);
Graham Parker.

See: DEVIL WITH A BLUE DRESS
ON for other Motown hits.

See: HOW SWEET IT IS for other
Holland/Dozier/Holland songs.

YOU CAN'T JUDGE A BOOK BY THE COVER

(Willie Dixon)
A timeless Willie Dixon blues made
popular by Bo Diddley, who also
recorded it with Muddy Waters and
Little Walter. The song had a gentle

message about racial discrimination a long time before Eddie Holland and Norman Whitfield's BEAUTY IS ONLY SKIN DEEP, the Temptations' hit (Gordy: 1966), and during the beginnings of the Civil Rights Movement.

Performed by Mike Nesmith in a 'live' Monkees concert which was filmed by director Bob Rafelson for the closing episode of the 1966–1967 season of the television series, "The Monkees" (NBC).

US HIT: Bo Diddley (Checker: 1962) Pop & Black

Other recordings: Tom Rush (Elektra); The Rolling Stones (UK Decca); Patti LaBelle (Epic); Stevie Wonder (Tamla); The Mugwumps (Capitol); John Hammond (Vanguard); The Merseybeats (Fontana); The Shadows Of Knight (Dunwich); Dion (Warner Bros); Willie Dixon; Hank Williams Jr (Curb).

See: I'M YOUR HOOCHIE COOCHIE MAN for other Willie Dixon songs.

YOU CAN'T SIT DOWN
(Dee Clark/Cornell Muldrow/Kal Mann)
Guitarist Phil Upchurch's group had the first record on YOU CAN'T SIT DOWN, an instrumental divided into both sides of a 1961 single. The five-man Dovells scored their first smash (BRISTOL STOMP) also in 1961 and, a year and a half later, were back in the Top 5 with the vocal version of YOU CAN'T ; the lyric was by Kal Mann who founded Cameo-Parkway Records in 1956 with fellow songwriter Bernie Lowe. (Incidentally, The Dovell's featured Len Barry who went on to fame with his solo hit 1-2-3.)

US HITS: The Philip Upchurch Combo (Boyd: 1961) Pop
The Dovells (Parkway: 1963) Black & Pop

UK HIT: The Philip Upchurch Combo (Sue: 1966)

Other recordings: Boots Randolph (Monument); Len Barry (Cameo); The Kingsmen (Wand); Brian Poole (UK Decca).

Instrumentals...with lyrics
YOU CAN'T SIT DOWN was just one of many instrumentals in the rock era to which lyrics were added and the vocal rendition made chart noise as well. One example, SOULFUL STRUT (Record/ Sanders) made its own piece of history when Barbara Acklin's vocal version, titled AM I THE SAME GIRL? (Brunswick: 1969), used the same basic instrumental track, recorded under its original title by Young-Holt Unlimited (Brunwick: 1968).

Among the other instrumental hits to which lyrics were later written: THE LONELY BULL (Lake) first by Herb Alpert and The Tijuana Brass (A&M: 1962) and then by Jack Jones (Kapp: 1963); TELSTAR (Meek) by The Tornados (UK Decca: 1962) found new life as MAGIC STAR by Margie Singleton (Mercury: 1962). Similarly, Mr Acker Bilk's British TV theme, STRANGER ON THE SHORE, was given a lyric by American publisher Robert Mellin and the song subsequently charted for both Andy Williams (Columbia: 1962) and The Drifters (Atlantic: 1962).

MERCY, MERCY, MERCY is the other instrumental-turned song that stands out in pop history; written by Josef Zawinul, keyboardist with jazzman Cannonball Adderley, MERCY was a hit for Adderley's group in early '67; a lyric was added and it was cut by rock group The Buckinghams, fresh off such hits as KIND OF A DRAG (Beisber/Holvay) (USA: 1967) and DON'T YOU CARE (Beisber/Holvay) (Columbia: 1967); their version (Columbia: 1967) made it into the Top 10 and a competitive release by Marlena Shaw (Cadet: 1967) made it inside the Top 60, while charting higher in the R&B listings, as did a version by the teaming of Larry Williams and Johnny 'Guitar' Watson (Okeh: 1967).

YOU DON'T HAVE TO SAY YOU LOVE ME
(Pino Donaggio/Vito Pallavicini/Vicki Wickham/Simon Napier-Bell)
Among Dusty Springfield's most dramatic and enduring ballads, this was a masterful adaptation of the Italian·song, IO CHE NON VIVO. The melody was written by Pino Donaggio who has since composed a number of significant movie scores, most notably the horror film "Carrie" (UA: 1976). English lyrics were the work of two key music industry figures: Simon Napier-Bell, who managed The Yardbirds in the 60s through to Wham! in the 80s, and wrote his biography under the title of this song; the other writer was Vicki Wickham, one of the guiding lights behind British TV's legendary "Thank Your Lucky Stars" TV shows in the 1960's; Vicki went on to foster the careers of artists like Patti Labelle and The Bluebelles, eventually managing former Bluebelle Nona Hendryx and, as full circles are often meant to meet in the most creative of ways, Vicki is now managing the re-emerged (and as talented as ever) Dusty Springfield.
  Song performed by Elvis Presley in the concert movie, "Elvis – That's The Way It Is" (MGM: 1970). Dusty's original record heard on the soundtrack of "Baby It's You" (Paramount: 1983).

US HITS: Dusty Springfield (Philips: 1966) Pop
            Elvis Presley (RCA: 1970) Pop
UK HIT: Dusty Springfield (Philips: 1966)

Elvis Presley (RCA: 1971)
Guys and Dolls (Magnet: 1976)

Other recordings: Cher (Imperial); The Miracles (Motown); Vikki Carr (Liberty); Jim Nabors (Columbia); The Four Sonics (Sport); Helen Reddy (MCA); Arthur Prysock (Polydor); Tanya Tucker (MCA); Mel Carter (Imperial); Eddie Fisher (RCA).

See: SON OF A PREACHER MAN for other Dusty Springfield hits.

YOU GOT WHAT IT TAKES
(Berry Gordy Jr/Gwendolyn Gordy/Tyran Carlo)
Detroit-born Marv Johnson was one of the first Motown stars. His initial

YOU GOT WHAT IT TAKES
Though Marv Johnson had a Top 10 UK hit from his later days on the Gordy label with the song I'LL PICK A ROSE FOR MY ROSE (Dean/Johnson/Weatherspoon) (1969), his earlier Berry Gordy-produced sides released are perhaps more memorable. This was the second of his three UA albums from the days when he was supported by The Rayber Voices, a backing group so named becuase they were led by Raynoma Liles and Berry Gordy Jr.

single, COME TO ME (Gordy/ Johnson), was originally released on the then-regional Tamla label, but Berry Gordy signed Marv directly to United Artists who had the added advantage of national distribution.

US HITS: Marv Johnson (UA: 1960)
Black & Pop
The Dave Clark Five
(Epic: 1967) Pop
UK HITS: Marv Johnson (London:
1960)
Johnny Kidd and The
Pirates (HMV: 1960)
The Dave Clark Five (UK
Columbia: 1967)
Showaddywaddy (Arista:
1977)

Other recordings: Spooky and Sue (EMI); Helen Shapiro (UK Columbia); Marvin Gaye and Tammi Terrell (Tamla).

YOU GOT WHAT IT TAKES, I LOVE THE WAY YOU LOVE (Gordy/ Mikaljon) and (YOU GOT TO) MOVE TWO MOUNTAINS (Gordy) were Marv's best-selling UA singles, and YOU GOT was covered seven years after Marv by The Dave Clark Five. Marv's very first chart record was COME TO ME (Gordy Jr/ Johnson) (UA: 1959) and the song was also recorded by Mary Wells (Motown).

The Dave Clark Five drew a lot of their single material from American songs, including OVER AND OVER**, DO YOU LOVE ME**, PUT A LITTLE LOVE IN YOUR HEART**, plus Chuck Berry's REELIN' AND ROCKIN' (UK Columbia: 1965).

See: DEVIL WITH A BLUE DRESS ON for other Motown hits.

YOU KEEP ME HANGIN' ON

(Brian Holland/Lamont Dozier/Eddie Holland)
Pulsating R&B song, driven by the infectious Motown beat, YOU KEEP ME HANGIN' ON was the eighth chart-topper for The Supremes, namely Diana Ross, Mary Wilson and Florence Ballard. It was featured by Diana and The Supremes along with The Temptations on their 1968 TV special called "TCB - Taking Care Of Business".

The US psychedelic-era group Vanilla Fudge, two members of which joined Jeff Beck in Beck, Bogert and Appice, made a fine, heavy rock hit of the song which was seven minutes long on their first album, *Vanilla Fudge* (Atco: 1967).

In 1970 Jackie DeShannon recorded the song in a duet with the Little Anthony oldie, HURT SO BAD. Seven years later, another American girl singer, Roni Hill, charted in the UK with her medley this time combining YOU KEEP ME HANGIN' ON with another Supremes standard STOP IN THE NAME OF LOVE. The most recent significant revival is by Kim Wilde, daughter of former British rocker Marty Wilde who, in his day, covered American hits by such as Ritchie Valens, Jody Reynolds and Bobby Vee.

US HITS: The Supremes (Motown:
1966) Pop
Vanilla Fudge (Atco:
1968) Pop
Joe Simon (Sound Stage 7:
1968) Black
Wilson Pickett
(Atlantic:1969) Pop
Jackie De Shannon:
Medley with HURT SO
BAD (Imperial: 1970)
Pop
Ann Peebles (Hi: 1974)
Black
Kim Wilde (MCA: 1987)
Pop
UK HITS: The Supremes (Tamla
Motown: 1966)
Vanilla Fudge (Atlantic:
1967)
Roni Hill (Creole: 1977)
Kim Wilde (MCA: 1986)

Other recordings: Rod Stewart (Warner Bros); Tom Jones (UK

Decca); Gloria Gaynor; Sam Harris (Motown).

See: DEVIL WITH A BLUE DRESS ON for other Motown hits.

See: HOW SWEET IT IS for other Holland/Dozier/Holland songs.

Vanilla Fudge's other best-selling singles were also revivals of other writer's songs, including Junior Walker's SHOTGUN and Donovan Leitch's SEASON OF THE WITCH, plus TAKE ME FOR A LITTLE WHILE (Martin) which had initially been a semi-hit for Patti Labelle and The Bluebelles (Atlantic: 1967).

YOU REALLY GOT ME
(Ray Davies)
After two singles on Pye that went nowhere, The Kinks found them- selves on the bottom of the bill of a tour with The Dave Clark Five and The Hollies. With 'sheer determination', Ray Davies put together a 'watered-down' version of all the songs in their stage act. The Kinks performed mostly American R&B hits, but the riffs that particularly influenced YOU REALLY GOT ME came from LOUIE LOUIE by those punks from Portland, Oregon...The Kingsmen. Even Ray's demented vocal shows traces of the drunken slur of LOUIE LOUIE vocalist Jack Ely. The result was the most primal, mind-frying rock 'n' roller ever to come out of England. YOU REALLY GOT ME has since influenced thousands of rock 'n' rollers and was revived for the first hit by heavy metal group Van Halen in 1978.

As with a number of UK hits, The Kinks' original version of YOU REALLY GOT ME was re-released (PRT: 1983) and on that occasion, it made it just inside the Top 50 in the UK.

The Van Halen version was on the soundtrack of "Over The Edge" (Orion: 1980), and in the Tony Danza comedy, "Out Of Control" (1989), the original Kinks' record was used.

UK HIT:	The Kinks (Pye: 1964)
US HITS:	The Kinks (Reprise: 1964) Pop
	Van Halen (Warner Bros: 1978) Pop

Other recordings: Robert Palmer (Island); Buddy Miles (Mercury); The Silicon Teens (Sire); Thirteenth Floor Elevators (International Artists); Eclipse (Casablanca); Helen Schneider; Phil Manzanera (Polydor); Mott The Hoople (CBS); Johnny and The Hurricanes.

Another of the most recorded of Kinks' songs which, ironically, they never recorded themselves, is Ray Davies' I GO TO SLEEP. Published in 1965, it wasn't a hit until The Pretenders included it on their second album (Real: 1981) and the track was released as a single. 1960s British pop group The Applejacks, of TELL ME WHEN (Stephens/Reed) fame, had cut it on a UK Decca single in 1965 and former big band thrush (they called them that, way back then!). Peggy Lee also released it on a 45 on Capitol that same year. Other versions were by Cher (Imperial); The Truth (Pye); Fingers (Polydor); Lesley Duncan (Mercury); Marion (Page One) and also Adrian Pride (Warner Bros), which was produced by The Everly Brothers!

In 1989, Kirsty MacColl successfully revived DAYS (Davies), which was originally a Kinks' single on Pye in mid-1968. Covers are nothing new to Kirsty (daughter of folksinger Ewan) MacColl who scored a major hit on Stiff in 1985 with a remake of Billy Bragg's A NEW ENGLAND and whose own song, THEY DON'T KNOW, was restyled by Tracey Ullman on Stiff in '83.

YOU SEND ME
(L. C. Cooke)
Sam Cooke's smoothest of smooth

vocals was never so beguiling as on this, his first hit, his first Number One on the R&B chart *and* his first Number One on the national Hit Parade!

Written by Sam under his brother's name, it's a love song which was covered immediately by Teresa Brewer, and in later years, a mini-hit for such as Aretha Franklin, The Ponderosa Twins and The Manhattans, but the most successful revival to date has been by Rod Stewart.

US HITS: Sam Cooke (Keen: 1957) Black & Pop
        Teresa Brewer (Coral: 1957) Pop
        Aretha Franklin (Atlantic: 1968) Black & Pop
        The Ponderosa Twins Plus One (Horoscope: 1971) Black
        The Manhattans (Columbia: 1985) Black
UK HITS: Sam Cooke (London: 1958)
        Rod Stewart (Mercury: 1974)

Other recordings: Steve Miller Band (Capitol); Diana Ross and The Supremes (Motown); Mavis Staples (Stax); Roy Ayers (Polydor); Percy Sledge (Atlantic); Richie Havens (Elektra); Paul and Paula (Philips); Nicolette Larson (Warner Bros); Rufus Thomas (AVI); Z. Z. Hill (Kent); Bonnie Bramlett.

YOU'RE ALL I NEED TO GET BY
(Nickolas Ashford/Valerie Simpson)

US HITS: Marvin Gaye and Tammi Terrell (Tamla: 1968) Black & Pop
        Aretha Franklin (Atlantic: 1971) Black & Pop
        Dawn (Elektra: 1975) Pop
        Johnny Mathis and Deniece Williams (Columbia: 1978) Black & Pop
UK HITS: Marvin Gaye and Tammi Terrell (Tamla Motown: 1968)
        Johnny Mathis and Deniece Williams (CBS: 1978)

Other recordings: Barbara Mandrell (Columbia); Booker T. and The M.G.'s (Stax); Diana Ross (Motown); Nancy Wilson (Capitol); Chris Christian and Amy Holland (in a medley with AIN'T NOTHING LIKE THE REAL THING**) (Boardwalk); Gloria Gaynor (Polydor).

YOU'RE NO GOOD
(Clint Ballard Jr)
Originally an R&B hit for Betty Everett, it was covered at that time by The Swinging Blue Jeans and a decade later, Linda Ronstadt took the same song to Number One in America. Latest revival is from Elvis Costello, who earlier covered another mid-sixties song which had been introduced by Betty Everett...that was Van McCoy's GETTING MIGHTY CROWDED (Vee-Jay: 1964).

US HITS: Betty Everett (Vee-Jay: 1965) Black & Pop
        Linda Ronstadt (Capitol: 1975) Pop
UK HIT: The Swinging Blue Jeans (HMV: 1964)

Other recordings: The Swinging Blue Jeans (HMV); Elvis Costello (Warner Bros); Van Halen (Warner Bros).

Clint Ballard Jr's other hits have included GOOD TIMIN' (Ballard/Tobias) by Jimmy Jones (Cub: 1960), THE GAME OF LOVE (Ballard) by Wayne Fontana and The Mindbenders (Fontana: 1965) and I'M ALIVE (Ballard) by The Hollies (Parlophone: 1965).

YOU'RE SIXTEEN
(Richard Sherman/Robert Sherman)
'You're sixteen, you're beautiful and

you're mine...' soft rock hit written by the same Sherman Brothers who wrote the award-winning movie scores for Walt Disney's "Mary Poppins" (1964) and "Jungle Book" (1967). Song later became the second American Number One hit for ex-Beatle Ringo Starr.

US HITS: Johnny Burnette (Liberty: 1960) Pop
Ringo Starr (Apple: 1974) Pop
UK HITS: Johnny Burnette (London: 1960)
Ringo Starr (Apple: 1974)

YOU'RE SIXTEEN
Johnny Burnette, shown here during his hit-making days at Liberty about 1960. Together with his brother Dorsey and their friend Paul Burlison, he formed The Johnny Burnette Trio and they made some classic rockabilly sides for Coral in the late 1950s. In 1961, following the huge success of his records, DREAMIN' (DeVorzon/Ellis) and YOU'RE SIXTEEN, Johnny toured Britain with Gary US Bonds and Gene McDaniels.

Johnny Burnette, who died tragically in a boating mishap in 1964, was also an accomplished songwriter; his JUST A LITTLE TOO MUCH went Top 10 in the States for Ricky Nelson in 1959. He led his own group, The Johnny Burnette Rock 'n' Roll Trio (including brother Dorsey) on some classic rockabilly recordings for the Coral label in 1956, for whom he also recorded some solo sides. In 1958, as The Burnette Brothers, Johnny and Dorsey cut four sides for Imperial and in 1959, Johnny went solo again on Liberty's subsidiary label Freedom; he then switched to Liberty itself in 1960, where producer Snuff Garrett and arrangers like Ernie Freeman created the crisp pop productions which gave Johnny his three biggest sellers: DREAMIN' (DeVorzon/Ellis) (Liberty: 1960), YOU'RE SIXTEEN and LITTLE BOY SAD (Walker) (Liberty: 1961). Johnny's son, Rocky, has clocked up one solo hit to date, namely TIRED OF TOEIN' THE LINE (Burnette/Coleman) (EMI America: 1980).

YOU'VE LOST THAT LOVIN' FEELIN'
(Phil Spector/Barry Mann/Cynthia Weil)
The ballad which turned The Righteous Brothers' career around (they had previously been recording uptempo R&B songs) and the record which proved another milestone for producer Phil Spector.

US HITS: The Righteous Brothers (Philles: 1965) Black & Pop
Dionne Warwick (Scepter: 1969) Black & Pop
Roberta Flack and Donny Hathaway (Atlantic: 1971) Black
Daryl Hall and John Oates (RCA: 1980) Pop

YOU'VE LOST THAT LOVIN' FEELIN'
Bill Medley (*left*) and Bobby Hatfield were The Righteous Brothers; known primarily for their dramatic ballad hits: LOVIN' FEELIN' produced by Phil Spector and (YOU'RE MY) SOUL AND INSPIRATION which Bill Medley produced himself.

UK HITS: The Righteous Brothers (London: 1965)
Cilla Black (Parlophone: 1965)
The Righteous Brothers (London: 1969 Re-release)

302 • WHO SANG WHAT IN ROCK 'N' ROLL

Daryl Hall and John Oates
(RCA: 1980)
Telly Savalas (MCA: 1975)

Other recordings: Elvis Presley
(RCA); Long John Baldry (UA);
Martha Reeves (Arista); Kenny
Rogers and Dottie West (UA); Floyd
Cramer (RCA); Delaney and Bonnie
(Atco); Unit Four Plus Two (UK
Decca); King Curtis (Atco); Andee
Silver (UK Decca); Smokey Robinson
and The Miracles (Tamla); Freda
Payne; The Checkmates Ltd
(Capitol).

Mann and Weil songs

Husband-and-wife songwriters,
Barry Mann and Cynthia Weil were
another hugely successful team to
emerge from New York's famed
music publishing facility, The Brill
Building. Among the hit records of
other Barry Mann and Cynthia Weil
songs:

BLAME IT ON THE BOSSA NOVA
by Eydie Gorme (Columbia: 1963)
BLESS YOU by Tony Orlando (Epic:
1961)
COME ON OVER TO MY PLACE by
The Drifters (Atlantic: 1965)
CONSCIENCE by James Darren
(Colpix: 1962)
HE'S SURE THE BOY I LOVE by The
Crystals (Philles: 1962)
HERE YOU COME AGAIN by Dolly
Parton (RCA: 1977)
HOME OF THE BRAVE by Jody
Miller (Capitol: 1965)
by Bonnie and The Treasures
(Phi-Dan: 1965)
HUNGRY by Paul Revere and The
Raiders (Columbia: 1966)
I JUST CAN'T HELP BELIEVIN' by
B.J. Thomas (Scepter: 1970)
I'LL TAKE YOU HOME by The
Drifters (Atlantic: 1963)
I'M GONNA BE STRONG by Gene
Pitney (Musicor: 1964)
IT'S GETTING BETTER by Mama
Cass (Dunhill: 1969)
JUST ONCE by Quincy Jones
featuring James Ingram (A&M: 1981)

KICKS by Paul Revere and The
Raiders (Columbia: 1966)
LOOKING THROUGH THE EYES OF
LOVE by Gene Pitney (Musicor:
1965)
by The Partridge Family (Bell:
1973)
MAKE YOUR OWN KIND OF
MUSIC by Mama Cass Elliot
(Dunhill: 1969)
MY DAD by Paul Petersen (Colpix:
1962)
NEVER GONNA LET YOU GO by
Sergio Mendes (A&M: 1983)
PATCHES by Dickey Lee (Smash:
1962)
ROCK AND ROLL LULLABY by B. J.
Thomas (Scepter: 1972)
UPTOWN by The Crystals (Philles:
1962)
WE GOTTA GET OUT OF THIS
PLACE by The Animals (UK
Columbia: 1962)
(YOU'RE MY) SOUL AND
INSPIRATION by The Righteous
Brothers (Verve: 1966)
Also:
ON BROADWAY (written by Barry
Mann and Cynthia Weil with Jerry
Leiber and Mike Stoller) by The
Drifters (Atlantic: 1963)
by George Benson (Warner Bros:
1978)
ONLY IN AMERICA (written with
Jerry Leiber and Mike Stoller) by
Jay and The Americans (UA: 1963)
WALKING IN THE RAIN (written
with Phil Spector) by The
Ronettes (Philles: 1964)
by Jay and The Americans (UA:
1969)
SOMEWHERE OUT THERE from the
movie, "An American Tail"
(Universal: 1986)
by Linda Ronstadt and James
Ingram (MCA: 1986)

YOU'VE MADE ME SO VERY HAPPY

(Berry Gordy Jr/Frank Wilson/
Brenda Holloway/Patrice Holloway)
What became the breakthrough

song for the so-called jazz-rock band
Blood, Sweat and Tears, had actually
been co-written by west coast R&B
singer Brenda Holloway and her
sister, Patrice.

US HITS: Brenda Holloway (Tamla:
             1967) Black & Pop
             Blood, Sweat and Tears
             (Columbia: 1969) Black
             & Pop
             Lou Rawls (Capitol: 1970)
             Black
UK HIT: Blood, Sweat and Tears
             (CBS: 1969)

See: DEVIL WITH A BLUE DRESS
ON for other Motown hits.

YOU'VE REALLY GOT A HOLD ON ME

(William Robinson)
Aka YOU REALLY GOT A HOLD
ON ME, this was another slice of
pure Smokey magic and, not only
did the original Miracles' record
crest the top of the R&B charts in
America, but the song was one of
three Motown compositions on The
Beatles' second album, *With The
Beatles* (Parlophone: 1963) with John
Lennon turning in a superb lead
vocal.

  The original Miracles' record was
heard on the soundtrack of Philip
Kaufman's gang movie, "The
Wanderers" (Orion: 1979).

US HITS: The Miracles (Tamla:
             1963) Black & Pop
             Eddie Money (Columbia:
             1973) Pop
             Mickey Gilley (Epic:
             1984) Country

Other recordings: Small Faces (UK
Decca); Dusty Springfield (UA);
Laura Nyro (Columbia); Gayle
McCormick (Dunhill); The Gamblers
(UK Decca); Cliff Bennett and The
Rebel Rousers (Parlophone); The
Zombies (UK Decca).

See: DEVIL WITH A BLUE DRESS
ON for other Motown hits.

See: SHOP AROUND for other
Smokey Robinson songs.

YOUNG BLOOD

(Jerry Leiber/Mike Stoller/Doc
Pomus)
'I saw her standing on the corner...'
Performed by Leon Russell in
"Concert For Bangladesh" (1972).

US HITS: The Coasters (Atco: 1957)
             Black & Pop
             Bad Company (Swan
             Song: 1976) Pop

Other recordings: Wayne Fontana
(Fontana); Bruce Willis (Motown).

See: JAILHOUSE ROCK for other
Jerry Leiber and Mike Stoller songs.

See: A TEENAGER IN LOVE for
songs Doc Pomus wrote with Mort
Shuman.

YOUNG, GIFTED AND BLACK

(Nina Simone/Weldon Irvine)
Under its original title, also known as
TO BE YOUNG, GIFTED AND
BLACK, this became a major reggae
song as recorded by Bob and
Marcia, their record reaching the
Top 5 of the British pop chart.

US HIT: Nina Simone (RCA: 1969)
             Black & Pop
UK HIT: Bob and Marcia (Harry J:
             1970)

Other recording: Aretha Franklin.

(YOUR LOVE KEEPS LIFTING ME) HIGHER AND HIGHER

(Carl Smith/Gary Jackson/Raynard
Miner)
This song was Jackie Wilson's last
major hit before he collapsed on
stage in 1975 and eventually died
from unknown causes in early 1984.
From his first major hit REET
PETITE (Gordy Jr/Carlo)**, Wilson
had become a finely tuned rhythm-
and-blues performer, both in concert
and in the recording studio. Though

lacking the soul-filled dramatics of his earlier hits like LONELY TEARDROPS (Gordy Jr/Carlo/Gordy) (Brunswick: 1958) and the same composing team's TO BE LOVED (also Brunswick: 1958), HIGHER AND HIGHER nevertheless shows off the versatility of Jackie Wilson's voice as he soars above the driving rhythm section and the chanting backup chorus.

Song was heard twice in the movie "Ghostbusters II" (Columbia: 1989), firstly in a sequence where Jackie Wilson's original record is played to stimulate the slime! Secondly, it's heard in a contemporary remake by Howard Huntsberry.

US HITS: Jackie Wilson (Brunswick: 1967) Black & Pop
Rita Coolidge (A&M: 1977) Pop
UK HITS: Jackie Wilson (MCA: 1969)
Jackie Wilson (Brunswick: 1975 Re-release)
Rita Coolidge (A&M: 1977)

Other recordings: Bette Midler (Atlantic); Esther Phillips (Kudu); Barbara Mandrell (MCA); Dolly Parton (RCA); Bobby Darin (Motown); The Charlie Daniels Band (Epic); Bonnie Bramlett (Capricorn).

YOUR SONG
(Elton John/Bernie Taupin)
From Elton John's debut album (DJM: 1970). The cover version by soul singer Billy Paul came originally from his *360 Degrees of Billy Paul* album (Philadelphia International) in 1972, which included his international smash, ME AND MRS JONES (Gamble/ Huff/Gilbert).

UK HITS: Elton John (DJM: 1971)
Billy Paul (Philadelphia International: 1977)
US HIT: Elton John (Uni: 1971) Pop

Other recordings: Al Jarreau (Reprise); Cissy Houston (Private Stock).

Other cover recordings of Elton John songs include BAD SIDE OF THE MOON (John/Taupin) by April Wine (Big Tree: 1972) and BORDER SONG (John/Taupin) by Aretha Franklin (Atlantic: 1970).

Z

ZIGGY STARDUST
(David Bowie)
Bowie's alter ego, 'Ziggy Stardust' first surfaced on his 1972 album *Ziggy Stardust and The Spiders From Mars*. Featured in his legendary 'last' Stardust concert at the completion of a world tour at London's Hammersmith Odeon in 1973. The show was filmed by D. A. Pennebaker, but remained uncompleted until Bowie himself finally mixed the soundtrack in 1982 prior to the film's first public showings a year later.

UK HIT: Bauhaus (Beggars Banquet: 1982)

By contrast to the Top 20 version of ZIGGY by Bauhaus, one of the more obscure versions of a David Bowie tune was SILLY BOY BLUE as recorded by the late Billy Fury (Parlophone: 1968).

ZIP-A-DEE-DOO-DAH
(Allie Wrubel/Ray Gilbert)
A Walt Disney movie song (performed by James Baskett in "Song Of The South" in 1946) and a hit parade success the year after for, among others, Johnny Mercer.

Phil Spector turned it into a rock

'n' roll song in 1963 when he recorded Bob B. Soxx and The Blue Jeans (alias Bobby Sheen, Darlene Love and Fanita James) along with Billy Strange's memorable 'fuzz' guitar.

US HIT: Bob B. Soxx and The Blue Jeans (Philles: 1963) Pop & Black

UK HIT: Bob B. Soxx and The Blue Jeans (London: 1963)

Other recordings (in the rock era): Dave Clark Five (UK Columbia); The Big Three (UK Decca); Freddie and The Dreamers (UK Columbia); Nilsson (A&M)

Selected Bibliography

BRITISH HIT SINGLES: Sixth Edition
Paul Gambacinni/Tim Rice/Jo Rice (Guinness Books, 1987)

THE CASH BOX BLACK COMTEMPORARY SINGLES CHARTS
1960-1984
George Albert/Frank Hoffmann (The Scarecrow Press Inc., 1986)

THE CASH BOX SINGLES CHARTS 1950-1981
Frank Hoffman (The Scarecrow Press Inc., 1983)

NEW ROCK RECORD: Third Edition
Terry Hounsome (Blandford Press, 1987)

TOP POP SINGLES 1955-1986
Joel Whitburn (Record Research, 1987)

TOP R&B SINGLES 1942-1988
Joel Whitburn (Record Research, 1988)

THE TOP TWENTY BOOK: THE OFFICIAL BRITISH RECORD CHARGES
1955-1987: Fourth Edition
Tony Jasper (Blandford press/Javelin Books, 1988)

Index of Artists